Real Money, New Frontiers
Case studies of financial innovation in Africa

Edited by
Mark Napier

Real Money, New Frontiers
Case studies of financial innovation in Africa

First published 2010

Juta and Company Ltd
1st Floor, Sunclare Building, 21 Dreyer Street, Claremont, 7708

© 2010 Juta & Company Ltd

ISBN 978-0-70217-771-2

All rights reserved. No part of this publication may be reproduced or transmitted in any form or by any means, electronic or mechanical, including photocopying, recording, or any information storage or retrieval system, without prior permission in writing from the publisher. Subject to any applicable licensing terms and conditions in the case of electronically supplied publications, a person may engage in fair dealing with a copy of this publication for his or her personal or private use, or his or her research or private study. See Section 12(1)(a) of the Copyright Act 98 of 1978.

Project Manager: Debbie Henry
Editor: Wendy Priilaid
Proofreader: Karoline Hanks
Typesetter: ANdtp Services
Indexer: Sanet le Roux
Cover designer: Drag n Drop, Jacques Nel

Printed in South Africa by Mills Litho

The authors and the publisher have made every effort to obtain permission for and to acknowledge the use of copyright material. Should any infringement of copyright have occurred, please contact the publisher, and every effort will be made to rectify omissions or errors in the event of a reprint or new edition.

Contents

Preface	v
About the authors	vii
About the sponsors	viii
Currency conversions	ix
Abbreviations	x
List of tables	xiii
List of figures	xiv
Case study summaries	xv
Introduction	1
Chapter One: Mass banking	23
Equity Bank: Listening to customers	23
ESSAY: Foreign banks: Do they help or hinder financial inclusion? – *Karen Ellis*	39
Absa Flexi Banking Services: Taking banking to the people	44
ESSAY: Randomised trials for strategic innovation in retail finance – *Nathanael Goldberg*, *Dean Karlan* and *Jonathan Zinman*	59
Tanzania Postal Bank: Revitalising a decades-old model	65
Bank Windhoek: Reaching out to Namibia's rural population	76
Chapter Two: SME banking	88
Banque Misr: Making the unbankable bankable	88
Burkina Bail: Building entrepreneurship in Burkina Faso	99
Chapter Three: Linkage banking	110
Barclays Bank Ghana: Global meets local – working with the *susu* collectors of Ghana	110
ESSAY: Linkage banking and insurance schemes: Formal and informal providers combine to deepen the markets – *Robert Stone* and *Abigail Carpio*	122
Ecobank: A regional approach to microfinance	125
Al Amana: Transformation against heavy odds	129
Afriland First Bank and the *mutuelles communautaires de croissance*: Commercial links with the rural informal sector	141
Chapter Four: Remote distribution	146
First National Bank and ATM Solutions: Providing services to the masses	146
Hollard and Pep: *Prêt-a-porter*, cash-based insurance	158

Chapter Five: Remittances and payments 164
Dahabshiil: Sending money home in a conflict area 164
ESSAY: Features and functioning of the *hawala* remittance system in sub-Saharan Africa – *Frederick Ahwireng-Obeng* and *David T Mutombo* 167
ESSAY: G2P schemes: A business opportunity for financial services at the very base of the pyramid – *David Porteous* 176

Chapter Six: Mobile phone banking 185
Mobile banking: Living up to its promise? 185
ESSAY: Technology trends that will drive base of the pyramid financial services: Why telecoms, not banks, are the key to the future – *Allen L Hammond* 204

Chapter Seven: Technology suppliers 212
Cointel: Enabling m-commerce 212
Ferlo: A smartcard solution in Senegal 215

Chapter Eight: Rural banking 221
ARB Apex Bank: Supporting rural banking services 222
Mbinga Community bank: Tailor-made financial services for rural clients 226
Stanbic in Africa: Broadening its reach to the unbanked 229

Chapter Nine: Insurance 234
Opportunity International's MicroEnsure: Providing a safety net for societies in need 234
MLife insurance company: Tackling microinsurance 238
Microcare: Insurance for affordable access to quality healthcare in Uganda 242

Chapter Ten: Sustaining markets 261
Faulu Kenya: Finding finance after grant funding 261
Summit Financial Partners: A rescue remedy 266

Glossary of terms 274
References 277
Index 285

Preface

Since the case studies in *Real Money, New Frontiers* were written, the global financial system has plunged into crisis. It is tempting to speculate that as one of the least globalised regions in the world, Africa may actually do less badly than other parts of the world, but it will not escape unscathed and nor will its financial system.

Readers of this book may therefore be pondering on what sort of impact the global downturn in the financial industry might have on financial sector innovation in Africa. Will we see a continuation of the sort of momentum these case studies describe or will Africa's financial system succumb to the sort of deep chill we are seeing gripping the financial systems of developed economies?

In truth it is probably too early to tell. Disentangling the various influences that contribute to the financial results now being reported by banks and insurance companies will require careful analysis. There are sharp differences in these financial results. For example, the large South African banks, though still very profitable, are reporting reduced earnings and significantly increased impairments in their domestic retail businesses while banks in Botswana are reporting spectacular profit increases.

Pessimists will point to the fact that the rapid deterioration in global trade really took root only in the last quarter of 2008 and so the secondary impacts on domestic African economies (and, by extension, their financial systems) are not being felt yet.

On the other hand, optimists will say that African economies are more broadly based these days, so a dramatic collapse in Zambia's copper industry will not necessarily affect that country's hotel, tourism, construction or services industries to the same extent. The step change that many African economies have enjoyed in recent years has put them on a different, and more resilient, footing.

The banking industry too, it could be argued, is on a stronger footing than it was – better regulated and increasingly well capitalised, benefiting from considerable 'rehabilitation' (to use the International Monetary Fund's word) in recent years. Africa's banks are among the most liquid, profitable and risk averse in the world. Thankfully, exotic financial instruments barely feature in the African banking landscape. This is not to say that individual banking institutions are not at risk but the systems to which they belong may be less vulnerable than their counterparts in the developed world.

This book, however, is chiefly concerned with people who are not banked or insured, or who have only recently become so. The main purpose of *Real Money, New Frontiers* is, firstly, to draw attention to the fact that the people who do not have access to financial services in Africa vastly outnumber those who do, and secondly, to suggest that providers can reach out to this market profitably.

This emerging market of the previously unbanked is the core market of many smaller financial institutions. The nature of the opportunity will not, in their opinion, have been affected by the global financial crisis and so they will stick with it. Their greatest risk will be securing finance for on-lending to the extent they are financed from international sources.

The larger financial institutions, for whom this emerging market is an add-on, may choose to pull back from new market opportunities where the returns are not obvious, preferring to simplify their business operations in the hope of an eventual return to more normal banking conditions. However, the investment required in these new market areas is often small and the returns considerable. I hope this book encourages those larger financial institutions that are inclined to restrict their support for innovation in the interests of short-term cost savings to reflect again on the opportunity from which they might be turning away.

Overall, I am inclined to think that the factors that have been driving the strengthening of Africa's financial markets – better macroeconomic governance and financial regulation, a stronger information base, and new technology advances, to name some – will keep encouraging innovators in spite of the financial crisis. We have also seen the emergence of some compelling role models – banks and other service providers that have demonstrated beyond doubt that the 'missing middle' is a part of the market that deserves to be taken seriously. Showcasing some of these success stories is the rationale for *Real Money, New Frontiers*.

Putting a book together with so many case studies from so many different sources inevitably means that timing is a challenge. Sometimes details, such as exchange rates and growth rates, changed markedly between when the case studies were written and when the book was edited. We have tried strenuously to update the information, but this has not always been possible. All the case studies have been approved for publication by the companies concerned and we have relied on this process as a means of verifying the content of the case studies. All other errors and omissions remain our own.

This book has been a collaborative effort. Those responsible for writing the case studies, Oxford Policy Management and the case study department at Wits University's Business School, probably underestimated the extent of the task when they agreed to embark on this exercise. I would like to thank them for their dedication and stamina.

I would also like to thank those experts who agreed to write the articles for the book. Their insights have helped to make sense of the disparate messages coming out of the case studies. I know that in some cases they agreed to fit in with our extended publication deadline rather than publishing on their own, and they deserve our gratitude for their forbearance.

FinMark Trust is grateful to the co-funders of the book, the UK's Department of International Development and the Development Bank of Southern Africa, for their foresight in agreeing to fund in the first place and for their patience as grantors on what turned out to be a longer exercise than we had bargained for.

Special thanks go to FinMark Trust's theme co-ordinators and staff. This book could not have been developed without the knowledge that I gained from them during almost five years as FinMark Trust's CEO. This has been an extraordinarily rich learning period for me, and I owe them a debt of gratitude for the way they shared their time and experience so generously.

I would particularly like to thank Janet Wilhelm, FinMark Trust's editor, for her tireless work in co-ordinating the production of the manuscript. Her experience and intelligently applied attention to detail have been invaluable.

Finally, to my wife, Fiona – thank you for sharing the experience of working on this book with me. As ever, I could not have done without your companionship.

Mark Napier
Johannesburg
March 2009

About the authors

Mark Napier

From 2004 to 2009, Mark Napier was chief executive officer of FinMark Trust, a South Africa-based independent think tank whose mission is 'making financial markets work for the poor'. During this period he worked closely with African policymakers and private sector financial service providers to encourage sustainable innovation in financial markets in support of greater access to financial services for the poor. Before moving to South Africa, he worked in investment banking in the City of London. He was educated at Cambridge University and is a British citizen.

Oxford Policy Management

Oxford Policy Management is an independent consultancy providing policy research, advice and implementation support on international development and issues of public policy in developing countries. Within the financial sector, OPM's work is increasingly focused on issues of access to financial services for poorer households and smaller businesses.

www.opml.co.uk

Wits Business School

The Wits Business School Case Centre, based at the University of the Witwatersrand's Graduate School of Business Administration, specialises in writing case studies for lecturers to use in teaching business skills and theory application. More recently it has branched out into conducting case-based research for other organisations.

www.wbs.ac.za

About the sponsors

FinMark Trust

FinMark Trust was established in March 2002 with initial funding from the UK's Department for International Development. Its mission is summarised in its slogan, 'Making financial markets work for the poor'. In practice this means promoting and supporting institutional and organisational development to increase access to financial services by the unbanked and underbanked of Africa.

www.finmarktrust.org.za

Department for International Development

The Department for International Development (DFID) is the part of the UK government that manages Britain's aid to poor countries. DFID operates in partnership with governments, civil society, the private sector and other multilateral institutions, and works to increase access to financial services, financial transparency and the development of strong financial sectors.

www.dfid.gov.uk

Development Bank of Southern Africa

The Development Bank of Southern Africa (DBSA) is a leading development finance institution in Africa south of the Sahara. The bank supports government and other development role players to improve the quality of life for people in the region through funding infrastructure projects, accelerating the sustainable reduction of poverty and dependency, and promoting broad-based economic growth and regional economic integration.

www.dbsa.org

Currency conversions

US$1 =	2006 Q3	2006 Q4	2007 Q1	2007 Q2	2007 Q3	2007 Q4	2008 Q1	2008 Q2	2008 Q3	2008 Q4
CFA franc Burkina Faso Cameroon Senegal	537.78	517.16	512.36	497.19	471.58	454.63	424.55	424.73	466.54	472.84
Egyptian Pound (LE from the French Livre Egyptienne)	5.43	5.52	5.70	5.63	5.63	5.22	4.69	5.34	5.43	5.52
New Ghana cedi (GH¢) On July 1, 2007 the cedi (¢) was replaced with the New Ghana cedi (GH¢), each GH¢ being 10 000 old cedis	9 484	9 589	9 674	8 477	9 636	9 961	9 922	11 034	11 790	12 970
Kenyan shilling (KSh)	72.76	69.57	69.27	66.57	63.62	63.16	54.94	63.90	71.71	77.92
Moroccan dirham (MAD)	8.68	8.44	8.42	8.32	8.09	7.79	6.32	7.36	7.87	8.28
Namibian dollar (N$) Currency tied to the ZAR	7.39	7.03	7.34	7.08	1.10	6.85	6.88	7.94	8.07	9.95
South African rand (ZAR)	7.39	7.03	7.34	7.08	1.10	6.85	6.88	7.94	8.07	9.95
Tanzanian shilling (TZS)	1 305.19	1 270.63	1 254.75	1 254.88	1 249.10	1 150.00	1 022.28	1 184.55	1 159.31	1 302.02
Ugandan shilling (USh)	1 851.45	1 771.04	1 752.42	1 644.49	1 674.51	1 711.70	1 458.55	1 602.20	1 640.72	1 952.48

Source: www.gocurrency.com & www.oanda.com

Abbreviations

ABIL	African Bank Investments Limited (South Africa)
ACCION	ACCION International
ACOD	Apex Certificate of Deposit (Ghana)
ADAF	Appropriate Development for Africa Foundation (Cameroon)
AMfB	ACCION Microfinance Bank (Nigeria)
AML	Anti-money laundering
AMPS	All Media and Product Survey (South Africa)
APR	Annual percentage rate
ARB	Association of Rural Banks (Ghana)
ASCAs	Accumulating Savings and Credit Associations
ATM	Automated teller machine
BAI	Bank Administration Institute
BCEAO	Banque Centrale des États de l'Afrique de l'Ouest
BEE	Black economic empowerment
BFI	Banking and financial institutions
BIB	Banque Internationale de Burkina (Burkina Faso)
BMCE	Banque Marocaine du Commerce Extérieur
BoN	Bank of Namibia
BoP	Balance of payment
BOP	Bottom of the pyramid (also base of the pyramid)
CA	Chartered accountant
CBK	Central Bank of Kenya
Cedi	Currency in Ghana
CEO	Chief executive officer
CETZAM	Christian Enterprise Trust of Zambia
CGAP	Consultative Group to Assist the Poor
CIH	Capricorn Investment Holdings Ltd.
Cordaid	Catholic Organisation for Relief and Development Aid
DFIs	Development finance institutions
DFID	Department for International Development (UK)
DoSD	Department of Social Development (South Africa)
DRC	Democratic Republic of Congo
EBS	Equity Building Society
EIB	European Investment Bank
EQI	Environmental Quality International (Egypt)
EU	European Union
FATF	Financial Action Task Force
FBS	Flexi Banking Services (Absa Bank)
FHI	Food for the Hungry International (Kenya)
FICA	Financial Intelligence Centre Act (South Africa)
FINCA	Foundation for International Community Assistance (Zambia)
FMO	Finance for Development (Netherlands)
FNB	First National Bank
FDCF	Financial Deepening Challenge Fund

FSDU	Financial Sector Deepening Project Uganda
FSM	Financial Services Measure
GCSCA	Ghana Co-operative Susu Collectors' Association
G2P	Government-to-person
GDP	Gross domestic product
GH¢	New Ghana cedi
GNI	Gross national income
GPRS	General Packet Radio Service
GSM	Global System for Mobile Communications
HMO	Health Maintenance Organisation
HSMS	Health service management system
HSN	Hunger Safety Net (Kenya)
ID	Identity document
IFC	International Finance Corporation
IFI	International financial institution
IFTS	Informal funds transfer systems
ILO	International Labour Organization
IMF	International Monetary Fund
IGVGD	Income Generation for Vulnerable Group Development
IP	Internet protocol
ISO	International Organization for Standardization
IT	Intermediate technology
IPA	Innovations for Poverty Action
LE	Egyptian pound
LDC	Least developed countries
LOA	Life Offices' Association of South Africa
LSM	Living Standard Measure (South Africa)
MBICU	Mbinga Co-operative Union
MCB	Mbinga Community Bank (Tanzania)
MC^2	Mutuelles Communautaires de Croissance (Community-based Mutual Funds
MFI	Microfinance institution
MFRC	Micro Finance Regulatory Council (South Africa)
MSMEs	Micro, Small and Medium Enterprises
MTAC	Medical treatment access card
MTC	Mobile Telecommunications Limited (Namibia)
NBFI	Non-bank financial institutions
NCA	National Credit Act (South Africa)
NGO	Non-governmental organisation
NHIS	National health insurance scheme
NPL	Non-performing loans
PAR	Portfolio at risk
PASP	Programme d'Appui au Secteur Privé (Burkina Bail)
PC	Personal computer
PIN	Personal identity number
POS	Point of sale
PRIDE	Promotion of Rural Initiatives and Development Enterprises
PULSE	Peri-Urban Lusaka Small Enterprise

RCB	Rural and Community Bank (Ghana)
RCTs	Randomised controlled trials
ROSCAs	Rotating Savings and Credit Associations
SACCOs	Savings and Credit Co-operatives
SADC	Southern African Development Community
SASSA	South African Social Security Agency
SBU	Strategic business unit (Absa)
SGMB	Société Générale Marocaine de Banques
SIEL	Société Internationale d'Equipements et de Leasing (Burkina Faso)
SME	Small and Medium Enterprise
SMMEs	Small, Medium and Micro Enterprises
SMS	Short message service (text message via mobile phone)
SPEED	Savings Promotion & Enhancement of Enterprise Development Program (Uganda)
TPA	Third-party administration
UCB	Uganda Commercial Bank
UEOMA	West African Economic and Monetary Union (Union Économique et Monétaire Ouest Africaine)
UIC	Uganda Insurance Commission
UK	United Kingdom
UML	Uganda Microfinance Limited
UNDP	United Nations Development Programme
UNICEF	United Nations Children's Fund
UEPS	Universal Electronic Payments Scheme
USAID	United States Agency for International Development
USSD	Unstructured supplementary service data
VAT	Value-added Tax
VCT	Voluntary counselling and testing (for HIV/AIDS)
VoIP	Voice over Internet Protocol

List of tables

0.1	Replicable models of innovation	20
1.1	Key economic data – Kenya	24
1.2	Overview of Equity Bank	28
1.3	Key economic data – South Africa	45
1.4	General household survey results, 2007	46
1.5	Salient financial features for Absa, 2005-2007	47
1.6	Flexi Banking Services' salient features	58
1.7	Key economic data – Tanzania	66
1.8	Key financial indicators for Tanzania Postal Bank, 2006	69
1.9	Key economic data – Namibia	77
1.10	Namibian banking sector – market share	77
2.1	Key economic data – Egypt	89
2.2	Poverty distribution in Egypt	90
2.3	Highlights from the Banque Misr Annual Report, 2005	91
2.4	Loans extended by Luxor Branch, 2004-2008	96
2.5	A cross-section of Banque Misr clients in Luxor	96
2.6	Key economic data – Burkina Faso	101
2.7	Key data for Burkina Bail	102
3.1	Key economic data – Ghana	111
3.2	Overview of Barclays Bank Ghana	115
3.3	Linkage schemes	123
3.4	Moroccan microfinance sector – key statistics	130
3.5	Loan portfolio profile of Al Amana	131
3.6	Highlights from Al Amana Annual Report, 2006	132
3.7	Branch network and staff evolution	134
3.8	Key financial information about Al Amana	137
5.1	Interviewed *hawala* agents operating in Johannesburg	172
5.2	Average value of funds transferred per transaction	174
5.3	Relationship between positive and negative characteristics	176
5.4	Relationship between positive characteristics and miscellaneous factors	176
5.5	Major schemes and their payment mechanisms	179
6.1	Mobile banking pricing – selected products, 2008	199
7.1	POS, ATM and internet charges	219
8.1	Mbinga Community Bank customer growth	228
9.1	Key economic data – Zambia	239
9.2	Key economic data – Uganda	243
9.3	Annual cost of Microcare insurance plans in Ugandan shilling, 2007	248
9.4	Microcare Group's financial profile, June 2007	257

List of figures

1.1	Growth in number of customers and staff	30
1.2	Percentage of bank customers who are poor	41
1.3	Proportion of the population who use financial services	42
1.4	Mzansi market share, March 2006	50
1.5	Formal mass-market size, 2007	51
1.6	Absa delivery footprint	55
1.7	Tanzanian population below the poverty line (%), actual and target	66
1.8	Deposit trends	68
1.9	Tanzania Postal Bank asset/income mix, 2005	70
1.10	Tanzanian T-bill and loan yields, 1993-2005	71
1.11	Composition of lending to clients, 2005	71
1.12	Bank Windhoek: Financial overview	78
2.1	The Banque Misr microlending organisation	94
3.1	The Barclays Bank Ghana/GCSCA on-lending scheme	116
3.2	Growth in total number of active microfinance clients	130
3.3	Al Amana's organisational structure	133
3.4	Global approach of MC^2 model	142
5.1	Schematic representation of *a hawala* transaction	170
5.2	The ladder of basic financial products	182
7.1	Transactions architecture	217
9.1	Microinsurance economic segmentation	247
10.1	The landscape of funding options for microfinance	264

Case study summaries

	Key dates	Kind of business	Key innovations	Target market	Total assets	Number of customers	External funding	Growth rates	People	Market capitalisation
Absa Flexi Banking South Africa	Began targeting the mass market in 2000	Bank unit offering savings, insurance, loans, mobile phone and internet banking, and the social grant Sekulula debit card	Used research to segment its target market into five distinct groups Has a variety of mass market products, including Sekulula, a debit card-based product for social grant recipients	Absa's Flexi Banking unit targets social grant recipients and people earning less than R5 000 a month	R7 067 million (Flexi Banking Services, 2006)	5.3 million (2008)		Flexi Banking Service's headline earnings grew by more than 400 % from 2003 to 2007	**Marius Ungerer**, general manager and strategy planner **Sonja van Vliet**, general manager mass market customer value propositions **Dave Liebenberg**, general manager segment management	
Afriland First Bank Cameroon	Launched linkage scheme with the Appropriate Development for Africa Foundation (ADAF) and the mutual societies in 1995	Financial and non-financial services offered through the two institutions, with Afriland providing financial services and ADAF the non-financial services such as capacity building	Launched a linkage-banking scheme with informal community-based mutual societies formed by village and rural members	By linking with community organisations, Afriland has significantly expanded its business and extended financial inclusion to previously unserved rural areas in Cameroon	Total funds mobilised: CFA 11 billion (2006)	63 participating mutual funds (2006)		Between 2006 and 2008, total funds mobilised grew by 27 %	**Dr Paul Fokam**, identified 95% financial exclusion in Cameroon in 1988 In 1992 he was appointed director general of Afriland (then CCEI Bank)	

	Key dates	Kind of business	Key innovations	Target market	Total assets	Number of customers	External funding	Growth rates	People	Market capitalisation
Al Amana Morocco	Established in 1997	Transformed from an NGO into a microfinance institution in 2000 providing loans to low-income solidarity groups and credit and housing loans to individuals	Carries out frequent market and impact studies in rural areas to build up knowledge of the market Created own-client identification records to deal with problem of lack of ID documents in rural areas	Low-income people in various sectors including commerce, artisans, services and agriculture Its goal is to reach the rural disadvantaged, especially in the desert and mountain regions where the population is sparse, to contribute to their social integration and economic development through microfinance and the promotion of small businesses	US$345 989 (2008)	At the end of the first 10 years of operating it had served almost half-a-million people, 50 % of who were women	Established as part of a USAID project Ongoing technical assistance Used DFI guarantees to help wean itself off donor funding and raise commercial loans	Steady growth from 1997 to 2004 of 15 % to 20 % a year using only development finance institution loans More rapid growth after 2004 Total assets grew by 141 % from 2005 to 2006	Fouad AbdelMoumni, chief executive since 1997	
ARB Apex Bank Ghana	Established in 2002	An apex bank for rural community banks It operates a payments system that enables these small banks to integrate into the national clearing system It also offers a money transfer service, the Apex Link Domestic Funds Transfer: a channel for foreign remittances	Launched *Efie Ne Fie*, enabling city workers to open savings accounts in their home villages, making remittances easy and encouraging saving	Rural and community banks	GH¢51.4 million (2008)	123 community banks and more than 560 banking offices	The bank was set up with the support of the donor community, primarily through the Rural Financial Services Project facility Funding from US Millennium Challenge Account helped the banks to computerise	Between 2007 and 2008, total equity grew by 13 %		

Case study summaries   xvii

	Key dates	Kind of business	Key innovations	Target market	Total assets	Number of customers	External funding	Growth rates	People	Market capitalisation
ATM Solutions South Africa and other countries	Established in 1999 Installed the first off-premise ATM in 2000	Private company deploying ATMs for different banks	Deploys mini-ATMs or ATMs in non-bank locations –32 % of the company's ATMs are located in previously underserviced areas	Retailers and corporates that want an ATM on their premises Retail banks that outsource deployment of ATMs		The company has a network of more than 4 000 machines dispensing R1.6 billion cash a month		Controls about 48 % of the off-premise ATM market in South Africa	Steven Kark and Rowan Swartz, inspired by the success of independent ATM deployers in the US, founded the company	
Bank Windhoek Namibia	Established in 1982 and began targeting the mass market in 2003	Retail bank offering a range of products	Set up community branches in the rural areas Introduced tailor-made banking products designed according to the needs of the rural target market	Lower-income rural people earning less than N$1 000 per month		More than 40 000 accounts opened with the launch of its EasySave product in November 2005	Awarded £1 million grant over four years in 2003 from DFID's Financial Deepening Challenge Fund to develop banking for the unbanked in rural areas		The bank's transformation was driven by Johan Swanepoel, group managing director Germanus Mate, head of business development, led the engagement with local communities	
Banque Misr Egypt	Microcredit business launched in 2004	State-controlled bank	Went out to micro-entrepreneurs to understand their businesses, using young graduates as loan officers	Micro and small enterprises in the less developed region of Upper Egypt	LE106 billion (2005)	112 201 loans disbursed (2008)	Developed plan to launch project in conjunction with the IFC	Total assets increased from LE62 billion in 2001 to LE106 billion in 2005	Microcredit programme driven by Dr Akmal Bassili	

	Key dates	Kind of business	Key innovations	Target market	Total assets	Number of customers	External funding	Growth rates	People	Market capitalisation
Barclays Bank Ghana and the *susu* collectors Ghana	In 2006 bank launched its *dwetiri* account for on-lending partnerships with credit unions, MFIs, savings and loan companies and *susu* collectors	Savings, wholesale loans, training	By using the traditional *susu* collectors as intermediaries, Barclays Ghana was able to extend its services to their clients and also build up a knowledge base of this new market for very low-value transactions	Barclays Ghana is reaching the unbanked segment of the market through the *susu* collectors	GHC1.2 billion (2007)	732 susu collectors are participating in the scheme (2008)	Seed grant of £160 00 from Barclays Bank plc	New deposits grew from US$2 million in 2007 to US$10.2 million in 2008		
Burkina Bail Burkina Faso	2005	A non-bank financial institution which provides loans, leasing and factoring services to small businesses. Co-owned by BIS, FMO and Cauris Investissement	Introduced leasing and factoring to SMEs, helping them to overcome traditional obstacles to getting finance. Personalised contracts	SMEs across most sectors	CFA7 957 million (2008)	More than 500 SMEs	Quasi-commercial funding by co-owners and Banque Ouest Africaine de Développement, Belgian Investment Office and European Investment Bank	Net profits grew from CFA95 million in 2005 to CFA116 million in 2008	**Gaspard Ouedraego**, managing director of BIS identified leasing as a way to bridge the financing gap for SMEs in 1996. **Abdoulaye Kouafilann Sory**, chief executive since 2000 also introduced factoring services	

Case study summaries xix

	Key dates	Kind of business	Key innovations	Target market	Total assets	Number of customers	External funding	Growth rates	People	Market capitalisation
Celtel (Celpay) Zambia, DRC	Launched Celpay in Zambia in 2002 and DCR in 2004	African mobile network operator Independent company since 2008, now headquartered in the Netherlands	Its mobile phone-based bank account Celpay offers deposit-taking and a range of payment services Customers can deposit and withdraw cash at participating banks and Celpay outlets			Accounts worth US$25 million per month in Zambia; two million transactions per month in DRC (2008)			Lazarus Muchenje, Celpay CEO	
Cointel South Africa	1996	Cointel provides enabling technology for mobile commerce Cointel's operations were incorporated into Vodacom in 2007	Simplus is a technology platform that makes it possible to effect payment using a cellphone instead of a credit or debit card						Gary Nunez, Mark Attieh, Leon Richards and Ahmed Ayob formed Cointel	
Dahabshiil Somalia	Family business founded in 1970 Established in the UK in 1989	Developed into a money remittance operation following the collapse of the Somali government and the displacement of Somalis	Set up a money transfer company by adapting the traditional *hawala* system of money transfer in Somalia	The Somali migrant community	Gross profit of £800 000 (2005)			Net assets almost tripled from 2004 to 2005		

	Key dates	Kind of business	Key innovations	Target market	Total assets	Number of customers	External funding	Growth rates	People	Market capitalisation
Ecobank West and Central Africa	Founded in 1988

Began offering wholesale products to MFIs in 1993 in Togo | Regional bank providing wholesale loans, cash management services, bulk microinsurance policies and non-financial services such as training and branch upgrading

Has a partnership with ACCION International to promote new MFIs | | MFIs, informal business networks | | Combined outreach of MFIs is 2.15 million MFIs, nearly 60 % of whom are women; 42 100 individuals (2008) | | In 2007, Ecobank grew revenues by 56 % to US$544 million and increased customer deposits by 89 % to US$4.7 billion | | |
| Equity Bank Kenya | Formed in 1984 as a building society

Began transforming in 1994 and became Equity Bank Limited in 2004 | Full-service retail bank listed on the Nairobi Stock Exchange, offering savings, lending, payments transactions and remittances services, trade, asset and security financing, foreign exchange, insurance premium finance | A fleet of solar-powered mobile banking centres allows Equity to reach clients in remote areas

Business loans are appraised on the client's capacity to repay and allow for alternative forms of collateral such as household items | The 'missing middle' – people ignored by the commercial banks as well as MFIs and SACCOs, such as self-employed traders, artisans and low-end government employees | KSh56 billion (US$698 million) (2009) | Three million (2008) | Received donor funding during transition phase from operating as a building society | Between 2004 and 2006, Equity's total assets grew by 70 % and its loans and advances by 95 % | James Mwangi led the transition from building society to commercial bank

He is now the bank's CEO and managing director | KSh56 billion (2009) |

Case study summaries

	Key dates	Kind of business	Key innovations	Target market	Total assets	Number of customers	External funding	Growth rates	People	Market capitalisation
Faulu Kenya Kenya	Started in 1992 as a pilot microlending programme Incorporated as a private company in 1999	A microfinance bank offering lending, business consultation and training	Moved from being donor-funded to securing KSh500 million in a local bond issue	The unbanked in Kenya		150 000 (2008)	Funding from USAID and DFID (1995) Raised US$5.1 million in external funding between 2000 and 2003 from the EU, two commercial banks and Dexia Microfinance Fund	Credit customers increased from 39 000 in 2005 to more than 151 185 in 2008		
Ferlo Senegal	2005	A joint venture between AfriCap, a MFI investment fund, and ByteTech, a Senegalese technology firm Providing a payments system for microfinance institutions	Developed a smartcard, MoneaCard, which offers membership, savings, credit, funds transfers and internal payments for MFIs	Financially underserved MFIs in Senegal		Almost 12 000 clients were using Ferlo services by the end of 2008, an increase of 169 % on December 2007				
First National Bank (FNB Cellphone Banking) South Africa	M-banking product launched in 2005	Bank offering the full range of banking products and services, as well as m-banking as another banking channel for its existing customer base		Clients with mobile phones		More than a million transactions a month (2007)			Yolande van Wyk, head of strategic programmes for Mobile and Transact Solutions	

	Key dates	Kind of business	Key innovations	Target market	Total assets	Number of customers	External funding	Growth rates	People	Market capitalisation
First National Bank's ATM division South Africa	Concept of Mini-ATMs launched in 2001	Division of FNB, one of South Africa's big four banks	Pioneered the use of Mini-ATMs in non-bank locations	People in rural, underserviced areas where customers are ATM cardholders; social grant recipients					Mike Arnold, CEO of FNB ATM (2003–2008)	
Hollard Insurance and Pep Stores South Africa	Partnership formed in 2006	Partnership between insurer Hollard and retailer Pep Stores to provide funeral and accidental death cover	Developed a cash-based retail insurance starter pack modelled on a mobile phone starter pack that uses the stores as an alternative distribution and payment network People do not need a bank account to buy the insurance	People with a monthly income of R2000–R5000		250 000 starter packs sold by the end of 2007		For the 2007 financial year, profit before tax increased 26 %	Robert Inglis, retail portfolio manager at Hollard Insurance when the product was first launched Derek Cikes, general manager of personal finance solutions Hollard Louis Brand, commercial director, Pep John Edwards, financial services manager, Pep	
MTN Banking South Africa	Launched in August 2005	A joint venture between mobile phone operator MTN and Standard Bank Group	MobileMoney, a mobile phone-based bank account with a cash card for withdrawals and deposits at Standard Bank ATMs; and a MasterCard debit card for other ATMs and POS payments	MTN's customer base Between 30 % and 50 % of its active clients are previously unbanked		300 000 registered users, 20 % of whom are active			Terry Timson, chief executive officer Dave Parratt, business development executive	

Case study summaries

	Key dates	Kind of business	Key innovations	Target market	Total assets	Number of customers	External funding	Growth rates	People	Market capitalisation
Mbinga Community Bank Tanzania	Opened in July 2003	Regional microfinance bank providing loans and savings products, and social assistance schemes	Launched *kifuku*, an overdraft account aimed at addressing the seasonal income fluctuations of smallholder farmers	Rural smallholder farmers and fishermen, and the artisans and microenterprises that serve them	US$1.2 million at the end of 2005	7 752 savings accounts, more than 14 000 loan accounts at the end of 2008	Licensed by the Central Bank of Tanzania as a Regional Unit Bank	Between 2207 and 2008, number of borrowers grew by more than 60 %	Shedehwa Optati, CEO	
Microcare Uganda	Microcare Limited founded in 2000. In 2004 formed Microcare Health Ltd and Microcare Insurance Ltd as profit-orientated businesses focused on health insurance	Microcare Health Ltd: Health plans, managed healthcare, health education and preventive health. Microcare Insurance Ltd: Commercial re-insurance, health insurance	Developed community-based and corporate schemes offering affordable health care to low-income groups	Low-income and corporate markets where they did not previously exist. A large market for quality private healthcare services has been created in urban and rural areas	Microcare Health: USh29.7million Microcare Insurance: USh80.7million (2007)	79 000 lives covered in 200+ employees/cultural/affinity groups (2008)	Donor funding for start-up and expansion	Premium turnover more than doubled year-on-year 2006–2007 and increased by a further 50 % in 2007–2008	Gerry Noble, physician and health-financing specialist and Francis Somerwell, IT specialist, founded Microcare Ltd in a bid to provide quality healthcare to the poor of Uganda	
MicroEnsure Subsidiaries in Ghana, Uganda, Tanzania, the Philippines and India, but works in 10 countries	2005	Wholly owned subsidiary of Opportunity International. Develops tailor-made insurance products for the clients of MFIs and informal financing operations	Developed weather index crop insurance for farmers. Provides compulsory credit life insurance with microloans. Offers cheap in-patient healthcare insurance	Poor households		About one million policies (2008)	US$24.2 million grant from the Bill & Melinda Gates Foundation for expansion		Richard Leftley, president of MicroEnsure	

	Key dates	Kind of business	Key innovations	Target market	Total assets	Number of customers	External funding	Growth rates	People	Market capitalisation
MLife Insurance Company Zambia Zambia	2006	Underwrites life insurance policies, gratuity policies, funeral policies and pension plans	Offers microinsurance products which are sold and serviced by partner MFIs These products are often mandatory with loans	Clients live mainly in peri-urban areas and are mostly self-employed, operating small or micro enterprises		130 000 clients (2007)		The microfinance arm of the business has grown by more than 300 % since 2002	Agnes Chakonta, deputy general manager of MLife	
Stanbic Bank Uganda Uganda	1993	Transactional accounts, microloans and credit life insurance	Accessed customers by recruiting new accounts through large employers Offers a warehouse receipts/ guaranteed financing system for farmers, and mobile banking in rural areas	Unbanked, low-income salaried people; the rural market		550 000 (2006)	Collaborated with USAID/ Rural SPEED to pilot warehouse receipts system	Profitability increased from USh28.4 billion in 2003 to USh39.5 billion in 2007	Marius Wait, director of personal and business banking, Standard Bank Africa	More than US$450 million (2007)
Summit Financial Partners South Africa	2004	Offers preventative financial literacy training, reactive financial counselling and administering and auditing of garnishee orders	Started out working in microlending but saw the negative effects of uncontrolled microlending and began advising and educating borrowers, and assisting the victims of exploitative microlenders	Nearly four million overindebted employees in South Africa		Employers who contract Summit to offer services to their employees Through partnership with ICAS has access to 400 companies, representing 500 000 employees Government employees		Summit's turnover has more than doubled annually since 2004, with a 75 % increase for the year ending February 2008	Clark Gardner, founder	

Case study summaries   **xxv**

	Key dates	Kind of business	Key innovations	Target market	Total assets	Number of customers	External funding	Growth rates	People	Market capitalisation
Tanzania Postal Bank Tanzania	State-owned retail bank, formed in 1992 from a post office savings facility	Savings and lending, including microcredit	Salary loans and group-based microcredit Introduced the Uhuru card which makes it possible to access cash away from the home branch	The mass market in Tanzania, particularly the rural poor	TZS73 279 million (2006)	At the end of 2006 the number of consumer loan borrowers was 25 291; number of Uhuru card holders was 72 851			**Alphonse Kihwele**, managing director	Tanzania Postal Bank
Vodafone/ Safaricom (M-Pesa) Kenya	M-Pesa pilot launched November 2005; full roll-out in March 2007	Safaricom is the Kenyan subsidiary of the UK-based international mobile network operator Vodafone	Its M-Pesa money transfer system allows people without a bank account to transfer money using a mobile phone	People in urban areas wanting to transfer money to family in the rural areas People in areas without banking outlets		More than four million (2008)	Funding for the pilot was received from DFID's FDCF		**Nick Hughes**, head of social products and enterprise, Vodafone (since moved on)	
Wizzit South Africa	2005	Mobile bank operating formally as a division of the South African Bank of Athens Limited, which provides the licence that allows Wizzit to operate Functionally, it operates as a separate entity	A mobile bank with no formal branches Has a sales team known as Wizzkids who service clients in rural areas, and has deposit-taking arrangements with the South African Post Office and Absa Bank	Unbanked and underbanked people in poor and rural communities		Wizzit opens up to eight thousand accounts a month (2008)	Receiving some start-up funding In 2007, the IFC, the financing arm of the World Bank, bought a 10% stake in the business		Wizzit is the brainchild of social entrepreneurs **Brian Richardson** and **Charles Rowlinson**	

Introduction

The case studies in this book illustrate abundant innovation and entrepreneurial pluck, which is reassuring coming from the continent with the worst levels of financial access in the world. In most African countries less than 20 % of the adult population uses a bank account. Lack of access to financial services means that people do not have safe places to store their money, cannot raise funds to invest in income-generating activities, and are vulnerable to financial shocks. Most people in Africa do not use financial products at all, not even informal products such as saving clubs. Their household economies are mainly cash based, often supplemented by in-kind forms of saving such as cattle.

That people do not use financial products does not always mean that they do not want them. The success of the M-Pesa money transmission product in Kenya *(chapter 6)* is proof that people want these kinds of services. M-Pesa is a way of moving money without a bank account, with only a cellphone and the ability to send text messages. After 18 months the service had attracted more than four million users, a remarkable figure considering that in 2006 only 2.5 million people in the whole of Kenya claimed to have an account with a commercial bank.

This book argues that there are ways in which banks, insurance companies and other profit-seeking organisations can build sustainable businesses around a growing opportunity in Africa for banking the unbanked or insuring the uninsured, and by doing so, improve the lives of people and communities previously excluded from formal financial services. The case studies demonstrate that the market can be 'a powerful instrument for doing good'.[1]

The book focuses on the activities of *providers* of financial services in Africa as they explore ways to serve new markets profitably. In bringing the role of the service provider to the fore, we are also demonstrating the important role that service providers can play as agents through which policies for economic growth and poverty reduction can be transmitted. It is hoped that by focusing on providers, this book will complement other writing on financial sector development, much of which has a regulatory, technical or macro-economic bias, and be of interest to both policymakers and other service providers.

The book has three primary aims. The first aim is to explore what makes successful providers succeed in often very challenging circumstances. Until recently Africa has performed poorly in economic terms, and although there are signs of progress, in many countries doing business is still far from easy. The financial sector in particular faces many challenges, so why are some providers able to break the mould and do well when others fail?

The second aim of the book is to document case studies of innovation that could be replicated. This is intended to encourage investment and promote competition. The case studies contain considerable detail on replicable business models, and describe the way operational challenges were overcome. The long-term funding strategies of some of these organisations are also described.

The third aim is to understand what motivates the service providers. Ultimately, incentives shape the way businesses conduct their activities. Profit seeking is at the heart of the incentive structure but, while this is important for all private sector providers, it may matter less to some organisations in the short term than to others.

Political considerations and notions of corporate citizenship also matter – but, again, more to some organisations than to others. Understanding the incentives that drive these organisations to engage with new markets is the first step towards understanding whether, and how, these incentives can be strengthened.

The social benefits of financial access are not the primary concern of the banks and insurance companies involved. In the main, these are not double-bottom-line organisations as such, but it is clear that most can combine the primary purpose of delivering a return to shareholders with a sense of social mission.

The case studies

The case studies have been selected from across Africa and from most sub-sectors, including banking, insurance, enterprise finance and remittances. Both long and short case studies have been incorporated to balance the more in-depth insights of the long cases with the greater representation that comes with the larger number of small cases. The long cases involved country visits and in-field interviews; the short ones were desk-based exercises.

There are some sector and geographical gaps in the selection. For example, there is little in the case studies on housing finance or private equity. There is also a southern African bias, but we believe this is justifiable. South Africa's powerful and overwhelmingly private sector financial services providers are innovating domestically, spurred by political pressure.[2] They are also seeking out growth opportunities across the continent, in some cases taking strategies that are successful in addressing the needs of South Africa's emerging consumers and applying them to other markets – such as the export of South African-style payroll-based lending, cellphone banking and funeral insurance.

Most of the content of the book is dedicated to the 24 case studies. We also asked some leading experts to write short articles to accompany them. Some are intended to be explanatory, providing a professional perspective on issues that the case studies might illustrate. They are all on issues that are pertinent to innovation in Africa's financial markets.

Only profit-seeking organisations were chosen for case studies. We were particularly keen to explore the role of those *privately owned* businesses that had made a deliberate strategic choice to target mass-market consumers, rather than organisations that were established *ab initio* as 'pro poor'. This approach therefore excluded microfinance institutions (MFIs), except for Faulu Kenya *(chapter 10)*, which has now turned itself into a bank, and Al Amana *(chapter 3)*.

The new markets being explored by these innovators are those at 'the bottom of the [financial] pyramid', to borrow from development strategist C K Prahalad; in other words, markets in which, on the demand side, people on very low incomes or small businesses are the main actors. In fact, the markets served are quite varied. Some organisations have set out expressly to target the poorest in society, while others are probably operating more in the middle of the pyramid: they are, as Kenya's Equity Bank *(chapter 1)* would describe them, the 'missing middle', people who by Western standards would be considered as poor, or near poor, and who manage their economic lives outside formal financial service provision. In short, they are economically active people, perhaps traders, artisans, fishermen, farmers, low-paid government employees and even the recipients of social transfers, who collectively represent the *financially underserved*. This introduction describes this market variously as the 'emerging' or 'mass' market.

The cases try to answer a number of questions. Who did what to get the innovation or product launched into the market? What obstacles had to be overcome, including internal institutional and organisational problems as well as external environmental problems? What helped the achievement?

The case studies also look at the benefits for the financial institution, the customer and the community as well as exploring the potential for future development and replication.

The case study approach has some clear advantages. It brings the subject matter alive through interviews with providers and customers, but it has some disadvantages too, which we acknowledge. A collection of case studies can only ever be a selection and, however well balanced it may be, this does not compensate for lack of representivity. Inevitably certain biases creep in. There are limits to the generalisations we can make using these case studies.

We also accept that the case study format tends to emphasise the positive at the expense of the negative. It is easier to persuade organisations to talk about what they have done well rather than what they have done badly. These case studies are mainly stories of success, although Burkina Bail (*chapter 2*) is finding it hard to sustain the initial success of its leasing venture. Microcare (*chapter 9*) recently ran into difficulties with its local regulator and was prevented from writing new business because it did not have the necessary capital to meet licensing requirements. The reality is that, for all the successful financial innovations, there are many more failures.

Many of the initiatives are also either very small or at a very early stage. We use the term 'innovation' broadly. The process of creative destruction (with which economist Joseph Schumpeter associates innovation) is not especially evident in these case studies although, as many of these initiatives are so new, time alone will tell if they prove to be examples of genuinely 'disruptive innovation'[3] that radically reshape Africa's financial markets. The mobile banking models in Chapter 6 may yet prove to be the exception.

What is indisputable, however, is that these successes show considerable early-stage promise. We are seeing a remarkable collective effort involving established players tackling new market opportunities for the first time (often in new places), new companies exploiting niche openings, new types of business relationships for distribution or funding, as well as the use of new technology. Capturing and presenting them now has value, even if long-term business survival requires that these business models be adapted or even replaced. Innovation is a process, not an event.

Finally, these case studies are almost all taken from reasonably stable countries, which underscores the fact that political and economic stability are probably the most important drivers for the investment and innovation that is taking place. With up to 40 % of Africa's population living in states that could be considered fragile, failed or failing, undoubtedly the strategies of formal sector providers in these environments merit closer scrutiny.

The context for the case studies

Africa can be an extremely challenging place in which to do business, as has been routinely confirmed by indicators such as the following:

- The World Bank's *Doing Business* 2007[4] indicators where, of the bottom 30 countries out of 178 participants 25 are from Africa, and only nine African countries are in the top 100,
- The Heritage Foundation's Economic Freedom Index, in which in 2007 only two African countries out of the 157 in the survey appear in the top 50 – Botswana and Mauritius,
- Transparency International's 2006 Corruption Perception Index, in which the same two countries, Botswana and Mauritius, are the only African countries in the top 50.

A similar picture emerges in a number of books. In *The Bottom Billion*, Paul Collier locates 70% of the world's bottom billion people in Africa. There are competing theories for why Africa's economic development has proved intractably slow. Collier blames a number of 'traps' such as wars, the 'curse' of abundant natural resources, geographic factors such as being landlocked and having bad neighbours, and weak governance.

In *The Trouble with Africa: Why Foreign Aid Isn't Working*, Robert Calderisi blames predatory leaders and profligate aid policies. Jeffrey D Sachs blames insufficient aid in *The End of Poverty: Economic Possibilities for Our Time*. Unquestionably, regardless of the underlying causes of Africa's economic malaise, it would be disingenuous to downplay the hostility of the environment in which businesses are investing.

But there is another story to tell, which may help to make sense of why financial sector innovators appear to be ready to explore the kinds of new opportunities described in these case studies. Political, economic, demographic and technology-related factors indicate the possibility of a more optimistic future, especially for the financial services sector.

Firstly, there has been increased political and economic stability. The aftershocks of decolonisation have diminished and so the incidence of political or ethnic conflict is far less than in the early 1990s.[5] Economic growth indicators show many countries in Africa to be on a steadily rising trend. More than a third of Africa's populations live in countries that have experienced average annual growth over 10 years (1996–2005) of over 4 % – including Rwanda (7.6 %), Tanzania (5.3 %) and Senegal (4.5 %)[6] – and these exclude the oil producers. The whole of sub-Saharan Africa grew more than 5 % between 2004 and 2005, and growth was projected to be at around 6 % for 2007 and 2008.[7] Population growth takes some of the shine off the gross domestic product (GDP) figures although even per-capita GDP grew on average by nearly 4% between 2004 and 2006. While the unequal distribution of this new wealth remains a stubborn problem, the growth picture from many African countries is remarkably positive.

Secondly, a number of other demographic trends are feeding into this growth story.[8] Chief among these is a rapid increase in Africa's population – quite simply, the market will grow fast as a young population becomes economically active. In 2008, 44 % of Tanzania's population was under the age of 15,[9] which is why the country's population is forecast to grow from around 40 million to more than 60 million by 2025. Similarly, Nigeria's population is forecast to grow from 146 million today to 203 million by 2025; 42 % of its population is presently under the age of 15.

Translating this population growth into a viable market for financial service providers presupposes that growth will be employment generating, and that young adults will have the economic opportunities that financial service providers are supposed to cater to. While we accept that unemployment among young adults is already a major issue for many African economies, it is surely safe to assume that many of today's under-15s will require banking and insurance once they grow up. While large growing populations create all sorts of negative pressures for developing economies, particularly in the areas of the environment, health and education provision, financial services could paradoxically benefit from population growth. And perhaps these younger adults will be more inclined to use technology to fulfil their banking needs than their parents were.

The population is also urbanising rapidly. Sub-Saharan Africa already has an urban population as big as that of North America, and this is predicted to double between 2000 and 2030. Although providing formal financial services in large informal settlements (72 % of Africa's urban population live in slums) will present unique challenges, it should be easier for providers to reach people living in these environments than in rural areas.

Thirdly, Africa is becoming a much more connected place. The explosion in cellphone use is well documented, offering migrant workers and people living and working far from urban centres the opportunity to determine their economic destinies more effectively. The overall increase in cellphone penetration on the continent is simply staggering, from 16 million mobile subscribers in 2000 to an estimated 300 million now *(chapter 6)*, and still there are only 21 mobile subscribers per 100 Africans[10] compared to the world average of 41 per 100. Of particular relevance to the banking industry is the number of *unbanked* cellphone users – for example, 31 % in South Africa and 17 % in Kenya,[11] a group representing an untapped potential for cellphone banking services.

Internet penetration in Africa is also much lower than world averages – 5 % compared with the global average of 17 %.[12] This suggests that in time the internet may become a widespread medium for accessing financial services, assuming infrastructure gaps in the provision of broadband will eventually be plugged.

The degree to which these trends have strengthened the ambitions of the innovators specifically profiled in this book is difficult to say, but it is unlikely that they will have been disregarded.

Of course, the positive trends we are seeing in some countries could weaken, or indeed go into reverse as the full effects of the global financial crisis unfold in Africa. It could be argued that many of the positive developments are off an extremely low base, that the improvements should be more dramatic as a result, and that many of the more successful or improving economies are either very small (Botswana, Mauritius) or were buoyed by sharp rises in oil and commodity prices (Zambia, Equatorial Guinea). Finally, many countries in Africa are simply extremely poor – Rwanda, Malawi and Mozambique all depend on foreign donors for more than 40 % of their revenues[13] – and so we have to be realistic about how quickly economic reform can be driven and how deep it will be.

Financial services in Africa

The business environment specifically for financial services – the primary focus of this book – is far from adequate in most African countries.

The problems faced by banks and insurance companies are not all exogenous, but those that are include a lack of market information, unfriendly laws and regulations, a limited payments infrastructure and sporadic power supplies. Markets are also affected by the continued existence of moribund state-owned organisations that are prone to capture by local élites and whose subsidised balance sheets give them an unfair competitive advantage.

Populism, too, especially in the area of pro-poor finance, can lead to financial initiatives, or schemes, that are very damaging for microfinance. At best, these are well-meant initiatives that are supposed to respond to a market failure but often lack the operational back-up needed for effective delivery. At worst, they are simply pre-election gimmicks that are a vehicle for corruption. The sudden influx of cheap money through these sorts of schemes undermines the real economics of microfinance.

Given this predictably depressing backdrop, it is therefore all the more intriguing that, paradoxically, Africa's financial sector is one of the most profitable in the world, with bank returns in Africa double or even treble what other emerging markets deliver.

Why is this? First, financial depth, measured by deposits mobilised or credit extended, has been on a rising trend since the mid-1990s, especially in deposit mobilisation.[14]

Secondly, African banking systems are highly liquid, partly because their success in mobilising deposits is not matched by success in lending to the private sector. Where East Asian banks allocate about 63 % of their assets to private sector credit, the corresponding figure for banks in sub-Saharan Africa is only around 26 %. Government borrowing in many African countries has crowded out private sector borrowing, although government bond rates are now declining in many countries in response to better economic management and debt forgiveness.

Banks also generate huge margins from the deposit-taking business,[15] charging fees to depositors, paying little by way of interest but profiting from huge spreads, skewing incentives towards this part of the business and away from lending. The consequences are that growth is held back because investment is low, and access levels also remain extremely low. Many consumers cannot afford even to deposit their money with a bank let alone take out a loan. To say the least, this is easy money – why change?

The combination of inefficiency in many banking systems in sub-Saharan Africa, in which high operating costs are not adequately compensated by productivity, with year-on-year profitability leads to the inevitable conclusion that lack of competition is a fundamental reason why banks in Africa are so profitable. Where economies are very small, there is a limit to how much profit in absolute terms can be extracted from them and so new entrants stay away and markets remain uncontested.

In summary, banks in Africa occupy fairly narrow niches but have benefitted from an environment of profitable inertia. Outside the narrow niches is a much more complex world of unsalaried or informally employed people, small businesses with no collateral and farming communities where the immediate prospects of a return are often uncertain.

This book investigates why and how, some service providers are developing an appetite for this more complex world. Perhaps it is too early to herald the arrival of a 'new dawn' in African banking but this should not stop us celebrating the entrepreneurship, or even chutzpah, of a few organisations that seem to be willing to break the mould.

With the global financial system now in turmoil, it will be extremely interesting to see how Africa's banking system fares. There seems little doubt that Africa's real economy will be affected by recessionary conditions in the developed world and by more muted demand for commodities in countries such as China and India, and this will feed into the trading performance of the service providers. However, there are reasons to hope that the predominance of domestic funding (perhaps necessitated by exchange controls as in South Africa) and the relative traditionalism of African banking compared to the more exotic practices in the developed world will protect Africa's banking sector from the dramatic developments we have seen in the US and Europe.

Succeeding against the odds – why some providers get it right

While the case studies in this book focus on success stories, this has to be countered by the reality that many innovations in African finance have failed. Understanding why initiatives fail is as important as understanding why others succeed, although comparing the case study successes with documented failures is complicated for a number of reasons.

Firstly, there are few documented case studies of failure. Secondly, many of the 'bottom-of-the-pyramid' initiatives profiled as successes in the case studies are small parts of much larger operations, whereas most of the failures that are documented tend to be the collapse of entire organisations, so we have few clear comparators.

Thirdly, bank collapses tend to be triggered by a specific event (for example an act of fraud) that overshadows the multiple external and internal challenges the organisation might have faced while operating as a going concern. In the main, the case studies focus on the choices that the promoters and managers of financial innovations make in response to these multiple challenges.

Although there have been an extraordinary number of bank collapses in Africa in the past 20 years, most collapsed for reasons that had nothing to do with bottom-of-the-pyramid strategies going awry. Almost all were victims of catastrophic lapses in governance, and general management failure at board level.

In his analysis of bank failures in Kenya, Nigeria, Uganda and Zambia in the mid-1990s, Martin Brownbridge[16] concludes, predictably enough, that a major cause of financial distress was 'moral hazard, with the adoption of high-risk lending strategies, in some cases involving insider lending'. The establishment of local banks in, for example, Kenya and Zambia started in the late 1980s and accelerated with the onset of liberalisation in the early 1990s. Banking licences proliferated: there were very low minimum capital requirements, and licences were awarded without banks needing to prove that their senior management was up to the job. There was political interference in bank boardrooms and in the central banks such that loans were granted to politicians' pet projects and not repaid; Kenya's Trade Bank, which folded in 1993, being a particularly egregious example. Poor oversight perpetuated the survival of institutions that were inadequate and a dire threat to the financial system.

The impact was disastrous: in Kenya, between 1984 and 1996, nine local banks and 20 non-bank financial institutions failed; in Zambia, three banks folded in 1995 alone.

Constance Apea and Jemime Sezibera, in their 2002 case study of the collapse of Ghana Co-operative Bank in 2000,[17] tell a less dramatic story – but essentially still one of persistent management failure in which ineffective credit management resulted in large bad debts, losses year after year and declining depositor confidence, with the inevitable result.

Banks that are badly or fraudulently managed will fail – this much is obvious. This indeed is the equal and opposite lesson from the case studies where we see repeatedly that there is no substitute for the sound application of basic banking disciplines. Successful innovation is not only the result of an exceptional idea or the introduction of clever technology. It is mainly about ensuring that the 'nuts and bolts' of the banking business are firmly in place.

It is probably fair to say that market positioning meant that many of these failed banks were more prone to failure because they were operating in a higher risk environment. These local banks were exploiting an opportunity which, these days, would be called sub-prime. Whether the underlying business models of these failed banks operating in their sub-prime markets were essentially sound, only to be undermined by a once-off incident, such as a particularly large bad debt, or inherently unstable is hard to say. But it is clear from banks such as Equity, case studied in this book, or South Africa-based Capitec, that rigorous application of banking disciplines, including risk management processes, can allow businesses that explicitly target apparently higher-risk customers to prosper.

The collapse of the Meridien BIAO banking group in 1995 is especially interesting because Meridien was a self-styled 'bank of the people'.[18] But, again, its downfall appears not to be the result of its mass banking strategies. Indeed, the populist innovations it introduced, such as interest on current accounts, cheque books for savings-account holders and even a smartcard (the Meridien Card introduced in Zambia) were highly successful for the bank. The major factors behind the collapse of the bank – the devaluation of the West African CFA franc, a currency dealing room loss at the London office and fragility in a number of the group's operating markets in Africa – were exogenous to the mass banking business. Nevertheless, it is hard to escape the conclusion that overstretch – too many activities in too many locations – made the group highly vulnerable to external shocks, and so we can conclude that management actions (or lack thereof) played a part in the collapse of the bank.

The South African experience

South Africa's political transition in the 1990s was a time of considerable experimentation in financial services with some successes in reaching out to previously excluded, primarily black, communities. It was also a time of many failures.[19] Different role players – government, donors, private sector and unions – recognised the need and the opportunity for new types of organisations to provide financial services to previously excluded South Africans.

A number of themes emerge from these attempts.

Pro-poor design features can get in the way of operating effectiveness: The infusion of social motives into the operating principles of a number of these initiatives led directly to their failure. This was particularly true of Community Bank,[20] which was founded a few weeks after the country's first democratic elections in 1994 and lasted only two years.

Community Bank aimed to provide low-income clients with a range of products including a basic savings account, small home loans and loans to the small and medium enterprise (SME) sector. But its structure mirrored its developmental and commercial purpose, and proved to be highly dysfunctional and disempowering for management. Lack of mission clarity was part of Community Bank's undoing. It is noteworthy that in all the case studies in this book, business sustainability comes first with the developmental benefits as a by-product.

Role clarity among multiple promoters is a prerequisite: New ventures may start with multiple promoters – for example a management team, investors or lenders, donor or government agencies, providers of technical assistance, and so on. The case of Nkwe Enterprise Finance,[21] established in 2001 to provide loans on a commercial basis to microenterprises in South Africa's North West province and closed only two years later, is a salutary reminder of how quickly a coalition of promoters and funders can unravel, especially if the business performs poorly against expectations.

A viable strategy for growing quickly to scale must be matched by a long-term funding strategy: Mass banking is, above all, a volume game requiring economies of scale and a funding strategy that allows the entity to achieve that scale. This is one of the most difficult challenges new ventures face, with severe risks in both over-rapid and excessively cautious growth strategies.

In Community Bank's case, 17 branches were opened in only two years in pursuit of operating scale. The bank proved successful at extending small mortgages but unfortunately not at mobilising retail deposits. Rapid growth across a broad base, aimed at achieving economies of scale, might be possible in relatively uncontested markets but proved impossible in South Africa in the mid-1990s.

Another South African pioneer from the 1990s was CashBank, which specialised in low-income mortgages backed by pension funds – a niche that proved successful for several years. The bank also grew rapidly, but became dependent on the continued availability of concessionary funding which had dried up by the time it needed fresh capital.

First National Bank's (FNB's) GrowthAssist product, a credit product for small businesses, marketed as a pilot between 2002 and 2003, never got near achieving sufficient scale. Its execution was perhaps too tentative from the start. Eight loan officers from four branches were able to disburse only 90 loans during the first year against projected loans disbursed of 90 *per loan officer*. According to an executive involved in the pilot, 'the reasons for closure [of the pilot] came down to volumes and profitability, not because the clients did not repay'. GrowthAssist was hampered by a highly centralised loan-approval process, where the branch managers had no lending approval authority. A conservative stance towards perfecting and protecting its security on its loans also meant that loans were disbursed as much as two to three months after credit committee approval. Although FNB relaxed its stance on security later in the pilot, it is suggested that these excessive delays damaged the reputation of the bank in the minds of prospective borrowers and contributed to low levels of take-up.

Location matters: While there is no template for how to balance market development and profit-making, it is critical that innovators get it right. As Nkwe was originally promoted by the government of North West Province, its location was arguably a foregone conclusion. Nevertheless the market proved to be weak, such that management even proposed moving the operation to the more densely-populated urban area of Soweto. The pre-launch market research was considered in hindsight by one of the stakeholders to be 'permeated by wishful thinking'; such was the government's eagerness to bring Nkwe to the province.

It is noteworthy that even though Banque Misr *(chapter 2)* chose to locate its microlending operation in Upper Egypt, away from the main urban centres in the north of the country, it nevertheless made a point of establishing its activities close to where its principal competitor was already operating. Thus, it was sure there was a market there to compete for.

Excessive exposure to government carries risks: Whether government is a customer or simply the architect of a policy environment on which the business model depends, exposure to government carries risks. A dramatic example of this was the South African government's abrupt decision to deny microlenders access to its payroll deduction facility, Persal, in 2000. This contributed directly to the failure of two banks working in the new microlending market – UniFer (absorbed in 2002 into Absa) and Saambou (which went into curatorship in 2002).

As the reviewers of the Nkwe experiment conclude, general lesson learning from case studies is difficult because outcomes are context specific and determined by decisions taken at a particular time. This is as true of the successes as of the failures although the difficulty of accessing information in relation to failed financial innovations makes one particularly hesitant to draw broad conclusions because the sample size is so small.

Although the case studies in this book are extremely diverse, some common success factors do make it possible to suggest some general observations on the nature of the innovation that is taking place in Africa's financial markets. Six general themes link most of these cases:

1. A cross-disciplinary approach is needed for successful innovation.
2. Technology helps but it is not everything.
3. Doing things differently can pay off.
4. There must be a profound understanding that the needs of these new customers are different.
5. New markets need to be developed.
6. Innovation often happens because of the commitment of a particular individual, but the support of senior management is essential.

A cross-disciplinary approach is needed for successful innovation: Successful innovation comes from effective collaboration across complementary business disciplines. The case studies illustrate that getting the business basics right is a necessary, and perhaps even a sufficient, condition for success. Investment in product design or technology will not in itself make good the absence of sound business management.

Equity Bank is the outstanding example of this, a financial organisation that has innovated well at the customer end but has also placed great emphasis on operating efficiency. To quote the Bank Administration Institute (BAI):[22] 'To be successful banks (and other financial institutions) need to be virtuosos of the everyday. [They] must "do" routine extremely well. Customers need to know their money is safe.'[23] As an institution that grew from a position of technical insolvency in 1993, Equity realised that winning the confidence of its customer base needed to be a clear priority. It is instructive that the bank still feels it needs to combat the perception of being a small, indigenous (and, by inference, risky) bank, even though it has a market value on the Nairobi Stock Exchange of over US$650 million. Countering this kind of negative perception needs years of reliable and consistent performance.

It is instructive that MicroEnsure *(chapter 9)*, which is capable of developing complex products such as crop derivative insurance, strives to simplify its products because this streamlines administration and keeps costs down, a necessity for this low-margin, high-volume business.

Technology helps, but is not a panacea: Technology, used especially for communication, is unquestionably stimulating much of the innovation that is profiled in this book, by enabling it to happen at all, by enhancing its chances of success and by giving the innovators a sense of what might be achievable in the future.

Effective and reliable communication is obviously a precondition to overcoming the challenge of bringing financial services to remote communities – the Mini-ATM, essentially a communication device, is a prime example *(FNB/ATM Solutions* in *chapter 4)*. Cellphones, while facilitating mobile banking (m-banking), are also routinely used in other ways: microloans and insurance products are processed with the help of cellphones *(Absa, chapter 1)* and insurance brokers currently reliant on MFI intermediaries may look to cellphones to facilitate direct service provision in the future *(MicroEnsure and MLife* in *chapter 9)*.

However, technology per se is not the reason the m-banking players *(chapter 6)* or Cointel *(chapter 7)* are making progress: it is the effective application of that technology for a business purpose that is innovative. Cointel's innovation was to see a way to take the mechanism for paying for airtime by cellphone into the unbanked environment using a prepaid card instead of a credit card, a new approach that required collaboration with both a bank and a card company. The Ferlo case study *(chapter 7)* is another good example of technology being adapted to fit a particular market context.

Good technology is a given for mobile bank Wizzit *(chapter 6)* – it could not function at all with inadequate technology. The bigger business challenge, it would appear, has been building a banking business from scratch that its customers would trust with their money. Wizzit is an exciting potential 'disruptive innovator' not because of its technology but because its positioning appeals to a large part of the population who have no experience of (or are disenchanted with) the mainstream banks.

Without doubt, technology advances, particularly in cellular technology, are giving financial services in Africa a massive boost, opening up new access frontiers that even recently would have been considered well out of reach. Though these developments should be celebrated, the case studies remind us of the numerous gritty operational realities that technology cannot spirit away.

Doing things differently can pay off: It goes without saying that innovation implies doing things differently. In financial services organisations, the pressure to do things the same way can be intense. It has been suggested that highly regulated industries such as banking and insurance tend towards cultures that value compliance more than risk taking. In 'thick cultures',[24] such as in banks, scale economies are extracted by standardising and aggregating millions of routine transactions, leaving little room for innovation. These dynamics are often then reinforced by hierarchical remuneration structures which do not reward short-term experimentation. However, in several of these case studies, we see organisations creating the space for innovation that would otherwise be counter-cultural.

Banque Misr is the clearest example of this. Its Upper Egypt SME lending operation departed radically from the bank's normal lending practices, firstly by choosing to start its microlending business in Upper Egypt (the south of the country) rather than in the populous urban centres of the north. Secondly, it hired enthusiastic graduates as loan officers rather than more experienced staff because it needed to have this new initiative run by people who were not doctrinaire in their views about how a banking business should be run.

FNB went against the grain by rolling out Mini-ATMs across South Africa. It was the only one of South Africa's big four banks to do so and is still the sole provider of these devices in the country.

When Bank Windhoek *(chapter 1)* decided to make a play for low-income consumers in remote rural areas of Namibia, the other banks must have raised their eyebrows. Here, grant funding from a donor encouraged Bank Windhoek to create the space for this strategic push, which has paid off for the bank in both financial and non-financial ways.

A number of the organisations profiled do not carry the ideological baggage that established players often do. Some have moved in to exploit a greenfield opportunity *(ATM Solutions* and *Burkina Bail)*, post-conflict Somalia being an extreme example *(Dahabshiil, chapter 5)*. Some carry a conviction about an opportunity, based on research or market knowledge, that has taken them into an environment that seems either highly unpromising at first blush *(MicroEnsure)* or potentially very competitive *(Wizzit)*. Others have transferred experience into a new environment *(Stanbic Uganda, chapter 8)* or have looked to create a new type of financing relationship *(Faulu)*.

At least two *(Summit, chapter 10* and *Microcare)* have taken a for-profit business model into an environment where service providers have traditionally been not-for-profit. Microcare also broke the mould by allowing policyholders a choice of service provider rather than tying them to one particular organisation as Uganda's Health Maintenance Organisations do. Whether Microcare's model endures remains to be seen.

But this is not just about business models – it is also about a style of doing business. As one of Burkina Bail's leasing clients remarks about the advice he receives from the company: 'I have never asked myself whether it is a "service" of theirs …. It's not like a typical office.'

There must be a profound understanding that the needs of these new customers are different: This is probably the insight that connects more of these case studies than any other. Almost all recognised that making a successful business out of this emerging market would depend on knowing their customers – that is, developing a profound understanding of their financial behaviour and needs. Quickly adapting existing products would not work.

Market research was the first step for some *(MicroEnsure)*. Absa and Bank Windhoek took the time to understand what the FinScope[25] data was saying about the target market.

Even community banks *(Mbinga, chapter 8)*, despite the advantage they have of being rooted in the local community, acknowledge the need for market research.

Knowing what customers can afford is evidently a critical output of the market research *(Bank Windhoek, Equity)* but so too is an understanding of the income profile of a customer through the year. Financial products that enable farmers to ride out the 'boom and bust' of the annual agricultural cycle *(Stanbic Uganda, Mbinga)* can help farmers to maximise the yield from their crops and so, over time, contribute towards building a stronger client base.

Microcare's familiarity with its customer base is built into its charging structure. A small consultation fee is levied to prevent overclaiming for benefits which would end up being too expensive for the business: 'Ugandans love health services and love to be treated whether by tablet or especially by injection, and this small fee is a way of screening,' Microcare says.

For the organisations adopting a more wholesale approach to financial service provision *(Barclays Ghana, chapter 2* and *Ecobank, chapter 3)* the business of knowing one's customer is effectively outsourced to the partner. Not using the traditional *susu* collectors as intermediaries, if Barclays Ghana ever chose to do this, would be a dangerous strategy. It is hard to imagine how it would ever be able to build a knowledge base on its customers as comprehensive as that which the *susu* collectors already have.

New markets need to be developed: Common to many of the cases is the recognition that new markets need to be developed, although perhaps not all in the extreme way that Bank Windhoek did so in transporting building materials, and even drinking water, into the remote areas where it wanted to build a banking business.

For many organisations *(Ecobank)*, market development means providing non-financial services, such as training, or a more general package of financial support (for example treasury services) to clients. One can see a direct business benefit to these services being offered. Clearly these services could be explicitly charged for, for example by bundling the costs into a loan, but it is not always clear from these case studies when this happens.

ARB Apex Bank's *(chapter 8)* entire *raison d'être* is to develop its market, on behalf of the rural banks which are its shareholders, with the aim of recovering all its costs and eventually making a profit. Afriland First Bank *(chapter 3)*, through supporting the Appropriate Development for Africa Foundation that provides non-financial services to its network of village-based mutuals, is also developing its own market. Al Amana *(chapter 3)* has used a combination of loan officers out in the field and market, and impact studies to expand its reach into the desert and mountain regions of Morocco where the population is sparse. It is difficult to reach women in the traditional communities in which they work, and women constitute 71.3 % of its clients.

Burkina Bail developed its market by working with government to adapt and introduce required new legislation governing leasing in Burkina Faso.

These are instances of 'enlightened self-interest' in which organisations contribute to the long-term development of a new market which is then commercially viable.

Poor consumer financial literacy across the continent is perhaps the biggest market development challenge. The insurance industry case studies *(MicroEnsure, MLife)* illustrate vividly the importance of investing in training intermediaries (typically, MFI loan officers) so that they understand how the insurance works and are then in a position to pass this knowledge on to the end customer.

Innovation often happens because of the commitment of a particular person, but the support of senior management is essential: Innovators are often driven individuals whose passion for their idea is the basis of the entrepreneurship behind a new business. For these people, the risks and rewards of business ownership are closely aligned with the realisation of their vision *(Cointel, Summit)* and so the seeds of a successful business are sown.

What is perhaps more surprising is how much successful innovation depends on the commitment of particular individuals within larger organisations, and a number of the case studies profile exactly this. These people do not have the capital incentives of the business owner and, as we discussed earlier, they often have to contend with organisational cultures that may not be especially supportive. Their motivations are complex: some may see in the new business initiative a serious platform for career advancement. Most appear to be motivated by a mixture of both pure intellectual interest and a desire to make a contribution to society, and at the same time wanting to make money for their employers. The Absa case hints at how its more developmentally oriented Flexi Banking Services attracts a particular kind of socially motivated employee, which is good for the employee and also for the bank, which benefits from that additional motivation.

It is also noteworthy that a number of these individuals are very experienced people who have already achieved success in their careers *(Banque Misr, Burkina Bail)*. This can be important for winning the confidence of senior management: several of the cases *(Absa, Banque Misr)* single out the support of senior management as vital.

Perhaps the most important lesson from this is that innovation is not something that larger organisations can leave to boffins or mavericks, although these may have their place. The successful innovators profiled in this book seem to be people who have considerable business experience and are authoritative enough to be able to command the respect and imagination of senior management and win the co-operation of the other departments within the organisation whose help will be required. The lesson for senior management is that if you are serious about innovation, you need to hire high-calibre people whom you can trust to carry out their mandate effectively even if their methods are unorthodox.

Having a champion is, however, no guarantee of a new venture's long-term success. Community Bank lost a key executive shortly before trading started. This person was considered experienced and authoritative enough to have been able to reconcile the profit-seeking and developmental motives of the bank. In its small way, GrowthAssist also suffered from changes in key staff as a result of which there was a loss of commitment to the pilot.

It is also worth noting that while exogenous factors may have contributed to the failure of some financial innovations, many were undone by the promoters or managers of businesses making the wrong choices, or none at all.

Understanding motivation

All the organisations profiled in this book are in business to make a profit, and profit seeking is overwhelmingly the driving force behind these innovations. Political economy considerations clearly matter but corporate citizenship alone is not a primary consideration in any of these case studies.

The profit motive

Some of the larger organisations *(Barclays Ghana, Banque Misr)* approach the opportunities as pilots, investing relatively little by way of capital and, in turn, making very little by way of a profit. While the payback on the investment may be quite quick, it will take several years for these initiatives to contribute materially to group profits. One can surmise, therefore, that non-financial gains such as political relationship building or corporate citizenship provide a good short-term justification for the cost of investment, even if the intent is to experiment with a view to building a substantial business in the long term.

Other large organisations *(Absa, Stanbic Uganda)* invest more up-front to make a significant return more quickly. The growth rates described in both these cases have been rapid. Absa's Flexi Banking Services started in 2000 and by 2006 contributed 3.4 % of group earnings, no mean achievement considering that Absa as a whole was growing strongly throughout that period.[26] The message is clear – the investment needs to make money for the group quickly and so the absolute cash contribution matters. Absa's Flexi Banking team make the point expressly: they are subject to the same investment criteria as any other part of the group.

In some cases, the path to profitability was fairly slow. What is striking is the number which reported they were profitable from a very early stage *(ATM Solutions* and *Hollard/ Pep, chapter 4, Absa, Bank Windhoek)*. While this demonstrates that these organisations researched the opportunity well, it also points to the strength of pent-up, unmet demand.

Most of the case studies make absolute levels of profit that would be considered modest by developed world standards, but common to practically all are the growth rates. A number can be considered to be coming off a low base but others *(Equity, Summit)* are now established businesses that are growing profits extremely fast. This speaks not just of well-implemented strategies but also of the quality of the business to be made in these emerging markets where repayment rates are astonishingly high *(Banque Misr, Barclays Ghana)*.

This is confirmed by a cursory look at the financial statements of some well-managed MFIs in other parts of the world, which are also generating above-average profit growth.[27] This is perhaps not so surprising given that the client bases share certain similarities, even if they are on different continents. Profitable distribution in these emerging markets hinges on being able to handle large volumes of small transactions or at least being able to provide services to the organisations that do.

Wholesale lending to MFIs is obviously one approach. In one case *(Ecobank)*, however, a purely wholesale offering is evidently not enough of a response to the opportunity and so, in partnership with ACCION International, this bank is actually promoting new MFIs so that it can get closer to the end clients.

Many of the business models profiled depend on the bank or insurance company being able to access *groups* of people efficiently and, where intermediation is involved, then sharing profits appropriately with distribution partners. One way to access groups of people efficiently is at their place of work – at offices, farms, factories or mines *(Summit, Stanbic Uganda, Wizzit)*.

Where services are offered indirectly, getting the incentives right for all the participants in the value chain is of paramount importance *(Barclays Ghana, MicroEnsure, FNB/ATM Solutions, MLife, Afriland)*. ARB Apex Bank, a kind of central bank for the rural banks in Ghana, is an intermediary providing the infrastructure that binds these 123 banks (with their 560 banking offices) and links them to mainstream financial markets.

In the case of Microcare, dealing with pre-existing groups (groups of employees, burial societies, clients of MFIs) is about more than simply aggregation: it is fundamental to its being able to avoid the risk of adverse selection and yet uphold the principle of equal access to healthcare.

The biggest intermediary of all is the telecommunications industry. As Al Hammond explains in his article in *chapter 6*, it is the mobile phone companies that are calling the shots through huge rollout programmes and the introduction of more sophisticated technology that will make the provision of financial services at scale much easier. M-banking does not necessarily need banks, as the success of the Vodafone/Safaricom M-Pesa product in Kenya demonstrates, and so there are great opportunities for mobile phone companies to encroach on traditional banking business, if they choose to do so and if permitted by regulation. Thus, the conjunction of mobile telephony and banking has created uncertainty for banks at the same time as creating huge potential. Several different business models are now up for negotiation, a number of which will no longer use banks as intermediaries in any way. The incentive for the banking industry to use mobile telephony to access new customers – the millions of unbanked mobile phone users – or provide enhanced services to mobile phone users who are already banked is enormous, but there are complex strategic choices to be made that will involve giving part of the value chain away to the mobile carriers.

In a number of cases *(MicroEnsure, Microcare)*, the non-profit and for-profit worlds seem to co-exist reasonably happily, although we can surmise that the stringency of operating in a for-profit environment has played an essential role in their success.

Political economy motivations

While the pursuit of profit is the primary driver, a country's political economy shapes the incentives. Most formal providers are regulated, and the laws of the land impinge directly on their businesses through acts of parliament, central bank regulations and so on. Because they are regulated, formal financial sector providers are mindful of their relationships with government.

The Absa and Banque Misr cases illustrate how political pressure can produce a result that works for both the government and the service provider. In both these cases, the unbanked have turned out to be an attractive source of new business. Thus, moral suasion – political pressure that falls short of coercive legislation – can fulfil a political objective and also stimulate innovation. If adequate profits can be made from these politically driven initiatives, this is surely not objectionable.

We maintain that increased moral suasion, such as South Africa's Financial Sector Charter, could be effective in other countries in Africa as a way to accelerate the momentum towards greater access that we are starting to see around the provision of financial services to the poor.[28] A charter approach would need to be tailored to local conditions but we believe that the provisions of the charter that can be easily exported are the commitments relating to improving access, even if the targets are difficult to define.

The main argument against moral suasion is the risk that it is a deterrent to foreign investment, and that foreign-owned incumbents will divest. We doubt this light form of pressure is a serious deterrent in markets that can deliver returns that, for banks, are among the highest in the world. And, indeed, requiring incoming banks to direct part of their business to low-income or rural communities may not be a deterrent at all as this is increasingly where the growth opportunities are seen to be.

Similarly, requiring incoming banks to make a reasonable contribution to market development as a condition for granting a banking licence should not be controversial either as most already understand that market development benefits them. Financial institutions contribute best to market development by actively competing for business, investing in infrastructure where necessary and introducing new products. However, more could be done to benefit the market as a whole – for example supporting publicly available market research or funding consumer financial literacy.

Corporate citizenship

Finally, it is clear that pure corporate citizenship plays only a minor part. One of the organisations profiled *(ATM Solutions)* points to aspects of its activities that are there simply to provide a community benefit – ATMs in very remote areas that are (presumably) loss making, but this is an exception. Bank Windhoek did not set out to serve rural Namibians for charitable reasons but because it wanted to find a profitable new market – and even used donor funding to defray the cost of investment.

Almost all these cases suggest that the profit motive can coexist with a sense of social mission. A clear example is Summit, turning a profit out of debt counselling services that many would argue is the natural preserve of non-governmental organisations (NGOs). Even after discounting that organisations want to portray themselves in a positive light, the reality is that few of these case studies ignore the social drivers. Unquestionably, profitability is the condition precedent but the social drivers seem to reinforce the profit driver, especially by providing a strong motivation to the employees directly involved.

Donors

There is a certain irony in the fact that donor funding for financial sector development in Africa has never been more plentiful while the private sector is innovating as if it needed no financial encouragement at all. The question of what role donors should play in driving innovation is an important one because the sums of money are so large: at the end of 2007, around US$4.2 billion had been committed by donors to financial sector development in Africa, an increase of 6 % over the previous year. The number of donor-supported programmes was also up – by 38 %.[29]

This introduction is not the place to debate the pros and cons of donor funding in any great depth – the dangers of market distortion and of the perverse incentives that donor funding can create are well documented, if not always acted upon.

In this small sample of case studies, those that have not used donor funding slightly outnumber those that have. Nevertheless, it is clear that donors or development finance institutions and multilateral agencies can play a significant role in supporting innovation:

- by subsidising operational expenses *(Vodafone/Safaricom, Bank Windhoek, Microcare, Stanbic Uganda, ARB Apex Bank, Banque Misr)*;
- as investors *(Burkina Bail, Equity)*;
- by guaranteeing a bond *(Faulu)*;
- by providing better market information *(Absa, Bank Windhoek)*; and
- by strengthening market capacity *(Afriland First Bank)*.

Generally, this soft funding has been made available to encourage financial institutions to expand their scope of business to include hard-to-reach segments of the population and, in these cases, the donors' strategy seems to have paid off (although, once again, we acknowledge that this is a very small sample).

Four of the initiatives described in the case studies benefited from funding from the UK's Department for International Development's (DFID's) Financial Deepening Challenge Fund *(Bank Windhoek, Microcare, Vodafone/Safaricom and Equity)*. The review of that project,[30] which committed £15 million to around 30 projects in 12 countries over a five-year period starting in 2000, suggests that the main purpose of the funding was to catalyse *(Vodafone/Safaricom)* or accelerate *(Bank Windhoek)* new projects. It concludes that very few of the projects would have gone ahead without the funding and so DFID's funding seems, in the main, to have been additive. The challenge fund approach is quite compelling.

Many find it troubling that donor funding is used to support profit-making ventures but, as the case studies show, the customer bases of for-profit and non-profit financial service providers are converging, and the more successful MFIs, often still donor backed, are making substantial profits. It is hard to see the logic in the argument that says donors should support one type of institution over another if both are serving the same sorts of clients. Donor support should rather depend on the developmental impact that is likely to eventuate, for example, better access to financial services for communities not previously served.

Investing in the capital of organisations *(Faulu)* involved in microfinance, perhaps indirectly through investment funds, is another way that donors can directly support innovation. There is a risk that the introduction of foreign capital into these markets crowds out local sources of funding,[31] although partial guarantee of Faulu's bond by Agence Française de Développement, the French development agency, did appear to be successful in mobilising local pension fund and bank funding that would otherwise not have been committed.

There are now several major financial sector reform processes under way in Africa, funded mainly by donors, in countries as diverse as Ghana, Zambia, Mozambique, Rwanda and Tanzania. These are important and wide-ranging initiatives aimed mainly at enabling a better market environment for financial sector providers. But they are also long-term projects that may have limited short-term impact on access levels and so it will be important for the donor community to keep offering direct forms of appropriate innovation support if the momentum towards greater access to finance is to be maintained.

There is always the risk that nothing much changes despite considerable investment in the enabling environment, perhaps because the market position of the incumbents is too strong or because the market is simply too small to attract hoped-for foreign investors. But if innovation can be directly supported, it is possible, as M-Pesa *(Vodafone/Safaricom)* has shown, for even a single organisation to revolutionise a financial market in a short time.

Liberalisation

Some of the case studies *(Stanbic Uganda, Barclays Ghana)* describe the interventions of foreign-owned firms in local African markets. The theory behind liberalisation is that allowing foreign firms to enter local markets can encourage competition and stimulate innovation. This is explored in Karen Ellis's article in *chapter 2*, which concludes that, while liberalisation may increase the efficiency of domestic financial markets, the evidence that it leads to improved access is less clear cut.

Corporate activity, including acquisitions, in the banking sector across Africa has been high, with banks such as Barclays, Rabobank and the leading South African banks making multiple acquisitions in the past few years. Undoubtedly acquiring or expanding footprint in a profitable market is behind this but the encouraging aspect of many of these acquisitions is that they appear to have been accompanied, or in some cases motivated by, strategies for mass banking. It is hard to escape the conclusion that there has been a massive reappraisal by some foreign-owned banks of the opportunities in mass banking in Africa.

It is probable that the positive impact of liberalisation on access has not yet filtered through.

How far will this innovation go?

Although the case studies paint an optimistic picture, suggesting momentum towards increased access across a broad front, we should nevertheless consider objectively how fast and how far this momentum will carry.

Although access to *formal* financial services is bad enough in African countries, perhaps the real scourge is absolute levels of financial exclusion – that is, people conducting their lives entirely outside the formal *or informal* financial system. In other words, we are only at the very, very beginning of a transformation process and it is not clear how complete the transformation will ultimately be. Perhaps users of informal services will gradually dispense with their merry-go-rounds, *tontines* and *stokvels* (informal saving clubs). Many informal product users already have bank accounts and insurance policies, so making the transition should not be difficult for them. But how much of a hard core of financially excluded people will there still be then? How far will market forces push the access frontier of financial inclusion?

Although there will always be elements in society arguing that access to financial services should be universal – a right rather than something to be bought – this is not realistic in developing economies, at least not in the short term. South Africa's experience with the Mzansi basic bank account *(Absa)* shows that even if the cost of accessing a bank account is very low, the numbers actually opening or retaining the bank account may still disappoint.

Market dynamics are such that suppliers will always seek out first the opportunities that seem the easiest and most remunerative. In the case of Microcare, the company is clear that it cherry-picks both service providers ('We pick the best of the bunch') and the groups of individuals to whom it extends insurance (although within the group, access to healthcare is universal and there are no exclusions for HIV/AIDS). This kind of selection is innate to all profit-making companies – some people will be left behind.

If market expansion left to its own, has limits, is there a place for coercion? The traditionally held view of financial market development is that coercion by governments should be discouraged. But persistently low levels of access call this purist view into question, suggesting that some form of regulatory intervention is necessary to overcome such obvious market failure. We believe that *dirigisme,* or market-led government activism, is not necessarily antithetical to sound principles of market enablement.[32]

The really important question is: *What forms of coercion, in the interests of market development, are not necessarily bad?* This merits more of an answer than we have space for in this introduction, but it is instructive that many developing economies, especially in Latin America and South Asia, are implementing market-led interventions in the interests of expanding access. African countries could learn from these initiatives.

Perhaps what we will see in Africa is continued innovation, such as is profiled in this book, feeding into an environment where the barriers to formal sector provision that create abnormally low levels of access are becoming better understood and tackled, and where policymakers are confident enough to demand, as a *quid pro quo* for the grant of an operating licence, realistic obligations from their regulated financial sector that both parties consider acceptable in the interests of building greater inclusion in the future.

Conclusion

Several of the case studies include direct quotations from beneficiaries as a way to make real what access to the financial product or service means to them. One of these is Nobukela Ndlothovu, a lady from South Africa's Eastern Cape, who now accesses the government grants she receives for her two children through a First National Bank Mini-ATM – previously, grants were distributed physically in cash by government vehicles. She explains: 'It is now better and faster and we can sit down while waiting. Before, we used to stand in a long line waiting in the sun for our money. Sometimes the government truck did not arrive.'

These case studies, though written from the perspective of the provider, are really about the transformation that access to affordable, convenient financial products and services products can have on the lives of poor people. With this newly acquired 'freedom to transact', to quote Amartya Sen,[33] people can not only lead their economic lives more effectively but they can do so, as Nobukela Ndlothovu suggests, in greater dignity.

Few (if any) of the service providers profiled in this book would regard the impact their services are having on the lives of the poor as merely incidental, even if they are in business primarily to make money. As we have seen, the social benefits seem, for most, to reinforce the profit motive. The end result of this coming together of profitmaking and social attentiveness is that innovation is honed not just by an understanding of what will sell but by what particular consumers really want.

This is about quality of service delivery, and what this book demonstrates is that quality of service matters intensely to poor people. For them, quality of service means that products and services must be convenient, sensitively tailored to their particular needs and affordable. But this book also demonstrates that where these elements are in place, the response from consumers can be exceptionally positive.

Mark Napier
CEO, FinMark Trust

Table 0.1 Replicable models of innovation

An objective of this book is to document case studies of innovation that could be replicated. This is to encourage investment and promote competition. This table highlights the approaches that stand out as being promising candidates for replication elsewhere.		
Approach	**Relevant case study**	**Comment**
The Equity Bank model	Equity Bank	The clearest proof from the case studies that an exceptionally profitable business can be built by providing appropriate and affordable banking services dedicated to economically active low-income consumers in Africa. Other banks on the continent, notably Capitec Bank in South Africa, have a similar vision even if the execution is different.
Leasing and factoring for small businesses	Burkina Bail	Small business demand for alternative forms of finance, including leasing, remains high. Factoring is an even less-used form of finance.
Privately delivered debt counselling	Summit	The rapid growth in consumer credit across Africa will lead to increasing demand for the sort of services Summit provides. For this model to be successfully replicated, there needs to be sufficient numbers of employers (which would include government) with whom a provider can contract.
Overdraft finance/ cash-flow smoothing for small businesses	Equity Bank, Mbinga, Stanbic Uganda	Unsecured overdrafts for small businesses are a fraught proposition for conservatively inclined banks but Mbinga's *kifuku* product shows it can be done. Equity's *biashara imara* product and Stanbic Uganda's warehouse receipts product are both serious attempts to address business cash flow fluctuations with alternative forms of collateral.
Private health insurance for the mass market	Microcare	While Microcare's community-based model brings services to some of the neediest people, its corporate model offers the prospect of more rapid growth.
SME lending	Banque Misr	Banque Misr proves it is possible to lend money profitably to very small businesses. In fact, other organisations such as Access Holding and ProCredit, both active on the continent, also demonstrate that it is possible to replicate a standardised approach to small business lending in different jurisdictions.

→

Bundling insurance through small loans	MLife, MicroEnsure	If consumers start to experience the benefits of insurance by seeing it pay off a microloan or compensating a farmer for weather-damaged crops, this will reinforce perceptions of its value among poorer consumers. Working through the continent's burgeoning commercial microlenders could be a significant growth opportunity for insurers.
Paying social payments through bank accounts	Absa/David Porteous article	Subsidising banks to open basic bank accounts into which social payments, such as an old-age grant, can be paid extends access while simultaneously providing beneficiaries with a safe, and cost-free, means of receiving money.
The Mini-ATM	FNB	As the devices are mobile enabled, no landlines are required. The small size of the terminals means they can be housed in very small retail outlets and the retailer, not the bank, dispenses the cash.
Mobile payments	M-banking	The demographics of mobile phone use, the early success of M-Pesa and other models, and the continuing flux around the types of business model that are evolving all mean that this continues to be a space that will repay careful monitoring. Although the operational complexities and required investment are significant, the potential for large-scale success is clear.

Endnotes

[1] Stiglitz (2003).
[2] In October 2003, South Africa's financial industry committed itself under the Financial Sector Charter to achieving specific targets in key areas: black ownership and management, procurement, lending in targeted areas (housing, small businesses, agriculture, infrastructure) and access to financial services. In essence, the charter embedded access to financial services within a broad-based black economic empowerment agenda.
[3] Christensen (1997).
[4] World Bank (2006a).
[5] Marshall (2005).
[6] World Bank (2007).
[7] IMF (2008).
[8] CGAP (2006).
[9] World Resources Institute and CIA World Fact Book (online).
[10] International Telecommunications Union (2007).
[11] FinScope South Africa (2006) and FinAccess (2006).
[12] Ibid.
[13] Fitch Ratings, quoted in analysis on Malawi in March 2008.
[14] Honohan & Beck (2007).
[15] Oxford Policy Management (2007).
[16] Brownbridge (1998: 173–188).
[17] Apea & Sezibera (2002).
[18] Meridien BIAO's founder, Andrew Sardanis, has written a colourful account of the rise and fall of the bank in *A Venture in Africa: The Challenges of African Business* (2007), Tauris.
[19] Porteous & Hazelhurst (2004).
[20] Ibid.

21 Christen & Pearce (2004).
22 BAI is a US-based professional organisation for the financial services industry focused on enhancing employee and organisational performance.
23 BAI (2001).
24 Ibid.
25 FinScope is a market research tool designed by FinMark Trust and now implemented in several countries in Africa that tracks how consumers engage with formal and informal financial systems. The survey in Kenya is known as FinAccess. See www.finscopeafrica.com.
26 According to group annual reports, Absa grew headline earnings at a compound annual growth rate of 23 % between 2001 and 2005.
27 Between 2005 and 2006, Compartamos (Mexico) had a profit growth of 66 %, Acleda (Cambodia) 58 %, Grameen (Bangladesh) 40 %, Brac (Bangladesh) 32 %, and Socremo (Mozambique) 32 %.
28 See Napier (2005) for a more detailed description of the charter approach.
29 From the CGAP donor-mapping exercise.
30 Financial Deepening Challenge Fund Strategic Project Review. Available at http://financialdeepening.org/data/documents/FDCF%20OPR%281%29.pdf.
31 Brigit Helms in the CGAP publication *Access for All* (2006) puts this succinctly: 'Building inclusive financial systems ... actually calls for a lot *less* money and a lot *more* technical support than is commonly believed.'
32 De la Torre, Gozzi & Schmukler (2006).
33 Sen (1999).

Chapter One

Mass Banking

A number of financial service providers are setting a trail and taking mainstream banking services to a low-income customer base. A common theme is the emphasis they place on understanding the particular needs of this emerging customer base.

Two of the banks profiled – Absa in South Africa and Bank Windhoek in Nambia – are downscalers. They have made a strategic choice to seek out the opportunities further down the pyramid, creating a new business segment to complement their more traditional business lines. One, Equity Bank in Kenya, chose to differentiate itself by specifically focusing on mass banking: the result is that more than half of all banked Kenyans now bank with Equity Bank. The Tanzania Postal Bank story demonstrates that having a privileged position as the long-established provider of choice for the poor, which many postal banks enjoy, is no guarantee of commercial success. The bank has revitalised its income profile by delivering affordable products that its customers want and by investing judiciously to deliver its services more effectively.

Two essays are included. Karen Ellis writes about banking liberalisation and its impact on domestic banking markets: liberalisation may increase competition but what impact does it have on access for those on low incomes? The essay concludes by suggesting that, while liberalisation should benefit African financial markets, additional policy measures may be needed to drive greater access. Nathanael Goldberg, Dean Karlan and Jonathan Zinman propose that financial institutions looking to innovate should take advantage of randomised controlled trials – essentially, innovation experiments – to optimise operational strategy, for example for a new product launch.

Equity Bank: Listening to customers

> Equity Bank is the success story of the transformation of an ailing building society into a fully fledged bank with a stock market listing and more than half of Kenya's banked population as its customers. Equity set out expressly to capture the 'missing middle' of the market – those not well served either by banks or microfinance institutions, and savings and credit co-operative societies – a customer base typically comprising self-employed traders, artisans and low-end government employees. Being different in offering affordable products and innovating was part of the success. But Equity also focused on getting the internal basics of the banking business right: strict operational performance measurement, risk management and automation.

Wanjohi is a young credit officer at a Nairobi branch of Equity Bank. He is a successful professional and he knows it. He joined the bank after completing his university studies, and in a country with 40 % unemployment he considers himself lucky. He finds the job tough and the targets set by the branch manager challenging, but he enjoys the pressure. The good quality of his loan portfolio, with zero defaults, has already earned him a salary bonus. But Wanjohi is hoping to be promoted to supervisor. He knows this is feasible – it is early afternoon and he has a room full of people hoping to open new accounts.

This is one of the key elements in the formula that transformed the ailing Equity Building Society of the late 1980s into the most successful domestic bank in Kenya. Equity Bank has changed the way banking is done in Kenya by creating a virtuous circle of providing tailored financial services for more people at an increasingly lower cost. These are being taken up by the 'missing middle', the millions of Kenyans who until recently had struggled to maintain a bank account, let alone obtain credit. Most of them had even been nervous about stepping into a banking hall.

Equity's new customers grew by 35 % in 2005 and 82.5 % in 2006, deposits have been growing at a rate of 80 % a year, and the loan portfolio has grown close to 95 % a year over the same period. By the end of 2008, Equity had built up its customer base to three million customers and now has over 52 % of all deposit accounts in the Kenyan banking industry. This is remarkable in such a short time span. Why is everybody queuing at Equity Bank? Should other banks in Kenya and Africa be worried about it? And more importantly, could other banks replicate this model?

Poverty in Kenya

Following a dismal economic performance from the mid-1970s to the 1990s, Kenya started a slow process of recovery. Only in recent years has the Kenyan economy seen significant improvement, bolstered by stable key macroeconomic indicators. The economy has also started to reap the benefits of increased private sector credit, and liberalisation of government utilities such as ports, energy, telecommunication and railways. Key economic data are in Table 1.1.

Table 1.1 Key economic data – Kenya

Population (in millions), estimate 2008	38.5
Urban population (%)	21
Poverty (% population below national poverty line)	53
GNI per capita (US$), 2006	680
GDP growth rate, estimate 2008	4.1
Financial depth (M2/GDP)* (%), 2004	40.3
Private sector credit to GDP(%), 2004	25.3
Loan to deposit ratio (%), 2004	73.2
Inflation rate (%), estimate 2008	25.5
Prevalent local commercial bank lending rate (%)	15–23
Agriculture sector as % of GDP	27
Industry sector as % of GDP	18
Service sector as % of GDP	55

→

Population in formal waged employment (millions)	1.85
Population employed in informal sector (millions)	6.4
% of population with a mobile phone, 2005	20
% of population with access to internet, 2005	3.2
% of population using a commercial bank, building society or postal bank	19

Sources: BBC Country Profiles; CIA World Factbook; FinAccess (2006)

Note: *M2/GDP is a measure of the money supply relative to the size of the economy

A key economic concern is the weakened level of country competitiveness because of poor infrastructure and the high cost of power. There is room for improvement in almost all areas of governance, including the public service, public financial management, procurement, transparency, media environment, privatisation and deregulation in the enterprise sector, as well as in the financial sector.

While absolute poverty in Kenya has declined in recent years, inequality remains high: 46 % of the population still lives below the food poverty line.[1] In 2001, the *Poverty Reduction Strategy Paper*[2] identified low economic performance, low agricultural productivity, landlessness, insecurity, unemployment, low wages and gender inequalities as causes for Kenyan poverty. Pervasive corruption has probably exacerbated income inequalities. Worryingly, Kenya has also seen a faster pace of urbanisation than Africa as a whole. Between 1982 and 2002, Kenya's average annual urban population grew at 6.3 %, more than double its annual national population growth rate of 2.8 %.[3] Despite recent macroeconomic gains, urban poverty is on the rise. This rapid urbanisation poses clear challenges for policymakers trying to reduce poverty.

Equity Bank, however, sees this is an opportunity. Senior management points out that the growing urban population opens up the market for financial service providers serving the lower end of the market to extend services to people who were previously unbanked because they lived in remote areas.

Financial sector

Kenya has introduced a variety of financial system reforms that date back to the early 1980s. Financial and monetary policy reforms in the 1990s liberalised interest rates and replaced direct controls on lending with open-market operations. Initially these reforms were damaging because they led to high government borrowing costs that increased the fiscal burden and created instability. This forced the government to abandon the interest-rate liberalisation.

Even though reforms were intensified by the National Rainbow Coalition government after 2002, the financial sector remains broadly uncompetitive, with a highly concentrated banking system. High spreads persist between lending and deposit rates, averaging between six and 12 percentage points, which reflects the perceived high level of credit risk and general lack of competition. Nevertheless, as the reforms have continued and begun to take effect, several insolvent banks have exited the market through mergers and liquidations, creating a more robust banking system in Kenya.

Favourable macroeconomic conditions have allowed banks to improve their asset quality and achieve high capital adequacy ratios. Capital adequacy in the sector, as measured by the ratio of total capital to total risk weighted assets, is 16 %, well above the minimum statutory requirement of 12 %.

The sector has also registered growth in deposits and profitability, resulting from increased income on loans and advances, and a significant inflow of foreign deposits. The share of non-performing loans (NPLs) in the portfolios of banks continued to decrease from 17.6 % in 2005 to 15 % in 2006. Commercial banks have been reluctant to channel resources to the private sector, preferring the more secure and still profitable alternative of purchasing treasury securities, although there are signs that this trend is reversing.

Access to financial services in Kenya

The formal banking sector comprises 43 commercial banks, one postal bank and four non-bank financial institutions. Kenya has a highly developed co-operative financial sector, with an estimated 3 800 semi-formal institutions, MFIs and savings and credit co-operatives (SACCOs), not regulated by the Central Bank of Kenya (CBK). The informal sector is made up mainly of rotating savings and credit associations (ROSCAs) and accumulating savings and credit associations (ASCAs).

The bulk of these clients are salaried, almost 75 %, and only a quarter are in rural areas. Considerable overlap exists between the services offered by commercial banks on the one hand and SACCOs on the other – in fact, 52 % of banked Kenyans use SACCOs as well as other informal services.[4] According to the CBK's 2004–2005 Annual Report, while many salary-based lending programmes have performed well, other SACCOs, particularly those in more rural areas and operating more informally, have serious problems with the quality of their loan portfolios. Not surprisingly, levels of trust in SACCOs, as well as other informal services, are rather low. FinAccess data shows that only 68 % of people using informal products and SACCOs trusted the providers they were using.

MFIs have expanded their activities in the past few years, though their reach is still limited compared to that of SACCOs. Estimates are that there are more than 900 MFI outlets offering a variety of services to about half-a-million clients and extending more than KSh17 billion (US$250 million) of gross new lending each year.[5] The Micro Finance Act (2006) gives the CBK the responsibility for regulating and supervising the 10 to 12 MFIs that presently accept, or are likely to accept, deposits from the public, which should improve the safety and reliability of public deposits mobilised through these channels.

The Kenyan Post Office Savings Bank is a formal financial institution also providing services to a broader segment of the market. It services one million Kenyans. Its alliance with the Postal Corporation potentially allows it to provide access in regions where few other financial institutions operate, given the more extensive network of postal outlets or branches across the country.

Despite this variety in the institutions serving the market, large segments of the population continue to have either no, or only limited, access to financial services. The 2006 FinAccess survey shows that the country's performance is roughly level with that of comparable African neighbours, but it falls short of what has been achieved in other parts of the world. In 2006, 27 % of the adult population was served by formal financial institutions, including those that operate as formal entities but without regulation, such as MFIs and SACCOs. A further 35 % enjoyed informal financial access through organisations such as ROSCAs and ASCAs, leaving 38 % of the population financially excluded. The bulk of credit still goes to larger enterprises, mainly in urban areas.

Equity Bank: The origins and today

The establishment of Equity Building Society (EBS) in 1984 was inspired by a vision of the potentially high demand for financial services in the underserved, low-income section of the Kenyan market. It was founded by five private partners as a building society with the purpose of pooling the resources of members for onward mortgage lending. Between 1984 and 1993, Equity operated through five branches in Nairobi and Central Province but it suffered from a deteriorating loan portfolio and continuing losses. By the end of 1993, Equity received a central bank rating as technically insolvent: it was noted that supervision by the board was poor, management control was inadequate, asset quality was unsatisfactory, capital was fully eroded by accumulated losses, and deposits were being used to meet operating expenses. At that point the CBK was ready to liquidate the institution.

However, in light of the achievements of EBS in creating affordable and easily accessible financial services for low-income people previously excluded from the financial system, CBK decided to allow EBS to initiate changes that would lead to a turnaround. As part of the turnaround plan, Equity was obliged to continue providing financial access to low- and middle-income people, or face closure. Building society legislation allowed Equity to offer savings and mortgages that were rarely used for housing. From 1994, under the leadership of a newly recruited change manager, James Mwangi, who is now the bank's CEO and managing director, Equity began to transform into an institution that expanded its range of products beyond housing loans, and focused on providing microfinance services. Within three years, Equity started to show positive results, growing at annual rate of 10 % by 1997.

From 2002, EBS engaged in an aggressive programme to recruit quality personnel to help steer the business forward as it rolled out new financial products. Seeing the huge opportunities offered by going deeper downmarket, Equity decided that year to offer loans to clients with even lower incomes using cash flow and credit scoring technologies. EBS was given significant help in transformation: donor grants and technical assistance supported the institution's drive to improve its outreach and develop new products. The growth in business volume and outreach prompted Equity to convert into a fully licensed commercial bank. In December 2004 it transformed into Equity Bank Limited with a mission to 'mobilise savings, term deposits and other funds to provide loan facilities to the microfinance and missing middle sectors, especially SMEs, to generate sufficient and sustainable profits, in order to contribute to the members' welfare and to the national economy'.

Equity is now a public company that was listed in 2006 on the Nairobi Stock Exchange and is regulated by the CBK under the Banking Act. In early 2009, it had a market capitalisation of KSh56 billion (US$698 million).

Equity's high profitability (see Table 1.2) demonstrates a remarkable turnaround from its ailing condition in the early 1990s. At the same time, the bank has demonstrated a firm commitment to affordable financial services and better access to finance for low-income people by lowering the cost of transactions. Surprisingly, by 2004, Equity's income from fees and commissions was higher than income from interest as the bank succeeded in creating a virtuous cycle of lower transaction costs and higher volume of transactions. Notwithstanding that, net interest income has continued to grow at a rate of more than 50 % a year while the net interest margin contracted, further reflecting the bank's strategy to provide more affordable credit to its customers.

Table 1.2 Overview of Equity Bank

Operational highlights	
Year established	2004 (bank, 1984 as building society)
Number of branches (2008)	95 branches, 54 village banks (vans), Internet, cellphone and POS transactions
Number of customers (2008)	3 296 000
Number of borrowers (2008)	628 000
Regional coverage	Seven out of eight provinces
Number of ATMs (2008)	500
Number of points of sale (POS) (2008)	1 100
Products and services offered	Savings; lending; payments transactions and remittances services; trade, asset and security financing; forex exchange; insurance premium finance
Ownership structure	Kenyan public, staff and management (64.23 %), Helios Investors, a private equity fund company comprising the International Finance Corporation, Commonwealth Development Corporation and Overseas Private Investment Corporation (24.45 %) and British American Investments (11.32 %)

Extracts from the balance sheet (2006)		
	KSh million	US$ million (US$1 = KSh65)
Total assets	20 000	295
Total loans to customers	11 000	170
Total deposits	16 000	246
Shareholders' funds	2 200	34

Extracts from the income statement (2006)		
	KSh million	US$ million (US$1 = KSh65)
Net interest income	1 500	23
Commission and other income	1 900	29
Expenses	(2 300)	(35)
Profit before tax (after depreciation)	1 100	17

Key ratios (2006)	
Return on equity	41 %
Return on assets	4.4 %
Net interest margin	11.2 %
Cost income ratio	67 %

Extracts from balance sheet (March 2007)		
		Growth rate in two months
Total assets	KSh25 billion	25 %
Outstanding loans	KSh13.46 billion	22 %
Number of active loan accounts	254 000	
Average loan size	KSh52 975 (= US$815)	
Value of deposits	KSh18.1 billion	13 %
Number of active deposits	1.1 million	10 %
Average deposit amount	KSh16 445 (= US$253)	

Source: Equity Bank

The figures for the year ended December 2006 indicate the exponential growth the bank saw in the first two years. Equity's total assets grew by 75 % from KSh11.5 billion in 2005. Loans and advances were up 95 % from KSh5.9 billion in 2005, driven by enhanced lending to the micro, small and medium enterprise (MSME) and consumer sectors. The pace of this astonishing growth does not yet show signs of flagging: in 2008 Equity Bank continued to grow, with total deposits approaching KSh49 billion, and loans and advances totalling KSh41.8 billion. In 2007 Equity was ranked the third best microfinance institution in the world in an analysis conducted by MicroCapital.[6] The ranking follows the Global Vision accolade jointly awarded to Equity Bank and the Grameen Bank of Bangladesh[7] during the 2007 G8 summit, where the Equity banking model was recognised as a 'concept of the future that will shape the world economy'. Similarly, the bank was voted by the premier Euromoney Awards for excellence as the Best Bank in Kenya in 2007 and 2008. In 2008 it was also voted the best microfinance bank in Africa, a Superbrand in East Africa, and Best Performing Ai Company in Africa.

Rebuilding Equity: From ruin to riches

The journey to success was not without obstacles. Its image had been tarnished and Equity had to battle with low public confidence; after all, it had been a failed institution. The bank has managed to overcome this lack of public confidence, though it still suffers from the public misconception that it is a small indigenous bank. But, given that its assets account for 6 % of the total assets of the banking sector in Kenya, and that it holds more than 50 % of the total number of deposit accounts, Equity is anything but small.

Mwangi's first task in rebuilding Equity was to review the institution's capabilities, both internally and externally. The internal capabilities were extremely poor, as evidenced by a non-performing loan rate of 54 %. This meant that the company was not in a position to conduct banking business until it had undergone a drastic change in its management. Mwangi also recognised that it would not be sensible to compete with 42 other banks for the same customers, so it had to do something different to survive.

Equity chose to differentiate itself from the traditional commercial banks by offering savings and credit products that were easily accessible to a mainly urban, non-salaried and collateral-less population. This was coupled with quick disbursement of funds, reliability of credit supply, and making customers feel accepted, especially those who were not familiar with formal banks and so might be intimidated. Equity also differentiated itself from the traditional MFIs by providing customers with products oriented towards individuals, in contrast to the group-based schemes offered by most MFIs. And quite significantly, in contrast to other financing programmes, Equity sought to build confidence in the market by emphasising its target of sustainability – it stressed that the bank intended to be in business for the long run and is not dependent on donor funding for its long-term continuity. It positioned itself to be a market-led as opposed to product-led institution. To borrow from William Easterly's *The White Man's Burden: Why the West's Efforts to Aid the Rest Have Done So Much Ill and So Little Good*, it was a 'seeker' rather than a 'planner', seeking to respond to signals from the market rather than to impose a predetermined development plan.

Equity adopted a three-pronged approach to overcome the negative perceptions of the early days.

First, Equity understood that it had to unlock the potential of the missing middle market by convincing it to trust the bank again. It decided to persevere in serving the unbanked and underbanked market, and to involve the customers in the transformation. The bank asked customers about their needs, and incorporated their views in all aspects of the business from bank charges to the design of the corporate logo.

Second, as soon as the bank was again solvent and profitable, it started recruiting new staff (see Figure 1.1), and building microfinance capabilities across the whole company, based on international best practice. Equity's strategy is to recruit young people at entry points with little or no experience. The emphasis is on moulding young entrants who will learn to embody the institution's corporate culture, operational norms and customer-focused approach. In contrast to other banks, Equity prefers to fill management positions from within. Since 2002, it has been obliged to recruit a number of experienced professionals from outside the institution to fill senior management positions, but these recruits were generally sourced through headhunting from outside the banking industry. Equity considers that traditional bankers may be less able to absorb and embody the institution's corporate culture and operational norms, given their previous experience in serving the higher end of the market.

Figure 1.1 Growth in number of customers and staff

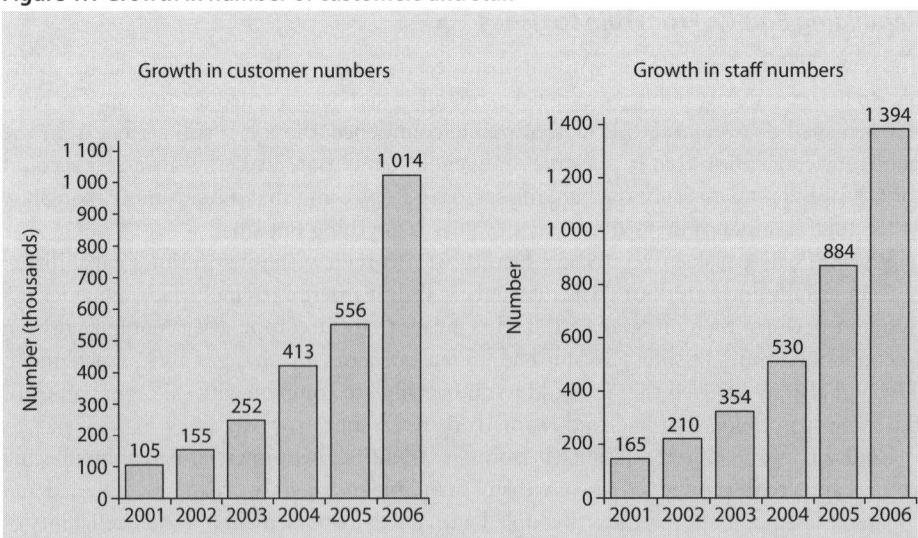

Source: Equity Bank (2006)

Third, Equity needed new capital to support the management pursuit of the institution's new business objectives. The initial institutional shareholders were handpicked by Equity's management to ensure a good fit between the owners and the social dimension of the business. This strategy minimised the potential for conflict between management and ownership in the delivery of the reform plans.

The bank's approach emphasised customers, staff and investors, and became core to its business model.

A new banking business model emerges

The Equity business model is based on three permanent focal areas:

- **Market research and innovation:** striving to move the financial access frontier further down the income scale. The Kenyan population is relatively young and a large proportion is unemployed or working informally, thus creating a massive market for Equity's products and services.
- **Customer service:** as the key differentiating factor.
- **Risk management:** early recognition and mitigation of risk factors that may lead to a repetition of the failure of the building society.

Market research and innovation: Affordability, affordability, affordability

Equity's slogan is 'Equity – the listening, caring financial partner', and its Innovation Centre works with the marketing department to ensure that its products match the needs of its customer base.

Equity's savings products include traditional savings and current accounts, a foreign currency account and the *jijenge* account, all of which share the following characteristics:

- There are no required minimum operating balances. In contrast to other banks in Kenya, Equity's savings and current accounts do not require a minimum operating balance, which most Kenyans find prohibitive, or which at least acts as a disincentive for many.
- All accounts have an ATM card facility on application – the card costs KSh300 (US$4.50).
- There are no account maintenance fees, for example monthly fees. The bank does not charge for monthly account statements, cash deposits and cheque handling or internal standing orders. Photos (for identity cards) on account openings are also free.

The interesting feature of the *jijenge* account is that it allows fast access to loans up to 90 % of the *jijenge* savings, and it earns an annual bonus interest on the balance. Moreover, there is no withdrawal notice on maturity. This account has some common features with what several other MFIs offer as 'security funds' for customers that are new to using financial products.

On the lending side, Equity's range of products includes:

- Business and development loans, including not only general business and agricultural loans, but also an innovative credit product called the *biashara imara* loan aimed at financing the working capital requirements of MSMEs.
- Personal consumer loans, which are often salary advances, such as the Equiloan product – an unsecured and affordable loan facility geared towards salaried clients,

which offers convenient access to cash through a check-off system. These loans are often used for smoothing consumption or responding to sudden household expenses related to the education and medical needs of clients and their families.
- Asset finance, which (a) allows clients to purchase investment assets like motor vehicles (cars, *matatus*, buses, lorries, etc) and machinery; (b) allows clients to make insurance premium payments for themselves and their assets; (c) allows clients to purchase shares at initial public offer and on the stock exchange. These loans are geared towards the small and medium enterprise market segment.

The common feature of these loans is that they are offered at an affordable interest rate with no extra hidden charges such as arrangement fees, which is consistent with the way deposit products are priced at Equity. Equity has reduced its lending rate from 18% to 15%, while traditional commercial banks have been offering rates above that.

In terms of traditional banking services, Equity has managed to price common transactions at the lowest level in the Kenyan market. This is in line with its strategy of increasing access to financial services. Cash deposits and ledger maintenance are free of charge rather than subject to a fee, as in all other banks. A bankers' draft is available to both Equity customers and non-customers for KSh100 (US$1.50), compared with the standard industry charge of KSh600 to KSh650 for customers and KSh1 250 to KSh1 500 for non-customers (0.3 % minimum). Standing orders to another Equity Bank account and cheque clearing are offered free of charge instead of charging the usual industry standard of KSh165 to KSh450, while inter-bank transfers are priced at only KSh300 (US$5), compared with the traditional industry-wide cost of 0.2 % to 0.5 % of the transfer value or a minimum fee of KSh1 000.[8]

Equity client: Dave Njoroge Mwangi

Dave Njoroge Mwangi is an entrepreneur who has been banking with Equity for the last four years. He is on his second loan, and making plans for a third. Dave belonged to a SACCO before he joined Equity. He did not like being in a SACCO as he is a car-hire driver, and this meant sacrificing time away from his business to meet with the group. The risk of having to step in for a group member on a late repayment also concerned him. Becoming an individual bank customer gave him the independence to concentrate on expanding his business, he says. He considered joining other banks but chose Equity because it was offering a lower-cost service with an added business-support element thrown in.

Dave uses savings and credit products. He finds the savings service convenient and speedy, as he can drop by an ATM any time when he is not serving customers and it does not cost him money to make deposits. For credit he mainly uses loans with a 12-month maturity but he was able to repay the first one of KSh590 000 in about six months and is trying to repay the second one of KSh640 000 in less than 12 months. The incentive is that the repayment amounts are flexible, and the interest accrues only on the outstanding balance. He is able to obtain loans for up to 70 % of the value of the cars he buys with the loans. His minimum daily takings operating two cars with one employee are around KSh2 000 net of all costs. He reckons that in a year he makes about KSh700 000. Prospects for his business are good and if he can find reliable drivers to expand his car pool, he plans to buy his third car soon.

What is particularly innovative about Equity's business loans, especially compared to loans offered by other banks, is that each loan application is appraised on the basis of the client's capacity to repay rather than on the value of the security or collateral presented. Equity's most popular loan product, the *biashara imara*, allows for alternative forms of security such as chattels (household items and business stock), which makes the loan appealing to micro-entrepreneurs who do not own fixed assets that can be pledged as collateral. The requirements for accessing loans allow ease of entry for new unbanked clients: borrowers are required only (a) to have had at least six months' experience carrying out their economic activities, and (b) to have maintained their business deposits with Equity Bank for at least six months. After review of the loan application, security requirements and repayment terms are determined by both the bank and client.

The bank lends amounts equivalent to a certain percentage of the business's cash flow, which in most cases is about 60 %. This measure is designed to ensure that the entrepreneur is able to save and build capital from the receipts of the business while still being able to repay the loan with some comfort. This flexibility has enabled the bank to make realistic credit appraisals that ensure low levels of default. Nonetheless, while Equity adopts this flexible approach, it still specifies a minimum loan size of KSh1 000 (US$15), which it reckons is the minimum the bank needs to be able to operate sustainably. There is no prescribed maximum loan size – it depends entirely on the client's ability to repay. So far, the largest loans the bank has made fall within the KSh5 million to KSh10 million range (US$75 000 to US$150 000), although there was one instance when it extended a KSh200 million (US$3 million) loan to one client. Its closest competitor in terms of loan sizes for SMEs offers group lending and individual lending with similar characteristics to Equity, but Equity's appeal is in its focus on the individual. Another competitor offers SMEs unsecured individual loans to up to KSh500 000. This is an attractive offering, but most of the clients interviewed thought that the total cost of finance with other banks was higher than with Equity Bank and that it was less easy to qualify for such loans.

Equity also tries to cross-sell its products. For example, the bank has been working to persuade its small-business customers to pay the salaries of their staff through Equity's facilities, thereby creating another income stream, while possibly reaching even more clients who may be potential salary loan and Equiloan borrowers.

Customer service: Knowing your clients and reaching out to them

Equity's clients are a mix of people who have either left their old banks or who are newcomers to the banking system, including perhaps those moving away from solidarity groups, or who previously operated purely in the cash economy. The bank estimates that it has a 50/50 mix between these two types of clients. Although its corporate mission specifies its aim to serve low-income groups, Equity does not use poverty-profile or gender criteria in selecting clients. Nonetheless, especially given the characteristics of the financial products being offered by the bank, its target client may still be classified as 'skilled working class' and 'working class'. These two groups mainly comprise self-employed traders, artisans, smallholder farmers and low-end salaried workers such as teachers and city council workers. Equity clients also include SMEs and a small number of larger enterprises.

Because Equity does not specifically target women customers, unlike some MFIs, its client base is split evenly between male and female clients. This contrasts favourably with the sector as a whole, in which 61 % of banked adults are male and only 39 % are female.[9] Notwithstanding this strategy, in 2007 Equity rolled out a KSh5 billion lending programme for women in a joint plan with the United Nations Development Programme (UNDP), which included the opening of three branches in Nairobi to serve women only. This initiative seeks to increase the competitiveness of businesses owned by women. An initial 2 000 businesswomen have been selected for training in the joint programme organised by the bank, UNDP, the International Labour Organization and the United Nations Industrial Development Organisation. The UNDP resident representative has expressed an interest in replicating the programme in the entire east African region.

Equity Bank CEO James Mwangi talks to the president of Kenya, Mwai Kibaki, and other delegates about the bank's Fanikisha loan products for women entrepreneurs at a launch.

A group that Equity deliberately targets is the youth market. To empower young people who have finished formal education but find it hard to find work, Equity has created a special group-lending scheme to address the needs of young budding entrepreneurs. Equity believes that these young individuals will form a loyal base of customers for the bank in future.

How Equity tries to reaches its clients

The marketing thrust of the early transformational days has changed. The bank no longer needs to create brand awareness, and 60 % of Equity's new business is now generated through word-of-mouth and customer referrals. Equity still advertises to keep high visibility, but the bank's strategy is not focused on persuading customers to join Equity. The priority now is to improve customer service and to decongest branches by encouraging customers to use ATMs, internet banking, SMSs and cellphone banking rather than queuing in branches. A new account applicant can queue for up to 45 minutes before being attended to (see the story about Rachel in the box on p. 35). At a certain point long queues will deter customers and undermine Equity's impressive growth. For many entrepreneurs, time spent away from their business is a considerable transaction cost.

> **Equity client: Textile trader**
>
> Rachel is a new customer and she has been waiting for 45 minutes in the customers banking hall where Wanjohi works. She is not pleased with the wait but she is willing to sacrifice her lunch hour to apply for her first *biashara imara* loan. She used to bank with a different bank but left because she could not maintain a KSh50 000 minimum deposit and did not qualify for loans. Rachel has been in business for three years selling textile cuttings, but has never taken a loan as she does not own a home or other property to be used as collateral. She is confident about her business prospects and wants to increase the amount of stock to sell. She cannot afford to finance the extra stock from her daily takings. When her turn comes she will speak with Wanjohi, who is processing the applications in her queue, about her business and the chattels that she owns that could be used as collateral. Then Wanjohi will set up an appointment to visit Rachel at her home and business, and observe how she goes about her trade. If the loan is approved, Wanjohi will continue to visit Rachel's business weekly to ensure that she is able to meet the repayments and hopefully help her to grow her business, which will need larger loans.

To reduce waiting times Equity is increasing frontline staff and investing heavily in more ATMs and point-of-sale (POS) devices to divert as many transactions as possible to non-branch channels. The marketing and educational drive to shift simple transactions out of the banking hall and into the auto branches has already diverted most withdrawals to ATMs. Through this facility, customers can make deposits into their accounts and transfer money between Equity accounts free of charge, while withdrawals cost only KSh30 (US$0.42), the lowest withdrawal charge of any bank in Kenya.

Individual customers tend not to use internet banking but this channel is important for a number of Equity's corporate customers.

To complement its full-service branches, and further increase access to financial services, Equity built a fleet of 54 mobile van banking centres, with state-of-the-art IT and security systems, to reach clients in more remote areas. The vans used are suitable for all terrains and fitted with solar panels. Regrettably, criminal activity targeting these vans means that the future of this facility is in doubt. Central bank regulations designed to ensure staff safety now require a second vehicle to accompany the mobile branch.

Equity is also rolling out POS terminals at petrol stations and supermarkets. The latest addition to the non-branch channels is cellphone banking. Equity has teamed up with mobile bank Wizzit of South Africa to develop M-Transact as a different model to Safaricom's M-Pesa money transfer product. M-Pesa does not require a bank account – value is stored in the phone account, and cash is handled by Safaricom agents. M-Transact needs a bank account and is cashless. The Equity customer transacts with other Equity customers or the bank itself, and deposits/withdraws at the branch or ATM. Equity uses the standard charges and only charges an additional KSh9 per top-up from the telecom operator.

Equity is also expanding its branch network using the cash generated from improved profitability, increasing the number from 41 in 2006 to 98 in 2008. Initially Equity established branches in commercial areas where other banks had a presence, making the bank resilient to competition and allowing it to capture customers who were being served by MFIs or banks, or were new to the system. Having tested the business model in banked areas, new branches are being established in locations where there are no other banks operating, thus reaching areas where people are largely unbanked or where existing clients incur high transaction costs to travel to the nearest bank branch.

In common with most African countries, Kenya lacks the physical bank infrastructure that developed countries take for granted. World Bank research suggest that there are only 0.77 bank branches per 100 000 square kilometres, and only 1.4 branches per 100 000 of the population.[10] Further, there are significant regional differences: Nairobi province has around one branch for every 9 700 adults, whereas Kenya's Western province has only one branch for every 128 900 adults.[11]

As the more densely populated areas are being covered, the bank is moving towards the more sparsely populated areas. It does not immediately open in unbanked areas. First, it tests a new area with its mobile van banking units, and only after establishing a customer base will a new branch be opened. Branches have been modelled into an easily replicable product. All branches are designed with the same features and layout, costing between KSh10 million and KSh20 million (US$150 000–US$300,000) for an average-sized branch or between KSh20 and KSh30 million (US$300 000–US$445 000) for a bigger one.

Risk management

In the turnaround years Equity was hamstrung by large loan losses that impaired its ability to bring down the cost of its loans. Since 2004, Equity has seen a steady recovery of non-performing loans (NPLs) despite significant asset growth. According to Global Credit Rating's 2004 rating report, in spite of a 79 % increase in lending, gross NPLs fell remarkably from 33 % of the loan portfolio in 2003 to 12 % by December 2004. During this period, Equity had to adopt a conservative approach to loans and advances to improve portfolio quality, which meant that hard security in the form of land and vehicles was then required. For salaried loans, security equivalent to 200 % of the loan value was required, while agricultural loans advanced only 40 % of the final expected value of the crop. By 2005, given the favourable performance in the quality of loan portfolio, Equity began relaxing these requirements, which helped to drive its high growth strategy. Even so, NPLs still fell from 10 % as at December 2005 to 5 % by December 2006.

The recovery in 2006 was underpinned by the risk management team conducting a branch-by-branch review of NPLs. This exercise showed that one of the reasons why NPLs were so high was the high level of temporary overdrafts. These facilities were provided to customers quite liberally to help them meet a loan repayment if their cash flow was delayed by a few days. Customers felt it was better to access an overdraft to keep up with the repayment schedule than miss a payment and damage their credit score for further loans. Because of the close relationship between the loan officer and the customer, the temporary overdraft did not pose an extra risk for the branch, though it was nevertheless included in the NPL ratio. Based on these findings, the risk management team implemented NPL targets and quarterly reviews at branch level. At the start of the financial year, all branch managers are given targets for NPLs and are provided guidance on what to do to reduce or avoid NPLs. At headquarters, all branch managers are peer reviewed in a group meeting to make the process transparent. This acts as an incentive for the managers to avoid being at the bottom of the NPL league. Moreover, Equity is considering linking the branch staff's promotion and salary bonus to the successful management of NPLs. This would reduce the possible moral hazard if all the incentive is based on extending credit, which may result in reckless lending to unsound customers.

In terms of liquidity risk, Equity is working to manage the mismatch between deposits and loans and advances very closely. By the end of 2004 the cumulative liquidity gap was positive up to 12 months. But beyond 12 months, the liquidity gap becomes negative due to the large number of savings accounts which are callable on demand. These deposits are diverse in nature and cover more than 500 000 clients. They are considered stable and the CBK has approved the mismatch.

A mitigating factor for Equity is its highly liquid balance sheet. It has an average liquidity holding of 30 % of total assets, although management is targeting an increase to 40 % to keep reassuring customers that the bank can withstand any credit shock and that it is a solid institution. Currently, the industry average in Kenya is 45 %, which is way above the statutory liquidity reserve required by the CBK of 6 %.

Operational risk in Equity is reasonably well monitored with all the key risks mapped, along with their assigned measurements and targets. These risks are measured daily or monthly and compared with the bank's targets. In 2000 a manual system was replaced by a computerised one. This automation of the risk management system has helped manage its operations more effectively. The bank has a dedicated risk management department and a risk management framework that sets out guidelines for the identification, assessment and management of risks. It has also put a business continuity plan into place to ensure that operations are not completely disrupted if there is an emergency.

In 2005, the bank made another major investment in its systems, purchasing an Infosys core banking system with the potential to handle up to 35 million accounts. This, too, has helped bring down the cost of transactions and speed up transaction processes.

The bank also actively tracks operational performance through a complex set of indicators based on what it sees as critical success factors. These include financially based indicators such as return on assets and return on equity, and also those linked to organisational culture, innovation, strategy execution and customer service.

Building for the future

As Equity Bank's critics are quick to point out, a fundamental risk for financial institutions undergoing rapid asset growth is the increase in NPLs when sound risk management practices are not effectively conducted by a rapidly expanding workforce. This is further exacerbated when growth overwhelms a bank's management information system and so loan performance is not monitored properly.

Other non-performance measures can sometimes be helpful in revealing instances of loan defaults that have not yet been reflected in the NPL ratios. Assessing the quality of Equity's loan portfolio using portfolio-at-risk (PAR) over 30 days and over 90 days, however, shows the following results:

- PAR > 30 days: 10.3 % end February 2007 compared to 20 % end July 2006.
- PAR > 90 days: 5.4 % end February 2007 compared to 6.7 % end July 2006 (net of provisions).

These PAR ratios are relatively high by international standards – but they are better than other players in the Kenyan market, where the banking sector has an average NPL ratio of about 15 % and the local microfinance sector has an average PAR > 90 of 22 %. Notwithstanding these local industry averages, Equity aims to continue improving the quality of its asset portfolio, and has internally set PAR targets of 7.5 % for > 30 days and less than 5 % for > 90 days.

CBK, as the regulator, has naturally expressed concern over the rapid growth of Equity, especially since it remains unprecedented in Kenyan experience. On-site visits are carried out regularly to monitor portfolio quality more closely despite favourable opinions by independent credit agencies regarding Equity's robustness.[12] The CBK's bank supervision department acknowledges that Equity has passed the annual on-site examination since it made its transformation, but points out that as it accounts for 6 % of the financial assets of the banking system and holds deposits for more than half of the banked population, it poses a high systemic risk. The average Equity deposit balance is $250, up from $50 in 2004. This amount represents almost half the country's gross national income (GNI) per capita.

Even though Equity has risk mitigation measures in place, such as keeping low NPL and PAR rates, and is managing its reserves prudently and maintaining a highly liquid balance sheet, the entire banking sector has been affected to the global economic downturn and the post-election violence of 2007–2008. Kenya's economic performance has been volatile with the effect of small businesses struggling to stay afloat and savers withdrawing deposits.

The competition

Equity's main competitors are those MFIs and other domestic commercial banks that target the same market. However, a huge part of the target market remains untapped, which allows ample room for these competing institutions to coexist.

The enactment of the new Micro Finance Act in 2006 does not concern Equity, even though it will allow other non-bank MFIs to take deposits and fulfil other functions similar to banks. This law sets lower core capital requirements, which will limit the number of deposits such institutions can take. The lower limit is likely to deter MFIs from the business model followed by Equity, which has been based on accumulating a large numbers of transactions.

Given the success of the Equity model, other traditional banks have started to look into tapping the microfinance market. Currently, however, these banks' microfinance activities have been limited to offering consumer loans.

Equity's main competitor seems to be of a different kind: it is 'keeping money under the mattress'. There are 15 million adults in the country who do not have a bank account at all. If Equity wants to tap the unbanked market, it will need to persuade those 15 million people to take their money out from under the mattress and deposit it with Equity. This will mean convincing them that Equity offers greater convenience, affordability, reliability and accessibility – in short, a better value proposition than their mattress.

Keeping the focus on the underserved

As Equity continues to grow and expand its range of services, it may be tempted to slowly deviate from its original core target customer base – the low-income unbanked market. Some of the bank's former micro-enterprise clients have already grown in size and are generating higher incomes. As Equity is still able to meet the changing financial needs of these clients, most remain loyal to the bank. It is hard to assess the number of micro-enterprise clients which have now graduated into larger businesses, though Equity's management claims that a good proportion of its clients are SMEs that used to be micro-enterprises when they started banking with Equity. Equity can hardly be expected to reject such clients once they become successful.

The bank's senior management is clear about its mission to serve the low-income target group, and do not see any threat of a mission drift. Nevertheless, as their clients' businesses evolve, Equity may face a situation where an increasing proportion of its funds are allocated to its better-off clients, given that such clients require more funds per head than lower-income clients. Moreover, these clients will have established a track record with the bank, and their asset profiles will also have improved, making them a lower credit risk, and therefore more attractive as borrowers. In this context it becomes essential for a bank like Equity to seek ways to balance an orientation to providing services to the low-income unbanked market with a desire to respond to the changing needs of its customers, especially those who have chosen to remain loyal to them.

Conclusion

The model's success factors are general principles that do not depend on country-specific conditions and it should be possible to replicate this in other countries. Having consolidated its position in Kenya, Equity is looking at a growing in footprint in Africa. It began implementing its regional expansion strategy with the acquisition of Uganda Microfinance Limited in 2008. In the medium term it is planning to become a regional bank and in the longer term perhaps even a pan-African bank.

If current trends continue, it looks as if young Wanjohi will not be lacking in opportunities to fulfil his ambition and to extend his horizons within Equity Bank well beyond his Nairobi branch. It is no wonder that he is smiling.

ESSAY
Foreign banks: Do they help or hinder financial inclusion?

Karen Ellis – *Business and Development Programme Leader and a Research Fellow at the Overseas Development Institute*

Access to financial services is important for growth and poverty reduction. Access to credit or a bank account that enables an individual to accumulate funds in a secure place over time can strengthen their productive assets by enabling them to invest in micro-enterprises; in new tools, equipment or fertilisers; or in education or health, all of which can play an important role in improving their productivity and income. However, in many African countries, access to formal financial services for the poor majority of the population remains very limited.

Historically, governments have made attempts to promote access, for example through interest rate ceilings designed to make finance more affordable, through directed lending, or through requirements for banks to set up branches in rural areas. These have often caused distortions in the market and have been counterproductive and destabilising.

These government attempts to promote access have often been replaced by more market-friendly policy prescriptions to promote financial sector development, which have focused on (i) deregulation – including the withdrawal of government intervention through the privatisation of state-owned banks, the freeing up of interest rates, the removal of directed lending and reduced reserve requirements; and (ii) financial liberalisation – the removal of restrictions on market entry for domestic and foreign financial providers.

Promoting new entry and greater competition is expected to result in more dynamism, innovation and efficiency in the financial services sector – and the evidence supports this claim. Cross-country evidence shows that foreign entry has helped to stimulate improvements in domestic banking performance, and has generated significant benefits for consumers through improved service delivery, and for the economy as a whole because of the more efficient allocation of capital which occurs as a result of improvements in the evaluation and pricing of credit risks.[13]

'Foreign banks may be able to operate in a more efficient way than domestic banks, mainly because they are likely to have a longer experience operating in a competitive environment than domestic banks in African countries. Foreign banks are therefore, for instance, used to dealing with variable prices, e.g. interest rates, fees, commissions, to assessing the risk of projects and, more generally, they are used to choosing activities in a way as to maximise profits. They may also be aware of more sophisticated financial instruments than domestic banks and of more advanced management methods. As a consequence foreign banks are expected to provide different types of financial services to African clients and may be able to offer their services at a better price-quality relationship.'[14]

Banking practices and regulation may also improve through the diffusion of skills and best practice, as domestic banks imitate more efficient practices, or acquire staff with more sophisticated skills from foreign entrants. The presence of foreign banks helps build a domestic banking supervisory and legal framework, and enhances overall transparency in the sector. Foreign banks also tend to be less politically connected and may therefore be less likely to exert self-promotional influence on the regulatory authorities.

Foreign entry may also stimulate innovation and the provision of new products or better services by the foreign entrants themselves and by local banks. For example, competition from new foreign entrants in Hungary stimulated the main domestic bank to develop new products such as bank cards and ATMs.[15] Foreign banks can also use their international experience to introduce innovations. For example, Citibank overcame the lack of credit information on enterprises in many developing countries by introducing a new mechanism for establishing creditworthiness based on an estimate of growth prospects in particular industries.[16]

Empirical evidence supports the contention that opening up the financial sector contributes to improved financial sector performance with knock-on benefits for the rest of the economy. A good number of empirical studies confirm that in developing countries foreign banks tend to be more efficient than their domestic counterparts,[17] and that entry of foreign banks increases the efficiency of the domestic banking sector, by reducing the costs and profitability of domestic banks.[18] According to one study, countries that were open to trade in financial services achieved growth rates up to 1.2 percentage points higher in other countries over the period 1990 to 1999.[19]

However, the financial crisis which started in 2008 undermines some of the arguments in favour of openness to foreign banks. Some of the innovative new products they have developed have resulted in excessive risk taking, and regulatory structures in developed countries have been found wanting. It may also be the case that countries with relatively closed financial sectors may be less vulnerable to financial contagion. Previous evidence, however, suggests that in the long run at least, the presence of foreign banks has reduced financial instability.[20] This may be because they are associated with lower incidence of non-performing loans, have internationally diversified asset portfolios that are less susceptible to economic difficulties in any one country, and are less likely to retrench their lending significantly during financial difficulties in the host country.

Given the perceived benefits of market opening, the expectation has been that it would also promote better access to financial services by reducing spreads and hence reducing the cost of credit, and by incentivising financial services providers to expand their client base. The evidence to support this, however, has been much weaker.[21] This is because foreign banks have tended to focus on serving market segments where local profit opportunities are perceived to be the greatest – providing financial services to large firms in urban areas – and it is mainly in these sectors where competitive pressures drive down costs and profit margins for domestic banks. There has been relatively limited involvement by foreign banks in the low-income end of the market, thus their presence may be expected to have a fairly limited impact on financial inclusion.

There has been a concern about the impact of foreign bank entry on access to finance for SMEs.[22] Large, multinational banks may not be well placed to provide relationship-based lending services to small businesses. They are likely to prefer standardised methods for assessing creditworthiness based on readily available information. Thus if foreign competition forces some small domestic banks to exit the market, access to credit for small businesses, which have previously relied on relationship banking services with these smaller local banks, and which may not be able to provide the standardised information that large banks require, could decline.

However, there is evidence that access to credit for SMEs is actually improved, albeit indirectly, by foreign entry, as the increased competition from foreign banks in the corporate sector forces domestic banks to seek new markets that they might not previously have served.[23] A study of banks in 78 countries shows that 44 % of those banks that lent to small and micro enterprises said that changed market conditions and stronger competition in lending to large and medium-sized enterprises were the two most important reasons for doing so.[24]

The impact of foreign entry on access to financial services for poor households is even less clear, and the poor majority of the population often still has very limited access to formal financial services even after liberalisation in many countries, particularly in Africa.

Figure 1.2 Percentage of bank customers who are poor

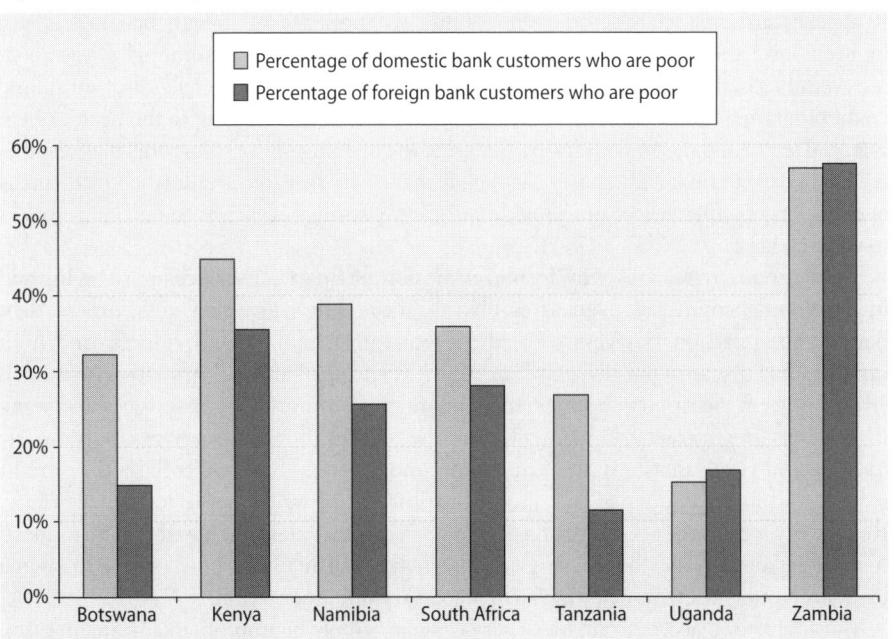

Source: Eighty20 using FinScope survey data

Many African countries have liberalised the financial sector to a significant degree, and foreign banks already account for a substantial proportion of financial intermediation in many countries. However, evidence from recent FinScope surveys shows that foreign banks tend to have fewer poor customers in their client base than domestic banks in most countries (see Figure 1.2).

Thus, despite a high degree of foreign bank participation in many African countries, financial exclusion remains very high (see Figure 1.3).

Figure 1.3 Proportion of the population who use financial services

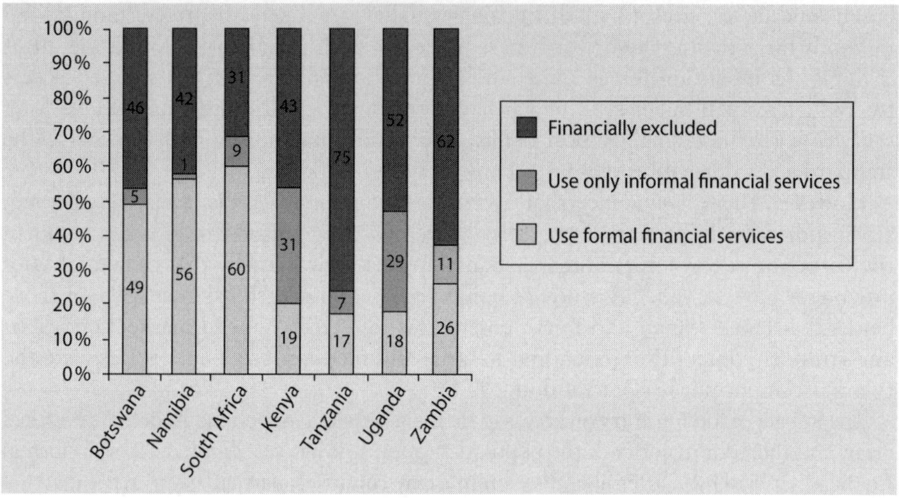

Country	Use formal financial services	Use only informal financial services	Financially excluded
Botswana	49	5	46
Namibia	56	1	42
South Africa	60	9	31
Kenya	19	31	43
Tanzania	17	7	75
Uganda	18	29	52
Zambia	26	11	62

Source: FinScope survey data

It appears that financial sector openness and the presence of foreign banks does not by itself solve the problem of financial exclusion. Even though traditional government interventions in the financial sector to promote access through directed lending, subsidised credit programmes and interest rate ceilings may have been damaging to the health of the financial sector, if they are withdrawn alongside the opening of the sector, this may result in reduced access to financial services. At the same time, market forces unleashed by financial opening may by themselves not provide sufficiently strong incentives to encourage banks to widen access.

There are many reasons why formal provision of financial services may be limited in developing countries, even after liberalisation. High levels of government debt have often constrained access to credit for private firms and individuals, and high inflation has discouraged saving. Poor physical and institutional infrastructure, such as intermittent electricity supplies, inadequate telecommunications services and weak institutions for contract enforcement, raise the costs of providing services, particularly to poor and rural areas. At the same time, most people have no collateral or credit record, and many countries lack credit bureaus, all of which serve to deter lending. Regulatory requirements such as Know Your Customer rules that have been introduced to guard against money laundering can also make it difficult for poor people to open a bank account as they may not have the necessary documentation.

Thus, widening access to financial services may simply be unprofitable in many cases. Indeed, given the many types of market failures present in financial services, the market is likely to underprovide. It is also the case that weak competition policy in some countries has resulted in quite a concentrated financial sector even after liberalisation, allowing high spreads to persist, which blunts incentives to expand access to new, unfamiliar and risky market segments, even where they may be potentially profitable. And a lack of detailed information about the characteristics of these market segments has made it difficult for financial institutions to correctly assess the costs and risks associated with expanding access.

In many countries, any access that the poor do have to financial services may be through semi-formal or informal financial providers, such as credit unions, microfinance institutions or moneylenders. While these kinds of providers may be able to meet the needs of poor households more easily than banks, they are often unable to mobilise and on-lend funds on a large scale, or pool risks over large areas in the way that formal financial institutions do. Thus they are usually small in scale and patchy in coverage, and offer a limited range of services, which can be relatively risky and expensive. The lack of access to the deeper, formal financial sector constrains the ability of the poor to participate fully in markets, to increase their incomes and to contribute to economic growth.

There is often a significant disconnect between these alternative financial services providers and the formal financial sector in terms of operational methods, the customers they serve and the regulatory constraints they face. This disconnect partly explains why additional competition as a result of market opening in the mainstream banking sector has a limited knock-on impact on those parts of the market serving the wider population, including low-income clients. It also makes it difficult for these alternative financial providers to expand. Often they themselves do not have adequate access to finance with which to scale up their operations.

Governments can develop a regulatory and incentive framework that facilitates greater linkages between these different types of financial providers, thus bridging the gap that prevents the knock-on benefits of markets opening in the formal financial sector to be realised. For example, policy, legal and regulatory changes can be introduced that enable formal financial institutions to more easily use informal and semi-formal agents as delivery channels, thus reducing the costs of expanding access, and which also enable informal and semi-formal institutions to more easily access formal finance with which to expand their own operations.

It is possible for large foreign commercial banks to serve low-income customers directly, but the evidence suggests this is most successful when they have established relatively independent microfinance operations. 'Banks with specialised independent microfinance units or subsidiaries found it easier to institute microfinance lending policies, procedures and methodologies and avoid interference from the larger bank culture.'[25]

As already noted, past government interventions to promote access have often been distortionary rather than helpful. But the foregoing discussion suggests there is a role for government beyond liberalisation. First, it is clear that governments need to create an appropriate enabling environment to promote financial inclusion, and tackle market failures. While action on these fronts is under way in many countries, it requires far-reaching improvements in a number of areas, which will take time to achieve. Additional intervention may therefore be required to create stronger incentives for banks to serve the lower-income end of the market. Such intervention needs to be implemented carefully, however. Market-friendly mechanisms need to be found. A variety of interesting approaches have been adopted in developed countries that could be considered.[26] For example, the US Community Reinvestment Act focuses attention on access by publicly rating banks on their performance in making loans to people with low and moderate incomes. Other countries, including the UK, have established a requirement or model for a basic bank account, which sets the framework for banks to provide a simple, low-cost, no-frills bank account for lower-income customers.

Voluntary charters or codes of practice developed by the banking sector can also help provide the necessary incentives. Even then, moral suasion from the government, perhaps accompanied by providing better information about lower-income market segments, may well be needed to help kick-start the process. Early indications suggest that the South African Financial Sector Charter, which was developed voluntarily by banks in response to moral suasion from the government, and which set targets for improving access, has helped to encourage significant growth in access to financial services, which has in turn demonstrated that it can be profitable for banks to sell to lower-income groups. This was assisted by the provision of detailed data on patterns of demand for financial services across the population through FinScope surveys, which helped banks to identify potentially profitable customers and design new, more suitable products.

Governments may also be able to facilitate the use of existing networks, such as post-office branches or retail outlets, to allow the delivery of financial services without the need to establish expensive new bank branches in all areas. New technology, including smartcards, mobile phones and the internet, can help reduce costs and broaden access if the appropriate infrastructure and regulation is in place. Governments can also encourage the use of formal financial services by making transfer payments electronically. As this is likely to be cheaper than other methods of distribution, the savings could potentially be used to subsidise the establishment of additional access points, as has been tried in the US.[27]

Government intervention to incentivise a widening of access to financial services should be implemented carefully, in a market-friendly and non-distortionary manner. The last thing that governments want to do is deter new entry altogether. But harnessing the market dynamism and innovation that financial liberalisation can bring is likely to be a great deal more successful than the state-led approaches of the past in tackling the problem of financial exclusion.

Absa Flexi Banking Services: Taking banking to the people

> After tentative overtures to the bottom end of the market, Absa is now reaping the rewards of products tailored to suit this segment. By segmenting its target market into five distinct groups, Absa was able to focus on particular needs, gear its marketing and education programmes more accurately, and introduce products that fulfil customers' needs. Among these is its transactional debit card Sekulula, developed in partnership with government specifically for social grant transfers, which gives grant recipients the choice of whether to receive their money in cash at a pay point or via a direct deposit into a bank account.

Absa Bank, the youngest of the big four banks in South Africa, is the country's second largest bank by assets and the largest in its geographical footprint. In 2000, Absa started tentative overtures to the mass market in South Africa, initially targeting the 1.8 million of its customers who fell into this bracket. Its experience in this market was such that in the same year it formed a separate business unit, Flexi Banking Services (FBS), to deal specifically with the low-income end of the market. By September 2008, it had 5.3 million customers from this sector.

Political and socio-economic background

A lasting legacy of the apartheid policy of the nationalist government, which led South Africa from 1948 to 1994, is a dual economy. David Porteous, former CEO of FinMark Trust and author of the book *Banking on Change – Democratising Finance in South Africa 1994–2004 and Beyond*, describes South Africa at the end of nationalist party rule as a country with 'highly sophisticated first-world financial markets and a third-world social infrastructure'.[28] The democratic government that came into power in 1994 recognised the role that the financial services sector could play in redressing this imbalance, not only with empowerment and transformation initiatives, but also in social issues, such as providing finance for housing as well as the development of the small, medium and micro enterprise (SMME) market.

Table 1.3 Key economic data – South Africa

Population (million), 2007	47.9
Urban population (%), 2007	60.2
Unemployment rate (%), March 2007	25.5
Poverty (% population at US$1 per day), 2000*	10.7
Poverty (% population at R322 per month), 2000**	53
GNI per capita (US$), World Bank 2007	5 760
GDP (ZAR billion), 2006	1.74
GDP growth rate (%), 2006	5.4
Forecast GDP growth rate (% per annum), 2007–2012	4.8
Inflation rate (%), estimate 2008	11.3
Average one-year deposit rate (%), November 2007	10.1
Prime overdraft rate (%), December 2007	14.5
Credit extended to households (ZAR million), 2006	726.2
Short- and long-term domestic deposits (ZAR million), 2006	743.7
% of population with a mobile phone, 2007	42.3
% of population formally banked, 2008	63

Sources: Stats SA (2007); SA Reserve Bank; Industrial Development Corporation; World Bank World Development Indicators; CIA World Factbook; FinScope SA (2008); Mix Market; UNDP

Notes: *World Bank statistics

**Tentative, national poverty line estimate of the SA National Treasury. No more recent data available.

The call to cater for unbanked South Africans has been gathering momentum since the early 1990s. In October 2002, for example, the then Minister of Finance, Trevor Manuel, noted in a speech to the investment community: 'Our banking halls glisten invitingly while the vast majority of our population remains unbanked. Our investment markets stand shoulder to shoulder with the best in the world. Yet, many of our people rely on the vagaries of informal markets for their livelihoods. We must seek to bring all South Africans into the financial environment so that every South African who wants one can have a bank account.'[29]

Another feature of this dual economy is that the population remains divided between those who use sophisticated financial products with ease and comfort, and those who are excluded from the system. However, according to FinScope South Africa 2008, a national household survey which focuses on financial services needs and use across all sectors of the population, access to financial services is improving: 63 % of the 31.5 million adults over the age of 16 in 2008 were formally banked, compared to only 46 % in 2004, an annual increase of more than 1.5 million people.

The drive for greater financial inclusion culminated in the signing of the Financial Sector Charter on 17 October 2003, in which the financial sector voluntarily committed itself to transformation and black economic empowerment (BEE). The charter includes undertakings on ownership, management representation and procurement. Section 8 of the charter committed the financial sector to substantially increasing effective access to first-order retail financial services to a greater segment of the population within Living Standard Measure (LSM) 1-5.[30] First-order retail products and services include transaction and savings products and services, credit for low-income housing, financing agricultural development and SMMEs, and insurance products and services.

At the same time, the standard of living of the average South African has been steadily improving since 1994. With a total population of 47.9 million people in 2008 and a GDP per capita of US$5 907[31] for 2008, the real annual GDP at market prices increased by 5.1 % in 2007. According to Statistics South Africa (Stats SA), the percentage of working-age employed people rose from 41.7 % to 43.5 % of the labour force for the year to September 2007 and the unemployment rate dropped from 25.5 % to 23 % for the same year.

The *General Household Survey*[32] bore out the trend of improved standards of living (see Table 1.4). FinScope's quality of life index shows a strong correlation between those whose lives are generally good or satisfactory with those who are banked, indicating that these positive economic trends will eventually be reflected in more people entering the formally banked arena.[33]

Table 1.4 General household survey results, 2007

	2002	2005	2007
Live in informal structures (%)	12.7	15.9	15.5
Have cellphone for regular use (%)	35	59.9	73.7
Use electricity for lighting (%)	75.7	80.3	82.5
Have access to piped water (%)	66.1	68.5	71.3
Have no flushing toilets (%)	13.2	10.2	8.3
Have an adult who goes hungry (%)	6.9	4.3	2
Have at least one child going hungry (%)	6.7	4.7	2

Source: Stats SA (2007)

Absa in context

In December 2007, the financial sector had total assets of more than R2.5 billion.[34] According to Stats SA, finance, real estate and business services accounted for roughly 20.7 % of South Africa's GDP in 2007.[35] By comparison, mining and quarrying contributed only 4.9 % of GDP.[36]

With 18 registered banks in the country,[37] four banking groups dominate the market, controlling almost 86 % of the total banking assets and deposits in the country. In January 2007, Standard Bank was the largest, measured by total assets and deposits, with 25.6 %, Absa was next with 21.6 %, followed by Nedbank with 19.7 % and FirstRand with 18.7 %.[38]

The Absa Group came about through the merger of a number of banking groups in 1991 and 1992, which included the Allied, Trust Bank, United and Volkskas brands. Initially, all the brand names of the amalgamated entities were retained. In 1997, the group changed its name to Absa Group Limited, and in 1998 it consolidated the banks into a single brand. At this time Absa adopted a new corporate identity and started to move away from its more conservative corporate culture of the past.

The Barclays Bank deal, in which the UK bank bought a majority stake in Absa in late 2005, was highly significant for the banking sector. Not only was Absa the first of the big banks to be owned by a foreign company, but the deal was also the largest direct foreign investment into South Africa until then. By December 2007, Absa had 892 outlets, nine million customers, 7 693 ATMs and 36 893 permanent employees. Headline earnings for the financial year to December 2007 increased by 19.6 % to R9 413 million, and attributable earnings for the same period increased by 18.4 % over the previous financial year (see Table 1.5).

Table 1.5 Salient financial features for Absa, 2005–2007

	Nine months ended 31 December 2005 (audited)	Twelve months ended 31 December 2006 (audited)	Twelve months ended 31 December 2007 (audited)
Income statement (Rand million)			
Headline earnings	3 443	5 861	9 413
Profit attributable to equity holders	3 431	6 051	9 595
Balance sheet (Rand million)			
Total assets	376 687	453 726	640 909
Loans and advances to customers	292 955	368 320	455 958
Deposits due to customers and banks	289 113	348 934	n/a
Financial performance (%)			
Return on average equity	22.8	25.1	27.2

	Nine months ended 31 December 2005 (audited)	Twelve months ended 31 December 2006 (audited)	Twelve months ended 31 December 2007 (audited)
Return on average assets, excluding acceptances	1.31	1.42	1.68
Loans-to-deposits ratio	101.3	105.6	107.1
Operating performance (%)			
Net interest margin on average assets	3.29	3.42	3.37
Net interest margin on average interest-bearing assets	3.64	3.71	3.38
Impairment losses on loans and advances as % of average loans and advances to customers	0.27	0.44	0.58
Non-interest income as % of total operating income	46.3	45.4	47.0
Cost-to-income ratio	62.5	58.1	51.8
Effective tax rate – excluding indirect taxation	30.1	28.4	28.7
Share statistics (million), including 'A' ordinary shares			
Number of shares in issue	332.9	337.3	678.6
Weighted average number of shares	321.0	336.3	671.5
Weighted average diluted number of shares	321.0	336.3	716.4
Share statistics (cents)			
Headline earnings per share	1 072.6	1 742.5	1 401.9
Diluted headline earnings per share	1 085.4	1 742.5	1 316.1
Earnings per share	1 068.8	1 799.0	1 428.9

	Nine months ended 31 December 2005 (audited)	Twelve months ended 31 December 2006 (audited)	Twelve months ended 31 December 2007 (audited)
Diluted earnings per share	1 081.8	1 799.0	1 341.4
Dividends per share relating to income for the period	1 309.7	591.9	560.0
Dividend cover (times) n/a	0.8	2.9	2.5
Net asset value per share	6 545	7 630	5 537
Tangible net asset value per share	6 508	7 586	5 493

Sources: Adapted from documents provided by Absa

Banking at the bottom of the pyramid

The FinScope 2006 report asserts that the drive from South African banks to meet the charter objectives has probably led to the increase in the number of banked people over the past few years. It adds that despite this, poor people still say that banks are too far away or too expensive, or that they do not have a regular income and therefore have no need to be banked.

The survey notes that although the mass market understands that banking in branches is more expensive than using ATMs, it still prefers to deposit cash at branches, where it feels more secure that the cash is safely in the designated account. The FinScope report goes on to point out that although affordability is important to this market sector, the choice of bank is strongly influenced by whether the bank is seen as trustworthy and a status symbol. As such, it is critical not to erode a product or brand by positioning any extensions as 'cheap'. The market at this end is highly aspirational.

Although a number of the banks introduced products for the low end of the market prior to the launch of the low-cost Mzansi bank account in October 2004, the Mzansi initiative is mainly responsible for the increase in the number of banked people.[39] The big four banks and PostBank initially built Mzansi on a consortium-type model, which originated in the idea of a national bank account. After consultations with various stakeholders, including government, Mzansi was launched competitively to avoid a monopoly developing. The result is that the Mzansi brand has become a standard in terms of minimum functions provided, but fees differ from bank to bank. Absa has the largest share of Mzansi accounts out of the big four banks, although PostBank enjoys the biggest slice of them all (see Figure 1.4).

Figure 1.4 Mzansi market share, March 2006

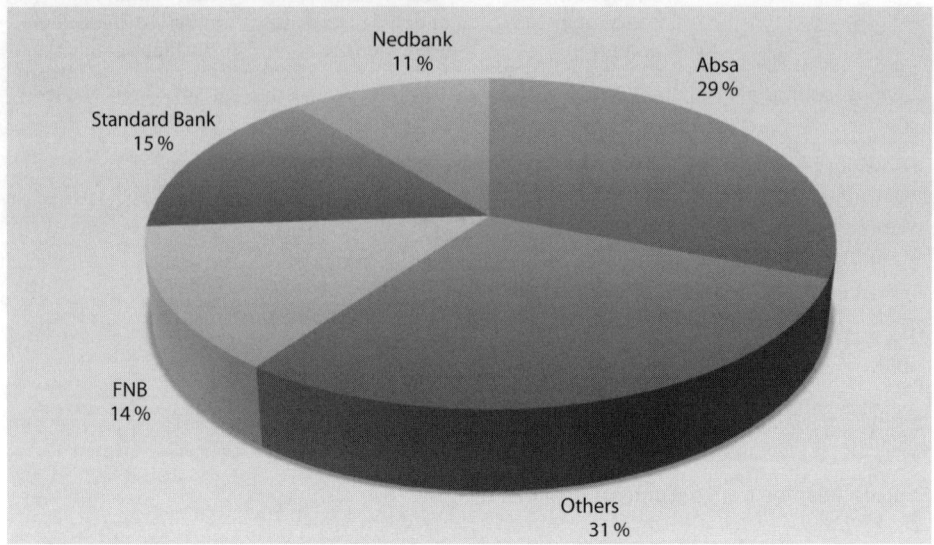

Sources: Adapted from documents provided by Absa

Note: These are the most recent figures available. The Banking Association South Africa is collating new numbers which will enable each bank to calculate its own market share, but not that of its competitors.

Absa valued the formal mass market at R73.5 billion in 2007, with microloans accounting for R30.4 billion of that market, deposits R23.2 billion, and money transfers and social grants (applicable prior to 2007) making up R19.1 billion (see Figure 1.5). It valued the informal mass market at R15.9 billion in 2007, indicating the significant opportunities that both the formal and informal mass market present, particularly as 53 % of this market is unbanked.

Microlending is an important and increasingly competitive sector of the mass market, although FinScope points out that borrowing money falls fairly far down the list of what it sees as important in a bank relationship. At the same time, stockbrokers Barnard Jacobs Mellet stated that only 8.1 % of the mass market has home loans, while 47 % has some form of debt, indicating that opportunities still exist to extend this base.[40]

The big four banks, formal microlenders who may or may not be banks, large retail groups and informal lenders, including burial societies, stokvels (savings clubs) and investment clubs, all operate in this sector. Traditionally, retailers had the greatest share of this market, followed by African Bank Investments Limited (ABIL). However, with full introduction in 2007 of the National Credit Act (NCA), which aims to regulate granting of credit by all credit providers, the big four banks are expected to move more aggressively into the microlending market where, says Barnard Jacobs Mellet, they will in all likelihood become the strongest players.

The act addresses, among other things, overindebtedness, the reckless granting of credit and unlawful provisions in agreements. It promotes disclosure of the form and effect of credit agreements, and prohibits any form of debt settlement other than debt enforcement.[41] It defines a small agreement as R15 000 or less, an intermediate agreement as one between R15 000 and R250 000, and a large agreement is anything in excess of R250 000.[42]

Figure 1.5 Formal mass-market size, 2007

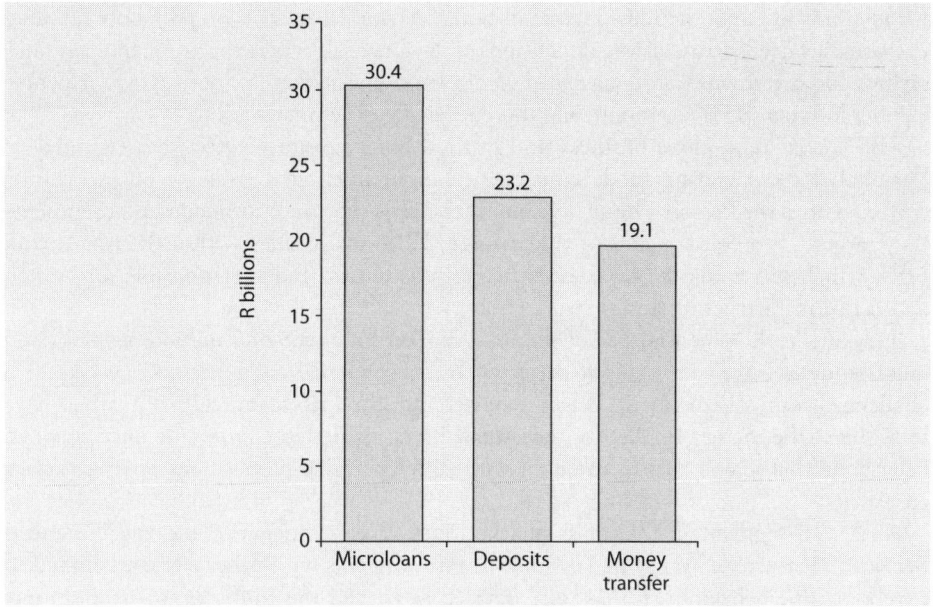

Sources: Adapted from documents provided by Absa

Absa's mass-market challenge

Absa started its journey into the mass market in 2000, well before the charter came into being. Marius Ungerer, general manager strategy and planning for FBS, says this followed a strategic analysis of the personal retail market which identified this as a competitive space not being used. This was confirmed in 2005 at the time of the Barclays merger, when the bank once more carried out a strategic portfolio review that demonstrated that the mass market showed opportunity for further development.

Ungerer says this business unit was fortunate enough to be supported at the highest levels within the group from the outset. Nevertheless, it had to legitimise the mass-market segment with the bank's internal stakeholders, and prove that it is not only a significant growth area but that it can also be profitable.

Sonja van Vliet, general manager mass market customer value propositions, notes that profitability at this end of the market is a function of how you make it part of your business model. She adds that what makes mass-market banking exciting is that you have to think more innovatively to make the models work. 'That is why most innovation happens at the low end of the market, because you are dealing with limited disposable incomes and you are challenged to think,' she says.

Dave Liebenberg, general manager segment management for FBS, says that one of Absa's challenges has been to understand how customers prefer to engage with the bank. In the early 2000s, the idea was to service the mass market primarily through third parties in the belief that customers would prefer familiar surroundings, such as retail stores. It soon became clear that customers wanted interaction with the bank. This realisation left Absa scope to leverage off its own extensive infrastructure.

Flexi Banking and segmenting the market

FBS's aim is to target the mass market in South Africa. Its focus is on profitably fulfilling mass-market needs across all four dimensions of the financial services spectrum: transactional, savings and investments, insurance, and credit. Its target market in South Africa is people earning less than R5 000 a month and those receiving government grants.

FBS was a stand-alone business unit at first, but in August 2007 Absa changed its Personal Bank operating model and created eight integrated strategic business units (SBUs) within the Personal Bank division, each defined by the customer market segments they target. As a consequence of this change, FBS now resides within the retail bank SBU, which serves mass- and middle-market customers, and is responsible for branch and ATM infrastructure and network strategy.

'Looking at the potential size of the mass market [of about 24.9 million people][43] and questioning how we were going to service it and become real as bankers to it, was quite a challenge,' admits Liebenberg. When it started out, the FBS team realised it would have to segment the market further to understand its needs better. It was only once this had been done that it was able to come up with different value propositions for the various customers.

Absa sub-segmented the mass market into five segments using the Financial Services Measure (FSM) as its key tool, fine-tuning this with other elements linked to psychographic behaviour. FSMs were devised as part of the FinScope tools, and grew out of the fact that LSMs did not provide enough insight into the financial behaviour of consumers, as they were heavily income based. The FSM model has four broad components – financial penetration, attitudes to money, physical access to banks, and connectedness and optimism – and people are classified into one of eight tiers for these components.

The first segment used by Absa includes people who typically come from FSMs 1 and 2. There are about 13 million people in this sub-segment, three-quarters of the total population; 60 % are urban, and they are equally split between men and women. Most are unbanked and unemployed, and the recipients of social grants. Sub-segment 2 includes people falling predominantly into FSMs 3 and 4, who are either formally employed, or contract workers or temporary employees. They earn their own incomes and about 1.5 million in this segment are still unbanked.

Sub-segments 3, 4, and 5 consist of people in FSMs 5 to 8. Van Vliet says there is limited potential for opening new accounts in these segments as penetration by formal products has been successful, and the 65 000 unbanked people in sub-segments 3, 4 and 5 may be there due to choice rather than exclusion. Those in sub-segment 3 tend to be more disciplined, patient savers who are credit averse. Those in sub-segment 4 take more risks and seek more credit. People in sub-segment 5 are traditional families with multiple earners, who make responsible use of credit and have reached their maximum earning potential. They are all ambitious for their children's education and future, take pride in their homes and dream of a better life.

By sub-segmenting the market in this way, Absa has been able to focus on particular needs, gear its marketing and education programmes more accurately and effectively, and introduce products which fulfil customers' needs. Van Vliet notes that getting to the finer detail has been important. Thus because FSM 1 is so large, Absa has had to conduct more analysis at the bottom end to enable it to slice the cake better. Although it has used FSMs in other countries in Africa, it has found that more research at FSM 1 level has also been necessary there.

Products for the mass market

Absa's entry-level product in 2000 was a standard transactional-savings account called FlexiSave. The aim was to build a customer base by targeting the market with a permanent income to attain a certain level of sustainability. 'Once you have this firm base,' Van Vliet explains, 'you can start looking at how much you can afford to go up the chain and how deep you can afford to go down it. Through smart pricing and innovation, you can then work on extracting more value from your base, always bearing in mind its affordability constraints.' At the outset, customers had to produce a payslip or some proof of income, but FBS has now waived this requirement because the business is sufficiently well established. For the first three years, while busy with further sub-segmentation of the market, FlexiSave was the bank's only offering for low-income customers.

The Mzansi account, launched in October 2004, was also designed to take care of transactional and savings needs. By the end of September 2008, FBS had opened 642 000 Mzansi accounts, but with around 440 000 of these active it has a high dormancy cost. FBS has therefore initiated a strategy to improve the use of the Absa Mzansi account base, which includes cross-selling insurance to Mzansi customers, sending proactive SMSs (mobile phone text messages) to activate customers, and eliminating fees on mobile phone banking transactions.

FBS products have been built along a continuum of needs:

- Mzansi, as the entry-level savings and transaction option;
- FlexiSave (with or without Money Builder, a discretionary savings product), which offers account holders a set of free value-added services (each worth about R50 if the customer bought them individually), such as R2 000 funeral cover, a 24-hour healthcare advice line, emergency medical evacuation, legal assistance benefits and funeral support services; and
- FlexiSelect, a debit card-based transactional account, launched in 2006, with overdraft and other optional savings. Investment facilities can be linked to the primary card account. FlexiSelect also provides insurance and assurance options, such as a funeral policy, a personal accident policy, short-term insurance and life insurance with different payment options. By September 2008, 96 000 accounts had been taken up. The debit card allows Flexi Banking Services to monitor FlexiSelect customers' transactional behaviour so as to give them access to credit in future, based on their track record. All customers can, however, apply for an overdraft, a microloan, a personal loan or a credit card.

Microloans

A key focus for FBS in 2006 was re-entering the microlending market. Prior to 2004, Absa had offered microloans through UniFer, a third party in which Absa initially had a majority stake. This venture was not successful, and UniFer ultimately collapsed, with the result that Absa effectively withdrew from microlending. However, Liebenberg maintains that the credit market at the bottom of the pyramid is too large to be ignored.

The introduction of the NCA and the certainty that goes with it (as well as the high returns generated by ABIL) has encouraged the big four to strengthen their presence in the microlending market. Other noticeable trends in this sector are increases in loan sizes, the number of loans outstanding and the increasing size of the total loan book.[44]

Absa loans to this sector are between R2 000 and R15 000, and they are all granted in line with the NCA regulations. Anyone can get a loan provided they meet the risk assessment criteria of the bank. The re-introduction of a lending product in the mass market was supported by an internal communication and education campaign to positively mobilise Absa's branch staff to sell the new offering. Today, microloans are an integral part of the mass market product portfolio, with microloan unit sales averaging between 20 000 to 25 000 a month.

Sekulula

Sekulula is a transactional debit-card-based product, developed specifically for social grant recipients. Absa, in partnership with participating provincial governments, provides cash distribution of grants in Gauteng and parts of the Eastern Cape through a wholly owned subsidiary, Allpay Consolidated Investment Holdings (Pty) Ltd (Allpay). Absa is tendering to handle the distribution for the other provinces.

The South African Social Security Agency (SASSA) is a government agency created in 2004 which falls under the jurisdiction of the national Minister of Social Development. Its aim is to improve service delivery in respect of social grants. Gerry Rees, an executive manager of SASSA, explains that, in 1996, the government looked into the possibility of outsourcing the payment of social grants, and awarded the contract for Gauteng and parts of the Eastern Cape to Allpay in 2000. Although the payment system started to work far better with this new arrangement, there were still lengthy queues at pay points. For this reason, Allpay and the Department of Social Development (DoSD) jointly came up with the Sekulula account concept. Launched in 2003, this product gave grant recipients the choice of whether to receive their money in cash at a pay point or via a direct deposit into their bank accounts. If they chose the bank account option, beneficiaries had the additional convenience of access to their grants via Absa ATMs, branches, Mini-ATMs and POS merchants, as well as two free cash withdrawals a month.

Population distribution and the proximity of banking facilities determines whether grant recipients prefer to receive cash, or to have their grants paid directly into an account. 'We have 727 359 beneficiaries with accounts in Gauteng and the Eastern Cape,' Liebenberg says. 'Most urban beneficiaries now prefer the account option, as there is sufficient banking infrastructure and they are never too far from an ATM. In rural areas, however, it is still predominantly cash based.'

Rees says that the introduction of Sekulula has led to considerable cost savings for the DoSD because the payment per beneficiary to Allpay for Sekulula account holders is 65 % of its payment for beneficiaries who receive cash. In both instances, there is no cost to the beneficiary. Other benefits have been reduced congestion at pay points and increased convenience for Sekulula account holders.

Edith Mekoa, a pensioner who has chosen to have her pension paid into a Sekulula account, notes that she no longer has to go to a pay office to receive her money, nor does she run the risk of criminals attacking her for cash – a real threat for elderly people in South Africa. Added benefits of the Absa card, she says, are that she can use it to buy groceries, pay her bills and save money.

Delivery of services

Liebenberg is clear that the bank's success in the mass market is dependent on proximity to that market (see Figure 1.6 for Absa's delivery footprint). Part of FBS's strategy has been to build remote capability to take banking to the people. Absa has remote and mobile sales teams, staffed with people drawn from the areas they service, who speak the local language and use innovative technologies to open new accounts. They can also process microloan applications and insurance products on the spot.

The teams also educate customers about the features and benefits of the account they have chosen to open. Remote vehicles are equipped with training ATMs, and new customers conduct simulated transactions until they are comfortable with the process and can confidently undertake real transactions in the future. Liebenberg says that Absa opened many of its Mzansi accounts and all Sekulula accounts remotely using this technology.

Figure 1.6 Absa delivery footprint

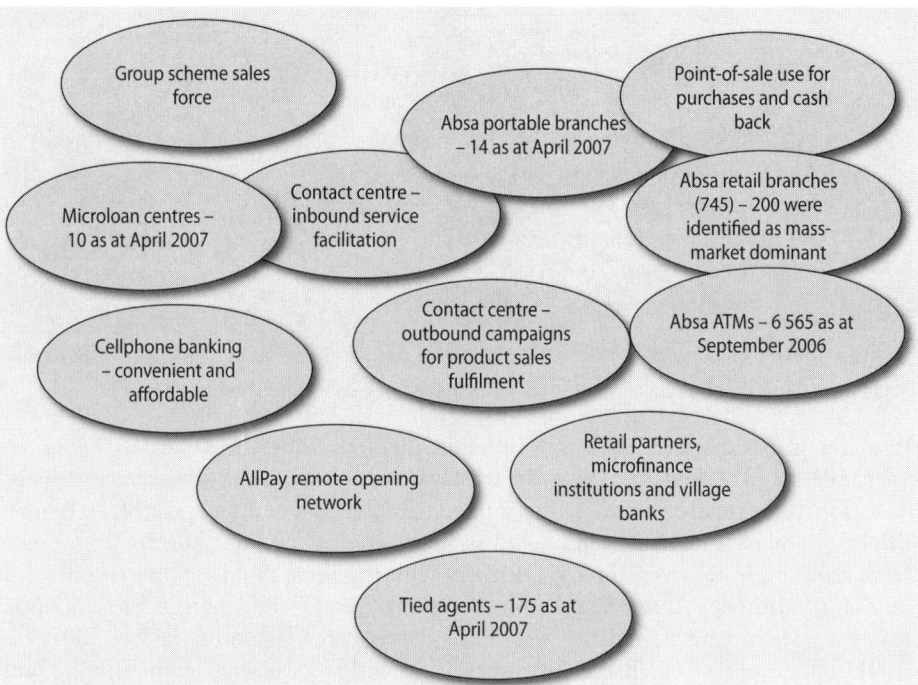

Sources: Adapted from information provided by Absa

Group schemes benefit from remote opening because of convenience to both members of the group and the group itself. Group schemes refer to a number of different possibilities such as company schemes creating value propositions for individual employees, *stokvels*, church groups and professional groups. Sales teams may, for example, engage with the employees of an organisation at their place of work, where discussion ranges from opening new accounts and processing microloan and insurance applications to advice and education on banking in general and Absa products in particular. Debt rehabilitation through a mandated third party is also offered for those who may need it.

Portable branches are another new concept. Portable branches operating from containers provide a full range of banking services. They can be deployed quickly, usually within six to eight weeks, and provide alternatives to branches, which take longer to plan and deploy, depending on the availability of premises or of land for construction. A typical example is near the Chris Hani-Baragwanath Hospital in Soweto, the largest hospital in the southern hemisphere, where a portable branch was deployed for about a year while a mall was being built nearby, where Absa now has a branch. Once a portable branch has fulfilled its purpose, it can be moved elsewhere.

Absa's portable branches are a quick, economical way of expanding the bank's reach.

Absa has also expanded its reach through alliances with third parties. Some are independent and others, like Allpay, are wholly owned by Absa. Absa customers can also draw cash from retailers such as Shoprite and Pick n Pay, and any post office branch. Mobile phone banking has been offered as an addition to account holders for the past three years and is delivered through alliances with the three mobile phone operators in the country. Initially, Absa offered mobile banking free of bank charges for six months from the date of launch, and this was subsequently extended to the end of 2007. The mobile phone operators charge for airtime and SMSs associated with banking, and Absa is negotiating with some of them to dispense with these charges. Ungerer says the criteria for selecting alliance partners is firstly that their capabilities complement Absa's core competencies, and secondly that they have a footprint that increases access to the mass market.

Absa has been selective about devices used to expand its network, finding that full ATMs are often preferable to those serviced by a store operator. 'It depends on how much cash store owners or operators have, their appetite for wanting to provide additional services and the fact that attention is drawn to them because people know they have cash in the store,' Liebenberg explains. Although Absa has an extensive POS network in place, it believes it can still get better leverage off this network. 'The key is to put ATMs in the right areas, leverage more off alliances and create the awareness with our customers that they can use our alliance partners.'

Absa also acts as a link bank for some village banks, which fall within the ambit of third-tier banking in South Africa, and which will be regulated by the Co-operative Banks Act once it comes into force in 2009. Such banks have been established by communities mainly due to the lack of formal banking services close to the community. Each village bank opens an account with a link bank of its choice, which gives it access to the formal banking system. Absa is also providing advice and capacity-building initiatives, and may use some of its products and services to supplement the village bank's offerings.[45]

Liebenberg says that Absa follows a multi-channel distribution approach because mass-market customers, like any others, need choices. He says that more and more mass-market customers are also using internet banking as they gain access through computers at work and at home. Mobile phone banking is also increasing in popularity, but Liebenberg maintains that because South Africa is a cash-based society, mobile banking will not provide for all customer needs in isolation and will have a limited role until alternatives for obtaining cash become entrenched.

Education

FBS incorporates education into much of what it does to tackle a general lack of financial literacy. Eight of the 11 official languages are available on its ATMs, and the Absa Contact Centre can assist clients in their language of choice. Education takes place when an account is opened. Local events, community radio and the workplace are used for existing customers. Roving teams also provide education, and frontline staff takes customers out of the queues in banking halls to show them how ATMs work. A number of Absa products also have educational elements, and FBS conducts educational forums in community centres, through industrial live theatre and videos.

Risk

FBS has identified specific risk factors in this market. Ungerer says that UniFer was a huge learning experience and the company is determined not to make the same mistakes again. 'In the re-introduction of the credit solution, we have ensured that we have built a business model and a value chain that alleviates the risks that we previously experienced,' he notes.

Credit risks are not the only ones in this market. Abandoning products leaves the company with an opening cost that it cannot recover. For this reason, FBS has established customer-retention strategies which attempt to engage customers by addressing their needs.

Business outcomes

FBS has the same return on equity targets as the rest of the bank, and, says Ungerer, it is in the market for the long term because, more than any other area of retail banking, it takes time for new products to deliver returns. Although Absa budgeted on making a loss in its first year of entering the market, it actually made a profit. FBS's headline earnings were separately reported from 2003 to 2005, and grew from R96 million in 2003 to R125 million in 2004, and to R203 million in 2005. By 2007, earnings had grown to R410 million. This in turn represented a 2.8 % contribution to group headline earnings for 2003 and 2004 respectively, a 3.7 % contribution for 2005, 3.4 % in 2006 and a 4.4 % contribution in 2007 (see Table 1.6).

Table 1.6 Flexi Banking Services' salient features

	2003	2004	2005	2006
Headline earnings (R million)	96	125	203	265
Contribution to group headline earnings	2.8	2.8	3.7	3.4
Total assets* (R million)	5 796	4 777	4 865	7 067
Total advances (R million)	1 805	1 020	497	2 070
Total deposits and current accounts (R million)	3 175	3 526	3 991	6 586
Return on average equity (%)	113.0	240.4	202.9	180.3
Cost-to-income ratio (%)	68.7	81.8	77.7	73.4
Permanent employee complement	664	464	448	456
Number of customers (million)	2.3	2.6	3.1	4.5
Number of Mzansi accounts			202 955	377 509

Source: Absa Group (2007)

Note: Total assets include intergroup balances

At the same time, Absa's market share and customer base has grown significantly. The company started its strategic journey into the mass market in 2000 with a customer base of 1.8 million. This grew to five million in 2008, with a total number of accounts (due to cross-selling) of 6.4 million. Van Vliet notes that 3.3 million of its mass-market customers bank only with Absa. Absa's share of the mass market grew from 25.5 % in 2000 to 37.9 % in 2007.[46]

Absa is also recording good growth in microloans: from a starting point of 1 % on re-entering the market in 2006, by the end of that year it had captured 4 % of this market. An estimated growth of between 8 % and 10 % was recorded for 2008.

Barnard Jacobs Mellet expressed the view that 'Absa has the footprint, size, client base, brand recognition and management buy-in to be a serious force in the mass market'. The company goes on to state that 'FBS is entrenching itself in the lower-income segment of the market by building a clear understanding of its customers, their needs and the business environment. This is enabling FBS to develop compelling value propositions for targeted segments and deliver affordable and appropriate financial and lifestyle products and services to the lower-income segments of the market'.

Conclusion

FBS has learnt three key lessons during its eight years in the mass market. The first is that low-end customers know what they want from a bank, and a company must engage with its customers to obtain this important information. Second, mass-market customers tend to be extremely loyal and reward service suppliers who look after their interests. And third, the market is highly aspirational and prepared to wait patiently for the best.

Ungerer attributes Absa's success at this end of the market to a customer-centric approach, support from the highest levels within the bank, a belief on the part of the people it attracts to work in the unit that increasing financial services to the bottom of the pyramid will make a difference to society in general, and a corresponding commitment to making that difference.

Van Vliet maintains that the Absa brand has played a huge role in its success with low-end customers. Explaining that sub-branding is often perceived as discrimination of sorts, particularly in South Africa, she says that one of Absa's strengths is that it has not diluted its brand and has served the mass market through its primary banking channels.

While Absa regards serving the mass market as a social imperative, it also answers to its shareholders, and making money remains the main business focus. By the end of 2007, FBS had proved that the two objectives are not necessarily mutually exclusive. 'Absa top management has identified the growth of a profitable mass market franchise as a priority for the group. This has influenced behaviour at the front end dramatically,' notes Liebenberg. 'Our customers generally have better and better experiences; they spread the word to their friends in an environment where viral marketing is hugely influential. A lot has been about focus, without which we would not have been able to develop the right value propositions for the right sub-segments, or deliver them in the right way through the right channels to the right audience.'

ESSAY

Randomised trials for strategic innovation in retail finance

Nathanael Goldberg, Dean Karlan and Jonathan Zinman – *Nathanael Goldberg is at Innovations for Poverty Action; Dean Karlan is at Yale University; and Jonathan Zinman is at Dartmouth College*

The financial world is full of indications that microfinance has 'arrived'. 2006 saw Muhammad Yunus and Grameen Bank win the Nobel Peace Prize. 2007 saw the US$1.5 billion initial public offering of the Mexican microfinance institution Compartamos. Now rumours swirl that the next watershed may be the entry of investment giants such as the Carlyle Group and Blackstone into microfinance.[47]

Yet 50–80 % of the adult population in developing countries remains unbanked. Hundreds of millions of working, poor households and entrepreneurs still lack access to basic financial products and services.[48]

How will this vast untapped demand be met? Already, retail financial institutions are reaching out to poor households and entrepreneurs. But clearly meeting this demand is not as simple as hanging a sign and ushering the poor into branches. Poor customers have particular financial needs: they need to be able to deposit and borrow small amounts of money, often at irregular intervals; many live in remote areas; and many are illiterate. How are banks to overcome these obstacles? Innovations for Poverty Action (IPA) has been working with both for-profit and non-profit financial institutions in a variety of settings to explore techniques for expanding financial access for the poor.

Our advice to financial institutions wishing to serve the poor is to *scale down but emulate up*. Many leading firms (for example Capital One, H&R Block and Amazon) have adopted systematic experimentation as part of their risk management, marketing, pricing and innovation strategies. Our partners in developing countries are finding that using scientific rigour to create a 'learning organisation' is a source of strategic innovation and long-run comparative advantage. IPA has worked with banks and microfinance institutions to study marketing, risk assessment, product development and more. In this article we will describe how retail financial institutions can use randomised controlled trials to improve both profits and broader social objectives

Why randomised trials?

Suppose you want to know how successful a new type of savings account is at bringing in new clients and increasing savings balances. One naïve approach is simply to track account activity following the launch of the new product. Say you do this and find that 1 000 new accounts were opened since the launch, and that savings balances increased by 10 % on average. Does this mean the new product was a huge success? Not necessarily. Maybe demand for saving products increased in your market for reasons unrelated to the new product. Maybe you improved sales or customer relationship management practices as part of the new launch.

The impact question simply stated applies both to measuring impact on poverty as it does to measuring impact on profits for the firm: 'How did the lives of the clients and the profits of the bank change relative to how they would have changed had the policy not been implemented?' The first part of that question is typically easier to answer. One can follow clients to see how their lives changed (and measure myriad outcomes to one's heart's content), and one can measure profits of the firm. The trick is measuring how these things would have changed had the policy not been implemented.

Establishing causality is important to avoid drawing wrong conclusions. Wrong conclusions can harm clients, and it can also be costly for firms to change operations (or not change operations) when they should not (or should). So it is essential to verify whether innovations truly achieve the desired effect, and to learn about how and why they are (not) working well in order to maximise effectiveness. There is almost always more than one way to design a product, market a service and run a business. Even if one could be confident that the product or service is working well, is it the *best* way to do it? Is it the *most* profitable, does it have the *greatest* impact on clients? Only through accurate evaluation is it possible for firms to make such comparisons and determine their optimal operational strategy.

But establishing causality is hard to do. A scientific approach is a must because human behaviour is so complex. Customer decisions are driven by many factors, and we typically cannot measure all of these factors perfectly (or even close to perfectly).

Randomised controlled trials (RCTs) solve this problem by randomly varying the business proposition we want to evaluate – for example the offer of a new product or the features or marketing of a product – and holding everything else about the offer fixed. So in our savings product example, an RCT would randomly assign some existing bank clients to be offered the new product. Other clients would be randomly chosen not to receive the offer (yet). A large enough sample ensures that the 'treated' clients (those who got the offer) are essentially identical to the 'control group' (those who did not get the offer). After all, the only thing that determined who got the offer is a random number generator (the computer code equivalent to drawing names out of a hat). The bank could then compare client retention and balances over some period of time – six to 12 months or sometimes even longer – to measure whether the new product had a *causal* effect on client behaviour and profitability. Then if the product was indeed a success, the bank could offer it to everyone.

RCTs are the 'gold standard' research methodology because they allow us to establish causality. Non-experimental methods typically require strong assumptions about *why* some people use a product in order to conclude that the product itself – and not some unobservable characteristic of the individual, or some environmental influence – *caused* a change in an outcome of interest. The randomisation takes care of both of these issues because individuals do not *choose* whether to be randomly offered the product or not, and because there is no need to control for environmental influences since they influence both the treatment and the control groups. So whether we are studying the marketability of a new product or the effect of a new human resources policy, an RCT evaluates the *causal impact* of that innovation. By impact we mean the effect of the innovation *compared to its non-existence*. Only this approach identifies the true value of an innovation, whether the innovation is in the product, marketing or product space, and whether the metric of value is profits or social impacts, or both.

The rest of this article is devoted to demonstrating through several examples that RCTs can provide a source of strategic innovation for financial institutions. These studies are part of a larger trend in scientific experimentation among innovative organisations.

Direct mailing: Pricing and marketing

Some settings are more natural than others for conducting RCTs. There is perhaps no more opportune setting than a direct mailing – mass emailing, phone banking operations or text messaging – to potential customers. Direct communications can provide a large sample size, and a carefully controlled environment in which several versions of a marketing or pricing pitch can be evaluated simultaneously. Even better, when an institution is already conducting direct individualised communications, the only additional cost of an RCT is in managing the permutations and carefully tracking their response rates.

We conducted an RCT with a South African consumer finance company in which we used a direct mailing of more than 50 000 credit offers to former clients to evaluate the lender's pricing, marketing and risk strategies. Each of these presents problems for financial institutions, especially when expanding into new markets, because there is surprisingly little evidence available to guide them in making key decisions in these areas: how to price products, who to lend to, and how to sell it to them. Sure, it is simple enough to mimic competitors' products and pricing, and to lend only to obviously qualified customers, but a socially or profit-minded firm should aim for a higher bar: what is the *optimal* strategy in each of these cases? How do we maximise returns?

To explore these questions the lender mailed 'pre-qualified', two- to six-week limited-time offers to all former clients in 86 urban and rural branches who had borrowed from the lender within the past 24 months. The client base was largely working poor. The mailing was limited to former clients who were in good standing with the lender, and did not have a loan outstanding. The offers contained randomised interest rates ranging from 3.25 % to 14.75 % a month,[49] 96 % of which were lower than the lender's standard rate.[50] Former clients eligible for maturities longer than four months also received a randomised example of a four-, six-, or 12-month loan.

In our sample frame, 4 540 clients out of 53 810 applied for a loan at the offered interest rate, for an 8.4 % take-up rate. Among the 99 % of the sample who received offers at or below the standard rate for their risk category we found a 100-basis-point decrease in the monthly interest rate increased take-up by 3/10 of a percentage point. This implies that a price decrease from the maximum rate offered to this group (11.75 %) all the way to the minimum (3.25 %) would only increase take-up by 31 %. Raising rates, however, had a much larger effect, with price sensitivity six times as great. One potential explanation is that when customers know your standard rates, they perceive an increase as 'unfair' and react accordingly.

While borrowers turned out to be rather insensitive to price cuts, we found that they were much more sensitive to the maturity of the loan. Though they would ultimately pay much more interest with longer loans, poorer clients increased the amount borrowed when offered a longer maturity loan, a finding which suggests the poor are severely liquidity constrained. The wealthier half of our sample did not increase their loan size when offered a longer-maturity loan, and were more sensitive to the interest rate offered.

We used the same direct mailing to test out the effectiveness of several marketing approaches drawn from the psychology literature.[51] By simultaneously testing price and marketing within the same experiment we were able to calibrate each marketing feature to the change in interest rate one would have to offer to achieve the same effect in take-up. The results were surprisingly large. We found that some marketing treatments – at no cost to the lender – were as powerful as dropping the interest rate substantially. One in particular, the simple inclusion of a female photo on the mailer, was equivalent, for male clients, to dropping the interest rate by 4.5 percentage points. For some clients the lender would have to cut the interest rate in half to achieve the same effect!

In another test we compared the presentation of a single example loan offer to a table with several choices of loan sizes and monthly payments. While economic logic might suggest that more information is better for the consumer, our results corroborated a psychology theory which suggests consumers can be overwhelmed by 'choice overload'. We found that employing a simple description of the offer has roughly the same effect on take-up as decreasing the interest rate by 2.3 percentage points (a 25 % reduction in the interest rate for some).

Risk assessment

How do you identify a creditworthy client? How should one balance 'soft' information (human judgement) with 'hard' information (quantitative models), and is there a way to get the best of both worlds? This section first looks at how to use credit scoring both to make better credit assessments and to measure impact on clients' welfare and poverty. Then we discuss how one can set up randomised trials to determine the most effective decision-making process.

Lenders use information available to them such as borrowers' credit history, income and assets to estimate the risk of default for each credit applicant. But where is the optimal place to draw the line between creditworthy and not creditworthy such that lenders are not leaving money on the table? In other words, how do banks know for certain that the next client below the approval cut-off would not be likely to bring in more revenue than he or she would cost in collections and unpaid arrears? Since credit scores are imperfect, the best way to find out is to take some calculated, controlled risks by actually lending to riskier clients in an RCT that allows you to measure where to draw the line between creditworthiness and uncreditworthiness.

We did a second RCT with the South African consumer lender described above to optimise its risk assessment criteria. In this case, the senior management felt its branch staff was being overly conservative. By randomising some approvals for riskier clients who were rejected under the lender's previously standard procedures, but not deemed obviously uncreditworthy by loan officers, we were able to limit the lender's risk exposure while measuring the profitability of the riskier loans, both in an absolute sense, and compared to loans that were just above the bar.

We found that the riskier loans were profitable, although substantially less profitable than those made under the standard, stricter criteria. The loans extended to applicants just below the bar were less likely to have been paid back in full than loans that were just *above* the bar (71.5 % versus 76.4 %). With costing input from the lender, we were able to calculate the profitability of the below- and above-the-bar loans as well. The marginal loans were profitable in an absolute sense, yielding R201 (US$32) per loan, but less profitable than the standard above-the-bar loans, which yielded R284 (US$45) per loan.

Risk assessment RCTs can also shed light on the *best* way to expand. Take the simple case where profitability is the only metric of success. Then a mid- or large-size MFI could compare the profits obtained from systematically liberalising risk assessment within branches, as in the RCT above, to the profits obtained from opening new branches. The key would be to randomise whether branches or other types of field operations, including village banks, 'dig deeper' – that is, make riskier loans – or 'spread farther' by expanding into new areas or segments where there are potential clients with more typical risk profiles.

Risk assessment RCTs are also a natural place to evaluate the piece of a double bottom line that pertains to impacts on the borrowers. In the risk assessment RCT described above, IPA hired a survey firm and used follow-up credit reports obtained by the lender to measure a range of economic and subjective well-being outcomes in both the treated and control groups. Despite concerns about the welfare effects of consumer credit we found that treated applicants were better off than their control group counterparts six to 27 months after initially applying for the 200 % APR (annual percentage rate) loan. Treatment group members were significantly more likely to retain their job over the study period, and their incomes were significantly higher. They were less likely to report hunger, and were even less likely to be below the poverty line.

All the findings from this study suggest expanding financial access can be good for the 'double bottom line' of profitability and social welfare. As such the findings from this RCT provided important evidence to the policy community and valuable operational feedback to the lender.

Credit scoring can include hard and soft information, and in particular one can set up randomised trials to learn the most effective decision-making process. What training is effective in guiding decision-makers to emphasise the most important borrower characteristics? Who should get the final decision, the computer or the credit officer? If the computer, what are the 'human' inputs (in other words, perception of trustworthiness, perception of financial sophistication and planning capabilities) that the credit officer can provide that can guide the quantitative model the best?

Product development

Rolling out a new product is a risky proposition for a financial institution, and RCTs provide a methodology for taking carefully controlled and measured risks in order to produce effective product innovations. One example of this approach was a savings product IPA developed in co-operation with a rural bank in the Philippines. The design was built on cutting-edge research at the intersection of psychology and economics. This work suggested that two of the main obstacles people face in meeting their savings goals are self-control and spousal control. We designed a product that provided clients with more control: a 'commitment savings' product called SEED. SEED clients established a goal, a commitment to reach a target balance within a pre-specified time period, upfront and voluntarily restricted their right to withdraw any funds in their own accounts until they reached a self-specified goal. Clients could opt to restrict withdrawals until a specified date (for example, in a month when school fees were due), or until a specified savings amount was reached (for example, a certain amount of money for a new roof). The clients had complete flexibility to choose which of these restrictions they would like on their account. However, once the decision was made it could not be changed, and SEED clients could not withdraw funds from the account until they met their chosen goal amount or date.

To evaluate the impact of this new product the rural bank implemented an RCT where it randomly assigned about 1 800 individuals to either receive an offer to open the SEED account or not. The bank's primary metric of success was savings balances, and here we found a strong effect: after 12 months, average balances increased by 80 % in the treatment group, those who got the SEED offer, compared to the control group. We were also interested in measuring whether the spousal control channel was important, and found a significant increase in women's decision-making power within the household, which we attribute to the account helping women to gain control over household assets.

Conclusion

These examples represent only a few of the randomised trials we have conducted with retail financial institutions. We have used RCTs to evaluate door-to-door deposit collection, emergency savings accounts, health insurance, and more. Our current work includes projects testing loan collection strategies, deposit reminders via SMS, and crop-price insurance for poor farmers. We hope we have demonstrated both the flexibility of RCTs and their utility in helping financial institutions to improve their operations, profitability, and impact.

Of course, RCTs will be easier and cheaper to implement in some settings than others. The simplest RCTs, such as direct mail, text messaging and phone banking, can be implemented by banks themselves using a spreadsheet to randomise and their own accounting software to track clients. Where randomisations are more complicated, outcomes are harder to measure, and there is less direct control of the process, such as where marketing is performed outside the bank branch, RCTs will be more expensive and better left to experienced researchers. Still, for key decisions the benefits of better information can easily outweigh the costs. The trend towards commercialisation of microfinance will provide firms with incentives to get these decisions right. We predict firms will follow the lead of consumer finance companies in America and begin integrating randomised trials into everyday operations. These RCTs can be used to develop product and process innovations that are both profitable to financial institutions, and beneficial to their clients.

Tanzania Postal Bank: Revitalising a decades-old model

> Postal banks in Africa are among the largest financial institutions on the continent in terms of clients. Their infrastructure outreach and their explicitly pro-poor mandates mean they are important players in the fight against financial exclusion. But upgrading from the traditional model of providing only passbook-based savings services into a fully fledged bank that can offer credit as well as connection to the wider financial system is no trivial matter. Changing strategy raises important questions about the choice of business model, product pricing and how best to invest scarce capital.

All over Africa, people from all walks of life can remember a postal savings account that either they or someone else in their family had. Postal financial services in Africa still typically provide almost as many access points as the whole banking system combined, and they still often service as many accounts as all of the rest of the banks combined. Ask Alphonse Kihwele, managing director of Tanzania Postal Bank, what is special about his bank and he can tell you of a million account holders in a country where only two to three million adults have ever had a bank account. He can also tell you about a network of 172 outlets reaching right out into a country of nearly a million square kilometres, whereas almost all of the 230 branches of commercial banks operate virtually in urban areas.

But you will not find any complacency about the challenges ahead for his bank. There is an enormous shortfall in access to finance in Tanzania. For every Tanzanian adult with a postal bank account there is another with an account at another commercial bank, but there are also 15 other adults without any account at all. This matters to Tanzania Postal Bank because universal access is written into its corporate mandate – it is a key part of the bank's founding legislation, and its corporate logo, vision and mission statement all reinforce this.

Tanzania Postal Bank has shed a restrictive, colonial-era model and has become a full-spectrum retail bank. It is slowly tailoring its credit and payments services so that they are perceived as 'usable' by the target market. 'Usable' may be an inelegant term but it captures the need for banks to design products that are not rendered unusable by the mass market because of basic terms and conditions – a savings passbook may not be as useful a product as a full bank account but it is often the only product in the market that can be used by the less well off. By keeping the centuries-old savings passbook product viable, there is still a place where hard-won savings can be kept safely by anyone – however poor, wherever they live – and without those savings being eaten up by high recurring bank charges.

Poverty in Tanzania

Tanzania is a country of more than 40 million people, living on average just over five people to a household and with an annual per-capita income of only US$400 in 2007. The average household size is standard for sub-Saharan Africa but the GDP indicator places Tanzania firmly in the bottom half of that region's countries and in the bottom tenth of countries worldwide, according to World Bank data.[52] Key economic indicators are given in Table 1.7.

Table 1.7 Key economic data – Tanzania

Population (million), UN 2008	41.5
Urban population (%)	25
Poverty (% population below national lower poverty line)	36
GNI per capita (US$)	400
GDP growth rate (%), estimate 2008 CIA	7.1
Forecast GDP growth rate (% per annum), 2005–2009	5.8
Deposits to GDP, 2006 (%)	18.6
Inflation rate, 2008 (%)	10.3
Deposit rate > 3–6 months (%)	4.7
Loan rate < 1 year (%)	15.1

Source: World Bank World Development Indicators; Government of Tanzania (2003); IMF International Financial Statistics; BBC Country Profiles; CIA World Factbook

Figure 1.7 Tanzanian population below the poverty line (%), actual and target

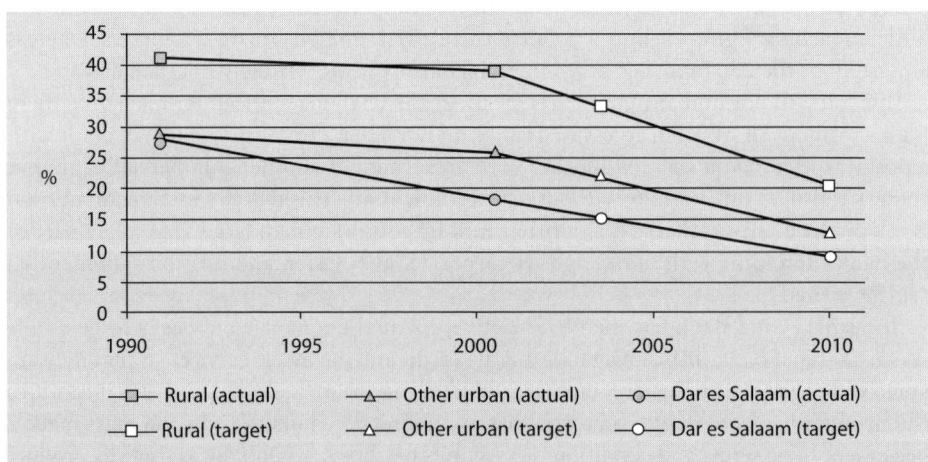

Source: Government of Tanzania (2003)

There are wide disparities in poverty levels between rural and urban areas of Tanzania (see Figure 1.7). About 87 % of people living below the basic needs threshold reside in rural areas. This mostly reflects the dominance of rural dwellers in the overall population (84 %). More importantly, rural poverty seems more entrenched than urban poverty. A comparison of national Household Budget Surveys for 1990/91 and 2000/01[53] shows that the proportion of the rural population living below the basic needs threshold had hardly changed in a decade. Only in the country's capital, Dar es Salaam, was there any chance of hitting targets of halving the incidence of poverty between 1990 and 2010. Even these slight improvements were not enough to offset the rise in population. The absolute number of people living below the basic needs threshold rose from 9.5 million to 11.4 million over the decade between the two surveys. Radical new thinking was needed in designing the Poverty Reduction Strategy in 2002.

Banking and the poor in Tanzania

To put poverty into a financial services context, at the start of the Poverty Reduction Strategy the basic needs threshold was estimated at roughly US$9 a month for an adult, of which US$6.50 was needed to sustain a daily calorific food intake at 2 200 calories. For financial services to reach the poor at all, an account has to be capable of being run at very low charges, and ideally with zero charge for zero use. It also has to be capable of being opened with very small amounts of money.

Affordability is therefore absolutely central to reaching the poor; but some interesting differences arise between the urban and rural poor. The urban poor need a lot more money to achieve the same living standard as poor people in rural areas. This is partly to do with differences in prices[54] but also reflects the reduced opportunities to produce for own consumption in urban areas. Paradoxically, this means that even though the urban poor may be more bankable, they can have lower living standards than poor people living in the rural areas.

Reaching the rural poor has its own problems. On top of affordability issues, people use cash less and the cost of reaching a bank to access their money is higher. The FinScope Tanzania 2007 survey shows that only one in five of all Tanzanians live within an hour's travel of a bank branch. Given that four out of five adults live in rural areas, this must mean that virtually all of the rural poor have no branch within easy reach. At these sorts of distances the true cost of actually getting to a bank branch can be as much as the financial cost of accessing any account held there. Hardly surprising, therefore, that only one in 10 adults has a bank account – and in rural areas this drops to one in 20.[55] Most people who do save do so either in a 'safe place' at home or in kind.

This suggests that any strategy to reach poor people must have a dual focus – first, a service that does not exclude the poor through pricing and, second, products that the rural poor find worth travelling long distances for.

Tanzania Postal Bank

Tanzania Postal Bank was established in 1925 but its roots date back to the British takeover of mainland Tanzania from Germany after World War I. As a savings scheme ran as an integral part of the post office, it shared a common heritage with postal savings schemes and postal banks across Africa.[56]

Typically, the inherited form allowed for only very simple passbook deposits and withdrawals plus a basic postal money order. Some schemes have not changed much but others – including Tanzania Postal Bank – have evolved into fully fledged banks with their own branch networks. The model is not without its problems, not least the challenge of distributing financial services through an intrinsically non-financial service provider, namely the post office. Cash flow management is important, and problems with this hit the precursor to Tanzania Postal Bank in the 1980s. Deposits made by customers went hopelessly astray within the general cash flow of the postal service, and government had to intervene to hive off the savings scheme into a properly regulated stand-alone bank in 1992.

This transition was marked with difficulties. Just as the position on unremitted customer deposits was regularised, the Postal Corporation unilaterally raised the amount it charged Tanzania Postal Bank to process each customer transaction by 300%. Nevertheless, over time the two organisations negotiated a workable service level agreement between them[57] and by the late 1990s Tanzania Postal Bank had recovered the momentum lost in the late 1980s (see Figure 1.8).

Figure 1.8 Deposit trends

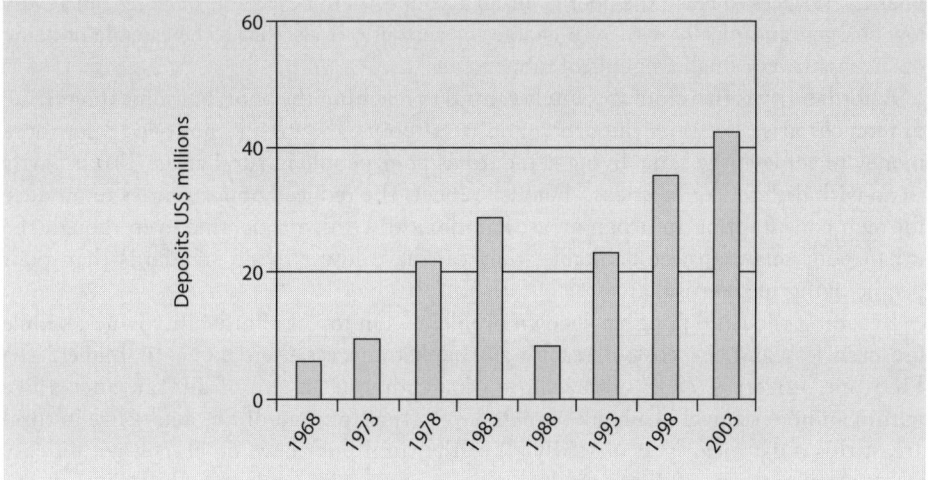

Source: IMF International Financial Statistics and Tanzania Postal Bank (2006)

Tanzania Postal Bank's loan portfolio at the end of 2006 was more than US$17 (see Table 1.8). This is not large by Tanzanian standards, where total gross bank lending was US$1.2 billion at the end of 2005; but it was an achievement for an institution that had spent 65 years *not* lending at all. It was also the right long-term strategic move. Lending is done by all of the big savings banks around the world that support high levels of national access in their home markets (Germany, Spain, France, Brazil, Chile, China, Thailand).[58]

Starting a credit business has risks but for Tanzania Postal Bank it was not the disaster that commentators sometimes predict when a non-lending bank enters the credit market for the first time. The bank provides mostly small-scale consumer credit and some SME lending. It had a 1.5 % NPL ratio on an international accounting standards basis at the end of 2005, down from 4 % in 2004. Lending in any country, but particularly in poor developing countries, involves periods of profitability followed by periods of retrenchment as losses have to be recognised and provisions need to be made. This was true of Tanzania Postal Bank in 2003/2004.

Table 1.8 Key financial indicators for Tanzania Postal Bank, 2006

Year ended December	TZS million	US$ million
Balance sheet		
Total assets	73 279	55.51
Deposits	63 075	47.78
Shareholder's equity	5 859	4.44
Gross loans to customers	23 260	17.62
Loan loss provisions	1 656	1.25
Provisions as % of gross loans	7.9	
Income statement		
Net interest income	6 841	5.18
Net fees and commission income	4 653	3.53
Operating profit before tax	1 574	1.19
Profit after tax	925	0.70

Source: IMF International Financial Statistics and Tanzania Postal Bank (2006)

Note: At December 31 2006 exchange rate US$1 = TZS 1 320.

The bank's capital has increased to TZS5 billion (US$4 million), up by a factor of four on launch levels when it was capitalised with TZS1 billion of share capital and a modest amount of additional reserves. This does not imply that there is more than enough capital. Savings banks are rarely endowed with excess capital when they are launched and they always operate on tight margins. They are, however, generally profitable despite typically being state owned.[59] This has been true of Tanzania Postal Bank, which needed to balance making a profit with the goal of improving access to finance for all and tie in with the government's 1997 *National Poverty Eradication Strategy*, the new *Development Vision 2025* that followed it in 1999, and the *National Strategy for Growth and Reduction of Poverty* of June 2005.

Strand 1 – Balancing the income stream

At the time of the relaunch, Tanzania Postal Bank was registered under the same Banking and Financial Institutions (BFI) Act 1991 that governs all commercial banks. The statement of objectives and functions included two subsequently crucial elements allowing the bank to:

- provide, in accordance with the provisions of the BFI Act, adequate and proper banking services and facilities throughout the United Republic; and
- undertake any other functions performed by commercial banks.

These clauses created the legal and regulatory space for the relaunched bank to become a properly supervised full-service retail bank, not shackled by the traditional constraint of having to invest all savings in government securities. Government debt was not unimportant,[60] but it gave Tanzania Postal Bank a chance to rebalance its income away from relying on interest from government securities and fees from customers (see Figure 1.9).

Figure 1.9 Tanzania Postal Bank asset/income mix, 2005

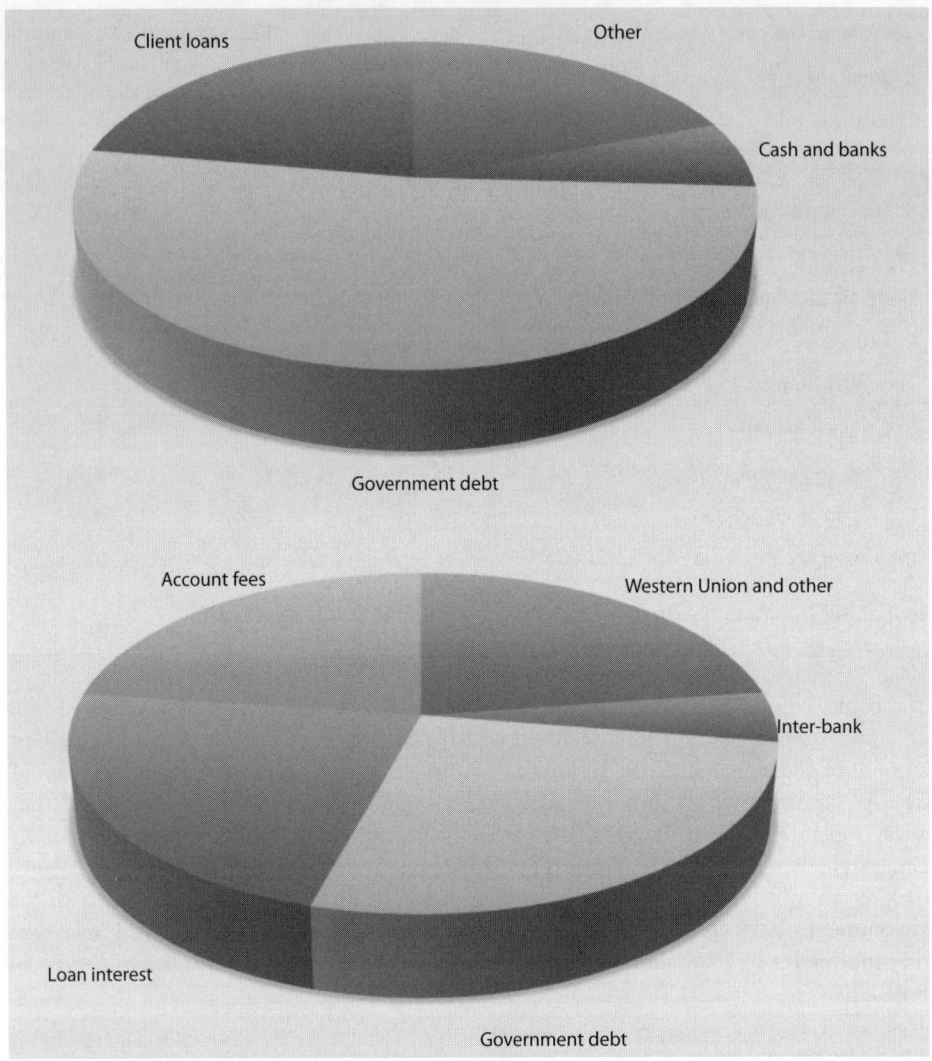

Source: Tanzania Postal Bank (2005)

This turned out to be important in securing the bank's financial sustainability. Figure 1.10 shows how sharply treasury bill yields have dropped since Tanzania Postal Bank was re-launched compared with the much smoother trend in prime lending rates.

By 2005, the bank was earning as much from its loan portfolio as it earned from government securities (about US$2 million from each) and about as much again from each of fees and charges on customer accounts and Western Union international money transfers. Two important points emerge about access from this income split:

- Most loan income is from salary loans, which dominate the loan portfolio (see Figure 1.11). This equates to an average lending rate of around 20 % to 25 %, which is not unreasonable when compared to a prime lending rate of around 15 %. Lending against automatic deduction from salary is not risk free but it is relatively low risk compared to other loan products. It is encouraging that Tanzania Postal Bank can carry out this sort of lending at such affordable interest rates.

- Within the fees charged on customer accounts, the US$2 million or so charged on deposit accounts equates to only 3 % to 4 % of average total deposit balances. Comparing similar banks in the region, the Kenya Post Office Savings Bank also earns as much from fees as it does in interest income. However, all of the interest income is derived from treasury bills, and yields on these have fallen just as sharply as in Tanzania. As a result, in Kenya, the fee yield has been pushed up to around 7 % to 8 % of average deposit balances to keep the Kenyan bank profitable. What this suggests is that consumer lending allows Tanzania Postal Bank to keep its deposit account charges to around half the level it would be at if the bank were to only invest in treasury bills. The cross-subsidy implicit in this is not a crude transfer of funds, but instead involves the credit product carrying part of the cost of the infrastructure that houses the deposit customer base – from which the loan customer base is drawn.

Figure 1.10 Tanzanian T-bill and loan yields, 1993–2005

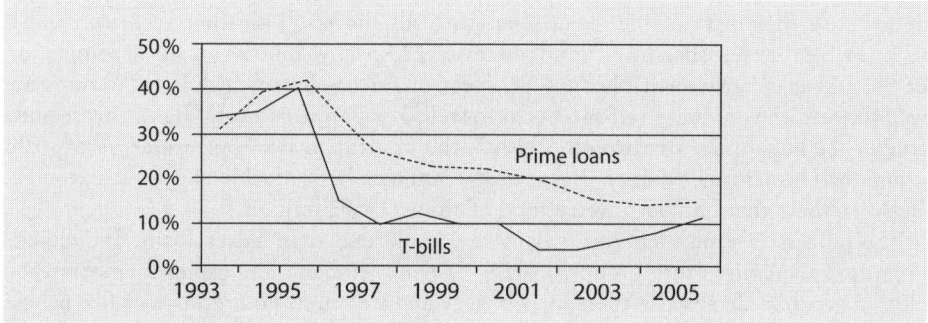

Source: IMF International Financial Statistics

Figure 1.11 Composition of lending to clients, 2005

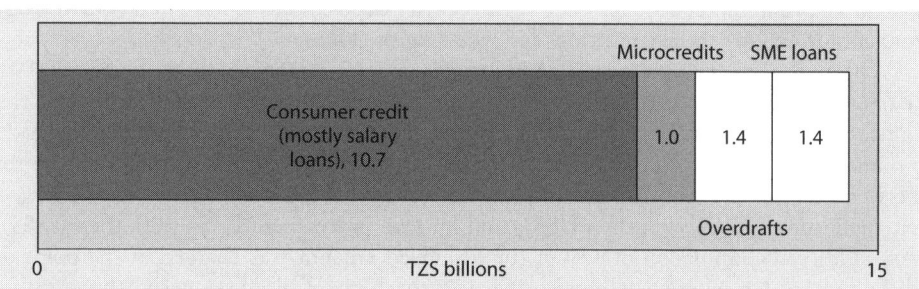

Source: Tanzania Postal Bank (2005)

Strand 2 – Getting the right credit portfolio

Having identified the importance of diversifying by introducing credit products, the products Tanzania Postal Bank chose reflected the wider economic background. Ever since independence, governments in Tanzania have aimed to reduce acute poverty.

Many of these efforts lacked co-ordination. The launch of Tanzania's *National Poverty Eradication Strategy* in 1997 gave the first real cross-government coherence to policy in this area.[61] Just as important, its preparation was more open than had traditionally been the case. It was given impetus by Tanzania being one of the first countries to qualify for international debt relief under the Highly Indebted Poor Country initiative a couple of years later. Tanzania Postal Bank responded with the launch of the salary loan for people with regular employment. For those outside formal employment, it offered group-based microcredit.

The salary loan has been a great success for customers and the bank alike. Customers get the agreement of their employer to guarantee the loan and deduct payments at source directly from their salary. One value of this product is that it can be standardised, making it less expensive to evaluate and administer. By the end of 2005, nearly 18 000 clients had loans outstanding worth an average of US$500. The double-risk mitigation of capturing loan repayments out of salaries before they can be spent and guarantees provided by employers mean that this unsecured lending is low risk. The regulator has therefore relaxed early restrictions on total exposure and allowed the salary loan portfolio to expand to a multiple of three times Tanzania Postal Bank's capital.

Group-based microcredit is also unsecured but repayment rates are supposed to be enhanced by the peer pressure aspect of any group-based lending. If one group member defaults on their part of the group loan then all the rest lose their security deposit (5 % of what they have borrowed), and they lose a prospective interest rebate on completion of the full loan repayment plus any prospect of further borrowing. If the groups are well formed, the product itself can perform well. For Tanzania Postal Bank this seemed true in the beginning. By the end of 2002, the first full year of operations, nearly 700 groups had been formed comprising almost 4 500 members, of which 80 % were women. Between them they had borrowed a total of almost US$2 million.

The process of group lending was more complicated than salary loans. Individuals organised themselves into groups, usually of five members. The group members then elected group leaders: a chairperson, secretary and treasurer. Four groups of five people then formed one larger solidarity group of a maximum of 20 people called a Microcredit Members Centre. This helped reduce administration costs and further enhanced the mutual guarantee mechanism. After the formation of groups, Tanzania Postal Bank officers trained group members ahead of loan approval. Loan disbursement happened only if all group members had made their security deposit (5 % of individual borrowing) and conformed to all the conditions for accessing the loans.

Within the groups, members could borrow amounts ranging from TZS50 000 to TZS600 000 (US$50 to US$600 – equivalent to 14–170 % of per-capita GDP), and the outstanding balance at the end of 2002 suggests that most borrowing must have been made in amounts equivalent to what is more or less top of this range. Maturity could be set between six and 12 months, and interest was set at 2.5 % a month. Fees were charged on application (TZS1 000, then US$1) and for loan processing (TZS5 000, then US$5). An additional commission of 1 % of the disbursed amount was charged at the point of disbursement for subsequent monitoring. On the basis of all these costs, the effective borrowing rate for a typical $500 individual debt ranged from 70 % over 12 months to 90 % over six months.

This should have produced good-quality lending over the long term and initial default rates, at around 1.5 %, were as good for this sort of microcredit, but the fact that the average individual debt was starting out at the same level that the salary credit now delivers (US$500) should perhaps have sounded alarm bells.

The explanation offered by the Tanzania Postal Bank management is that commercial bank lending officers were recruited at that time put together rather disparate groups of established small entrepreneurs. These entrepreneurs were really interested in and wanted individual loans but did not have the regular income to qualify for a salary loan nor the collateral needed for a conventional SME loan. While the scheme was growing fast, the incentive of further borrowing and rebated interest on loan repayment was enough to hold groups together. However, the scheme had to operate within a cap set by the regulator, with total microcredit exposure held to a quarter of the bank's capital. As growth slowed, the scope for group tension and breakdown became more apparent, and loan performance quickly deteriorated. The regulator insisted on retaining the cap, whereas the cap for salary loans was relaxed given the good performance in the salary loan portfolio.

As a result, the salary loan programme grew to three times the size of the capital and continued to perform well, with administration costs kept low. On the other hand, the microcredit programme stagnated and could not grow much beyond the TZS1 billion (US$0.8 million) mark at which it stood at the end of 2005. Only groups with an existing track record can now borrow and the microcredit programme is effectively in abeyance. It does still, however, have strategic importance. It remains a model of savings banking that most consistently delivers broad access to finance, including an explicitly pro-poor microcredit product. Tanzania Postal Bank is therefore working on how to relaunch a workable microcredit product.

Strand 3 – Freeing up the deposit product

The old passbook product is extremely robust and can be operated on an entirely non-technological platform. Almost everyone knows how to use it and literacy is not an issue – several banks in Africa and elsewhere run these accounts on thumbprints. It is, however, time consuming to process, and the lack of technology does not allow it to be operated flexibly. It is also open to fraud and therefore its use often has to be limited, such as tying it to a fixed 'home' branch or by limiting withdrawals so that any fraud or overdrawing can be contained before it gets out of hand.

Tanzania Postal Bank started broadening its deposit base some years ago. In 1999 it introduced its Domicile Savings Account, which removed the limits on the size and frequency of transactions but reduced the flexibility of where a customer could gain access to their home branch. The account could be accessed through a basic card that could be supported locally on un-networked PCs. Service was much quicker than the passbook product, and it was rebranded the Quick Account. The product was popular and by 2004 balances on the account had grown to almost a third of total deposit balances.

The real breakthrough came in 2005. Tanzania Postal Bank completed the connection of all its 22 branches to its new Equinox banking system. The Equinox system cost just over US$1 million to install – a large commitment for a bank with only US$4 million of equity capital, but made it possible to dramatically change the products it offered. The Tanzania Postal Bank teamed up with a local upmarket bank, the Federal Bank of the Middle East, to allow the card used to access the Quick Account, thereby making it a fully fledged debit card.

In April 2005, the Uhuru card was launched, and balances on the Quick Account exploded, growing by 74% in the same year. Growth in its twin Call Account, which targeted small-scale entrepreneurs, was even faster, with balances doubling in a year. In money terms, the increase in balances was equivalent to about US$10 million. This is a huge increase considering a total deposit base of under US$50 million at the start of the year. What is particularly interesting is that most of this was switched money – balances on traditional accounts fell. The rest of the inflow represented faster growth on an already popular product.

Uhuru is the Kiswahili word for 'freedom' – and the account gave customers the freedom to access their money through all 22 branches, plus 11 new Tanzania Postal Bank ATMs, the Tanpay network of ATMs, as well as 200 Tanpay POS terminals where cash can be withdrawn at some of the terminals and purchases may be made using Tanpay's Pesa Chapchap service.

What investment was needed to achieve this? In addition to the US$1 million main software, the software linking the bank's Equinox software to its partner bank's systems cost an additional US$50 000. About US$1.5 million was invested in new hardware, which can be amortised over five years, thereby bringing the cost per year to around US$500 000. This cost is, however, doubled, given the requirements for licensing, maintenance and telecommunications expenses.

The real issue is how this cost should be spread. Even with the rapid growth of Quick Account customers, loading the entire systems cost onto this product would give a false long-term picture of the product's viability. The Equinox system provides an account management platform for all of the bank's accounts even though it is not yet feasible to do online transactions processing at the post offices. Spread over the whole customer base of roughly one million, the unit cost comes down to around US$1 per customer per year. This will then need to reflect the cost of the card product, where each card is spread over a life of three years, but this should not raise the overall unit cost by more than another US$0.50 per customer per year.

Potential outreach

There is a second, and perhaps, more important approach to judging the affordability of Tanzania Postal Bank's card-based strategy, which is the potential outreach to a large number of poor people. The poor live on less than US$10 a month and the most they can afford to pay for banking services is perhaps 10 to 20 US cents a month or around US$1.50 a year. It is, however, hard to imagine that someone living on less than US$120 a year is able and willing to surrender voluntarily even a single dollar in exchange for having access to banking services. But what if they were provided with a card as part of a social welfare programme?

Such programmes are being tried more and more around the world. There is growing evidence that given the low minimum basic living standards in Africa, that social welfare programmes costing perhaps 1 % to 2 % of GDP have the potential of significantly reducing acute poverty. They must, however, be delivered accessibly, and a version of the Uhuru card could do this for Tanzania – at least for those poor households living within reasonable range of the district town centres where the postbank branches or post offices are located.*

This is not factored into the plans for the Uhuru card, but to pay US$1 to US$2 a year to receive benefits of at least US$20 a year and have a safe basic bank account is possible. US$1 to US$2 a year would be enough to pay for a card and contribute towards improving the technology needed to support it, plus any other transaction costs.

* *Given the spatial distribution of Tanzania's population and the size of the country, it will be difficult to reach a good proportion of the target beneficiaries who are rural based with social cash transfers that can be accessed through ATM cards. This will require significant investment in telecommunications, roads and energy infrastructure that is very much lacking in the rural areas.*

Given a total cost of around US$1.50 to US$2 per customer per year, Tanzania Postal Bank now has the potential to offer any of its one million customers who are within reach of a district town centre the chance of using a banking product that can be accessed in any reasonably urbanised area across the whole country. Looking at the cost of basic services in this pooled way is intrinsic to savings banks around the world. The charge made may be in the form of foregone interest but can also be in the form of a monthly fee. The other way pooling works for savings banks is that they often have a lot more inactive or very low-usage accounts than very active accounts. This is somehow seen as a failure by many outside observers, but why should savings accounts be actively used? Customers, particularly poor ones, deliberately put aside money so as not to use it until they really need to. What matters is that they should be able to do this at very little cost.

The affordability of the US$1.50 a year compares to the equivalent of about US$2 per customer that is earned in deposit fees per year. Another US$3 per customer per year can be earned in net interest just by investing deposit balances in government securities. Taking the balance between fixed systems costs and combined fee and interest income suggests how the strategy for deposits has been fairly prudently configured. The implicit system's cost-to-income ratio of 30 % still leaves room for a staff cost-to-income ratio of 40 %. It does not, however, leave much room for profit after other operating costs, although there is also significant fee income from Western Union to help defray some of the other operating costs. This case study does not cover a detailed product costing and profitability analysis, but the key point is that Tanzania Postal Bank has launched a competitive, modern deposit product, and has not incurred losses for the bank. Having invested in creating the platform to support the delivery of the Uhuru card product, the scope for scaling up is huge and potentially profitable.

The other interesting aspect of the bank's strategy is that it has not been designed entirely to replace the old passbook product. That remains the platform for most of Tanzania Postal Bank's clients, including those in the rural areas – and customers still using the old passbook product are not excluded from using the new modern bank premises in the urban areas.

Conclusions

A number of lessons can be drawn for other savings banks in Africa. The first is that Tanzania Postal Bank's success came from providing its existing customers with the freedom to get their money when and where they wanted to – and not from looking for growth from some better-off customer base. There is nothing wrong in launching a successful product for the top end of the mass market if it makes the bank strong enough to provide services for the poor as well. Launching a salary loan product that served the middle to higher end of the market gave Tanzania Postal Bank the profit slack to pay for a modernised branch network and IT platform without having to push all the cost onto deposit fees in a way that would have made the savings product unaffordable for many people.

The second lesson follows from this: cross-subsidisation is not necessarily the result of failure of an institution if this makes it possible to modernise the business model. It is a problem only if it allows the inefficient aspects of the business to limp on unreformed.

The next step for Tanzania Postal Bank: taking the Quick Account forward by revitalising the ordinary postal savings product to be delivered through a network the bank does not control. The bank can offer its Uhuru debit card at a cost that fits within the income yield of an ordinary deposit. It now has a model to build on and a product to market, plus an infrastructure that is already being paid for. The switch in customers from the old ordinary postal savings to the new card product shows they respond to this approach, and the task now is to help more of them do so by steadily linking more and more of its outlets to the POS network.

The final lesson is that the unbanked will only become genuinely bankable when the industry stops designing its core products in a way that makes them unusable for poor people. For this to happen, the unbanked need the price of ordinary banking to be brought low enough by smart management that knows how to configure its business in way that makes the core products not just useful but also usable. That is what Tanzania Postal Bank is doing.

Bank Windhoek: Reaching out to Namibia's rural population

> Namibia is extremely sparsely populated so expanding banking services into remote rural areas is expensive because the volumes of people do not justify a big investment in fixed branch infrastructure. Still, Bank Windhoek, Namibia's only domestically owned bank, has chosen to make banking the country's poor and remote communities a priority and the strategy seems to be paying off. Understanding the needs of these poorer consumers has been critical and the bank has made valuable use of market research to inform its product design. The new initiative was also partially subsidised through donor funding, a good example of how donor funding can help to expand outreach.

In November 2005, Namibian Bank Windhoek launched EasySave, a new, entry-level transactional product, in all of its branches as well as its newly established community branches in rural Namibia. The product was unique at the time, tailored to meet the needs of the low-income market. It had been based on thorough research into the needs of this unexplored market, with the assistance of a grant from DFID. The venture paid off, and the success of EasySave motivated the Bank to develop other products to serve this market.

As Gida Sekandi, at the time executive director of Capricorn Investment Holdings Limited, the main shareholder of Bank Windhoek, remarks: 'We never properly understood what the market potential was although we had been in banking for over 23 years at the time that we entered this market.'

The Republic of Namibia

The Republic of Namibia, formerly called South West Africa, is a democratically governed country on the southwest coast of Africa. The country achieved full independence from South Africa in 1990. It is large, spanning 824 292 square kilometres, and sparsely populated, inhabited by only about two million people, most of whom are clustered in the capital city, Windhoek, and in one or two other major towns. Namibia's population density of around 2.5 people per square kilometre, which compares with its neighbour South Africa's population density of around 39 people per square kilometre, has important implications for the delivery of financial services.

The Namibian economy is based on services, including financial services, making up 58.1 % of GDP in 2006, industry (especially mining), accounting for 30.2 % of GDP and agriculture, accounting for 11.8 % of GDP. About 54 % of the population aged 15 years and above falls into the labour force, of which 69 % was employed at the time of the census conducted in 2001.[62] However, the Human Development Report[63] indicates that 34.9 % of the Namibian population lives under the breadline, on US$1 a day, and 55.8 % live on US$2 a day. Nevertheless, estimated GDP per capita in 2006 was US$7 400,[64] very high for sub-Saharan Africa.

Table 1.9 Key economic data – Namibia

Population (million), UN 2008	2.1
Urban population (%), 2007	33
Unemployment rate (%), 2004	36.7
Poverty (% population at less than US$1 per day), 2007	35
GDP (N$ billion), 2006 (US$6.1 million)	44.4
GDP growth rate (%), estimate 2008	3.9
Inflation rate (%), estimate 2008	10.3
Agriculture sector as % of GDP 2008	10.6
Industry sector as % of GDP 2008	30.8
Service sector as % of GDP 2008	58.6
Average deposit rate (%), August 2007	7.68
Prime overdraft rate (%), December 2007	15.25
Household debt: GDP (%), 2005	40
% of population using formal financial services, 2007	46.8

Sources: CIA World Factbook; BBC Country Profiles; FinScope Namibia (2007); Namibian Government; Bank of Namibia; National Planning Commission; National Labour Force Survey; UNDP

Namibia's financial sector

The Bank of Namibia (BoN), established in 1990, is the central bank of Namibia and supervises the banking industry. The Namibian Financial Institutions Supervisory Authority is the regulator for the non-bank financial sector.

Namibia's banking industry is small and competitive, with four major commercial players: FNB Namibia Holdings, the largest bank in Namibia, followed by Standard Bank Namibia[65], Bank Windhoek, which alternates between second and third position with Standard Bank in terms of market share, and Nedbank Namibia (see Table 1.10). With the exception of Bank Windhoek, which is locally owned, all the other commercial banks are owned by South African parents.[66]

Table 1.10 Namibian banking sector – market share

1.1 Total deposits	April 2007 share %
Bank Windhoek	26.3
First National Bank	30.6

→

Standard Bank	30.8
Nedbank	12.4
Total	100.0
2.1 Total loans and advances	**April 2007 share %**
Bank Windhoek	26.9
First National Bank	32.6
Standard Bank	27.6
Nedbank	12.9
Total	100.0

Source: Bank Windhoek (2007)

Bank Windhoek background

Bank Windhoek was established in 1982 when a group of Namibian businessmen took control of the local branches of what was then Volkskas Bank[67]. Capricorn Investment Holdings Limited (CIH) became Bank Windhoek's holding company in 1996, and for many years, Absa Bank, one of the largest financial services groups in South Africa, held a minority stake of 34.4 % in CIH. Since 8 November 2006, however, when the Namibian shareholders acquired the Absa stake, CIH and Bank Windhoek has been wholly owned by Namibians.

Figure 1.12 Bank Windhoek: Financial overview

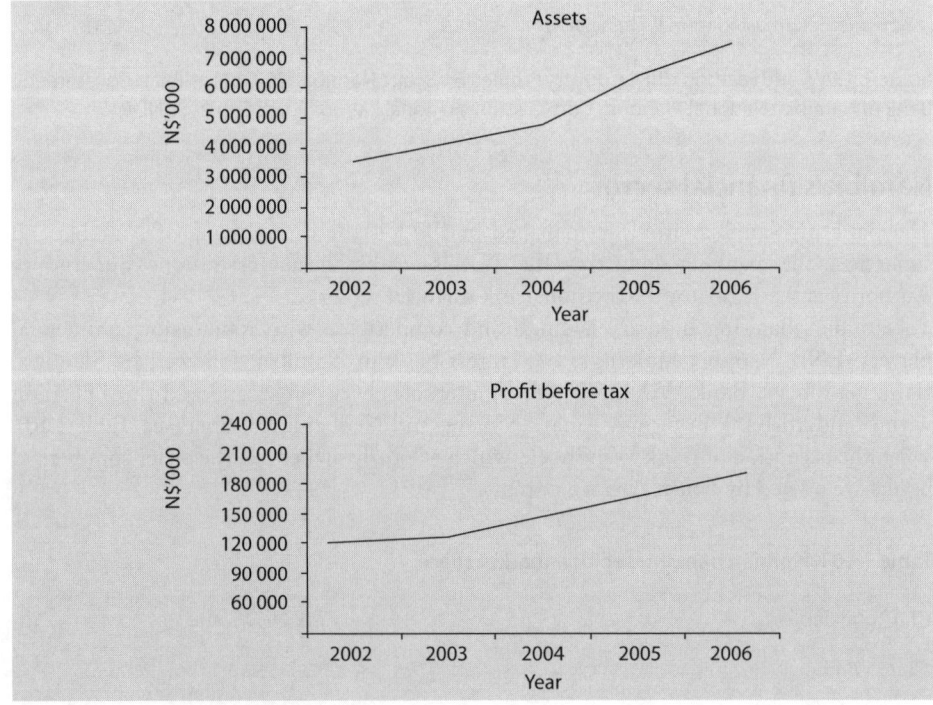

Source: Bank Windhoek (2007)
Note: N$1 = US$7.05 as per the end of June 2007

CIH started spreading its wings to other parts of Africa in May 2005 when it lodged an application for a banking licence in Botswana: Bank Gaborone Ltd starting operating in September 2006. In early 2007, CIH also secured a 24.9 % interest in a Zambian banking operation, Cavmont Capital Bank (Pty) Ltd.[68] Since 2003, the bank's profits have increased steadily, making N$275 million in pre-tax profits in the financial year to 30 June 2007 (see Figure 1.12).

Repositioning Bank Windhoek

The bank's first transformation was driven by Johan Swanepoel, shortly after he was appointed group managing director of the Bank and CIH in 1999. Swanepoel's changes were twofold: he introduced locally-owned technology which could be managed in Namibia, rather than from South Africa, and attempted to reposition the bank to serve the emerging markets – often referred to as the 'post-independence markets'.

However, the bank was still hampered by the perception that it was an Afrikaans bank serving primarily the agricultural and small business communities – a legacy which it had long outgrown as a result of various mergers and acquisitions with other banks and local businesses. As a result, in October 2003 the bank launched a new corporate identity and slogan, 'Together we do better'. Jerry Elago, brand manager of Bank Windhoek, says this repositioning was highly significant, as the bank has since become one of the most recognised brands in Namibia[69].

Bank Windhoek has gradually extended its distribution network over 25 years to 38 retail branches and agencies and more than 140 ATMs across the country, with a total staff complement of 983. The bank's ATM network is the largest in Namibia.

Taking banking to remote areas

In 2002, BoN published a report on plans to introduce second-tier banks that would address the poor levels of access to banking in the low-income market. It was under the impression that the commercial banks would not be interested in addressing this need because the sparse population and remoteness of the towns would not make it sufficiently profitable. As a consequence, it proposed that second-tier banks should fill the gap. Coincidentally, Bank Windhoek was already talking to DFID about providing banking services to low-income rural people. The government had already started applying pressure on the banks to cater for the unbanked and the talks with DFID were a direct result of this, says James Hill, managing director of Bank Windhoek. According to Sekandi, the bank was delighted to find a partner willing to share the risk and the costs in setting up the infrastructure in a new market, and the confluence of events led to Bank Windhoek responding to BoN's challenge.

In 2003 the Financial Deepening Challenge Fund (FDCF), sponsored by DFID, awarded Bank Windhoek a grant of £1 million over a period of four years to take banking to the unbanked in the rural areas of Namibia. The grant enabled Bank Windhoek to conduct a comprehensive study to understand consumers' use of, and need for, financial services in rural areas. The outcome of this initial research, which measured effective access to financial services, identified market segments, and assessed opportunities for expansion of financial services, was to direct Bank Windhoek into particular target areas.

Understanding the unbanked

Sekandi explains that contrary to their expectations, the research showed that to be underbanked and underserved in rural Namibia did not necessarily mean being poor. 'We actually found that there were various reasons for being unbanked in the remote areas. Either people do not bank because they have no physical access [to banks or ATMs], but they do have money; or they do not bank because the amount of money they have is not sufficient to warrant a bank account; or they cannot afford the products; or they do not bank because the products do not meet their needs,' she says. These findings came as a complete surprise to the bank. Contrary to the more popular belief that there were only poor people residing in the remote areas, the research found lots of people who have a sizable income from small businesses, but who were unable to access formal banking systems in their areas.

Another significant finding was that, more than anything, low-income households want their money to be secure. Unlike clients at the higher end of the market who are interested in a high return on investment, clients at the lower end of the market are more interested in protecting their money from fire or theft, while at the same time being able to access it when they need it.

The FinScope Namibia 2004 survey showed that 43 % of all Namibians did not use either the formal and informal financial products or services available in Namibia. Yet, it became clear that there was a need for banking in the rural communities for those employed in both the formal and the informal sectors. 'Any financial activity indicates a need for banking services,' maintains Sekandi.

Having established the need for banking in the remote areas, the next step was a financial feasibility study in each of the targeted communities. The bank had to determine whether a commercial branch would be sustainable, based on the economic activity of the area in question. Key factors considered were the population of the village and surrounding areas, the number of people employed in the public, private and agricultural sectors of the region, and the number of SMMEs, as well as the number of NGOs operating in the area. The feasibility study also involved a thorough investigation into infrastructure: factors such as suitable premises for branches, the presence of a police station, schools, hospitals or clinics and the scope of the telecommunications infrastructure, including cellphone coverage, were all taken into account.

Engaging with local communities

Running parallel with the feasibility studies were discussions with the traditional leaders of the various communities. Germanus Mate, head of business development at Bank Windhoek at the time, led these discussions. He explains that this was a cumbersome process which required much perseverance and patience, as it often involved gathering various members of the community to the meetings. He says that the bank went to great lengths to explain to the community leader why it wanted to set up business in his area and to demonstrate how an ATM worked. It was crucial for the bank to have the leader's blessing, as his support would determine whether or not his community members would use and trust the local branch.

The bank learned some valuable lessons in communicating with the rural market. Mate says it was crucial to plan and communicate thoroughly and to repeat the message. The local radio stations gave the bank free airtime to remind the people in the area about the meetings and their purpose, not charging because they regarded these messages as educational. 'In the end it all boils down to honouring a region's customs and its culture,' says Mate. 'The Herero people would not respect a person who mixes his languages or who does not adhere to the proper dress code for a meeting, which at the very least means a jacket at the start of the meeting, even in the heat of Namibia.'

This communication process in the rural areas started in 2004 and ended in 2006, but eventually paid off. Mate remarks that eventually 'they [the rural people] started to believe in us, that we would suffer with them or prosper with them, regardless of what happens in the country.'

Setting up business

Bank Windhoek claims that its decision to set up physical branches in the communities rather than ATMs only was not motivated so much from a brand perspective, as from the desire to fulfil a social need. The initial research showed that rural people want to talk to someone when they transact, and as such the branch cultivates communication between the bank and its clients. The branches became a place where clients could drink water and use the toilet facilities, even if it was only to hide the money they had just withdrawn.

During the initial stages of the project, while still in discussions with the local communities, the bank had set up mobile branches in the areas as a first step towards establishing a presence while investigating suitable premises for brick and mortar branches. The mobile bank was meant to be a temporary arrangement for no longer than three months while the branch was under construction, but in some instances this extended to a much longer period. This seemed to have fuelled a perception that the bank's presence was only to be temporary, and the people feared that their money could disappear overnight with the bank. In one town, Eenhana, about 10 kilometres from Namibia's border with Angola, other banks used to visit once or twice a week, for example, but the visits tapered off to once a month and eventually stopped due to the costs involved in travelling the distance. Bank Windhoek therefore had to entrench the message that it was there to stay, by pointing out that it was a Namibian-owned bank, operated by Namibians and it was there to support the locals. As a result of this experience, the bank decided to use mobile banks only in areas where the building or renovation of the branch had already started.

Establishing brick and mortar branches was not that easy. Although the ideal scenario for the bank was to buy either a site or a property, it found that in most instances it was prevented from doing so by bureaucratic problems, such as registering titles in the Deeds Office. The option of renting premises presented its own set of problems, as land owners exploited the situation by charging exorbitant rents. In some instances, the rented buildings were in a total shambles which meant that the bank had to upgrade and refurbish them at a high cost.

Some non-negotiable necessities, such as air-conditioning, considering that temperatures of 40°C and above are not uncommon in Namibia, generators to back-up in case of power supply cuts, water tanks with a capacity of 5 000 litres at the branches and at the senior employees' homes in case of water supply cuts, and the requisite security measures, all added to the cost. Even building material had to be transported to rural areas at great expense because little was available locally. Perseverance had by this time become second nature to the bank, says André Nel, executive officer: banking services at Bank Windhoek.

A perpetual challenge is finding suitable people to man the community branches, which need between five and eight staff members. Trained city staff are not especially willing to move to these remote areas. By 2006, Bank Windhoek had established a bankers' training school in Oshakati in the north of Namibia to help solve the problem. The bank recruits matriculants (school leavers) from the communities, trains them in Oshakati, and then places them back to work in their own communities.

The first of the 10 community branches opened up in Noordoewer in November 2003. Eenhana followed closely in December 2003, Outapi in August 2004, and Opuwo in December 2004. In 2005 there was less activity, with only the Okakarara branch opening in August 2005, but 2006 was once again very busy with Aranos opening in February, Aminius in July, Ongwediva in June, and Oshakati North in November of that year. Nkurenkuru opened in the middle of 2007 with two other community branches in the pipeline for 2007 at Luderitz and Omaruru.

Products for the lower end of the market

Initially Bank Windhoek offered this market its traditional products, such as its regular entry-level savings account. It did not take long, however, for the bank to realise that physical infrastructure was not enough, and that it needed to develop specific products to meet the needs for the low-income segment of the market. Using FinScope Namibia 2004 data, it developed a range of products and services for the lower end of the market – which it defined as earning less than N$1 000 a month. Between 2005 and 2007, therefore, the bank introduced EasySave, EasyCredit, GroupSave, SeniorSave, CellPhone Banking and Solo. These products are all unique and not simply an adaptation of existing banking products.

Developing these products was time consuming. Further research was needed to understand the target group's transactional behaviour, their credit needs, their investment needs and, most importantly, their market environment. Jaco Kruger, manager of national sales at the bank says that client behaviour in a rural setting differs substantially from that in an urban setting. Rural clients, for example, being mainly subsistence farmers,[70] deposit large sums of money irregularly whenever they sell their cattle, and therefore transact only once or twice a year. Urban clients typically transact several times a month. For this reason the bank is less concerned about the seemingly dormant accounts in the rural areas than about such accounts in the urban areas.

Transactional accounts

EasySave, a transactional account, was developed around five client benefits: it needed to be easy to open so no payslip is required when this is done; it needed to be affordable, so a low monthly service fee of N$2 (US$0.28) applies; it had to encourage saving, and so no deposit fees are charged on the account; it would offer the benefit of free life cover of N$2 500 (US$353); and it needed to be easy for clients to maintain and so a low minimum balance of only N$20 (US$2.82) is required.[71] Even the promotional material for EasySave reflected the simplicity of the product.

The launch of EasySave in November 2005 exceeded expectations, with more than 40 000 accounts (of which 7 000 are 'dormant') opened across the country. In only 18 months, EasySave was able to garner deposits for Bank Windhoek of between N$12 and N$13 million from the low-income, informally employed market.

Credit accounts

The 2004 research showed that poor people in rural areas rely mainly on cash, and do not borrow as often as urban clients. When they borrow, they tend to do so in smaller amounts, between N$1 000 and N$1 200, and repay as quickly as possible. These loans are used mainly to pay for school clothes and school fees, or in the case of the subsistence farmers, for seed or animal feed.

Based on this research, Bank Windhoek developed EasyCredit in March 2006, an easy-access loan facility. To qualify, the client has to be 21 years of age or older, and have had an EasySave or transactional account at Bank Windhoek for at least three months. The loan facility is unsecured, thus the client is not required to provide collateral or security.

DFID's grant also helped the bank develop a credit-scoring model, which it used to determine whether the deposits made by a client over a period of time would sustain the loan. EasyCredit allows clients to borrow any amount between N$500 and N$2 500 over a period of 12 months, and no service fees are charged on the account.[72] By 2007 the Bank had extended N$830 000 in EasyCredit loans. Less than 6 % of the loan payments are in arrears, which, according to bank standards, is quite acceptable, says Kruger.

Senior citizens' accounts

To cater for senior citizens' banking needs, Bank Windhoek next came up with SeniorSave for clients older than 55 years. With a SeniorSave account, clients earn interest at the rate of 7 % on a positive balance and pay reduced banking fees. Because research showed that older people preferred conducting their banking business inside branches, the bank dropped its charges for over-the-counter withdrawals for SeniorSave clients.

Mobile phone banking

The 2004 research showed that regardless of the economic circumstances of people in remote areas, cellphone technology was gaining in popularity, particularly in areas outside the reach of fixed-line telecommunications infrastructure. It revealed that more Namibians had access to a cellphone (45.6 %) than to a landline telephone at home (26.6 %).

This, together with the success of the community branches, motivated Bank Windhoek to apply for an additional £100 000 from FDCF/DFID, which it used to establish cellphone banking in December 2006. It was the first bank in Namibia to offer this service to its clients, and since the launch of this channel – promoted as 'my bank in my hand' – more than 600 000 transactions had been conducted. According to Kruger, cellphone banking is the bank's most affordable channel.

Group savings accounts

GroupSave, launched in May 2007, is a product which fulfils a function similar to that of *stokvels* (saving clubs) in South Africa. It was developed to accommodate a saving culture collectively for a common goal such as a wedding or funeral, or to buy property. Members of the group contribute a minimum monthly amount, set by the bank, towards the account and are allowed to borrow against those savings.

The Bank's latest product, CreditSave, was developed to cultivate a savings culture by requiring a fixed monthly deposit, but clients are free to withdraw their money at any given time. However, if they can keep saving for three years, they may apply for an unsecured loan for up to N$50 000 (US$7 098), payable over a three-year term.

New product development

New product development is an extremely important aspect of the bank's activities at this end of the market. To this end, it has a policy of developing a new product every three months, although the product does not necessarily have to be launched within that time. In line with this policy, an emerging SME transaction package is in the pipeline.

A strong campaign to educate clients at the low end of the market in the proper and responsible handling of any banking account runs parallel with the development of the products.

Business outcomes

According to the bank's feasibility study, branches were expected to become profitable within three years of opening. While this was achieved in some cases, it was not in others. For example, Outapi, with 3 200 debit cards issued to local people, and Eenhana, with 4 056 debit cards, both broke even after 18 months and are operating profitably.

Opuwo, Aminius and Okakarara, on the other hand, are still struggling to survive. Nel believes that this can be attributed to the absence of brick-and-mortar buildings in both Opuwo and Aminius, where the bank has not been able to secure suitable land or buildings to buy. Although Okakarara does have its own bank building, only 1 500 cards have been issued. The reasons for the slow uptake are unclear, says Nel, although the bank is investigating the issue.

At the beginning of 2007, the total staff count for all community branches was 59. By the middle of the year, however, both the Outapi and Eenhana branches required extra staff members due to the unexpected demand for banking services, and were looking for new and larger premises.

In 2007, more than 80 % of Bank Windhoek's individual clients fell into the low-income category – the so-called 'new bankers'. As at June 2007, the banking activities of these clients contributed 11.6 % of the bank's annual turnover, which translates into almost N$1.3 million.

Unfortunately, Bank Windhoek did not succeed in spending the whole of the DFID grant by the end of May 2007 when the partnership ended. Nel notes that one of the reasons for this was that the research and the feasibility study took a lot longer than originally anticipated (up to two years in this instance). He adds that given Bank Windhoek's own contribution of £2.5 million, it is not surprising that the grant could not be fully used in the given period. Seen overall, however, the bank believes the low-income strategy was an opportunistic one which paid off, not only in terms of the additional accounts, but also in terms of the acknowledgement, both at government and at community level, of what the bank is doing in the remote parts of the country. 'That encouraged us a lot and being a local bank, born and bred here, it made sense that we should have taken the initiative,' says Sekandi.

Challenges

The bank now has an established footprint in the rural areas. However, other banks such as FNB, Standard Bank and Nedbank have subsequently also established themselves in the same areas. This means that Bank Windhoek's market share in these areas has inevitably shrunk. Competition may be helping consumers by providing them with greater choice but it leaves Bank Windhoek, as the first mover, with the challenge of retaining its customers.

However, Hill maintains that the most pressing challenge for the bank – more pressing than competitive pressure – is still the enormous distance between villages and towns. There is a cost to transporting money, and naturally it escalates with every additional branch, as does the cost of constructing or renovating a new branch, because most of the building materials need to be brought in from elsewhere.

Should the bank decide to extend its microlending activities, Sekandi identifies a further challenge: that of a lack of credit information on clients. While there are credit-checking facilities available in Namibia with private credit bureau cover of adults in Namibia at around 35 %,[73] it is still impossible to know whether a client is overextended. Although the Namibia Revenue Services has plans to build a large database to meet this demand, this particular kind of credit information remains a challenge to all financial institutions in Namibia.

Future plans

Bank Windhoek continues to receive requests from other regions and communities to provide banking services in their areas. While it plans to continue expanding into the rural communities at its own cost, subject to the outcome of market research and financial feasibility studies, the bank realises that it has to invest time and money in the low-income market first, as that market could grow into the bank's future business clients.

On entering the microlending market, Sekandi notes that the bank is considering forming partnerships with some of the foreign banks which have applied to the BoN for licences to set up microfinance services in the country.

Conclusion

Bank Windhoek has benefited from this project. Not only has the bank extended its footprint and grown its client base by thousands, but the deposits in the new accounts have helped the bank to raise retail funding against which it can grant loans. Moreover, according to Sekandi, to manage the bank's liquidity and to reduce risk, it is far better to attract large numbers of smaller accounts than to be dependent on a few really big accounts.

No doubt volumes determine profitability in the low-income market. Bank Windhoek's experience is that the poor can be served profitably if their needs are properly met. Hill notes that the bank has learned that to continue to meet those needs, it needs to think more innovatively and form smart partnerships which are managed to offer cost-effective products.

The benefit has not only been for the bank. The presence of Bank Windhoek has made a difference in the lives of the rural people, quite apart from providing access to banking services. Besides creating job opportunities by either contracting local builders or renting property from local people, the bank has also played a role in getting the telecommunication authorities to invest in better infrastructure in the remote areas so that the bank can operate there.

Money lubricates the economy, says Mate, and indeed, in the places where Bank Windhoek has established a community branch, the villages have started to develop economically. In Eenhana, for example, where the local salaried people had to travel 100 to 200 kilometres every month to the nearest branch to cash their salary cheques, they could save up to N$40 (US$5.65) in taxi fares by using a local branch. Because the local people no longer have to travel so far to the major centres to cash their salary cheques, they spend more of their disposable income in their own communities. Property developers have picked up on this, and have invested in building new business premises, where retailers such as the furniture group Beares and clothing retailer Pep Stores have established themselves. The result has been growth for the villages.

Sekandi suggests that the most important outcome of this project has been an intangible one. 'The bank gained a lot of political and social goodwill that is invaluable. One cannot put a price on goodwill,' she says. 'It has been an exciting journey, not because we realised profits but because we began to understand the market potential. It may not be profitable at first but you have to serve the lower end of the market in a way that suits them, in order to be profitable.'

Endnotes

1. DFID Country Profiles (online).
2. IMF and World Bank (2001).
3. See Center for Sustainable Urban Development, http://www.earthinstitute.columbia.edu/csud/projects/nairobi_studio.html.
4. FinAccess (2006).
5. The loans are of short maturities, and turnover of loans is high, which makes the economic impact less than the US$250 million figure implies.
6. Coppoolse (2007).
7. Grameen Bank was founded in Bangladesh by Professor Muhammad Yunus. Its group-based approach model has been a model for microfinance institutions worldwide. The organisation and Yunus were jointly awarded the Nobel Peace Prize in 2006.
8. Kabbucho, Sander & Mukwana (2003).
9. FinAccess (2006).
10. Beck, Demirguc-Kunt & Peria (2005).
11. FinAccess (2006).
12. PlanetFinance, Microlit and Global Credit Rating Co., among others. Also, Equity has been ranked the third most robust bank in Kenya after Citibank and Standard Bank in 2006.
13. Claessens, Demirguc-Kunt & Huizinga (2000).
14. Jansen & Vennes (2006).
15. Bonin & Abel (2000).
16. World Bank (2005).
17. For example Demirguc-Kunt & Huizinga (2000); Clarke, Cull, D'Amato & Molinari (2000); Barajas, Steiner & Salazar (2000); Kiraly, Majer, Matyas, Ocsi, Sugar & Varhegyi (2000); Bhattacharya, Lovell & Sahay (1997).
18. For example Claessens, Demirguc-Kunt & Huizinga (2000).
19. Mattoo, A, Rathindran, R & Subramaniam, A (2001).
20. Barth, Caprio & Levine (2001); Demirguc-Kunt, Levine & Min (1999); Levine (1999).
21. Brownbridge & Gayi (1999).
22. Clarke, Cull & Peria (2001).
23. Ibid.
24. Jenkins(2000).
25. Peachey & Roe (2006).
26. Cali, Ellis & Te Velde (2008).
27. Claessens (2005).
28. Porteous & Hazelhurst (2004: 12).
29. Manuel (2002).
30. LSM or Living Standards Measure is a categorisation ranging from 1 to 10 used extensively by marketers and advertisers as a means to segment the population. It is crude proxy for wealth, with the lower LSM groups comprising the most impoverished end of the spectrum. Living Standards Measures have traditionally been used as the tool for analysis of the South African consumer market.
31. IMF (2008: 38).
32. Stats SA (2007).
33. FinScope South Africa (2007).
34. Banks DI 100 returns, available at http://www.resbank.co.za.
35. Stats SA does not sub-segment the finance, real estate and business services category, save to state that annualised increases in the contributions towards GDP growth by this sector in the first six months of 2007 'was mainly due to increased activities in the finance and insurance services'.

36 Stats SA, (online). Gross Domestic Product, Second quarter: 2008, available via http://www.statssa.gov.za.
37 Porteous & Hazelhurst (2004: 12).
38 Banks DI 900 returns for December 2006, available http://www.resbank.co.za.
39 FinScope SA (2006).
40 Barnard Jacobs Mellett (2006).
41 The recoupment of payments through legal means, for example, debit orders.
42 Townsend & Mosala (2006).
43 South African Advertising Research Foundation's All Media and Products Study (AMPS) (2007).
44 Bernard Jacobs Mellet (2006).
45 http://www.finmarktrust.org.za forums link.
46 AMPS 2007, SAARF (2007).
47 MicroCapital (2007).
48 Demirguc-Kunt (2007).
49 Readers unfamiliar with the South African consumer credit industry may be surprised at these rates. They are high by global standards but, at the time of the experiment, normal for South Africa.
50 Slightly more than 1 % of the offers were higher than the normal interest rate and 3 % were at the normal rate.
51 We did this by independently randomising price and marketing features to the same sample. Each household in the sample received a single mailer with a randomised loan offer and a separately randomised marketing pitch selling the offer. The pricing experiment does not affect the marketing experiment because in the aggregate clients received each pitch across the full range of prices. In effect the high and low prices cancel each other out. The same logic holds in the other direction: the marketing experiment does not affect the pricing experiment because those who received low rates would get *all* the marketing pitches, as would those who received high rates.
52 Per-capita GDP in dollars from selected World Development Indicators (online).
53 Government of Tanzania (2003).
54 The 2000/01 Household Budget Survey shows that in Dar es Salaam, 30 % more cash was needed just to buy the minimum food basket than was the case in rural areas.
55 These figures may slightly understate actual penetration of banking services in that they may miss some people who think they are saving with the 'post office' and not a bank.
56 This is a model inherited in broadly similar forms down the British, French and Portuguese lines.
57 Despite, or perhaps even because of the early difficulties, these two organisations became acknowledged leaders in the field of negotiating service level agreements in Africa.
58 Peachey & Roe (2006).
59 Peachey (2006).
60 By the end of 2005, government debt still accounted for half of the total assets and almost a quarter of loans.
61 This has been superseded by the *National Strategy for Growth and Reduction of Poverty* of June 2005, but the underlying principles remain the same.
62 Namibia Trade Directory (online).
63 UNDP (2005a).
64 CIA World Factbook (online).
65 Namibia Trade Directory (online).
66 SA Department of Trade and Industry (online).
67 In 1991 in South Africa, Volkskas, Trust, United and Allied banks merged to form Absa Bank.
68 Bank Windhoek (2006).
69 Bank Windhoek Money Matters Issue 48 (2007a).
70 Subsistence farmers live off their land or livestock, selling only as and when they need money. They are not necessarily poor as some have substantial stock.
71 Bank Windhoek, Money Matters Issue 7 (online a).
72 Bank Windhoek, Money Matters Issue 20 (online b).
73 According to http://www.nationmaster.com.

Chapter Two
SME banking

Providing financial services for small businesses in Africa is recognised as important for development in view of the crucial role small businesses can play in creating jobs, especially at a micro or community level. Although donor agencies have been supporting this sector for years, through guarantees or subsidies, few of their interventions have been an unqualified success. Small business banking seems to be a sector that is intractably complex and ultimately resistant to rapid scale-up, although organisations such as ProCredit and AccessHolding are beginning to challenge these assumptions. Both these Germany-based organisation are testing new models and providing finance to the small business sector in developing countries.

The two case studies in this chapter offer very different approaches to the challenge of small business banking. Banque Misr is a classic example of a downscaler, exemplifying that in order to be successful in a new market it is essential that the business model is changed fundamentally, even down to the type of loan officer employed in the new business. Using recent graduates as loan officers rather than seasoned bank staff is central to the success of Banque Misr. Banque Misr's results, making 'unbankable businesses bankable', are dramatic, with a rapidly growing loan book and exceptionally high repayment rates, from 'the smallest companies in the poorest part of Egypt', as the case study says.

The other case study charts Burkina Bail's success in developing both a leasing and a factoring business. It is well known that small businesses often cannot borrow because they cannot offer banks adequate collateral for loans. Alternative forms of lending, including asset-based lending such as leasing or factoring, can plug this gap. Although Burkina Faso is a very poor country, Burkina Bail has shown that this kind of funding can aid development.

Banque Misr: Making the unbankable bankable

> Banque Misr's microcredit programme in Upper Egypt has already reached thousands of microenterprises and small businesses in the poorest part of the country. The bank departed from its normal lending practices to launch the programme outside of the urban areas to take advantage of the repayment culture and social solidarity that characterised the region. It then built its credit portfolio by using young graduates as loan officers, and by going out into the markets and streets to talk to small entrepreneurs to understand their businesses.

When we first asked Dr Akmal Bassili to explain Banque Misr's microcredit business, he smiled and said, 'Our strategy is to make the unbankable bankable.' Dr Bassili is the architect of a lending business that serves micro and small enterprises in Upper Egypt. The bank begins in each case with a very small loan, developing an ongoing relationship with each entrepreneur, and extending further credit to the business as required. This model enables the bank to transform businesses that would otherwise be too small to interest a commercial bank in the Egyptian environment into 'bankable' clients.

The programme was launched in April 2004. By October 2008 it had profitably extended around 112 201 small loans totalling LE416 million (US$75.6 million), with a repayment rate of 99.9 %.

Poverty in Egypt

Egypt is a country of 74 million people, whose annual income per capita was US$1 250 in 2005. It is classified by the World Bank as a lower-middle-income country, like most Middle East and North African countries.[1] Key economic data are shown in Table 2.1.

Table 2.1 Key economic data – Egypt

Population (million), estimate July 2007	80.3
Urban population (%), estimate July 2007	45.2
Poverty (% population below national lower poverty line), February 2008	19.98
GDP per capita (US$), 2007	5 899
GDP growth rate (%), estimate 2007	7.1
Forecast GDP growth rate (% per annum), 2005–2009	5.8
Deposits to GDP, 2007 (%)	96.4
Inflation rate, 2007 (%)	9.5
Overnight deposit rate, December 2006 (%)	8.75
Overnight lending rate, December 2006 (%)	10.75

Sources: World Bank World Development Indicators; Central Bank of Egypt; CIA World Factbook; UNDP (2005b)

There are wide disparities in poverty levels in the different regions of the country (see Table 2.2). In Upper Egypt in the south of the country, more than a third of the population is poor, whereas in Lower Egypt outside the metropolitan areas, 14 % are poor, and in the four big cities of Cairo, Alexandria, Port Said and Suez, this figure is only 6.2 %. Banque Misr has successfully launched its lending programme for microenterprises in Upper Egypt – the poorest part of the country.

The Egyptian government's poverty reduction strategy includes economic development and reducing unemployment as major components, with a particular emphasis on micro, small and medium enterprises (MSMEs) – companies with fewer than 50 employees.

In Egypt, for various reasons related to the regulatory and tax regimes, the MSME sector is heavily concentrated at the smaller end, with most microenterprises of four employees or fewer. Such microenterprises constitute 93 % of all MSMEs in Egypt.[2] Banque Misr's microlending programme focuses on these enterprises.

Table 2.2 Poverty distribution in Egypt

Region (% of national population)	Poor people as % of total population in the region*
Urban governorates (18.3 %)**	6.2 %
Lower Egypt (43.4 %)	14.0 %
Upper Egypt (36.7 %)	34.0 %
Frontier governorates (1.4 %)	5.4 %
Egypt as a whole (100 %)	20.2 %

Source: UNDP (2005b)

Note: *People falling below the national lower poverty line

**Cairo, Alexandria, Port Said and Suez

Banque Misr

A group of Egyptian businessmen led by the great nationalist entrepreneur Talaat Pasha Harb founded Banque Misr in 1920 to compete with the foreign banks that dominated the country's economy at the time. The bank was nationalised in 1960, and by 2004 it was the second largest of the big four state-owned banks dominating the Egyptian banking scene, between them accounting for 55 % of banking sector deposits. National Bank of Egypt accounted for 22 % of deposits, Banque Misr for 17 %, Banque du Caire for 9 %, and Bank of Alexandria 7 %.[3] Since 2004, as a result of the Egyptian government's extensive financial sector reform programme, the position of the state-owned banks has changed radically. The Bank of Alexandria was successfully privatised in 2006 and is now controlled by the Bank of Sanpaolo from Italy. In September 2005, the Egyptian government announced the merger of Banque Misr with Banque du Caire. Eventually, after many twists and turns in the planning, it was decided that instead of a merger of the two banks, Banque Misr would acquire Banque du Caire, an acquisition which was completed at the beginning of 2007.

Banque Misr has greatly improved its financial position in the context of the reform programme, increasing its total assets from LE62 billion in 2001 to LE106 billion in 2005, and steadily improving its profitability. But the legacy of old non-performing loans still affects the bank (see Table 2.3). Provisioning used up nearly two-thirds of the bank's net income in 2004/5, and provision for bad loans remained at 9.7 % of the value of loans on the balance sheet.

The improvements are the result of the strategy adopted by the new Banque Misr board appointed in 2001. The strategy recognised the need to diversify the bank's customer base, especially on the lending side. Until the turn of the 21st century, public-sector banks in Egypt traditionally focused their lending on large loans to a small number of large clients, mainly in the metropolitan areas such as Cairo and Alexandria. The past failure to diversify their loan portfolio had contributed to the problem of non-performing loans. Banque Misr also had to respond to pressures from the government for the banks to make a greater contribution to economic development and increasing employment. The microlending programme was proposed to the board as an innovative component of the bank's response.

Table 2.3 Highlights from the Banque Misr Annual Report, 2005

For the year ending 30 June 2005	LE million	US$ million
Balance sheet		
Total assets	106 754	18 583
Shareholder's equity	3 377	587
Loans to banks and customers (before provisions)	36 355	6 323
Provisions for loans	3 517	612
Provisions as % of loans	9.7	
Income statement		
Net income from activities	3 867	673
Provisions	2 473	430
Provisions as % of net income	64	
Profit after tax	140	24

Source: Banque Misr

Note: At June 2005 the exchange rate was US$1 = LE 5.75

The microlending proposition put to the board

Dr Bassili joined Banque Misr as its development consultant in 2000, with a remit to develop new forms of business for the bank. He immediately recognised the promising possibilities of microcredit. It would enable the bank to enter a new business and diversify its risks, while at the same time potentially contribute to economic development and employment, which are always serious issues for a state-owned bank in a country like Egypt. Dr Bassili studied the experience of others that had worked in microfinance, including the National Development Bank, Banque du Caire and a number of NGOs. He also undertook market research and consulted other experts, both Egyptian microfinance specialists and specialists in the international community.

It was clear to him that it was not appropriate for Banque Misr to establish a microcredit programme aimed at the very poor. As Dr Bassili put it, 'We could not compete with the NGOs in serving people at the deepest levels of poverty, and we did not set out to do so. We planned to target people, specifically entrepreneurs, at the next level – poor rather than very poor. The NGOs were not our competitors. On the contrary, to the extent that they lifted people out of the deepest level of poverty, they put those people in a position in which we could serve them.'

In 2002 Dr Bassili presented the new board with a detailed plan to develop a microlending business in conjunction with the International Finance Corporation (IFC), the private sector development arm of the World Bank. The plan was based on pilot lending programmes that would be developed in five Banque Misr branches in the governorate of Qena in Upper Egypt. The board was happy with a cautious approach based on pilot projects, but the plan turned out to include three radical elements that startled some of Dr Bassili's colleagues.

- The business would be started in Upper Egypt, the rural south of the country, not in Cairo, Alexandria or the Nile Delta.
- The pilots would be run only in locations where they would compete with other commercial banks, and especially with Banque du Caire.
- The loan officers would be new graduates, not experienced bankers.

The suggestion that the pilots be conducted in Upper Egypt and not in Cairo, Alexandria or the Nile Delta was radical because the north of the country is generally thought of as the powerhouse of business in Egypt. Another reason is that conventional wisdom supposes that it is easier to launch microfinance activities in metropolitan areas rather than in rural areas, given the economies of scale that can result from working in big cities. Dr Bassili, however, did not shy away from challenging conventional wisdom. In this case, he argued that Upper Egypt provides more fertile ground for microlending, mainly because of a significant difference in culture between the south and the north. In Upper Egyptian society there is still a very strong emphasis on family and community solidarity. There is also a repayment culture – as Dr Bassili put it, 'In the south, my word is more secure than any cheque!' If someone is unable to pay a debt, family and community will usually pay rather than face the shame of default. Such constraints are thought to be weaker in the north, for a number of historical reasons. In Greater Cairo, for example, of a population of about 16 million people, around eight million commute several kilometres every day to work in the centre. Microcredit in Cairo would often mean lending to someone whose business is in the centre of a metropolis while their home is far away in a different community. The borrower's home environment therefore would not be known to the bank, while the borrower's business may suddenly disappear to a new location – a very different case from an entrepreneur in a small town, who would be much easier to trace.

The second element of the proposal was that the pilot schemes be launched in places where competing commercial banks had already set up microlending programmes, and specifically where programmes had been established by Banque du Caire, which was targeting the same kind of micro-entrepreneur as Banque Misr. Some people thought this a daft idea – why put the bank at a disadvantage from the start, competing with a rival who had all the advantages of first entry? The two responses to this objection were, first, if Banque du Caire has gone to a location, then that confirms the judgment that it is a good market for the product; second, a pilot is by its very nature an experiment, and an experiment must replicate all the relevant conditions found in the real world, including competition. If the Banque Misr model succeeds where there is competition, then it will certainly succeed where there is no competition, whereas the opposite may not be true.

The third element was perhaps the most radical of all. In 2002 Banque Misr, like many state-owned banks throughout the developing world, was overstaffed. Some people at Banque Misr headquarters perceived a microcredit scheme as a good opportunity to siphon off some of the surplus staff and give them something to do.

Dr Bassili firmly rejected such suggestions: 'How can you take someone who has been sitting behind a desk for 15 years and is now biding his time until he retires, and send him out into the field to work the 12 to 14 hours a day needed to launch a microcredit programme?' What was proposed instead was a model in which each branch would have a microcredit team of five, including three new graduates – bright young people recruited fresh from university – who would market the loans and manage the relationship with the borrowers; and two more experienced bankers who would supervise the work, assess the creditworthiness of the clients and help structure the loans. The three graduates would work full time on the microcredit programme, while the more experienced bankers would combine their microcredit work with other branch banking duties, devoting perhaps 30–40 % of their time to microcredit supervision. The three loan officers would be given incentives to grow the microcredit business, their remuneration and their promotion being dependent on the number of good loans they brought into the bank.

The proposal was vigorously debated in the Banque Misr boardroom. The board eventually agreed to it, but set a tough target – within a year the programme was to achieve three times the level of lending achieved by Banque du Caire in each of the five pilot areas, and with a repayment rate of 100 %. These targets were actually achieved within 10 months of the launch of the pilot programme in April 2004.

Launching the programme

IFC advised Banque Misr on the design of the microlending programme, and helped to procure and fund specialist consultants for the bank. The selected consultants, Environmental Quality International (EQI), helped the bank:

- Develop its business plan and its microfinance operations manual;
- Assess current performance and prepare projections;
- Develop programmes and policies;
- Design the lending product;
- Design institutional capacity building for the bank, including delivery of basic and field training for loan officers and identifying managers for the programme;
- Provide the El-Mohassil Loan Tracking programme[4] together with training for bank staff in its use; and
- Provide technical assistance and workshops for follow-up and performance assessment.

The EQI team provided support to initiate activities in the branches, and installed software capacity in the head office of the bank to monitor and manage the activities of the branches. This specialist loan-tracking software was upgraded to include credit-scoring fields, enabling Banque Misr to capture borrower data necessary for the credit scoring of borrowers. Five supervisors and 24 loan officers were then trained.

The bank started disbursing microloans in the first week of April 2004. By the end of December 2004, more than US$2 million had been disbursed through more than 4 500 loans. The success of the pilot phase encouraged Banque Misr and IFC to extend the project to other areas in Upper Egypt as well as to the Delta region. The second phase commenced in April 2005, and with technical assistance from EQI, MSME lending was introduced in an additional six branches. By May 2006, the 11 branches had disbursed 23 584 loans, amounting to more than US$8 million. By September 2008, 54 branches were providing microloans – 27 in the Delta and 27 in the Upper Egypt. By that time, EQI had trained 90 loan officers and supervisors.

Both head-office staff and those in the branches pay tribute to EQI's contribution, not only in terms of the software and training they provided, but also for the way they shared their extensive experience in the microfinance field. One of the team leaders told us, 'I have worked with EQI from the beginning and now I regard them as my mentors. I often turn to them to discuss my plans as well as my problems.'

Programme management

Figure 2.1 shows how the microlending programme is organised. The teams report directly to the management team in Cairo led by Dr Bassili. The software provided by EQI gives the management team comprehensive real-time information, down to the level of individual loan officers. In addition, three Banque Misr middle managers have been designated as roving supervisors. They have other jobs within the bank but devote part of their time to moving from branch to branch for short visits, examining the records, checking the quality of the branch programme and, where necessary, troubleshooting. They help the teams to work with clients who are experiencing difficulties and resolve problem loans.

Figure 2.1 The Banque Misr microlending organisation

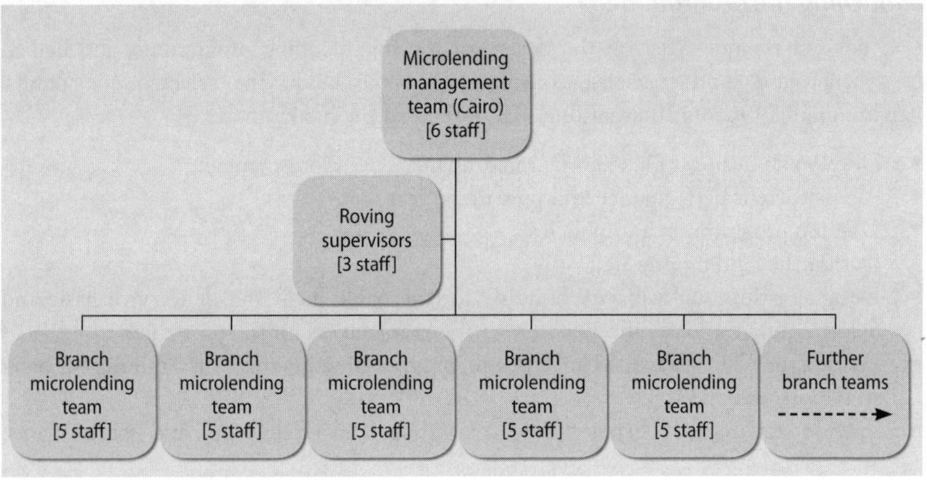

```
                Microlending
                management
                team (Cairo)
                  [6 staff]
                       |
              Roving
              supervisors
              [3 staff]
                       |
   ┌──────────┬──────────┬──────────┬──────────┬──────────┬──────────┐
 Branch     Branch     Branch     Branch     Branch     Further
 microlending microlending microlending microlending microlending branch teams
   team       team       team       team       team
 [5 staff]  [5 staff]  [5 staff]  [5 staff]  [5 staff]
```

Source: Dr Akmal Bassili, Banque Misr

The business model

The size of loans Banque Misr extends to microenterprises varies from LE1 000 to LE15 000 (about US$180 to US$2 600), all at a fixed interest rate of 16 % per annum. The lending sequence is highly structured. The maximum for a first loan is LE5 000 (US$900) for up to six months; for a second loan, 150 % of the first loan for up to one year; and for the third loan, 150 % of the second loan for up to one year. From the fourth loan onwards, the size and duration of the loan is for the judgment of the loan officer, up to a maximum of LE15 000, though loans are very rarely for more than one year.

This structured progression is at the heart of the programme's mission to 'make the unbankable bankable'. Dr Bassili explained, 'Our loan officers are going out into the markets and the streets and finding small businesses to work with. Most of these potential clients have never had a relationship with a bank, let alone taken out a bank loan. We need to train them gradually to be good borrowers – to husband their resources and to manage their cash flows. Often, we are giving the clients less credit than they ask for, maybe even less than they need, but this is part of the educational process, helping them to learn how to manage their borrowings and their repayments. Eventually, the clients graduate to bigger loans, open cheque and savings accounts with the bank, and even pay their loans by direct debit. I measure our success by the number of clients who achieve that graduation, who become truly bankable businesses. I love microfinance – working the pyramid from the bottom is very satisfying for me.'

The model is also highly profitable. Funds are lent at 16 %. The internal cost of funds for the programme is 8 %, overheads work out at around 2 % on a full recovery basis, and the repayment rate is 99.9 % – so the net return is almost 6 %. This compares very favourably with other bank activities, according to Amr El Mahdy, the managing director of Banque Misr, who is a strong advocate of the microlending programme. Says El Mahdy: 'It brings new clients into the bank; it helps to develop the economy of Upper Egypt and to decrease unemployment; and it makes us a good profit'.

The bank attributes its success to two features of its business model in particular. The first is its use of young graduates, whose enthusiasm and drive have enabled them to grow the business. Both the incentive system and the supervision by the more experienced members of the team are designed to encourage the loan officers not to increase the quantity of loans at the expense of quality, hence the excellent repayment record. The second feature is the practice of offering a succession of loans, enabling clients to graduate to bigger and more flexible loans. Some of Banque Misr's rivals have been less successful, according to Dr Bassili, either because they have fallen into the trap of using the microcredit programme, at least in part, to absorb surplus staff or because once they make a loan they follow up only or mainly to collect the repayments. They do not focus enough resources on building a growing relationship with the client.

The microlending programme in Luxor

Luxor is an important tourist and trading centre in Upper Egypt, with a population of about 450 000 people. If you visit Luxor as a tourist, you may ride in a *hantoor* – a horse-drawn carriage – through the town. If you do, it is likely that any street you pass along will include at least one Banque Misr borrower, as the bank had more than 1 698 microlending clients in the city by the end of October 2008.

The microcredit team at the branch office consists of Tariq Abdul Latif, the acting team leader, who has been in the bank for 15 years, and two new graduates who have been at the bank for two years, Ahmed Abd Al Satar and Mahommed Al Satar. At the time of the research, the team was down to three because the team leader was on sick leave and one of the three graduates had proved unsuitable for this work and had been moved to another job in the bank. A new graduate was being recruited. To fill the gap, Tariq Abdul Latif was working full time on the microcredit programme, helped by Abdelsalam Elshahazly, one of the three roving supervisors, who happened to be based at the Luxor branch.

By October 2008, the team had issued and managed LE14.5 million (US$6.7 million) in loans to 1 698 customers (see Table 2.4). It is notable that 27 % of the borrowers were women, which makes the branch a leader in lending to women, as a study by the IFC showed that women represent only 10–25 % of the business borrowers of the commercial banks nationally.[5]

Table 2.4 Loans extended by Luxor Branch, 2004–2008

	Number of clients	% of clients	Total loans (LE)	% of loans
Men	1 238	73 %	10 600 000	74 %
Women	460	27 %	3 900 000	26 %
Total	1 698		14 500 000	

Source: Banque Misr

Samir Bagib Yakoub (second left) used Bank Misr loans to expand and re-equip his workshop.

Most of the borrowers are microenterprises comprising one to four employees. Some fall into the definition of small enterprises – five to 14 employees – such as a car-maintenance business with eight staff, including the owner Samir Bagib Yakoub (see Table 2.5), who is already negotiating his fourth loan with Banque Misr. He used the first three loans to expand and re-equip his workshop, and grew the business in three years from four to eight staff, so he was a classic example of a business that was expanding with the support of the bank, graduating from a microenterprise to a small business.

Table 2.5 A cross-section of Banque Misr clients in Luxor

Name of client	Business	Staff including proprietor
Samir Bagib Yakoub	Car maintenance	8
Ahmed Amin Ali	Fruit retail and wholesale	4
Salah Salim	Restaurant	3
Romani Jerje	Barber	3
Ali Alfi	General store	2

→

Name of client	Business	Staff including proprietor
Ali Abda Latif	General store	2
Mogmin Fuad Abduletif	Shoe shop	2
Mastaga Desuki	Audio equipment store	2
Hamad Abdulghani	Fruit stall	1
Samir Sahid	Spice retailer	1
Abdul Bur Shaib	Barber	1

Source: Banque Misr

Smaller businesses include Abdul Bur Shaib, a barber working on his own, and Ahmed Amin Ali, a fruit seller who had three staff working with him. Ahmed Amin Ali was on his second loan from Banque Misr. The first was used to improve and stock his stall, and the second as working capital to enable him to develop a business selling fruit to hotels and restaurants, which is now becoming the major focus of his enterprise.

Ahmed Amin Ali is now also selling fruit to hotels and restaurants.

The micro-entrepreneurs are full of praise for the Banque Misr programme. They are enthusiastic about the support given by the lending officers, not only in extending credit but also in helping them improve the management of their cash flow and the use of their working capital. They were also surprised at how unbureaucratic the bank was. Previously unused to banks, they had expected a nightmare of forms and questions but instead had found the process of taking out and servicing loans relatively simple. As Tariq Abdul Latif explained, 'It was important to keep the processes simple. Remember that we were dealing with new customers and selling them a product that was entirely new to them. We had to go out into the town, visit the businesses and explain the loans to them. Ninety percent of our borrowers had never had a bank account before we lent money to them. Many of them had never even entered a bank, and some of them were quite afraid of banks, which were part of a world that was alien to them. If they had had to fill in mountains of paperwork they would never have taken out a loan, however useful it might be to their business'.

The only complaint about this programme is that the loans are too small. Although many clients are on their second or third loan, most started with a first loan of between LE1 000 and LE5 000 (US$200 to US$1 000) for six months. Some said they had asked for larger loans with longer maturities, but were unable to get them. They were particularly critical of the LE5 000 limit for the first loan, and the restriction of each subsequent loan to no more than 150 % bigger than the previous one.

This reflects the bank's lending strategy. Dr Bassili explained: 'It is good that the clients are straining at the leash. By the time a client gets to their fourth loan, we will have succeeded in making the unbankable bankable. Some of them will find that we are then willing to be more generous with the loans if they can make a good case'.

Rolling out the model

Following the success of the five-branch pilot programme in 2004–2005, the second phase was launched in April 2005 with six further branches added to the programme. In September 2005, however, after the government of Egypt announced the proposed merger of Banque Misr and Banque du Caire, the board of Banque Misr decided that while the details of the merger were being worked out, it would be unwise to expand the microlending programme beyond these 11 branches. The board therefore put on hold the introduction of further branches. Despite this restriction, the business continued to flourish and grow in the 11 branches.

After Banque Misr then acquired Banque du Caire at the beginning of 2007, the board agreed to resume the expansion of the microlending programme, not only in Upper Egypt but throughout the country. In 2007, the microlending team began a rapid expansion, opening the programme in eight new branches in May and accelerating the programme to reach 65 branches by October.

Conclusion

The Banque Misr case shows that it is feasible for a large commercial bank, whether private or state owned, to develop a successful lending programme targeted at microenterprises, and to work with those enterprises to make the unbankable bankable.

Ingredients for success will vary from country to country, but the most interesting ingredients in the Banque Misr programme included:

- Launching the programme in the poorer parts of the country to take advantage of the repayment culture and social solidarity that characterised the region;
- Using enthusiastic new graduates as loan officers, leavened by the advice and supervision of more experienced bankers;
- Not waiting for customers to come to the branch, but going out to the markets and the streets to talk to entrepreneurs, understand their businesses and sell them appropriate credit products;
- Building long-term relationships with borrowers, graduating them from loan to loan as they learnt the disciplines of financial and cash-flow management;
- Supplementing the team management structure by using roving supervisors to ensure quality and consistency in the programme and to deal with problem loans;

- Setting up a robust and comprehensive real-time reporting system to enable the programme managers in the head office to monitor the programme down to the level of individual loan officers; and
- Engaging experienced consultants, in this case with the assistance of the IFC, to customise and introduce the loan management systems, train staff in their use, and act as advisors and mentors to programme staff.

Burkina Bail: Building entrepreneurship in Burkina Faso

> Asset-based lending is not widespread in Africa even though many practitioners believe that this kind of finance is an ideal way both to overcome the absence of collateral that stunts the supply of enterprise finance and to smooth short-term cash-flow needs. Burkina Bail, which provides leasing and factoring services to small businesses, has shown how this can make a difference. A strong emphasis on quick service and personal relationships appear to be the main ingredients of Burkina Bail's success, despite leasing not being widely understood and, initially, the lack of a legal framework governing the leasing business. However, while the demand for its services is strong, funding continues to be a problem.

When he started his first business in 1986, Soudré Adaman hardly dared to dream that he would become the founding managing director of a group of businesses with an annual turnover of CFA800 million (US$1.6 million). As Soudré comes from a humble background in rural Burkina Faso, his family could only afford to ensure that he received primary education, after which he had to start earning money to support the family. His dream began to come true in 2001 when Burkina Bail, through its leasing service, helped him buy equipment to set up a dry-cleaning service. Adam's Pressing is now the leading dry-cleaning business in Burkina Faso, and the Adam's group of companies has grown to include an import-export business, real-estate sales and other shops.

Soudré Adaman's group of companies includes an import-export business, real-estate sales, shops and a dry-cleaning service.

SMEs in Burkina Faso, as in most developing countries, find it difficult to access traditional banking systems. People starting SMEs are often unfamiliar with banking practices and requirements, and many SMEs cannot meet bank-loan requirements such as providing collateral or an established track record. This lack of finance all too often inhibits business start-ups, starves new businesses of the working capital they need to flourish, and prevents successful SMEs from expanding.

Burkina Bail was created in direct response to this problem. Its financial services support the establishment, survival and expansion of SMEs, and at the same time contribute to Burkina Faso's overall economic development as well as indirectly benefiting the poor.

It is a non-bank financial institution (NBFI) whose main products are medium-term loans, microleasing, autoleasing and factoring. Its client base is diverse, covering businesses of different sizes from a range of sectors. Burkina Bail's main office is in the capital, Ouagadougou, with a branch in Bobo-Dioulasso, Burkina Faso's second city. Since its establishment, Burkina Bail has provided more than CFA16 300 million (US$32.6 million) of credit to SMEs.

Financial access in Burkina Faso

Burkina Faso is a landlocked sub-Saharan country in the heart of West Africa. Since independence in 1960 it has remained one of the poorest countries in the world. In the UNDP *2006 Human Development Index*[6] Burkina Faso was ranked 174th out of 177 countries. Much of this poverty is rooted in the country's lack of natural resources and an over-dependence on agriculture, which employs 90 % of the population and contributes about half the output. The key cash crop is cotton, which accounts for most of the country's exports, followed by shea butter and livestock. Burkina Faso has a small manufacturing sector producing textiles, sugar and flour.

Despite its poverty, the country enjoys political stability. As a result of this, and both internal and external adjustments since the end of the 1980s, its macroeconomic performance has been relatively good, with a real growth rate of more than 5 % a year in recent years. This growth is evident in bustling Ouagadougou, with new businesses, including internet cafés, plush hotels and international restaurants, springing up. There is a sense of a country fighting against the odds: determined to improve in spite of all the barriers to its development.

Despite recent improvements, Burkina Faso's financial sector lacks depth. There are 11 banks, five NBFIs and 43 microfinance institutions. While only 2 % of Burkinabés have bank accounts, it is estimated that 44 % of families use informal financial systems. Although microfinance services have grown quickly over the last decade and have provided around 1.3 million customers with credit, they remain marginal to the Burkinabé financial system, responsible for only 8 % of credit extension in the country.[7] Moreover, the country's poor infrastructure makes it difficult for much of the population to access finance. Key economic data are shown in Table 2.6.

In 1993, the government of Burkina Faso acknowledged the importance of SMEs for development by introducing the private sector support programme PASP (Programme d'Appui au Secteur Privé). This includes providing financial products adapted to the needs of SMEs, and reforming the institutional, legal, regulatory and fiscal frameworks to make them more conducive to private sector development.

Table 2.6 Key economic data – Burkina Faso

Population (million), estimate July 2008	15.2
Urban population (%), estimate July 2008	19.7
Poverty (% population below national poverty line), 2007	46.4
Life expectancy (years), estimate 2008	52.55
GDP per capita (US$), estimate 2007	1 213
% of GDP invested, 2007	19.4
Primary sector as % of GDP, 2007	29.7
Secondary sector as % of GDP, 2007	19.4
Tertiary sector as % of GDP, 2007	50.9
Inflation rate (%), 2007	2.4
% of population with a mobile telephone, 2008	10.5
% of population with access to electricity, 2007	14.3

Sources: UNDP (2007); Africa Project Development Facility; CIA World Factbook

In November 2005, as a key tool in the fight against poverty, the government adopted a national strategy for microfinance development. The strategy aims to widen financial access and improve the quality and quantity of services on offer. One issue identified during the development of the strategy was the limited range of financial services for entrepreneurs, most of whom have access only to short-term, traditional bank loans or small scale microfinance.

There are estimated to be between 1 200 and 1 600 SMEs in the country, defined by the ministry of commerce as enterprises with five to 10 employees, and around 3 000 microenterprises, with fewer than five employees. Few financial service providers offer medium- or long-term credit to SMEs, since such services are offered by banks or NBFIs mainly to large businesses in urban areas.[8] At the other extreme, the services offered by MFIs are small scale and generally aimed at individuals, households or co-operatives. Thus Burkina Faso's SMEs were caught between these two ends of the spectrum, unserved by either banks or microfinance. In this unpromising environment, Burkina Bail has pioneered the introduction of innovative financial products such as leasing and factoring.

Company background

Burkina Bail was established in 1996 as a joint initiative of Banque Internationale de Burkina (BIB), Burkina Faso's largest bank; Finance for Development (FMO), a development bank based in the Netherlands; and Cauris Investissement, a private equity firm.

It is co-owned by its founder shareholders: BIB (47 %), FMO (34 %), Cauris Investissement (18 %) and individual shareholders (1 %). It is regulated by the Banque Centrale des États de l'Afrique de l'Ouest (BCEAO), the central bank of West Africa.

In 1996 Gaspard Ouedraego, managing director of BIB, along with FMO and Cauris Investissement identified leasing as a possible way for banks to bridge the financing gap and support SME development. He took this idea to the BCEAO, which recommended finding a technical partner to provide expertise in an area that was new to Burkina Faso. FMO stepped in, providing vital funds, advice and contacts for the newly established company, Burkina Bail. Key data for Burkina Bail are in Table 2.7.

Table 2.7 Key data for Burkina Bail

	2005	September 2008
Total assets (million CFA)	8 137	7 975
Loans from creditors (million CFA)	5 703	5 619
Total portfolio value (million CFA)	6 067	7 289
Total disbursements (million CFA)	4 304	2 300
- Short-term loan disbursements (million CFA)	995	300
- Leasing disbursements (million CFA)	1 982	1 200
- Credit services (million CFA)	1 327	800
Loan repayments made on time (%)	76	85
Loan repayments outstanding for 60–90 days (%)	19	11
Loan repayments outstanding for > 90 days (%)	5	4
Net profits (million CFA)	95	116

Source: Burkina Bail

What Burkina Bail does

Bail means 'leasing' in French. Initially, Burkina Bail offered only leasing services, and this remains its main product. SMEs are able to obtain credit by leasing equipment with a low initial outlay, and paying for their equipment in monthly instalments rather than in one lump sum. The client does not have to provide a financial guarantee or collateral as the equipment serves as collateral. Many international organisations, particularly the IFC, see leasing services to SMEs as key to their development.[9] Having access to leasing strengthens the production capacity of SMEs and allows them to be more competitive in both national and international markets, which are becoming increasingly important because of globalisation.

A further problem SMEs face in Burkina Faso, as in many developing countries, is the management of their cash flow. If an SME is waiting for a large payment from a customer, it may not have sufficient cash to take on new orders and will therefore be unable to maintain or increase its business effectively. A solution to this is factoring, through which Burkina Bail buys the invoice from the SME and takes on the responsibility for collecting from the customer.

Another problem in Burkina Faso is that, despite the PASP, there are still elements in the legal, technical and fiscal environment that hinder the development of this sector. Burkina Bail has taken on a lobbying role in response to this.

Abdoulaye Kouafilann Sory has been chief executive officer of Burkina Bail since 2000. Before that he was head of banks and NBFIs at the Burkina branch of BCEAO. He says the company is trying to negotiate with government on behalf of SMEs using leasing to finance their equipment. M. Sory compares the use of leasing in Burkina Faso with other countries, such as Ghana and Tunisia, where it is more widely used, and claims that this is because there is a much more favourable tax regime in those countries. Some improvements have been made, such as with VAT payments, but more remains to be done. 'We are not just providing finance. We are trying to see how we can make the business environment better and more favourable for SMEs', he says.

In direct response to the needs of SMEs, Burkina Bail now also provides medium-term credit services. The company has provided credit to more than 600 SMEs – 97 % of Burkina Bail's clients are SMEs, About 60 % of its clients are based in the capital, Ouagadougou, about 30 % in Bobo-Dioulasso, and 10 % elsewhere in the country. Burkina Bail believes that, through supporting SMEs, it is indirectly benefiting the poor, both at a macro level by contributing to overall economic development and also through the increased employment and income-generation opportunities that SMEs provide. Burkina Bail is recognised as a key player in modernising the financial sector in Burkina Faso. In 2006 it became the first Burkinabé company to be awarded ISO certification.[10] Burkina Bail is profitable, with net profit increasing from CFA85 million (US$170 000) in 2003 to CFA119.5 million (US$239 000) in 2006.

Business model

Leasing: Burkina Bail leases both standard and sophisticated equipment to SMEs across most sectors. Eligible equipment includes industrial machinery and generators, IT hardware and medical equipment, as well as vehicles, including cars, buses and trucks. Vehicles make up 45 % of Burkina Bail's portfolio compared to 20 % for industrial machinery and 15 % for new technologies.

Once an application for support is accepted, the client orders the piece of equipment it needs. Burkina Bail pays for the equipment, and the client repays Burkina Bail over a period of 24 to 36 months, eventually owning the equipment outright. Burkina Bail is also starting to offer real-estate leasing, which it sees as a potential growth area.

Factoring: Burkina Bail was the first company in Burkina Faso to offer SMEs a factoring service, whereby Burkina Bail pays 80 % of an SME's bill immediately and takes responsibility for chasing payment from the SME's client. When the bill is paid, Burkina Bail gives the outstanding 20 % to the SME, minus their costs and charges. The company works out its margins for these services on a case-by-case basis, taking into account the anticipated costs of providing the service to the client, the interest rate they are likely to charge for their services and the level of risk involved. The margins are discussed openly with the client before the contract is signed.

While this confirms the existence of a market for the services offered by the company, the management stresses that it is too soon to reach firm conclusions about the sustainability of the business model as Burkina Bail is still using concessionary finance from FMO and others to fund its operations. FMO, like all Burkina Bail's lenders, provide commercial loans, with an average interest rate of 7 %, to Burkina Bail. Repayments are made directly by bank transfer to the lender either each trimester or semester. Whether it will be able to function as profitably on a fully commercial basis will depend on a number of factors, including the acceleration of economic growth in Burkina Faso, and improvements to the institutional, legal and fiscal environment.

Burkina Bail does not explicitly target the poor as its products are aimed at SMEs, which tend to be owned and run by the middle classes. Through supporting SME development, however, the company is contributing to macroeconomic development, creating revenue and jobs and thus providing people with regular income.

> **Burkina Bail's clients – Adam's Pressing**
>
> Adam's Pressing has been built up with the support of Burkina Bail into a company with 35 employees and has an annual turnover of CFA160 million (US$368 000).
>
> Adam's Pressing serves around 40 to 50 clients a day. Burkina Bail has provided Adam's Pressing with around CFA100 million (US$230 000) of credit through leasing its specialised dry-cleaning equipment and vehicles, and the provision of factoring services. 'Without Burkina Bail it would have been very difficult to work; with the classic banks you need guarantees', says M. Adaman.

Adam's Pressing has become the leading dry-cleaning business in Burkina Faso.

Other companies which Burkina Bail supports, such as Geofor (Société de Géologie et de Forages), provide services directly to the poor. Geofor drills for water and constructs wells throughout Burkina Faso and the wider West African region, thus providing essential water to villages across the parched Sahel. Geofor is also contracted by the World Bank, the European Union (EU) and the United Nations Children's Fund (UNICEF) for water projects. So although Geofor is exceptional as a Burkina Bail client in that it is no longer an SME, Mohamed P Sogli, its founding managing director, claims that Geofor 'helps all of Burkina Faso … as well as all the countries in which we work'. Another Burkina Bail client, Sat Télécom, has worked with Oxfam to provide satellite internet access to rural areas of Burkina Faso. Thus Burkina Bail is, indirectly, benefiting the poor by enabling SMEs to supply them with better products and services.

> **Burkina Bail's clients – Geofor**
>
> Mohamed P Sogli is the founding managing director of Sopam, a group of companies which includes Geofor. The company was established in 1994, and drills for water and constructs wells throughout Burkina Faso and the wider region.
>
> Geofor has worked in close partnership with Burkina Bail since 2005. Burkina Bail has supported Geofor through the provision of around CFA1 billion (US$2 million) in credit, both through their factoring service and in the form of leases for drilling equipment, including specialised lorries. M. Sogli thinks that 'Burkina Bail is like a source of oxygen [for SMEs] ... it allows us to breathe'.

How Burkina Bail developed its leasing market

Although the volume of leasing in Africa has grown rapidly in recent years, reaching US$6.3 billion in 2005, the business is extremely concentrated, 99 % being accounted for by four countries: South Africa (73 %), Egypt, Morocco and Nigeria.[11] So leasing was very new to Burkina Faso when M. Sory started as CEO of the company. Another company, SIEL (Société Internationale d'Équipements et de Leasing), had previously tried to launch leasing services in the country and had failed. M. Sory dedicated time and effort during his first year identifying potential customers and then meeting them at their offices. He says this enabled him to 'develop a relationship of trust' and 'enter into a partnership' with his clients. Geofor was one such client and, indeed, M. Sogli says that he had heard about Burkina Bail's products, but only realised their full potential for his business when M. Sory came to his office to explain them to him.

The decision to go directly to potential clients to discuss their business needs and Burkina Bail's products is an example of Burkina Bail's personal, one-on-one approach, which remains a feature of the company today. M. Sory claims that this is one of the company's competitive advantages: 'My office is always open to our clients. They can come in, sit down and discuss things openly with me. They can call me easily; they all know my direct line number'. Burkina Bail also features its clients in its annual reports, and celebrates their success. Clients appreciate this personalised approach. They see Burkina Bail as a valuable source of advice and support. M. Sogli says: 'I ask them about certain aspects of business and they advise me. I've never asked myself whether it's a "service" of theirs or whether it's because I know them now ... It's not like a typical office'.

Many of the challenges Burkina Bail encountered in launching its services arose because leasing was relatively new in Burkina Faso, and indeed in Francophone West Africa. It took some time for the concept of leasing to be fully grasped and accepted. SIEL failed in its leasing services because of the narrow range of its products; it was leasing construction equipment only. Burkina Bail learned from SIEL's mistake and was careful to widen its customer base by offering leasing for a wide range of equipment. It will consider purchasing any piece of equipment, from basic office equipment to highly specialised medical machines, provided the client can clearly demonstrate the business case. Burkina Bail's two biggest sectors are transport and industrial machinery, including construction equipment.

The second major challenge was that there were no laws or regulations relating to leasing. This made it difficult for all parties to know the legal parameters within which they were working. Burkina Bail, with the support of the Association Professionnelle des Banques et Etablissements Financiers du Burkina, the professional body for financial institutions in Burkina Faso, has persuaded the government to adapt existing laws and introduce new ones relating to leasing activity. Successes include the introduction of the Management of Finance law in 2004 and the creation of a *Maison de l'Entreprise*.

Finally, there was a shortage of people with the specific skills and competencies required to manage a leasing business. M. Sory therefore invested a great deal of time in acquiring these skills himself and then training his team. FMO helped M. Sory by putting him in contact with other leasing companies and arranging study tours for him to visit them, and by financing the required staff training.

Introducing factoring

Through working closely with their leasing clients, Burkina Bail became increasingly aware of the cash-flow problems SMEs face. Burkina Bail therefore carried out a study in 2005 to establish the best way of tackling this and, as a result, decided to offer factoring services to its clients. Burkina Bail is the first and only company in Burkina Faso to offer factoring services. Indeed, it is a pioneer in factoring in West Africa: factoring in Africa at present is concentrated in Egypt, Morocco, Tunisia and South Africa, and Africa as a whole represents only 0.6 % of global factoring compared to 6 % of global trade.[12]

Its first task was to gain permission from the regulator to introduce this new product to the market. It was then, once again, faced with the challenge of developing the necessary knowledge and skills to launch and manage this new product effectively. It achieved this by identifying a company, Omnifinance, which provides factoring services in the Côte d'Ivoire, and setting up an arrangement through which Omnifinance provided training for Burkina Bail's staff ,and shared its procedures manuals and specific software with them.

One of the first things Burkina Bail had to deal with after introducing factoring services to the Burkinabé market was clients' perceptions of the service. Several potential clients thought they could simply pass on long-standing debts to Burkina Bail and leave them to chase them up while continuing to bill the customers that settled bills promptly. The factoring team at Burkina Bail had to invest a great deal of time in explaining to potential clients exactly how the factoring service operates and also investigating the nature of any new clients' outstanding debts before agreeing to provide them with factoring services.

Burkina Bail now has a dedicated team specialised in factoring, and factoring services constitute 31 % of Burkina Bail's total disbursements. The factoring services have been positively received. As M. Sogli of Geofor says, SMEs 'don't have many resources and … have restricted cash flow … it is difficult when a client does not have the money to pay us. Factoring helps an enterprise to work without too much pressure and is a good thing for the economy'. Geofor, for example, has to carefully manage its liquidity.

The process Geofor follows from initially locating water sources to providing a village with a well and pump is expensive and complex, and takes between three and four months. If it had to wait for payment until long after the end of each job, it would be difficult to take on new jobs and grow the business. However, as M. Sogli explains, 'while we are awaiting payment we can send the bills on to Burkina Bail and they provide us with an advance on each bill … Without that, businesses would totally suffocate. It saves us.' He stresses that it is not just a matter of others paying for your business but also being able to pay suppliers. Paying on time helps companies gain and maintain a strong reputation, and win further business.

Clients' impressions of Burkina Bail

Clients are overwhelmingly positive about the benefits of working with Burkina Bail. Burkina Bail's products allow them either to start a business, as with Adam's Pressing, the dry-cleaning business, or, like Geofor, to grow more quickly than would have been possible using more traditional credit services. Clients appreciate the fact that Burkina Bail's products are more adapted to the specific needs of SMEs than those of the traditional banking system. In particular, they like the full service Burkina Bail provides.

In addition to offering financial services, Burkina Bail also follows up regularly, for example by checking the leased equipment, and offers helpful advice and insight into the Burkinabé market. M. Sogli says, 'In all my projects, M. Sory is there, he looks around, he advises me ... I like that.' This is in contrast to the most of the banks, which are generally perceived as simply lending the money to businesses and only following up if there are repayment problems.

Clients also credit Burkina Bail for the speedy processing of their applications for credit compared with the banks. M. Sogli says, 'When you submit a dossier it's really quick. This provides fewer constraints for us. They are very professional.' Burkina Bail attempts to review and respond to all applications within a week whereas banks, he says, can take months to respond.

As with any business, there are areas for improvement that customers would like to see. One of the few criticisms clients have about Burkina Bail is that its charges are relatively high compared to traditional banks, and they would, of course, like to see them lowered in future. M. Sory claims that most customers are happy to pay higher charges in return for better and faster service, and this appears to be borne out by experience. Burkina Bail sets its charges on a case-by-case basis, according to the perceived level of risk in investing in each SME. Therefore, it is usually the case that the longer the partnership with an SME, the lower the rates charged to that SME become. Some clients also claim that the formalities and bureaucracy they need to follow to submit a dossier to Burkina Bail, though less difficult than for the banks, are still too cumbersome, and they would like to see them simplified.

Challenges

Burkina Bail has a close relationship with BIB. BIB is its largest shareholder, and the managing director of BIB was the chairman of the board of directors of Burkina Bail from its establishment until 2008. This relationship can be seen as both a blessing and a drawback. Burkina Bail receives a lot of support from BIB, both financially and in terms of expertise and advice. Clients can also be referred to Burkina Bail by BIB, and vice versa. Similarly, Burkina Bail is considering working through BIB branches nationwide to reach a larger clientele. However, if it was also able to work in partnership with other banks, Burkina Bail could reach an even larger client base. Furthermore, the close links between the two companies means that Burkina Bail is not fully autonomous. However, the appoinment of Fogar T Sossah as Strategic Business Development Director in UEMOA (the West African Economic and Monetary Union) for the United Bank for Africa should improve this situation.

Burkina Bail has successfully attracted quasi-commercial funding from the BIB, FMO, Cauris Investissement, Banque Ouest Africaine de Développement, the Belgian Investment Office and European Investment Bank (EIB). Although FMO has facilitated much of this funding, it needs to withdraw its funding over time: its last tranche of funding came to an end in 2008. Burkina Bail is attempting to negotiate with FMO for further funding.

Funding is an ongoing challenge for Burkina Bail. Despite the initial success in providing medium-term finance for SMEs through leasing, the years 2007 and 2008 were difficult for Burkina Bail. Lack of access to new funding sources was the main reason for the decrease in Burkina Bail's volume of activity in 2008 compared to 2005 – about 40 % lower. Short-term operations were hit even harder – 70 % lower for the same period of time. The board has approved a business plan for 2009–2014 which includes a funding strategy. The plan predicts that Burkina Bail will be able to mobilise CFA5 billion in 2010.

M. Sory says the company is actively working to find new sources of funding for 2009. He mentioned that changes on tax regulation of leasing activities introduced in 2008 will act as an important incentive to attract new investors. It is foreseen that these changes will help Burkina Bail to start its real-estate leasing activities in 2009.

Burkina Bail has used the slow-down to work actively on improving the health of its loan portfolio. Thus, the number of outstanding loan repayments was significantly reduced to 15 % in 2008 compared to 24 % in 2005. Equally significantly, Burkina's net profits grew by 22 % in the same period. M. Sory explained that these developments were the result of two factors: a staff better qualified to manage a leasing business together with clients gaining a better understanding of the nature of leasing activities.

The future

What of the future of Burkina Bail? The company is aware that it constantly needs to improve, and M. Sory says that its real-estate leasing product has huge potential for future growth.

In the longer term, M. Sory believes that Burkina Bail will need to look beyond the borders of Burkina Faso and start to work with neighbouring countries, and at a sub-regional level. This is not just about growing Burkina Bail's own market – M. Sory is also keen to pass on the lessons they have learnt to expand microleasing to other countries and help their SME sectors. Leasing is a growth area in many developing countries, and Burkina Bail is receiving invitations to coach and partner new leasing initiatives, for example with a bank in Cameroon and companies in Senegal and the Democratic Republic of Congo. However, the worsening of the economic and institutional environment in Burkina Faso has meant that Burkina Bail's activities in neighbouring countries, like Mali, where it was starting to work through Geofor, have come to a halt, and the company's sub-regional expansion strategy has been suspended.

Conclusion

Burkina Bail has demonstrated that it is possible to provide medium-term finance for SMEs through leasing, and to support their working capital through factoring. A key element in its model is building a close business partnership between Burkina Bail staff and its SME customers, in which the loan officers act not only as financiers but also as financial advisors to their clients.

The leasing and factoring business has been built in a difficult economic and institutional environment in Burkina Faso, and at present Burkina Bail remains dependent on external funding to maintain its operations. Whether the company will be able to function as profitably on a fully commercial basis will depend on a number of factors, including the acceleration of economic growth in Burkina Faso, and improvements in the institutional, legal and fiscal environment.

Whatever happens in the future, however, Burkina Bail provides a significant case study of the development of financial products for SMEs in Africa. As Soudré Adaman put it, 'Without Burkina Bail, I could never have started my dry-cleaning business – I might still be a petty trader, unable to achieve my dream because of lack of finance'.

Endnotes

[1] Algeria, Jordan, Morocco, Syria and Tunisia are also classed as lower-middle income; Lebanon and Libya as upper-middle income; Saudi Arabia as high-income. See http://siteresources.worldbank.org/DATASTATISTICS/Resources/CLASS.XLS.

[2] IFC MSME Database, citing UNCDF – this figure is for 1998, but the proportion is considered similar today.

[3] World Bank (2006b).

[4] A loan-tracking software programme proprietary to EQI, installed in almost 200 microfinance institutions and bank branches in the Arab-speaking world (as at 2005).

[5] IFC (2007).

[6] UNDP (2006).

[7] Africa Project Development Facility (2005).

[8] 'SMEs … have little access to traditional bank loans and applications by existing firms and especially those starting up are often rejected. When they are accepted, interest rates are very high (10-18 %) and loans are basically for working capital and rarely long-term (only 1 % of all loans to the private sector).' OECD (2005).

[9] Fletcher, Freeman, Sultanov & Umarov (2005).

[10] The International Organization for Standardization is the world's largest developer and publisher of international standards.

[11] Euromoney (2005).

[12] Ayadi (2006).

Chapter Three
Linkage banking

Linkage banking describes how banks partner with other organisations, including informal ones, to deliver financial services to individuals or communities that are typically hard to reach. The bank benefits from accessing a new customer base, albeit indirectly, and the intermediaries in the financing chain also benefit from commissions and non-financial services from the bank, as well as being able to offer their own customer base an improved product range.

Linkage banking comes in various forms. A wholesale financing arrangement is a simple form of linkage. The Barclays Ghana case describes how the incentive structures work between one of the largest banking groups in the world and one of the most traditional informal structures on the continent – the *susu* collectors in Ghana. An essential advantage to the bank in these arrangements is that the bank benefits from the intimate knowledge that the intermediary has of its own customer base. This is an exceptionally valuable, intangible asset that the bank has to pay to access; in opting for an indirect form of banking arrangement, the bank has calculated that it makes more financial sense for it to give up part of the lending margin to the intermediary than to develop this knowledge base by itself.

A common thread across all the case studies in this chapter, also captured in Robert Stone's article, is the extent to which the bank invests in developing the market it is indirectly serving. Maximising the opportunity in these markets requires much more than negotiating a good deal with a village co-operative or microfinance institution. To be effective, the link has to be robust, and so investing in the capacity of its intermediaries is one way to ensure that the business develops in the right direction.

Barclays Bank Ghana: Global meets local – working with the *susu* collectors of Ghana

> The ubiquitous *susu* collectors of West Africa are informal providers of financial services who collect money at the end of day's trading and keep it safe, for a small fee, before returning it to the owner at a later date. Barclays Bank Ghana has developed a relationship with the *susu* collectors. They are depositing their clients' money with Barclays but are also on-lending loans from Barclays to their clients, typically microbusinesses with daily sales of less than US$25. Repayment rates on these loans are exceptionally high. For the *susu* collectors' clients, this represents a source of lending they would not otherwise have had. For Barclays, it is an entirely new market for both loans and deposits.

It is the end of a long day for Agnes, selling dried fish in Kaneshie Market – an unpredictable business with precarious profits. When Akusa, her *susu* collector, comes round, Agnes gives him GH¢3.5 (about US$4 at the time).[1] It is more than half her profit for the day, but Agnes is happy to hand it over. Akusa is providing a vital service by giving Agnes a safe means to put aside something each day for emergencies, hard times or special purchases like clothes for her children.

There are thousands of *susu* collectors in Ghana, each with hundreds of clients from whom they collect small amounts each day, charging a fee for looking after their savings.

The capacity of *susu* collectors to provide lending services has been limited, as most of them do not have the capital to become significant providers of credit to their customers. This is where Barclays Bank Ghana has stepped in. The bank has formed an on-lending partnership with the *susu* collectors as part of its microbanking operations in Ghana. The uniqueness of this partnership stems from the way two radically different financial intermediaries – at opposite ends of the spectrum in terms of size – have linked together in a way that enables each to benefit from the strengths and advantages of the other.

In November 2005, Barclays Bank Ghana launched a new product called the Dwetiri account in an effort to seek new markets and avenues to promote financial inclusion in Ghana. Dwetiri, meaning 'capital' or 'seed money', established partnerships between the bank and microfinance providers, including credit unions, microfinance institutions, savings and loans companies, and the traditional *susu* collectors. These partnerships allow Barclays Bank to reach out to the unbanked segments of the market that have been served by these intermediaries over the years while also gaining crucial information about the market, both the end clients and their agents or intermediaries. They also provide the bank with greater exposure to groups of clients that may not be familiar with the products and services offered by Barclays Bank, or indeed by any bank.

By February 2007, the partnership with the *susu* collectors had already generated almost US$2 million in new deposits for Barclays, and by September 2008 this had grown to US$10.2 million – and the partner financial intermediaries had benefited from having access to capital and to capacity-building programmes by the bank.

Access to financial services in Ghana

Ghana has a population of more than 23 million people, roughly half of whom live in the rural areas, and almost a third of whom fall below the national poverty line. The country's GNI per capita is US$590 a year (2007), which places it at the average level for sub-Saharan African countries excluding South Africa.[2] Key economic data are in Table 3.1.

Table 3.1 Key economic data – Ghana

	2007
Population (million)	23.46
Urban population (%)	44
Poverty (% population below national poverty line)	28.5
GNI per capita	590
GDP growth rate (%)	6.3
Inflation rate (%)	12.75
Local commercial interest rate (%)	12

Source: World Bank World Development Indicators, Bank of Ghana

The financial system in Ghana is made up of a variety of formal, semi-formal and informal institutions. Formal institutions include 18 commercial banks, 120 rural and community banks (RCBs) and a number of registered non-bank financial institutions, including 12 savings and loans companies. While the larger commercial banks tend to focus on the upper end of the market, catering for corporations and the public sector, RCBs serve people with relatively lower income levels, with RCB branches located in less affluent areas in the country.

The semi-formal sector comprises an estimated 50 institutions registered as NGOs with active microfinance programmes, as well as 250 co-operatives and credit unions. The NGOs are not allowed to take deposits from the public and therefore tend to depend heavily on external, mainly donor, funding. Co-operatives and credit unions can collect savings from their pool of members as well as issue loans.

The informal sector also includes individual moneylenders, *susu* collectors, *susu* clubs, associations and companies, as well as traders who provide credit and sometimes operate informal savings schemes. These are non-licensed, non-regulated operators, though some are organised into groups with a co-operative structure. Characteristic of the informal finance providers is their ability to provide small-scale financial services, including non-collateralised short-term loans. Their operations are also near to where their clients work.

Despite the variety of institutions supplying financial services in the market, available data suggest that most households in Ghana still fall outside the reach of the financial system. According to the latest estimate, only 15 % of adults in Ghana have any access to formal or informal financial services.[3] It appears that little has changed for most people since 1998/99, when the World Bank Living Standards Measurement Survey reported that only 39 % of the households said that they had borrowed money in the past 12 months from any source, of which only 3.27 % had used formal financial institutions.[4] MFIs have increased in numbers since the time of the survey, but in Ghana these institutions still tend to serve relatively better-off markets, and most of their branches are found in urban locations.

The linkage banking scheme – pilot projects in the 1990s

It was against this backdrop that a linkage banking scheme in Ghana was developed and initially tested in the 1990s with the support of the World Bank and other donors. As early as 1992, proposals were developed by the World Bank for on-lending schemes between a number of formal financial institutions, which included commercial banks, and savings and loans companies on the one hand, and informal finance providers such as *susu* collectors, *susu* clubs and/or companies on the other. Some of these pilot schemes failed, but others were successful – with high rates of repayment and significant outreach to new small depositors and borrowers.

The evaluation of the pilots underscored the need to further refine the agreements made between the formal financial institution (for example the bank) and the informal finance provider (for example the individual *susu* collector), especially about loan size, pricing and incentives. However, even with these refinements, not everyone was convinced about the viability of the scheme. Many bankers in Ghana concluded that the mixed results of the pilots showed that microclients are generally too risky. They remained doubtful of the claim that microbanking operations should be looked on as a business strategy and not just as a short-term community development programme of the kind sometimes undertaken by firms to boost their reputation for corporate social responsibility.

In more recent years, however, competition in the banking sector has accelerated, partly because of the influx of well capitalised Nigerian banks into Ghana, and the news has spread of specialised banks in other countries that have successfully developed commercial microfinance operations. These trends have stimulated formal financial institutions in Ghana to revive the idea of testing the linkage model as a first step in finding new markets and providing services to a new clientele.

Susu collectors in Ghana

The *susu* system has existed in Ghana for centuries, built on a relationship of trust between the *susu* agent and his or her client, something which develops with the frequency of their interactions over time. Until recently, virtually all *susu* collectors were men, though many of their clients were women. In recent years, however, women are beginning to enter the market.

In the *susu* savings system, the client gives the *susu* collector a fixed amount daily for 31 days. This amount is collected personally by the *susu* collector either at the client's place of business or at his or her residence. At the end of the 31-day period, the *susu* collector returns to the client the total of 30 days of savings, and retains the equivalent of one day's worth of savings which serves as the fee for the service. In his groundbreaking book, *The Poor and their Money*, Stuart Rutherford demonstrates the importance of enabling poor people to make frequent small deposits of money so that they can build up a 'usefully large lump sum' for life-cycle events, emergency needs and investment opportunities. This is precisely the service that the *susu* collectors provide.[5]

The *susu* collector visits clients daily, and collectors have from 300 to more than 1 000 clients, depending on seasonality in the demand for savings or loans. For each client, the *susu* collector keeps an account card where records of the collections are made. In carrying out the collection, the *susu* collector needs to be transparent, making sure that the transaction is recorded in front the client. The system is simple and flexible enough to accommodate the fluctuations in clients' income flows. *Susu* collectors are not alarmed if a client fails to make a contribution for a particular day as the same clients also often make advance contributions covering several days' worth of savings. Clients may access their savings in advance of the 30 days should the need arise. Such payments are conveniently given to the clients immediately on request.

The clientele reached by *susu* collectors are all, of course, economically active – they are engaged in economic activities that generate income for themselves and their households. They include market traders, artisans and other microentrepreneurs, mainly in urban centres and peri-urban areas. The *susu* system is a way to accumulate savings and access short-term loans or advances to smooth household consumption, respond to sudden changes in income flow or participate in opportunities to help improve their economic activities.

While their incomes may not be as predictable as those who have regular employment, most of these clients nevertheless generate a regular flow of income through the earnings of their microenterprises. To decrease transaction costs, *susu* collectors often concentrate on clients who are clustered in one area, such as the marketplace. Most of the *susu* collectors can be described as microbusinesses, with daily gross sales of

GH¢15 to GH¢20 (less than US$25). Their average daily savings contributions are between of GH¢1 and GH¢2 (roughly US$1–US$2).

Many *susu* collectors also include in their clientele a few relatively larger traders or entrepreneurs with daily gross sales greater than GH¢100 (US$110) who are able to save in amounts greater than GH¢5 (US$5.50) a day. In a typical marketplace setting, these entrepreneurs are usually those who either own or rent fixed stalls, and many have bank accounts even while they continue to save with their *susu* collectors. Such clients usually trade dry goods like clothes, textile products, accessories or processed items, whereas the smaller clients are normally retailers of fresh produce. The larger clients would typically represent between 5 % and 10 % of a *susu* collector's portfolio, depending on the location. This particular group of clients is important to *susu* collectors as they are often net savers and are useful as a means to diversify and ensure a steady cash flow.

Many of the *susu* collectors are organised into associations or co-operative societies, such as the Ghana Co-operative Susu Collectors' Association (GCSCA), which has 1 100 members nationwide.

A *susu* collector and his client

Akusa has been a *susu* collector for more than 12 years. Most of his clients are market vendors at the Kaneshie Market in Accra. On an ordinary day, Akusa makes his rounds with a bag containing the account cards of his clients and some cash. He crosses the street while counting the cash in his hand, which seems very risky. But he says that everyone knows that he is a *susu* collector because of his uniform and the cash he carries alone, and *susu* collectors will always be protected. 'We are important to the people in the market, just as they are important to us,' he says.

Akusa estimates that he has around 1 100 clients. One of them is Agnes, who sells dried fish in the market. On a good day, Agnes is able to sell 100 cedis worth of fish, from which she earns a profit between five and six cedis, depending on the price at which she can buy her stock. 'Some days fish is more expensive,' she says. Like the other small market vendors, she does not pay for her pitch outside the main building, so she can use her full earnings to support her family of six. She makes daily savings contributions of 3.5 cedis. Although her contributions so far are already three days ahead, she still gives Akusa a contribution today. She says, 'It's better to hand over my cash and let Akusa keep it while I have some to spare. Otherwise, it will be spent just like that!'

Barclays Bank Ghana enters the field

Barclays Bank Ghana, a wholly owned subsidiary of Barclays Bank plc, has been established in Ghana since 1917, and operates in eight out of the 10 regions in the country. With total assets of GH¢1.19 billion, it ranks among the four largest banks in the country (see Table 3.2).

Barclays Bank understood the strength of *susu* collectors as financial service agents to microclients and how they could mobilise small-balance deposits. The bank established a partnership with the *susu* collectors to reach the lower end of the market more effectively. Associations or co-operative societies like GCSCA gave the bank a way to reach out to the collectors without establishing partnerships with each of them individually, which would have been prohibitively expensive. With support from Barclays Bank Africa and Barclays Bank plc in London, Barclays Bank Ghana entered into a partnership with GCSCA to provide on-lending services through the association to its members.

Table 3.2 Overview of Barclays Bank Ghana

Operational highlights	
Year established	1917
Number of branches (February 2007)	63 branches, nine prestige centres
Products and services offered:	Credit facilities, cash management and transmission services, deposit products, business insurance and payroll management
Ownership structure:	Wholly owned by Barclays Bank PLC
Extracts from the balance sheet (2007)	
Total assets	GH₵1.19 billion
Total loans to customers	GH₵640.5 million
Total deposits	GH₵1.03 billion cedis
Profit for the year	GH₵36.3 million cedis
Return on assets	GH₵10.4 %

Source: Barclays Bank Ghana

Under the agreement, the GCSCA identifies those *susu* collectors who may be endorsed to participate in the Barclays Bank on-lending scheme, applying a set of criteria agreed between the bank and the association. The association has the advantage of knowing its members well enough to assess which of them has the capacity to administer loans and ensure repayment. The GCSCA takes on the liability for repayment of the loans to the bank through a credit guarantee fund. Each participating *susu* collector is required to contribute GH₵300 (about US$350) to the fund, which is deposited as security in an interest-bearing GCSCA account at Barclays Bank. The number of *susu* collectors participating in the scheme had grown from 300 in February 2007 to 732 in September 2008.

The scheme has complementary facilities which take it beyond lending to a more comprehensive relationship between the bank, the GCSCA and the *susu* collectors, based on what Barclays calls the 'ABC of microbanking' – awareness, banking services and capacity building.

The awareness programme is directed at both the *susu* collectors and their clients, who are provided with information about Barclays Bank and its services. The aim is not only to create goodwill between the end clients and the bank, but to also address the clients' need for information about financial services and how they operate so as to enable them to make informed decisions.

Banking services constitute the core of microbanking operations through which greater access to financial products and services is provided for end clients, in this case through *susu* collectors.

The third element, capacity building, is focused on training for *susu* collectors who take part in the on-lending scheme, which is provided by the bank free of charge. The training is designed to enhance the financial management capacity of participating *susu* collectors, especially about introducing loans into their range of products. The training is therefore focused mainly on credit risk and delinquency management. The level of financial literacy among the *susu* collectors varies, but the training is designed to equip all participating members with the capacity to deal with the new demands that will arise from their role as intermediaries in the Dwetiri on-lending programme.

As seed money to get the programme going, Barclays Bank plc provided Barclays Bank Ghana with a grant of £150 000 towards the costs of the non-financial services described above, and £10 000 to support GCSCA in their membership drive campaign.

How the on-lending scheme works

For the first two cycles of the on-lending scheme, Barclays Bank provides loans of GH¢3 000 (about US$3 300) to each *susu* collector, payable in six monthly instalments, at an annualised interest rate of 24.25 %. This loan amount represents about seven times the country's GDP per capita, and is almost four times the average monthly income of those targeted by Barclays Bank Ghana's premier and prestige banking operation. The loans are paid into the accounts that the participating *susu* collectors have opened at Barclays Bank. Loan payments, with interest, are automatically debited from these accounts at the end of each month.

As soon as the loan is available to the individual *susu* collector, the collector appraises end clients who have expressed interest in taking a loan. The flow of funds and guarantees within the scheme are illustrated in Figure 3.1.

Figure 3.1 The Barclays Bank Ghana/GCSCA on-lending scheme

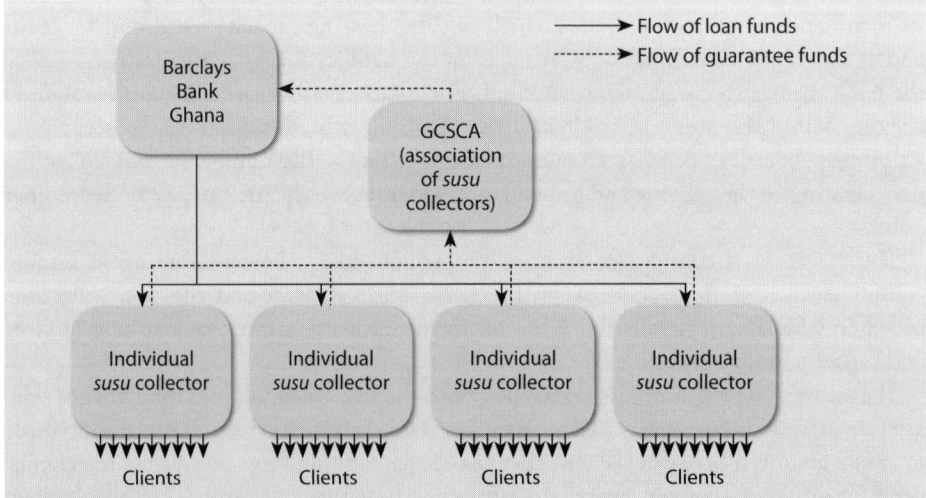

Source: Barclays Bank Ghana

Loan applications are usually processed in less than a week. The lending relationship for Barclays Bank is directly with the *susu* collector – GCSCA provides only a general guarantee. Neither GCSCA nor Barclays Bank is involved in the appraisal of the loans granted to the end clients. One person from both the GCSCA and Barclays does final checks on the client before the approval.

Given *susu* collectors' knowledge of each client's business and personal circumstances, they have the best information to judge the creditworthiness of their clients. This information is largely undocumented – individual end clients rarely maintain written records of their business and financial transactions, which would make their track record difficult for creditors other than *susu* collectors to verify. The history of savings maintained by clients with their individual *susu* collectors, in some cases spanning a period of 10 years or more, enable the *susu* collector to make judgments about what proportion of a client's income could be used for debt servicing and what sort of financial obligations the client already carries which might affect his or her capacity to repay the loan. As Barclays is not involved in the relationship between the *susu* collector and the end client, it is not in a position to track what the loans are used for, but anecdotal evidence suggests that they are used both for working capital for clients' businesses and as a way of smoothing household consumption.

The loans vary in size, depending on a combination of *susu* collectors' appraisal of each customer's capacity to repay and the overall demand for loans from their entire pool of clients. In practice, loan amounts granted to clients have been between 100 and 800 cedis (about US$100–US$800), payable in daily instalments for a total of 180 days at an effective annual interest rate of 25.285 %, which covers:

- The 24.25 % interest paid by the *susu* collector to Barclays;
- An arrangement fee (1 % per annum);
- An insurance fee (0.035 % per annum); and
- The *susu* collector's fee (4 % per annum). This is shared between the *susu* collector and GCSCA.

The arrangement fee represents the fee charged by the Barclays, which is separate from the fee collected by the respective *susu* collector. The insurance fee is also collected by Barclays, which insures all the loans, extended to end clients through a local insurance provider. Although the *susu* collector's fee is relatively low, producing an income of up to US$140 a year for on-lending of US$3 500, the facility enables the *susu* collector to satisfy an important demand for loans from clients. Without the facility, the *susu* collector would either be in danger of losing clients or would have to build an impossibly large base of net savers to provide loan capital.

Each borrower is allocated a separate account card in which the daily payment for the loan is recorded. These individual transactions are then tallied at the end of the day by the *susu* collectors, who deposit the total cash collections into their Barclays bank account.

In computing the daily instalments to be paid by each client, amounts are rounded up to simplify the transaction between the *susu* collector and the end borrowers. For example, given a loan amount of GH¢2 00 (US$220), the computed daily amortisation would amount to GH¢1.2 (US$1.30). To simplify the transaction, the amortisation is fixed at a rounded-up figure of GH¢1.5 (US$1.60). At the end of the 180-day cycle, the accrued difference between the computed loan payment and the rounded up figure is returned to the client as savings – in this example GH¢54.3 (about US$60).

In the last cycle, *susu* collectors reported that many of their clients were pleasantly surprised to realise that they had these funds at their disposal, because they had assumed that the whole of their payment was being applied to the loan. From the perspective of the *susu* collectors, this strategy has not only allowed the process to be simplified, but it has also been a route through which clients are encouraged to save more. It also helps the *susu* collectors gather additional information about a client's capacity to service loans of greater size.

The Barclays on-lending scheme was launched in July 2006. In the initial discussions between the bank, the GCSCA and its members in the months preceding the launch, Barclays Bank proposed a loan amount of GH¢5 000 (approximately US$5 500) for each *susu* collector. Interestingly, it was the GCSCA that argued that it would be prudent to begin by limiting the amount to GH¢3 000, with the understanding that as the scheme progressed to further cycles, the amount would be increased to reflect a readiness and ability of the *susu* collectors to administer the loans effectively.

The scheme was launched with a loan portfolio of about GH¢100 000 (about US$110 000) and had grown to GH¢340 000 (about US$375 000) by February 2007. Barclays Bank Ghana estimated to have reached about 1 000 clients during the first cycle of loans. Total deposits generated by the 300 participating *susu* collectors were estimated at almost US$2 million as of February 2007. The repayment rate has been consistently maintained at a remarkable 100 %, again highlighting the experience in many other microfinance environments across the world that poorer consumers can be an extremely good credit risk.

The first cycle of loans allowed some micro-entrepreneurs to purchase goods in bulk and benefit from wholesale prices, or to make their purchases before an anticipated price increase. In other cases, the loans enabled clients to cover household expenses that required larger sums and could not be paid in smaller amounts, such as school fees for children or the repair of roofing for homes in anticipation of the rainy season.

In the second cycle of loans, launched in February 2007, about 3 000 to 3 500 clients of *susu* collectors were expected to be provided with access to credit, some of whom were also borrowers on the first cycle.

Key issues

A number of issues emerged during the first cycle of the on-lending scheme that needed to be addressed by the bank, the GCSCA and its members.

Adjustments in banking operations: The first major adjustment had to be made by Barclays, which agreed to a more flexible approach to its banking hours. Early in the scheme, *susu* collectors expressed concern about the difficulties arising from the mismatch between their collection schedule and Barclays' normal banking hours. *Susu* collectors do not begin visiting their clients until shortly before noon to allow them enough time to generate some sales from which they could pay their loan instalments and/or make their daily savings contributions. This meant that *susu* collectors often completed their transactions after 3:30 in the afternoon, which is the time when most banks close their doors in Ghana. To accommodate the *susu* collectors, Barclays Bank responded by adjusting their opening hours, extending them to 4:30 in the afternoon. At some branches, *susu* collectors are allowed to make their deposits and undertake other transactions as early as 8:00 in the morning, or 30 minutes before the opening of the bank to the public. Bank tellers have also been instructed to prioritise the participating *susu* collectors, especially in banking halls that tend to have long queues. Moreover, two branches in Accra are now open even on Saturdays to serve the needs of those too busy to transact during the week, which may also be applicable to some *susu* collectors.

Some *susu* collectors tell of times when they have rushed to the bank with a bag full of cash at 4:30 in the afternoon, only to find that they were just too late and that the bank had closed. Seeing their distress, branch managers had reopened their doors to allow the *susu* collectors to make their deposits. In this sense, Barclays Bank has shown that it understands the constraints under which the *susu* collectors work and has been willing to make changes to accommodate their requirements.

A number of new initiatives to facilitate the activities of participating *susu* collectors have been introduced. Accounts can now be opened with a nil balance, and the cost per transaction has been lowered to a flat rate of GH¢2.5, although it is free if daily balance is at least GH¢1 000. A new insurance policy has been introduced in the event of the death or permanent disability of the client. Barclays is also working on a project to increase the outreach of the *susu* collector scheme using interactive theatre performances.

The need for capacity building: Adjustments have also been made by the *susu* collectors. For example, although capacity-building seminars and training are fully-financed by Barclays Bank, attendance requires an investment of time on the part of the collectors. Initially, the members were concerned that the amount of time that they would have to spend in training would hurt their business, because the collection of savings from hundreds of clients is very time consuming. In any case, those who qualified for the scheme were experienced – some of them had been in business for over 20 years. Many of them felt that there was little that outsiders could tell them about how their business works. Indeed, the trainers subsequently acknowledged that many of the *susu* collectors they trained had a solid basic knowledge and skills in the provision of financial intermediation services, even though they may not have had any formal training. However, Barclays Bank and the GCSCA worked closely together to ensure that the training modules were based on scenarios familiar to *susu* collectors while introducing the new language and concepts required for the administration of loans. They also decided to use a group of trainers with extensive experience in training NGOs and civil society groups rather than the bank's own banking trainers, recognising the need for the specific pedagogical skills that the outside trainers had developed. As a result, the capacity-building programme received very positive feedback from the *susu* collectors.

Loan size: As the on-lending scheme moved into its second cycle, the *susu* collectors asked Barclays Bank for an increase in the loan amount. The amount of GH¢3 000, according to them, was not enough to meet the growing demand among their clients. In a few cases, *susu* collectors used as much as GH¢2 000 to GH¢2 500 (US$2 200–US$2 800) of their own personal funds to add to the existing loan of GH¢3 000 made available by Barclays Bank. Others chose not to disclose the availability of the second cycle of loans, sharing the information only among those clients to whom they had chosen to provide loans.

Given the highly personal nature of the relationship between *susu* collectors and their clients, some collectors are concerned that should only a few clients be provided with loans, the non-recipients might look for other providers. There have indeed been cases in which clients have opted to stop saving with their *susu* collector and have chosen to join solidarity group-based microfinance institutions or even other *susu* collectors who have promised them access to loans.

Barclays has now agreed to increase the size of the loan amount for the third cycle, which has an upper limit of GH¢5 000. The new limit, which depends on the volume of the turnover of each individual *susu* collector, will allow them to meet this growing demand of credit among their clients.

Further business opportunities: It is still too early to expect any transformational changes in the economic circumstances of the *susu* collectors or their clients as a result of an improved level of financial access. However, there are signs that the scheme will bring additional benefits to both Barclays Bank and the end clients, as well as to the *susu* collectors. Barclays is still cautious about the full market potential for this business, but those who are operating the scheme are confident that it has the potential to become an important part of Barclays core business in Ghana.

Barclays Bank, like other banks in Africa, is moving in the direction of lowering the minimum level of opening balances for deposits. Some of the end clients of *susu* collectors would constitute part of the target market for small-deposit accounts. While these clients may generally perceive commercial banks as institutions which cater only to the upper end of the market, the on-lending scheme may alter that impression. The indirect relationship with Barclays may reduce resistance to setting up direct banking relationships in the future. This may also be facilitated by providing incentives to *susu* collectors to introduce new small-balance depositors to the bank.

The *susu* collectors also have clients who have a greater need for financing and the capacity to service loans in amounts that may be too large for the *susu* collector to provide, given that *susu* collectors' business requires them to diversify their loan portfolio and to channel the on-lending funds to a large number of their clients.

The more prosperous clients may be able to graduate to direct borrowing from the bank. By introducing such clients, *susu* collectors fulfil an important market development role. They may also act as a loan guarantor for individual clients, a practice that is already beginning to be tried by some MFIs in Ghana. In doing so, *susu* collectors are also able to build on the goodwill that has been established between themselves and their clients. Such moves are important steps in the integration of the informal and formal financial sectors.

Significant differences in the performance of the participating *susu* collectors emerge from the data collected by GCSCA and Barclays Bank, particularly about the volume of their turnover. A few *susu* collectors may be considered by Barclays Bank as potential individual loan conduits – that is to say, they may be capable of graduating out of the on-lending scheme to access normal loans of a size that is more in tune with the kind of demand they are capable of addressing. It may, however, be necessary for these individual *susu* collectors to provide a form of collateral, as is required by the bank in granting large loans to its other individual clients.

Conclusion

The initial success of this on-lending scheme between Barclays Bank Ghana and the *susu* collectors shows that the linkage-banking model can provide an innovative opportunity for large and very small financial intermediaries to co-operate in ways that enable them to benefit from each other's comparative strengths. The model allows both participants to overcome their intrinsic disadvantages, while retaining their tried and tested organisational form and culture.

Head of Corporate Affairs of Barclays Bank, Shola Safo-Duodu, confirmed that the 'experiment' between the bank and the *susu* collectors is well beyond the phase of pilot project, and it is now a sustainable and exciting reality to provide microentrepreneurs in Ghana with a wider range of financial services.

Barclays Bank, the GCSCA and its members have all acknowledged that the dialogue between the contracting parties needs to be continuous to address the issues resulting from the obvious differences in culture between a multinational bank and a small-scale informal deposit taker, as well as some differences that may at first be less obvious. So far, the communications between those involved in the Ghana linkage-banking scheme indicate that these institutions are well on their way towards realising the potential benefits of the scheme. Two immediate questions arise from the early success of the scheme:

- Can the approach be sustained, to ensure that clients who have been provided with access to financial services are able to reap the benefits of long-term banking relationships?
- Is the approach replicable?

The omens for sustainability are positive. Barclays Bank, the GCSCA and the *susu* collectors all show a high level of commitment. Barclays Bank Ghana hopes to build up its microbanking team in anticipation of a growing portfolio and an extension of regional coverage. The bank is also exploring the use of technology to reach branchless areas where some *susu* collectors operate.

That these efforts have been fully supported by Barclays Bank Africa and Barclays Bank plc has strengthened the Ghana bank's resolve to enter a market that has not been effectively reached in the past by other financial institutions in the formal sector. The availability of parent-company grant funds to cover the costs of non-financial activities in the on-lending scheme is considered necessary by all the parties involved, and has made this collaboration possible.

GCSCA and the *susu* collectors have also demonstrated a willingness to build the capacity of their association as well as that of the individual *susu* collectors. They emphasise that they have benefited from the on-lending partnership beyond merely having access to funds for on-lending to their clients. GCSCA appreciates the flexibility with which Barclays Bank has responded to its needs and those of its members, and is committed to a long-term relationship with the bank.

This is by no means the first example in Africa, or other parts of the world, of linkages between formal financial institutions with various other types of financial intermediaries. What makes this case special is that *susu* collectors are informal financial service providers motivated not so much by social development objectives as by the simple fact that these activities constitute their livelihood. Sustainability is a necessary condition for their existence from the outset, every day of the week. Should their clients fail to repay loans or stop contributing their savings, *susu* collectors will lose their means of livelihood.

This is in contrast to other types of informal institutions founded and organised with a social development mission, for which sustainability is less of an immediate issue. This is not, of course, to say that informal institutions with a social development orientation are not capable of being effective participants in a linkage-banking scheme. But in this case it is significant that the *susu* collectors are essentially commercial operators equipped with the knowledge and skills to attract deposits and issue advances to their clients. It is an important common bond between the commercial bank and the *susu* collectors. To put it simply, the partnership between these two intermediaries was established on the basis of crucial shared values and incentives.

ESSAY

Linkage banking and insurance schemes: Formal and informal providers combine to deepen the markets

Robert Stone and Abigail Carpio – *Robert Stone is Leader of Financial Sector Policy, and Abigail Carpio is a consultant, at Oxford Policy Management Limited.*

In much of Africa, the informal and semi-formal sectors are a crucial source of financial services for low-income clients, especially in rural areas.[6] A wide variety of individual operators and associations is involved. What they have in common is their close relationship with end-clients: whether in an association or in direct person-to-person transactions, the providers and the clients are linked in some way through livelihood or through a shared socio-economic profile. The main advantage of the informal and semi-formal providers, because of their knowledge and understanding of their clients, is that their operations are highly responsive to the needs of the specific markets they serve. Transactions usually involve very small amounts that are sometimes collected daily, reflecting and responding to the patterns of financial behaviour of low-income households and microenterprises.[7]

The widespread supply of financial services by the informal and semi-formal sectors is often viewed as a response to a demand that is left unmet by formal financial institutions. Commercial banks and insurance companies are usually concentrated in urban areas and tend to reach the upper end of the market, leaving unserved a large segment of the population. Such institutions are not generally in a position to provide poor people with the accessible, low-cost products they need.[8]

So, in most of Africa the banks fail to provide many poor people with what they need, while informal and semi-formal operators, who do provide appropriate services, are unable to extend the scale and scope of their operations. The informal operators are prevented from reaching a growing number of clients both because of the limitations in their available funds and because of their limited capacity to provide the full range of products these clients need.

There are encouraging signs, however, that the sub-Saharan financial markets may be becoming less fragmented. The last decade has seen the launch of a number of initiatives that have involved the creation of partnerships between formal financial institutions on the one hand, and informal or semi-formal financial service providers on the other. These linkage schemes have emerged as a response to various developments, of which three in particular are predominant.

- A prime driver has been a change in the market in some countries. In markets characterised by increasing competition and reduced interest rate spreads, banks have been forced to seek new markets and to diversify their offering. Linkage banking is seen by banks as a first step in developing a body of knowledge about the low-income market.
- This has in some cases been reinforced by the evolving requirements of the regulators, who have pressurised banks and other formal financial institutions to extend their exposure to the microfinance and small-to-medium enterprise sector. These pressures, whether by regulation or by moral suasion, have prompted banks to engage in wholesale lending to institutions that are more experienced at serving this particular market segment.

- Sponsorship has been made available by donors or other social investors that have an interest in providing financial services to poor segments of the population, which has resonated with the motivation of many banks to create an image as socially responsible actors in the financial markets where they operate.

There are notable cases of successful linkage schemes in Africa, a number of which are covered in the case studies in this book. These include Barclays Bank Ghana and its partnership with the *susu* collectors; Ecobank's provision of wholesale products and services to more than 60 MFIs in West and Central Africa; the provision by Opportunity International's MicroEnsure of microinsurance through links with local MFI partners and licensed insurance companies; and the partnership between Afriland First Bank and the village-based mutual funds in Cameroon (see Table 3.3).

Table 3.3 Linkage schemes

Linkage scheme	Country	Initiated	Network	Products and services
Barclays Bank Ghana + *susu* collectors	Ghana	2006	1 000 *susu* collectors; client base of about 800 000	• Savings • Wholesale loans • Training
Ecobank + MFIs	West, Central, East and Southern Africa	1993 (Togo)	More than 60 MFI partners; combined outreach in excess of two million	• Wholesale loans • Cash management services • Remittances subagency
Opportunity Micro Insurance Agency (OMI) + MFIs + insurance companies	Uganda, Ghana, Malawi, Mozambique, Zambia, Zimbabwe	2005	Operations in six countries in Africa and Asia, reaching about three million clients	• Market research and microinsurance product development • Training • Back-office support to MFIs
Afriland First Bank + ADAF + mutual funds (MC2)	Cameroon	1995	63 mutual funds; member base of 400 000	• Training • Savings and credit • Cash management services • Business development services for clients

Source: Authors

In each of these cases, the partners recognised their own limitations, and worked together to create a partnership in which each side complements the strengths and weaknesses of the other. This enabled the partnership to address the mismatch of resources and abilities in the institutions.

In Cameroon and Ghana, the informal and semi-formal finance providers, being the mutual funds and the *susu* collectors respectively, were limited mainly by the funds that they could generate through their own independent operations. By linking with larger commercial financial institutions (Afriland First Bank and Barclays Bank Ghana), they were able to access a much greater pool of resources that allowed them to expand services to the markets they serve. On the other hand, neither bank had been in a position to provide services directly to a widely dispersed low-income clientele, given their cost structures and their limited knowledge about this particular market segment. By linking with the informal and semi-formal providers, they could tap into a cost-effective delivery mechanism and into the much more intimate knowledge of the market that these partners had acquired.

In the case of MicroEnsure, the partnership was able to develop a financial product that partner MFIs as stand-alone entities had not been in a position to provide. It was then able to deliver it to clients that MicroEnsure alone had not been in a position to reach. With MicroEnsure's participation, not only were market research facilitated and appropriate products developed, but links with local insurance providers were also created to implement the microinsurance scheme. This partnership is thus built around the comparative strengths of the MFIs reaching low-income clients; and local insurance providers that are able to carry the risk. Moreover, MicroEnsure is able to invest in developing a suitable product and to broker the deal.

Through linkage banking and insurance, institutions are able to operate with greater economies of scale that help create a more efficient flow of funds. In Cameroon, the link between the mutual funds and Afriland First Bank facilitated the strengthening of the network of mutual funds, enabling interactions among institutions operating in different parts of the country. Thus, for example, the mutual funds that had greater advantages in terms of deposit mobilisation were able to provide liquidity to those operating in markets with greater demand for credit. Without the linkage scheme, mutual funds would have found it too costly to enter into individual partnerships with other mutual funds, and would be unable to facilitate a more efficient treasury management system. Interestingly, the presence of this strong network also paved the way for the mutual funds to establish an effective payments system with agricultural firms that contract with smallholder farmers in Cameroon, thus helping to reduce the transaction costs borne by both the farmers and the agricultural enterprises.

While the advantages of linkage banking and insurance may be enough to convince institutions to enter into such mutually beneficial partnerships, it is important to note that there are significant costs associated with establishing effective links. Strong institutions are needed for a linkage scheme to be successful. On the part of the informal/semi-formal finance providers, this means having the commitment to, and a track record of, providing sustainable financial services to low-income clients. This may be in the form of a socially driven institution such as an MFI or of informal operators that have a business interest in catering for the low-income market. In all four of the cases cited, the providers are characterised by their long-term presence in informal financial markets: some, like *susu* collectors, are an intrinsic element in the indigenous culture, and strongly linked to the way informal markets have been organised and operated for centuries. Nevertheless, linking these providers with formal institutions necessitates a common business platform. How can the practices of more informal financing relationships be reconciled with those of institutions operating in the formal sector?

The case studies show that, at both ends of the spectrum, the institutions have had to bear a part of the transaction cost to make the partnership work. The linkage scheme in Ghana provides a useful example to illustrate this point. In this partnership, Barclays Bank Ghana provides training in the administration of loans to *susu* collectors to support the latter in disbursing a greater volume of loans through the on-lending facility. Moreover, the bank also made adjustments in its operations by extending opening hours to accommodate *susu* collectors, who typically complete their transactions beyond traditional banking hours. For their part, the *susu* collectors had to devote significant time to the training, recognising that their strength lies in the mobilisation of small-scale deposits and that access to the on-lending facility required them to build their capacity in managing the provision of credit. This demonstrates how both parties were able to make the necessary investments of time and money to find common ground and ensure the alignment of their social and business interests and objectives.

It is important to note that most, if not all, of these successful linkage schemes have been, and continue to be, driven by a strong sense of social mission. In none of these cases, however, has this translated into an unprofitable set-up in which the provision of financial services to the low-income market on an unsustainable basis is justified by a social mandate driving the institutions involved. Instead, the strong sense of social mission has encouraged the channelling of investment towards what may be deemed as areas of market failure. This is evident in the experience of Barclays Bank Ghana, which provided training free of charge to *susu* collectors through the support received from its head office. In the case of Afriland First Bank's linkage scheme with the mutual funds, this form of social investment is evident in the creation of the Appropriate Development for Africa Foundation (ADAF), a non-governmental organisation that facilitates the provision of non-financial services, which include the training of officers of the mutual funds. ADAF sources its funding through contributions made by Afriland as well as by other international and national donors. Yet in all these cases, the activities are financially sustainable, providing a satisfactory source of income for both the formal financial institutions and their informal or semi-formal partners.

Ecobank: A regional approach to microfinance

> When does a regional banking concern become a multinational? Ecobank is surely close to this point. From a bank with dominance across West Africa, Ecobank has grown to become a pan-African bank operating in 29 countries – 28 in Africa plus France – and is the bank with the largest geographic footprint in Africa. Regionalisation underpins Ecobank's success. So too does its commitment to microfinance, both as a wholesaler and, in a retail partnership with ACCION International, as a promoter of new MFIs. This case study underscores how important it is for mainstream banks to invest in the development of markets further down the economic pyramid. Ecobank offers a range of services to its MFI clients, including wholesale loans, treasury and cash management services, and remittances subagency deals.

West and Central Africa continues to lag behind the rest of the continent in socio-economic indicators.[9] Much of the region is characterised by low governance capacity, weak economic output and limited financial infrastructure. The persistent threat of conflict spilling across borders and involving ever-greater numbers of actors is also a major factor deterring growth and turning away potential investors.

In these circumstances, it is not surprising that the track record of many financial institutions, formal and informal, in the region has been weak. Since 1988, however, one regional initiative has been slowly and steadily improving its financial stability and standing. Ecobank, operating in 28 African countries, has been a model of regional ownership and innovation. The bank is one of the most successful ventures coming out of West Africa, and its story has many important lessons for financial institutions in the region and beyond.

Ecobank Transnational Incorporated is a bank holding company founded in 1988. It is the parent company of the Ecobank Group, which operates across West, Central, East and Southern Africa at present – in Benin, Burkina Faso, Burundi, Cape Verde, Cameroon, Central Africa Republic, Chad, Congo Brazzaville, Cote d'Ivoire, Democratic Republic of Congo (DRC), Gabon, Ghana, Guinea Bissau, Guinea Conakry, Kenya, Liberia, Malawi, Mali, Niger, Nigeria, Rwanda, Senegal, São Tomé e Principe, Senegal, Sierra Leone, Tanzania, Togo and Uganda. In December 2008 Ecobank announced that it had formed a strategic alliance with the South African Nedbank Group, which will allow it to further expand its pan-African footprint.

Ecobank is a full-service bank, providing wholesale and retail financial services to governments and businesses – both large and small – and to consumers, with a network of more than 750 branches and offices built up over the last 20 years. As the bank has begun to consolidate its position, profits have started to increase substantially. Between 2005 and 2006, revenues grew by 47 % to US$348 million, while profit before tax grew by 75 % to US$129 million. This growth continued in 2007, when Ecobank grew revenues by 56 % to US$544 million and increased customer deposits by 89 % to US$4.7 billion and ended 2008 with total assets and deposits of US$8.3 billion and US$5.8 billion respectively.

The Ecobank Group seeks to combine its success as a commercial bank dedicated to increasing shareholder value with a strong social and developmental role. In pursuit of these aims, Ecobank has developed a two-tier approach to engagement in microfinance operations:

- The bank's entry into wholesale services for MFIs has indirectly enabled the provision of microfinance services to more than two million microentrepreneurs;
- A new strategic focus on retail microfinance will make the bank's services available directly to otherwise traditionally underserved markets in Africa.

Wholesale microfinance services

The bank has been working with leading MFIs in each of the countries of the bank's operations, providing wholesale products and services that enhance the capacity of the MFIs to serve a greater number of microclients. This began in the early 1990s, and has intensified in recent years along with the bank's growing involvement with retail banking.

There are many competitors active in the sector. West and Central Africa have numerous MFIs, many more prosperous than those in east or southern Africa, and these can be attractive clients for commercial banks. What makes Ecobank stand out from its competitors is its range of products and services specifically tailored for MFIs.

In particular, the bank is able to be much more active in lending to MFIs because it has developed an effective credit risk methodology that enables it to assess risks more confidently, and therefore price the loans more efficiently than its rivals.

Lending rates vary from country to country and from MFI to MFI, but in general the rates for each country are below the normal retail lending rate as Ecobank assesses MFIs as financial institutions – they are financial intermediaries after all – and applies a discount based on the credit risk score of the MFI.

The first MFI customer was signed up in 1993 by Ecobank Togo; today, Ecobank supports more than 100 MFIs in the region. These MFIs often have insufficient funds from deposits to cover their on-lending activities, and many of them also the lack capacity and skills to manage idle funds. As a result they face the high risk and cost of holding large amounts of cash. The financial and non-financial services and products designed for its MFI clients includes credit for on-lending, cash management and collection services to minimise vault cash holdings, and providing free training in banking skills such as tellering and cash management. Complementary services such as money transfers are aimed at the ultimate customer of the MFI. In these cases the MFIs are appointed as agents of the bank, which provides the fund transfer service to the MFI clients. Other services aimed at the end user include electronic banking and the joint use of ATMs and electronic cards, in effect converting and upgrading the branches of MFIs into joint branches of Ecobank and the MFIs.

These services have improved the capacity and strength of the bank's client MFIs in a number of ways. For instance, the credit facility has enabled MFIs, co-operatives and other informal business networks to extend microcredit to thousands of clients. The outstanding loan portfolio to MFIs in 2006 was about US$30 million, representing 1.5 % of the bank's total portfolio. Ecobank Group's total loans as at 2006 accounts were about US$2 billion, and these increased by 62 % to US$3.1 billion in 2007 and further to $3.8 billion in 2008. Typically, loans to MFIs vary between US$50 000 and US$3 million, depending on the size, risk profile and track record of the MFI. By contrast, Ecobank is managing about US$40 million in deposits from MFIs through its various cash management services. In addition, money transfer services have enabled many of Ecobank's MFI clients to earn additional income by being appointed as Ecobank subagents for its Western Union money transfer franchise. Under this arrangement, Ecobank acts as the head franchisee with Western Union, which allows the bank to create subagents under the head franchise. For this subagency arrangement MFIs share commission on fund transfers with Ecobank. Ecobank believes that its support to MFIs has boosted development, especially in job creation in the rural economy.

By developing a set of wholesale tools and services appropriate to MFIs, and rolling them out on a regional basis while adapting them to conditions in each country, Ecobank has been able to extend its outreach significantly. The combined outreach of the MFIs served by Ecobank is in excess of two million. This approach is strongly complemented by the second strand of Ecobank's microfinance activities, retail microfinance with ACCION International as the exclusive technical partner.

Retail microfinance

In November 2006, Ecobank formed a strategic partnership with ACCION International, a pioneer and leading global provider of microfinance funding and services, to jointly establish and operate microfinance institutions across Africa.[10] Ecobank's choice of ACCION as partner is due to ACCION's significant experience and success in commercial microfinance, spanning decades across Asia, Latin America and now Africa. This retail approach represented a fundamental shift for Ecobank, which had previously operated as a wholesale service provider rather than engaging directly with the clients at the bottom of the pyramid. The aim was to diversify its portfolio, while generating considerable socio-economic benefits for micro and small entrepreneurs in the region. The Ecobank-ACCION loans are provided to the public, and not through client MFIs. Two ranges of loans are being offered: microloans that range from US$250 to US$1 000, and small loans from US$1 000 to US$25 000. They will appear on Ecobank-ACCION's balance sheet and Ecobank-ACCION will be ultimately responsible for ensuring repayments and assume the default risk, unlike under the Ecobank wholesale scheme where MFIs bear this responsibility. By making individual loans directly, the bank hopes to provide much greater access to credit for microenterprises than it can do by providing funds on a wholesale basis through MFIs.

Some of Ecobank's MFI clients were worried about this move, fearing that the bank may become a competitor, but Ecobank emphasises that its plan is to continue to act as wholesale financiers for MFIs, even while moving into the retail market. As the microfinance head of Ecobank explains, 'This seeming clash is actually normal in the larger financial system. Banks compete, but they also collaborate with each other. It is perfectly normal to find banks in the same market supporting each other with loans, correspondent banking, treasury services, money transfer sub-agencies, network/payment services, card/ATM partnerships. So banks see each other not only as competitors but also as partners.'

Ecobank and ACCION have implemented their partnership by establishing microfinance initiatives in Nigeria and Ghana. The future plan is to jointly launch MFIs in all the countries where Ecobank operates in Africa.

ACCION Microfinance Bank (AMfB) started operating in Nigeria in May 2006. Ecobank is one of the partners in this venture along with ACCION, the IFC, the Nigeria International Bank (a subsidiary of Citigroup), venture capital company SME Managers, and Zenith Bank. By October 2007, AMfB had disbursed a total of 1 155 loans amounting to N143.5 million (around US$1.2 million), and mobilised deposits of N14.6 million from more than 1 763 savers, an average of US$70 per saver. Branches had been opened at Oke Arin, Oyingbo, Ladipo, Idi-Oro in Mushin and Balogun Business Association Trade Fair Complex. AMfB´s flagship loan product is 'My Own', a working-capital loan designed for microentrepreneurs and small business owners who want to borrow for business purposes but lack conventional collateral to secure their loans.

The bank launched Brighta in 2008, a new savings product designed to help poor customers to save while also granting them immediate access to their money. To suit the different needs of its customers, AMfB has launched different Brighta products. Thus, Brighta Account is designed for those clients who require only a few basic transactions per month; Brighta Future is more appropriate for those who have a lump sum to save or want to build up their savings day by day; and Brighta Togeda is designed for registered groups, associations and co-operatives. All of them include third-party withdrawals.

EB-ACCION Savings & Loan started operating in Ghana April 2008. It has a full licence to deliver a variety of financial services including microcredit, savings and microinsurance products. By October, six months after EB-ACCION opened, two branches were fully operational in the Accra market places of Tudu and Lapaz, and more than US$15 million had been disbursed to more 36 000 borrowers in the

MSMEs sector. Two more branches were opened by the end of 2008 with 6 100 savings customers through the four branches.

Conclusion

Ecobank is one of the first banks in West and Central Africa to break out of the mould of traditional banking. It has recognised the great potential in the market for microfinance services. The bank has also had the vision to see that it is possible to operate effectively and profitably at regional level, achieving economies of scale in the development of methodologies and the management of products and services. By recognising the bottom of the pyramid as a major bankable market and by widening its horizons in terms of geography and products, Ecobank has developed a successful business model with strong potential for scale and profitability while helping millions of microentrepreneurs, both men and women, to begin to work their way out of poverty.

Al Amana: Transformation against heavy odds

> Al Amana is the success story of how a small, donor-dependent NGO transformed into a self-sustaining, regulated financial services provider. Such development would be impressive in any country, yet Al Amana operates in Morocco, with its highly centralised banking system and strict regulatory framework, and a culture which makes lending to women entrepreneurs particularly challenging.

The microfinance sector in the Middle East and North Africa (MENA) region is relatively young, dating back to the 1990s when a few MFIs provided loans to finance the economic activities of people with low incomes. Morocco has the most vibrant microfinance in the region. In 1996, the government entered into a bilateral agreement with USAID to launch an eight-year US$15.5 million[11] microfinance project and set up a funding facility called Fonds Hassan II to increase the lending capital of existing MFIs. In 1998, in collaboration with the UNDP, the government set up the MicroStart programme to build the capacity of local associations to provide microfinancing services in a way that was financial sustainable.

The microfinance sector is regulated by the central bank, Bank Al-Maghrib, and governed by Law number 18-97, Loi Relative au Micro-Crédit, introduced in 1999 and modified in 2003 to allow MFIs to offer housing finance. By January 2007 there were more than one million microfinance clients, a 77 % increase from 2005 (see Figure 3.2), and MFIs were managing a collective outstanding loan portfolio of US$511 million, up from US$409 the year before. Most of these loans – 87.6 % – were distributed in urban and suburban zones. The main sectors benefiting from these loans were textiles and commerce, representing 34.3 % and 23.1 % respectively of the total number of loans. An encouraging feature of Moroccan microfinance is the large number of female clients, perhaps surprising given the difficulty MFIs face in reaching women in the traditional communities in which they work. In 2006, women constituted 71.3 % of the total number of active clients.

Figure 3.2 Growth in total number of active microfinance clients

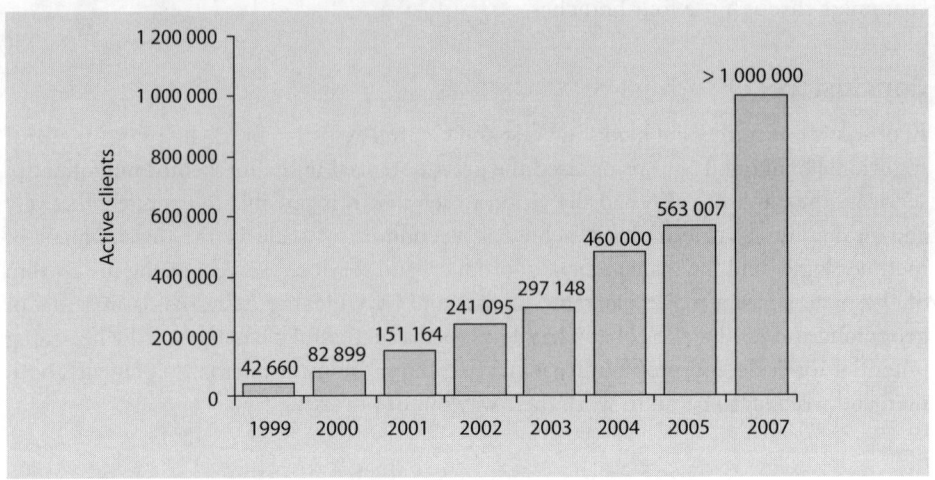

Source: PlaNet Finance (2007)

Table 3.4 Moroccan microfinance sector – key statistics

	2005	2006
Active clients (thousands)	563	1 034
Active clients (thousands)	73	119
Association Al Amana	39.5 %	39.2 %
Fondation Zakoura	31.4 %	35.6 %
Fondation Banque Populaire	13.1 %	12.7 %
FONDEP	7 %	7.4 %
Fondation Credit Agricole "Ardi"	3.2 %	1.2 %
The seven other MFIs	5.8 %	3.9 %
Portfolio size (millions of Moroccan Dirham)	1 557	3 491
Portfolio size (millions of US$)	181	406
Association Al Amana	52.5 %	52.2 %
Fondation Zakoura	14.5 %	21.8 %
Fondation Banque Populaire	20.3 %	16.7 %
FONDEP	6.9 %	6.4 %
Fondation Credit Agricole "Ardi"	1.4 %	0.5 %
The seven other MFIs	4.4 %	2.4 %
Total size of MFI sector (millions of Moroccan Dirham)	2 653	4 296
Total size of MFI sector (millions of US$)	306	495

Source: Société Générale Marocaine de Banques/Al Amana

Four institutions dominate the microfinance market: Association Al Amana pour la Promotion des Microentreprises (Al Amana); Fondation Zakoura; Foundation for Local Development and Partnership (FONDEP); and Banque Populaire du Micro-Crédit, an NGO offshoot of a state bank. These four MFIs serve more than three-quarters of the total active clients of the 12 MFIs in Morocco, and report a 99 % repayment rate. The potential for expanding the microfinance market in Morocco is estimated to be more than three million clients and US$1 billion in loans.[12]

Association Al Amana created to serve the excluded

Al Amana was established in 1997 in Rabat through a USAID project to provide financial services to urban microentrepreneurs. Paul Rippey, the chief of party for Volunteers in Technical Assistance, the US-based NGO awarded the contract to implement the project, brought his extensive microfinance experience to Morocco, and recruited Fouad Abdelmoumni to head the newly created Al Amana. It is now the largest MFI in Morocco providing microcredit to low-income solidarity groups and individuals in various sectors including commerce, artisans, services and agriculture. Since 2003 it has also offered housing loans.

Al Amana's evolution from a donor-funded NGO MFI into a larger institution was built on technical assistance from donors, coupled with investment in information technology, and a decision to keep head-office administrative staff to a minimum while increasing the number of loan officers in the field helped make this possible. This enabled the organisation to offer a wider range of loans and to reach people in remote rural areas. By 2006, the average number of borrowers per loan officer was 352, and in 2007 this was 365. By 2006, Al Amana's solidarity (group) rural clients made up more than one third (36 %) of its total portfolio. At the end of the first 10 years of operating it had served almost half a million people, and managed a loan portfolio of US$273 million (see Table 3.5).

Table 3.5 Loan portfolio profile of Al Amana

	2005	2006	2007
Number of active clients	249 531	404 956	477 267
Women clients	120 186	186 713	227 938
Solidarity rural clients	92 018	170 326	204 032
Solidarity urban clients	149 975	200 813	203 361
Number of loans to individual business clients	4 665	16 815	34 888
Number of loans to housing credit clients	2 873	17 002	34 986
Outstanding loans (million Moroccan Dirham)	763.8	1 849.3	2 354.4

Source: Al Amana (2006)

Al Amana's rapid growth is reflected in the figures in Table 3.6 from its 2006 annual report: its balance sheet shows a near trebling of the loan portfolio in 12 months. This has, however, inevitably led to some decline in portfolio quality but the PAR and other portfolio ratios remain healthy. Al Amana's growth is also reflected in the size of the average loan. By law the maximum loan is capped at US$5 580. By the end of 2005 the average loan size was MAD3 061 (US$356), and this increased to MAD4 915 (US$572) by the end of 2007. The average loan size is being driven up not only by loans to repeat customers graduating to larger loans but also by the housing loans which MFIs are now allowed to provide.

Table 3.6 Highlights from Al Amana Annual Report, 2006

	December 2005	December 2006	Growth rate (%)
Balance sheet (US$ '000)	MAD/US$9.246	MAD/US$8.442	
Total assets	86 376	227 933	164
Gross loan portfolio	83 000	219 000	164
Net fixed assets	1 463	3 000	100
Treasury assets	1 760	4 640	164
Shareholders' equity	24 632	33 875	38
Provisions	1 850	3 700	100
Financing, long-term liabilities	36 056	116 978	258
Financing, treasury liabilities	19 028	61 921	230
Other short-term liabilities	4 700	11 450	143
Portfolio-at-risk > 30 days' ratio (%)	0.16	0.48	
Loan loss reserve ratio (%)	0.99	1.37	
Risk coverage ratio (%)	632.64	283.94	
Write-off ratio (%)	0.37	0.49	
Income statement (US$ '000)			
Income from activities	17 135	32 900	75
Cost from activities	10 990	19 575	63
Net income from activities	6 143	13 322	98
Net result	4 077	6 899	55

Source: Al Amana (2006)

For microfinance organisations, Morocco is a particularly challenging context in which to operate. There is a continuing need to encourage a more market-oriented approach towards the provision of financial services to the poor, and MFIs need to offer a broader and more diverse range of financial services. However, the regulatory framework in Morocco is notoriously strict and does little to encourage such development. The cap on maximum loan size is a problem, and MFIs are unable to diversify into providing savings and insurance services, which is a source of frustration for Al Amana. The banking system is also highly centralised. At the end of 2007, Standard & Poor's Ratings Services issued a rating assessment of the Moroccan banking sector that indicates the need for caution. Morocco's banking sector has strengthened over the past five years, but has become increasingly vulnerable to rapid and untested credit growth. Also worrying was the high concentration of financial assets in a small number of leading institutions. Attijariwafa Bank, Groupe Banques Populaires and Banque Marocaine du Commerce Extérieur between them control about three-quarters of the system's assets.

Al Amana also had to deal with resistance from conservative groups. Moroccan regulations required MFIs to obtain a personal guarantee for business plans supporting a loan application in order to provide evidence of the sustainability of the business. It was often difficult for clients to meet this requirement, especially when women had to ask their husbands to be the guarantor. Al Amana's customers were therefore targeted by social radicals. The donors worked hard to promote the microfinance sector, and government champions played an effective advocacy role, which empowered female borrowers and reassured their husbands. Eventually, Al Amana was able to convince its customers that being an NGO that charged interest did not conflict with their Islamic beliefs or traditional values. In the end, only two of Al Amana's 20 000 clients terminated the loans on religious grounds and two other clients repaid only the principal. The rest maintained and honoured their loan agreements. This was a significant win for Al Amana and the microfinance sector in general. The public were convinced of the benefits of microfinance and were not deterred from obtaining credit from MFIs.

Al Amana works through a network of branches called antennas, which are supervised by regional co-ordinators. Each antenna is staffed by between one and six loan officers, depending on the stage of development and the size of the market being served. In 2005, Al Amana introduced a further organisational layer – agencies – aimed at increasing the productivity of solidarity loan officers by reducing some of their administrative tasks (see Figure 3.3).

Figure 3.3 Al Amana's organisational structure

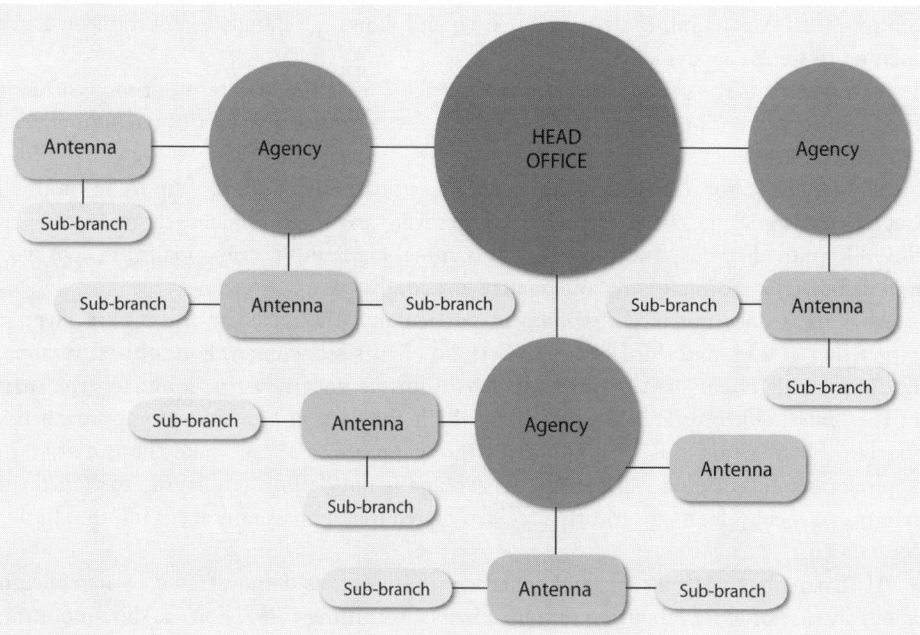

Source: Al Amana

From 2005 to 2006 the number of antennas decreased while the number of agencies increased as antennas were streamlined into agencies (see Table 3.7).

Table 3.7 Branch network and staff evolution

	2005	2006	2007
Total number of outlets	368	444	473
Antennas	362	352	259
Agencies	1	65	174
Attached offices (sub-branches)	4	0	6
Mobile offices (vehicles)	1	27	34
Total number of staff	1 062	1 845	2 373
Field staff	922	1 651	2 109
Loan officers	890	1 149	1 307
Central services and management	140	194	264

Source: Al Amana

Borrower groups are self-formed without Al Amana, and consist of between three and five people. Group members co-guarantee each other and they all pay the same interest rate on their loans. The loans are for a term of between three and 18 months. Individual lending is allowed for housing development and growth of small businesses, but solidarity loans are granted only for income-generating activities. Although there is a choice of repaying weekly, fortnightly or monthly, rural clients tend to choose monthly repayments and often opt to use Al Amana rather than an MFI which follows the Bangladeshi Grameen Bank method of weekly repayments.

An agent visits the group at least once or twice during the loan term, or more often if there are repayment problems. The audit team at head office also carries out spot checks on loans.

All branches offer individual loans, which generally have a term of up to 36 months, but this can sometimes be stretched for up to seven years.[13] Al Amana's target is to reach 800 000 individual customers by 2013. Individual loans and housing loans are approved and disbursed at both antenna and agency level daily.

Al Amana does not target women in particular, although loan officers are given a target that at least one third of their portfolio clients are women. For cultural reasons, finding female clients can be difficult. Loan officers generally first approach the man of the household to establish trust, after which they are in a position to approach the woman. Having said this, in some cases the women in a village take the initiative to apply for a solidarity loan. Although Al Amana is not deliberately trying to transform Moroccan society, loan officers often feel frustrated that men usually act as intermediaries for women.

Al Amana has a strong sense of social commitment, as demonstrated by its concern about the use of child labour among its clients. According to M. Fouad Abdelmoumni, 'We want to do our job but we want to do it on an ethical basis'. A potential negative side effect of supporting microenterprise development is that children are less likely to attend school because of the pressure to work in the family business. In response to this risk, Al Amana is acting against child labour, working in close partnership with the International Labour Organization (ILO), whose representative sits on its board. Al Amana has recently commissioned a study into child labour and is working on a strategy to combat the exploitation of children by its clients. From July 2007, it started asking all potential clients whether they have, or plan to have, children working for them – even if it does not look like children are, or will be, working for the enterprise, Al Amana feels it is still important to ask the question as a means of raising awareness about this issue. Al Amana is particularly concerned about cases of child labour that prevent the child from attending school. If this is the case, Al Amana will not grant the loan. For existing clients who use child labour, the loan officer will complete a simple template making recommendations about how to reduce the negative effects on the working child. Both parties sign the agreement, and the loan officer explains that future loans will not be approved if the recommendations are not met. Al Amana would like to get government support for this approach, with the MFIs in the country acting collectively.

Al Amana customer: Amenkach L'Akbier

Amenkach L'Akbier is a 60-year-old dairy farmer in Ain Aouda, a village 28 km south of Rabat. She is the main breadwinner in her household, supporting six adult children and their families. Amenkach is lucky to own her own farm, a modest, single-storey building with a stable for her cows and a small field, which was given to her by the previous owners, a Belgian farming family who employed her husband. Despite having property to offer as collateral, she could not borrow from a bank because she earned little and only wanted to borrow a small amount. Amenkach had been borrowing in a solidarity group from Fondation Zakoura when she heard in the village about Al Amana. She approached Al Amana's Ain Aouda antenna for her first individual loan of MAD4 000. This was a large loan for her compared to her firstever loan of MAD1 000. Although she is now in her third loan cycle from Al Amana, she still continues to take smaller loans from Fondation Zakoura. However, she prefers borrowing from Al Amana because the loan product and the lending process are more suitable to her needs – Al Amana loans are larger and repaid monthly, compared to Fondation Zakoura's, which are repaid fortnightly. Al Amana's interest rate is also lower. Before Amenkach used the Al Amana financing, she was sometimes forced to sell her calves too young in order to meet the repayment dates. She could not afford to wait a few weeks in order to command a higher price. She earns more money now for the same number of calves and still meets the repayment dates.

Al Amana's outreach strategy: Cities first, then the desert

Al Amana's strategy has been to expand in concentric circles: first establishing bases in big cities, expanding to the surrounding areas, then moving to mid-sized towns and then to villages in the region. Al Amana covers 100 % of urban areas at present and about 20–30 % of rural areas. Establishing financial services in rural areas is part of Al Amana's strategic plan to 2013, and its goal is to reach the rural disadvantaged, especially in the desert and mountain regions where the population is sparse. As part of its rural outreach programme, the organisation carries out frequent market and impact studies in rural areas. Obstacles to working in these remote areas include the lack of good roads, electricity and water supply. Security is also an issue for loan officers travelling alone. Al Amana differentiates itself from other MFIs in that its loan agents do not visit potential customers door to door. Potential customers generally approach officers, and the application is then processed at the branch or sub-branch.

Al Amana has a set system for opening new outlets. Staff from an established antenna spend a day visiting a possible new site, and carry out a study to validate the assumptions made about the area's potential. They ensure that sufficient infrastructure is in place for agents to get to the site, preferably by motorbike or car but at least on foot, that the site has a potential clientele who are unserved and willing to take on loans, and that the site will generate a sufficient volume of lending to be able to pay back the investment in establishing a permanent outpost. If it is decided that the site is viable, the originating antenna will decide on the best way to access clients at the new site. This can be done in different ways depending on the demand and difficulty of access:

- **Motorcycle:** The first step in creating a presence generally starts by itinerant agents creating a critical mass of customers in each new site.
- **Vehicle:** When the terrain is very challenging but the area is assessed as having good potential a specially fitted vehicle visits the site on market days, when inhabitants of the area congregate to trade.
- **Kiosk:** After the agent has created a group of clients in a particular area the originating antenna sets up a kiosk. Kiosks are dependent on the antenna, and provide an office space for the itinerant agent to receive customers at least once a week and create visibility. Depending on the population density of the area, the kiosk may, over time, become a full antenna.

Banking by mobile phone (m-banking) is a possible future outreach method for Al Amana. This is still under consideration due to its dependency on sufficient communications infrastructure. Al Amana has been working with the Poverty Action Lab at the Massachusetts Institute of Technology to carry out a survey to investigate the possibility of m-banking. The survey found that 40 % of the rural population in Morocco already have a mobile phone and that clients would benefit from the introduction of an e-purse, called *la carte monétique* by Al Amana, which would improve personal security as they would be able to carry less cash. It is estimated that it would take Al Amana nine months to develop a new management information system that will support the transactions of m-banking, e-purses and ATMs. However, it is not yet clear whether the strict Moroccan regulatory framework will permit these developments.

Al Amana agents often find that potential clients, both individuals and groups, in rural areas are not able to provide suitable identification documents. As MFIs do not have to follow the same stringent anti-money-laundering rules as banks, Al Amana agents have circumvented the lack of official records by creating their own client identification records, used for Al Amana purposes only. It is not a perfect solution, but Al Amana feels that, given the benefit of the client being given access to credit versus the small amounts being loaned, its self-produced records are of sufficient quality to monitor the loans and the client's credit behaviour. Al Amana also offers its clients non-financial services, aimed at strengthening their business capacity. This can either be through helping businesses form partnerships, or training programmes carried out by educational institutions.

MFIs have been able to extend their outreach by co-operating with each other. Although the competition for customers is fierce, the MFIs share information and discuss how they can provide more inclusive financial services within the current legal framework. The aim is to present a united front that conveys an image of financial solidity and viability, which in turn allows the MFIs to approach banks for funding as a cohesive business sector.

> **Al Amana customer : Bensadik El Hassan**
>
> Bensadik El Hassan is a local farmer who keeps cows, goats, sheep and chickens in his field, about five kilometres away from Ain Aouda. Bensadik's living conditions are basic: he, one of his wives and their child live in a small single-room hut without running water or electricity. He already had an established animal husbandry business before taking out his first Al Amana loan of MAD5 000 in 2006 to buy more goats. As a result, he is able to comfortably sustain two wives and send his children to school. Now he is on his second loan of MAD10 000, and he predicts that the pace of growth of his husbandry activity will allow him to take out larger loans to diversify into an artisan activity such as selling his wife's traditional woven carpets.

The business model

Al Amana's senior management and central functions are based at its head office in Rabat. Most of the management team have been with Al Amana since its inception and are passionate about its work. Al Amana's loan officers account for 89 % of its total staff, which is high compared to other MFIs. This is because the loan officers responsible for group lending also undertake the administrative work on these loans; the loan officers for individual borrowers do not carry out administrative tasks – these are done by supporting agents.

This structure has allowed Al Amana to achieve a manageable cost per borrower of US$64.80 a client in 2007 (see Table 3.8). It has enabled the institution to continuously lower its operating expense ratio to 9.83 % in 2007 compared to 14.36 % in 2005. The cost benefits of this have been passed on to clients as lower lending rates, thus the portfolio yield dropped from more than 24 % at the end of 2005 to 19.4 % in 2006. The rapid growth of Al Amana's loan portfolio has inevitably led to increased risk, but its risk profile remains healthy, with PAR (> 30 days) at 1.9 % at the end of 2007 and a write-off ratio of 0.85 %, as shown in Table 3.8.

Table 3.8 Key financial information about Al Amana

	2005	2006	2007
Capital/asset ratio (%)	28.52	14.86	12.71
Loan loss provision expense ratio (%)	0.12	0.33	1.13
Operating expense ratio (%)	12.72	8.59	10.68
Operating expense/loan portfolio (%)	13.30	8.94	11.48
Cost per borrower (US$)	44.05	48.34	73.62
PAR > 30 days ratio (%)	0.16	0.43	1.06
Write-off ratio (%)	0.17	0.31	0.75

Source: Al Almana

As well as investment capital, Al Amana needs working capital. Each branch (antenna or agency) needs a minimum weekly float of US$2 500 to finance its activities. The finance department also needs extra cash for the weekly loan cycle for antennas still in development – they need a larger float until they start receiving loan repayments. To manage this cash float, Al Amana uses money-market instruments that are highly liquid, and follows a strategy that tries to minimise the level of active treasury assets held.

Al Amana's initial lenders were development finance institutions (DFIs): the IFC; the International Co-operation Office of Spain; Agence Française de Développement of France; and the EIB. They provided subsidised rates at an average of 4.5 % or less, long repayment terms of up to 10 years, and grace periods of between two and five years. Banks were not prepared to lend to Al Amana while it was seen as an NGO receiving subsidised DFI lending. From 1997 to 2004, Al Amana's loan book grew steadily by at least 30 % a year using only the DFI loans. However, by 2004 it became clear that there was much greater demand for Al Amana's services than the credit supplied by DFIs could meet. This coincided with a change in the DFIs' lending strategy: they reduced credit support in a global drive to reduce MFI dependency on donor funds, and forced a move towards financial and operational sustainability.

In 2005, Al Amana was finally able to secure large loans from local banks, mainly as a result of the solidity of its balance sheet and, in some cases, DFI guarantees. This meant that Al Amana was no longer dependent on donor funding. In 2006, two changes took place which helped MFIs to access long-term bank lending: a new banking law was passed, and the financial supervision authority for MFIs passed from the ministry of finance to the central bank. This elevated the status of MFIs from NGOs to regulated financial institutions, still licensed by the ministry of finance. The more rigorous supervisory regime forced MFIs to improve their internal controls and reporting. For example, MFIs are now required to submit quarterly returns and harmonise financial reporting following the same financial accounting standards as banks.

In the MFIs' favour was the low default rate (write-off ratio) of less than 1 % of outstanding loans that they, and in particular Al Amana, had achieved, compared to an average default rate in the banking sector of 15 %. Al Amana also has a policy of writing off bad debts after 180 days. Banks became increasingly reassured that Al Amana was not a charity programme that was going to vanish and leave behind a trail of unpaid loans, and increased their lending to Al Amana, allowing it to grow dramatically. By the second half of 2006, demand for loans had surged to the extent that Al Amana was operating at 180 % over budget.

A Moroccan bank, Banque Marocaine du Commerce Extérieur, was the initial provider of funds and banking services for Al Amana. However, Al Amana has since diversified its funding sources so as not to be solely dependent on one bank. In 2007, Al Amana received a US$27 million guaranteed loan from Société Générale Marocaine de Banques (SGMB); a US$36 million guaranteed loan from Groupe Banques Populaires; a US$33 million unsecured loan from Banque Marocaine du Commerce Extérieur; a US$23 million loan from Crédit Agricole; and a US$16 million loan from Credit du Maroc. Besides these long-term loans of up to 10 years maturity, all from Moroccan banks, the banks also provided Al Amana with overdraft facilities that by the end of 2007 amounted to US$62 million. In July 2007, to strengthen its capital base, Al Amana signed a MAD100 million (US$13 million) subordinated loan agreement with SGMB which was fully guaranteed by PROPARCO, the investment arm of Agence

Française de Développement. As quasi-equity, the loan will facilitate future bank and bond financing.

In 2006, in recognition of the fact that Al Amana had outgrown its basic management information system capacity, an in-depth study was commissioned to make recommendations to improve the organisation and staffing. As a result, Al Amana was able to take decisive action to restructure by introducing agencies. In 2007, Al Amana engaged the Sopra Group of France to develop and install the MIS. The management information system has been developed further in-house, in partnership with Fondation Zakoura, to generate economies of scale.

In 2007, Al Amana invested heavily, using of its own resources to expand its network. The institution invested in feasibility studies, for example to examine the scope of new sites for branch expansion, or the effect of Al Amana's lending on reducing poverty. It also invested in communication, brochures and direct marketing. Despite this sizeable expense, most of the awareness about Al Amana has come about through word of mouth rather than the mass media.

The bankers' view of Al Amana

Société Générale Marocaine de Banques (SGMB) entered the microfinance sector in 1996. It provides finance to seven out of the 12 Moroccan MFIs with a combined lending portfolio of more than MAD600 million (US$62 million). SGMB requires audited statements and a business plan before considering a loan application, but after 10 years of dealing with MFIs in Morocco it has created close links with the largest four.

SGMB's first loan to Al Amana was motivated by compliance with its global strategy of corporate social responsibility rather than a firm belief in Al Amana's business. However, SGMB recognises that Al Amana has transformed its organisational structure and approach to become a professional financial service provider with a sound business plan.[14] It has a portfolio size that allows it to apply for increasingly larger loans, and has consistently shown PAR ratios of less than 1 %.

Al Amana's approach to dealing with banks evolved in part by the banks' own requirement for proof of MFIs' financial rigour before they would lend to them. SGMB charges an average of 8 % for its loans to Al Amana; and Al Amana's average on-lending rate is 15 %. The interest margin for the MFI is tightening and, as bank lending becomes more prevalent than DFI lending, the margin will continue to be squeezed. Al Amana's strategy of reducing the interest rate it charges to its customers means that it needs to secure greater levels of long-term cheaper finance to remain competitive.

Unlike SGMB, the Banque Marocaine du Commerce Extérieur (BMCE) lends to Al Amana without requiring DFI guarantees. When Al Amana first approached BMCE in 2005, the bank studied its financial statements and was impressed with the transparency of the data provided. Although the bank's main offices are in Casablanca, the financial centre of Morocco, the relationship with Al Amana was developed in Rabat. Al Amana had also decided to bank with BMCE so there was already a good customer–banker relationship. In 2005, BMCE recognised the great potential of the microfinance sector, and this, combined with the strong balance sheet of Al Amana, meant it was willing to grant substantial loans to Al Amana. Until then, BMCE had loaned Al Amana a maximum of MAD20 million (US$2.5 million). BMCE has some concerns about Al Amana's weaknesses. These include the inadequacy of its management information system, although the bank recognises that Al Amana has recently invested in its upgrade; the risk management function and weak internal controls; and the relatively high price of loans disbursed by Al Amana compared with mainstream banking. The bank feels it is questionable how much longer Al Amana will be able to command such high lending rates. However, the bank acknowledges that implementing the Al Amana lending methodology carries a higher operating cost than traditional banking. However, BMCE still views its lending to Al Amana as part of its corporate social responsibility programme, rather than a true business partnership, even though it is profitable for the bank. Compared to its other corporate banking activities, its lending to Al Amana is small.

Conclusion

Al Amana has shown that microfinance providers can grow organically and become successful and profitable formal financial service providers. Moreover, Al Amana is offering relatively low-cost financing to thousands of poor farmers, artisans and traders. There were criticisms within the industry in the early part of the decade that having such low PAR and default rates underscores Al Amana's conservative lending strategy. However, this was mainly because Al Amana was still establishing itself within the market and, as explained above, the organisation is now taking more risks, though managing them well. There is also a view that the MFI should be reaching out even more aggressively to the poorer segments of society instead of aiming to provide larger loan amounts to its existing customers. However, the average loan amount is still relatively low – around MAD5 000 (US$655) at the end of 2007.

Al Amana's low default rate has meant that scarce financial resources are being distributed among a financially excluded group that has previously had little or no access to finance. As this group of people obtains financial access and moves up towards bank finance or other loan cycles with MFIs, Al Amana is continuously reaching out to the next level down the income scale. It is investing in infrastructure in sparsely populated areas, taking greater risks, developing other loan products such as start-up finance, and monitoring not only its loan portfolio but also the effect of its lending in reducing poverty in the communities where it works.

Al Amana's net income in 2006 represented about 3 % of the average loan portfolio, while the global average for MFIs is 10 %, significantly reducing the cost to clients.[15] This cheapening of finance helps make it more affordable to the most disadvantaged. However, Al Amana may not be able to sustain the continuous efficiency gains for much longer. The prevalent lending rate from banks to Al Amana is 8 %, and Al Amana is able to keep a low cost of finance thanks to concessionary rates received from development funds. As the entity continues to grow, it will require more support staff to administer increasing numbers of individual and housing loans, and it will probably see its cost advantage eroded. Eventually the management will have to make a choice between keeping the strategy of increasing operating efficiency with rising borrowing costs (as it assumes increasing amounts of bank lending and less subsidised lending) versus the strategy of continuous lowering of lending rates to customers.

Having said this, Al Amana's success in transforming itself from a small MFI to a regulated financial institution is remarkable, not least because of the numerous challenges it has overcome and continues to face. Having already gained an excellent reputation in Morocco, Al Amana's fame is spreading further afield: it was recently identified as the tenth most successful MFI in the world.[16] This success can be attributed to a combination of factors: perseverance, hard work, patiently gaining peoples' trust, gaining the respect of the Moroccan banks, and working closely with the government to try to influence policy development related to microfinance. It has also benefited greatly from governmental and donor support, in particular USAID who founded Al Amana and maintained long-term support both in financial and operational terms. Finally, Al Amana has built up good relations with all the key players in the microfinance sector in Morocco – the government, donors and other MFIs – which have helped them to influence others and build their strong reputation.

Afriland First Bank and the *mutuelles communautaires de croissance*: Commercial links with the rural informal sector

> Afriland First Bank, Cameroon's fourth-largest bank, has teamed up with village-based mutual societies to allow them to provide a more diverse and better quality range of services to a mainly agricultural client base. For the bank, maintaining this linkage structure means it is a channel for finance and also a source of deposits because surplus funds from this growing network of mutuals are banked with it. First Bank is also actively developing its own market by co-funding, with donors, a non-profit organisation that builds the capacity of the mutuals and ensures the network works efficiently.

Following the financial sector crisis in Cameroon in 1986–1988, a study was carried out by businessman Dr Paul Fokam, which revealed that 95 % of the population in Cameroon were excluded from access to services provided by the banking sector. Given their lack of access to formal financial services, people in the rural areas saved and managed their financing requirements through informal types of institutions, such as the *mutuelles*. These member-based institutions are formed by the village population as mutual funds built through the contributions made by each member of a particular village. However, despite the services provided by *mutuelles*, many of the financing requirements in the rural areas still could not be met as these informal institutions operated on a very limited scale. Thus, individuals and households were often still forced to borrow from loan sharks and *tontines*.[17]

In 1992 Dr Fokam was appointed CEO of CCEI Bank, which was renamed Afriland First Bank in 2002 and is now Cameroon's fourth-largest bank. The bank sought to expand its reach to unserved markets, especially to the rural informal sector, by linking with the *mutuelles communautaires de croissance* (community-based mutual funds) or MC^2.

At the bank level, a team was formed which is responsible for linking with the different MC^2 units: they provide training for the MC^2 officers who act as agents to the banking system, they determine the surplus liquidity within the different MC^2 units that can then be deposited with First Bank, and handle the cash requirements of the different mutual funds as well as their refinancing.

To further support the development of MC^2, the Appropriate Development for Africa Foundation, or ADAF, was formed. It is registered as a non-profit NGO that acts as an intermediary between the different MC^2 units and various national and international organisations. Its main role is to build the institutional capacity of the MC^2: it conducts feasibility assessments for the setting up of MC^2 units; provides support in the creation, development and control of procedures in place at the MC^2 level; and co-ordinates the activities of, and provides assistance to, the MC^2 network. ADAF operations are partly funded by First Bank, along with several national and international donors.

The mutual funds or MC^2 units are defined as associations by law.[18] Each one has a general assembly that represents all the members of the mutual fund; a board of directors that oversees the administration and management of the mutual fund; and an executive secretariat, which is responsible for the day-to-day management and operations of the mutual fund and is accountable to the board. This secretariat often includes a treasurer, an accountant and a cashier, who are members of the community and the mutual fund. All MC^2 units have separate advisory committees that are elected by the general assembly and formed by members who have a certain social standing in the community, such as traditional leaders or local authorities who are community members. This advisory committee is in charge of settling conflicts and disputes.

Figure 3.4 Global approach of MC^2 model

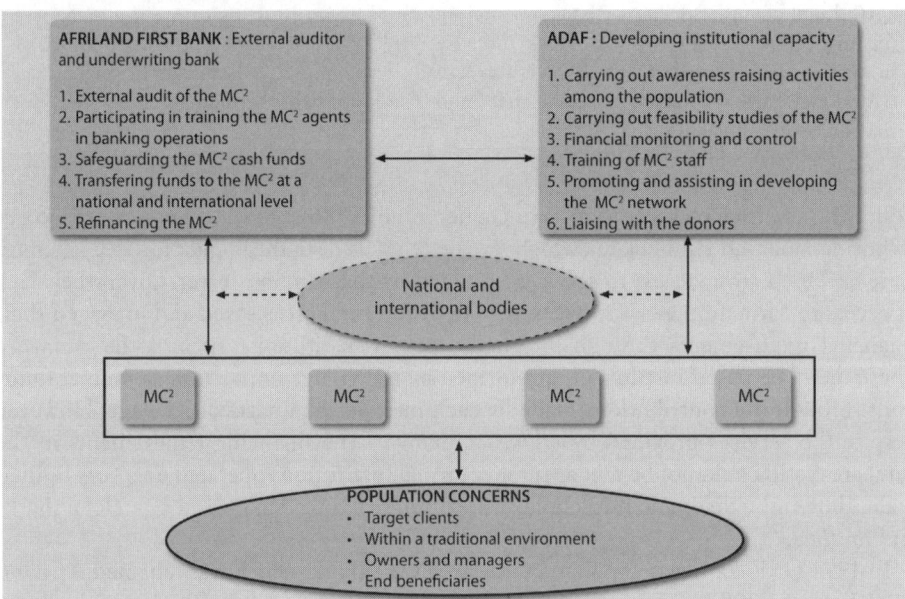

Source: Afriland First Bank

At the start of the linkage scheme in 1995, Afriland and ADAF worked with existing mutual funds, but they gradually started to encourage the formation of new MC^2 units to cover unserved areas in the country. At the outset, fewer than five mutual funds participated in the scheme; by the end of 2006, this number had grown to 63. By January 2008, the MC^2 network had a membership base of 8 941 clients. Between December 2006 and January 2008, total funds mobilised increased by 27 %, amounting over CFA14 billion (more than US$27 million). The total loan portfolio exceeded CFA24 billion (more than US$45 million).

Through the linkage mechanism, individuals and households – especially from the remote villages and rural areas – previously excluded from banking are slowly being introduced to the formal financial sector. This is being done within their customary environments, so that people are not asked to undertake their financial activities in an unfamiliar setting. The use of a village-based institution ensures that these individuals maintain a sense of ownership that is crucial to the success of MC^2. Thus, while support is provided in setting up and developing the capacity of the mutual funds, it is a strict rule that MC^2 units may be formed only by the village population and the community members. On the other hand, the support provided under the linkage scheme, especially human resource training and management in the different MC^2 units, is designed to ensure that the mutual funds are a safe haven for deposits and that the funds mobilised are allocated in the most efficient way possible. Moreover, members are also supported to ensure that they are able to make effective and efficient use of the financial services. The combination of all these interventions helps make the scheme successful. This community-based model aims to make rural populations aware of their management skills: it helps them understand that they are in control and are the only ones capable of providing lasting solutions to their problems.

Another important feature of this linkage scheme is the clear distinction made between the provision of financial and non-financial services through two separate institutions: First Bank (the bank) and ADAF (the NGO). ADAF administers the capacity-building activities for the mutual funds and their members. While these activities are important to ensure the long-term sustainability of the institutions with which Afriland is partnering, they carry a cost that cannot be borne by the bank and therefore has to be covered through grant funds generated by ADAF as an NGO. Providing these non-financial services also acts as an incentive for the different mutual funds, and encourages participation in the scheme.

It is also important to note that while the mutual funds maintain poverty reduction as a clear objective, they are not ideological in their approach to client targeting. Thus, many of the MC^2 units include in their membership village leaders and people who are considered economically better off or not especially poor, but who are influential. The MC^2 movement considers this an effective strategy to ensure that an adequate savings base is generated and maintained, and to guarantee credibility, especially during the initial setting up of the mutual fund. When the people in the villages see that their leaders and the elite in their communities are participating in the scheme, they become convinced that their money will not be lost or misused or that the scheme will simply disappear or fold up in a few months.

Significantly, the credibility of the mutual funds is strongly reinforced through their association with First Bank. Having a bank behind the scheme gives it a certain reputational capital that provides a competitive advantage over other typical informal savings and credit schemes. The deposits made by individuals at the MC^2 units earn interest in the range of 2.5 % to a little over 4 %, which is below the average rate in the commercial banking sector in Cameroon (5 %). These funds are then used to finance lending activities in the mutual funds, and surplus funds are invested with First Bank.

Recognising the dominance of agriculture-based activities in the rural areas where many of the mutual funds operate, First Bank through ADAF also helped to develop a contract farming model that makes use of the links established between the MC^2 network and agri-businesses in Cameroon. In this scheme, ADAF and the participating MC^2 units act as both banker and advisor to their farmer-clients: they provide useful advice on ways to minimise crop risk and increase output. Business development services such as training in financial and business management are also provided. Agri-businesses make use of the network of mutual funds to disburse payments to smallholder farmers with whom they contract. Without such a scheme, payment disbursement and collection would be exposed to risks as individual farmers or their representatives would have to collect the payments themselves and travel long distances while carrying cash. In many cases, people have been robbed and lost cash payments, and there have also been a number of deaths. The linkage mechanism is more reliable and safe as well as being a more efficient payments system for the smallholder farmers.

Afriland First Bank is also working with two other double-bottom-line financial institutions to provide support services to those who have no access to the banking system: Mutuelle Financière des Femmes Africaines (MUFFA) and the Micro Trust Fund Trust. The former is a savings and credit co-operative meant especially for women, to help them raise savings and have access to traditional banking services. By December 2007, MUFFA had more than 5 000 members, and the total loan portfolio exceeded CFA300 million (more than US$0.5 million). Savings collected by MUFFA amounted to CFA625 million (more than US$1.2 million).

Micro Trust Fund is a venture capital vehicle, which invests in microenterprises with significant growth potential, supporting their medium- to long-term financing needs once they have reached the stage of being capable of increasing production. The rationale behind setting up the fund is to enable MFIs such as the mutual funds to grant loans that have longer maturity periods, which the *mutuelles* are generally not able to do, given the short-term nature of the deposits they mobilise. This initiative addresses the demand for long-term resources for enterprises engaged in innovation and those seeking higher levels of productivity. By the end of 2006, total funds mobilised amounted to over CFA11 billion (more than US$24 million), with a total outstanding loan portfolio of US$10.9 million.

ADAF is also expanding its network of partners. It is conducting professional exchanges with the Project of Support to the National Program of Microfinance, the Popular Centre of Education and Animation for Development, the Women Investment Club, and several universities. ADAF has also developed close relations with a number of international funders.

By linking with community organisations, First Bank has significantly expanded its business, and extended financial inclusion to previously unserved rural areas in Cameroon.

Endnotes

[1] The Ghana cedi (¢) was replaced by New Ghana cedi (GH¢) on 1 July 2007, each new cedi being 10 000 old cedis. Although most of the research for this case study was completed before the redenomination, for consistency the new cedi is used in this publication.

[2] The 2005 average GNI per capita for sub-Saharan Africa excluding South Africa was US$451, calculated from World Bank World Development Indicators. The 2005 GNI per capita figures for Ghana's immediate neighbours are, Ivory Coast US$650, Burkina Faso US$400 and Togo US$350.

[3] Honohan (2007).

[4] Ghana Statistical Service (1999).

[5] The clients of the *susu* collectors in Ghana are less poor than those of Jyothi, the deposit taker in India, but the function is the same (Rutherford 2001).

[6] This is demonstrated by FinScope surveys undertaken in the region. Ernest Aryeetey (2005) provides an interesting discussion about the informal and semi-formal financial sectors.

7   These patterns are vividly described in Rutherford (2000). This book is out of print, but a summary is in Rutherford (1999).
8   The limited reach of formal financial institutions is demonstrated Beck, Demirguc-Kunt, Peria & Soledad (2006). The authors show that in a number of African countries there is only one bank branch per 200 000 people. See also Honohan (2007).
9   Two thirds of the countries in the region (10 out of 15) are in the lowest category, Low Human Development, in the 2007/2008 Human Development Index compared to less than half (12 of 26) in the rest of sub-Saharan Africa; 40 million adult West Africans and one-third of under-fives in the region are malnourished (UNDP, 2007).
10 ACCION has created joint ventures with four commercial banks, SOGEBANK (Haiti), Banco del Pichincha (Ecuador), Banco ABN-AMRO Real (Brazil), and Ecobank (West Africa) to begin lending to the self-employed poor.
11 The initial total budget was US$15.5 million although only US$10.5 million was ultimately needed.
12 Tanji (2006 : 17).
13 Mix Market (online).
14 Interview with SGMB staff (March 2007).
15 Microfinance Information Exchange (2007).
16 Ibid.
17 *Tontines* are a form of rotating savings and credit associations in Cameroon, sometimes referred to as *njangis*. *Tontines* are based on shared social characteristics (ethnic groups, socio-professional category, sector of activity, location of residence). Each member contributes on a regular basis and, in turn, has access to the capital formed: distribution is done on the basis of a lottery, or the consensus of the group or even in some cases through auctions.
18 In some of the literature, MC^2 are also often loosely referred to as *rural development microbanks* as they provide quasi-banking services to the population in rural areas. They are, however, at present, unregulated institutions providing financial services in both urban and rural areas of the country.

Chapter Four
Remote distribution

Advances in technology and successful models of remote distribution in countries such as Brazil have made remote distribution a hot topic in the broader debate about access to financial services. Essentially, remote distribution, or branchless banking, is about delivering formal financial services without having to invest in the infrastructure of a bank branch, perhaps because it would be prohibitively expensive to do so. Some banks believe that face-to-face contact in a branch, between a customer and a member of its staff matters. For example, Bank Windhoek is rolling out bank branches in remote areas in Namibia; other banks are using prefabricated, or modular, bank branch designs to drive down the cost of their physical infrastructure.

Other organisations have taken the view that some transactions do not need a human interface – a simple cash withdrawal being one. In both these case studies, existing infrastructure – typically retail outlets – is being used as a distribution channel. The social benefits of easily accessible financial services are documented in these studies but it also seems to be good business for all the organisations concerned, including the retailers through which the services are offered. The Hollard/Pep case tests whether insurance, which is a more complex product to offer than transactional banking, lends itself to this kind of remote distribution.

Remote distribution is an especially important area for financial services in Africa. The dramatic rate at which the continent is urbanising suggests that investment dollars (or rands or shillings) in financial services will increasingly be directed towards those urban areas where the customer base is growing, such as in the settlements around the continent's capitals. Alternative, cost-effective forms of outreach will be necessary if Africa's rural areas are not to be left behind.

First National Bank and ATM Solutions: Providing services to the masses

> The transforming impact of ATMs on access to banking services needs no explanation. This case study profiles how two organisations have harnessed the ATM concept in very different ways and have not only made money in the process, but have also brought profound benefits to communities in remote areas. First National Bank (FNB), one of South Africa's big four banks, eager to seek out new markets, has pioneered the use of Mini-ATMs. These relatively inexpensive devices are typically installed in a small shop or petrol station. ATM Solutions manages the deployment, service and maintenance of remote ATMs for Southern African banks other than FNB. From inception, growth was rapid, showing how great the demand for cash can be at different times of day and night and in different locations.

The ATM is an example of how technology can change the way people live. Simple to use, but able to offer complex transactions, the ATM is being used to improve access to financial services for the unbanked and for people living in remote locations.

FNB, one of South Africa's big four banks and subject to banking and industry regulation, and ATM Solutions, a non-listed, privately owned company, are two organisations in South Africa that illustrate different ways of deploying ATM devices in rural areas. Whether by design or by default, both players are making a difference in poor and underbanked communities.

South Africa's banking services in context

According to FinScope, a national household survey which focuses on financial services needs and use across all sectors of the South African population, access to financial services in the country is improving: in 2008, 63 % of the 31.5 million adults over the age of 16 were formally banked, compared to only 46 % in 2004, an annual increase of more than 1.5 million people.

The 2006 survey found that, even though access to banking was improving, poor people still say that banks are too far away or too expensive for them, or that they do not have a regular income and therefore have no need to be banked. And, although the mass market understands that banking in branches is more expensive than using ATMs, it still prefers to deposit cash at branches, where it feels more secure that the cash is safely in the designated account.

Despite this, David Cracknell, author of *Electronic Banking for the Poor – Panacea, Potential and Pitfalls*, outlines several advantages that the roll-out of ATMs has over branches in all markets, and in low-income markets specifically. ATMs are flexible and can be fully functional teller machines that accept deposits, dispense cash and offer a range of other functions, such as inter-account transfers and cellphone airtime purchase. Or they can only dispense cash. Although they are expensive to own and operate, they are much less so than branches, and offer a much cheaper way of processing large volumes of withdrawals than over-the-counter services.

He adds that when using an electronic banking solution, including ATMs, customers take several factors into account, including the accessibility of the service, affordability and ease of use. Walking many kilometres to access banking services is inconvenient, and transport is costly for customers. Saturating an area is preferable to a wider, thinner distribution. Furthermore, transactions must be affordable. Finally, the systems should be user friendly. Services should be standardised so that wherever the solution is used, customers are familiar with the procedure they have to follow. Customers should also have access to advice, whether this is through call centres, publicity or a physical presence.

Cracknell adds that from an institutional perspective, the electronic banking solution should increase profitability. He says that banks therefore need to give careful consideration to a number of factors: functionality, building volume through segmentation, fees and charges, efficiency, controlling development costs, distribution channels and partnerships.

The big bank – First National Bank

Originating as the Eastern Province Bank when it was formed in Grahamstown in 1838, FNB is the oldest bank in South Africa, and now trades as a division of FirstRand Bank Limited. It provides a full range of banking products and services, including individual, commercial, corporate and public-sector banking. For the 2007 financial year, the bank's profit before tax increased by 26 % from R4.5 billion to R5.6 billion.[1] As a financial services organisation, FNB is a signatory to the Financial Sector Charter, signed on 17 October 2003, in terms of which the sector voluntarily committed itself to transformation and black economic empowerment (BEE). Section 8 of the charter addresses access to financial services, stating that 'the financial sector commits itself to substantially increase effective access to first-order retail financial services to a greater segment of the population within Living Standards Measure (LSM) 1–5'.[2] LSM1–5 covers the population groups at the poorer end of the market.

First-order retail products and services include transaction services. In essence, the charter contains an undertaking by the banking industry to take banking services to rural communities. Specifically, the charter targets the deployment of branches and ATMs to make banking more accessible. The target was that by 2008, 80 % of the population in LSM1–5 must have access to a bank branch within a 15 km radius and an ATM within a 10 km radius.

FNB's Mini-ATMs

FNB has chosen to use Mini-ATMs in this market, and the company officially launched the concept in 2001. The Mini-ATM is an ATM emulation device, and works just like a normal ATM, except that it does not dispense actual cash. Instead, installed at a retail outlet, the machine works with any local South African bank card that is issued to the customer with a personal identity number (PIN). The customer swipes the card, enters the PIN and stipulates the amount he wants to withdraw. The machine issues a slip, which the customer takes to the store owner, who then pays over the amount. FNB electronically calculates the total cash amount paid out by the merchant and then pays this amount directly into the store's account.[3] This means that Mini-ATMs do not need to be supplied with cash. Clients can also use the devices to obtain balances and to buy prepaid services from the telecommunications service providers Vodacom, MTN, Cell C and Virgin Mobile,[4] and in addition, they can buy Eskom electricity.

The evolution of FNB's Mini-ATM

As far back as the early 1990s, FNB had been exploring ways to reach people in the low-income market and make it easy for them to withdraw cash. Through its soccer sponsorships, FNB enjoyed significant brand equity among low-income consumers, and the bank realised it had a large customer base that it was not servicing as well as it could.

FNB therefore entered into a relationship with mass-market retailer Score to install first-generation non-ATM devices in its stores. FNB conducted several pilots with Score, but problems with telecommunications forced the bank to abandon the project.

At the time, internationally, retailers and banks were offering cash back at the point of sale. While this service would have satisfied a need, it was not yet available in South Africa. Without cash-back at point of sale, FNB regarded the Mini-ATM as a good solution to a market opportunity, because it had distinct advantages over the conventional ATM.

When it originally introduced its ATM machine, FNB recognised an opportunity to use the device to provide financial services in rural areas. Deploying ATMs in remote, underserviced areas has its challenges. It is expensive to manufacture and buy ATMs, and they also have a high-cost servicing model. Logistics are complex and difficult to control. Cash has to be replenished regularly, and poor roads make access difficult for cash vans. Moving large volumes of cash into rural areas is a security risk and because of the distance travelled, cash-in-transit delivery fees are higher. As such, conventional ATMs have to perform more than 5 000 transactions a month to break even.

FNB's Mini-ATMs have improved access to financial services in remote areas.

Moreover, technological difficulties made using conventional ATMs in remote areas more difficult. ATMs need to work seamlessly, but are likely to fail more often in dustier areas and then need a technician to go and service them – which is more difficult and expensive in remote areas. To receive and dispense cash, ATMs must have a specific quality of currency notes, but in remote areas, notes tend to be worn or limp. ATMs operate online, and need reliable and affordable telecommunications networks and a power supply. However, telecommunications infrastructure in these areas was not well developed, took months to install and was often less reliable.

The Mini-ATM provided the solution. The device works in a similar way to a conventional ATM, but on a lower cost basis. The machine is small enough to sit on a retail counter, in a 50 cm by 46 cm space, and can run on a 12-volt battery without electricity. The infrastructure required is also less demanding, allowing FNB to install machines in hard-to-reach areas.

Technologically, the Mini-ATMs broke new ground by using the common Internet Protocol (IP) as opposed to IBM's proprietary Systems Network Architecture protocol, which is used in normal, full-sized ATMs. The IP protocol enables the terminals to use communication networks such as GSM and GPRS[5] used in cellphones, and the VIP dial service of Telkom, South Africa's fixed-line provider. FNB saw several advantages in using GPRS in that it does not rely on landlines and therefore they would not have to wait for these lines to be installed. It also eradicated service interruptions caused by cable theft,[6] and lowered communication costs.[7] Because of these savings, Mini-ATMs require less than 1 000 transactions a month to break even.[8]

The bank decided to pilot the Mini-ATM again, and approached Score to offer the pilot sites. The success of this pilot marked the beginning of FNB's Mini-ATM deployment, and since the official launch in 2001, FNB has deployed 1 295 Mini-ATMs in South Africa, 79 in Botswana, 98 in Namibia, 12 in Swaziland and nine in Lesotho.[9]

Mini-ATM business model

Mike Arnold, CEO of FNB ATM from November 2003 to March 2008, explains that ATM economics fix the costs of installing an ATM and influence how many machines can be deployed. 'So as the population density decreases, there will be fewer machines,' he says. 'The trade-off occurs around the break-even volume and density of the population. But, the lower the break-even point the more machines we can install.'

At the same time, he says, banking is about ongoing relationship management. 'Banks have points of interaction with their clients and the distance to an ATM device is critical for this,' he says. Thus, for FNB, the deployment of Mini-ATMs is not only about being able to install a greater number of machines to enable customers to use the bank more frequently, but also to travel shorter distances to do so.

FNB therefore had to design a business proposition so the retailer would see the value of having a Mini-ATM in the store. In developing this proposition, FNB wanted to ensure that the retailer could enjoy tangible benefits from housing the machine. Among these is that turnover can increase by as much as 15 % to 20 % when there is an ATM in-store, and that the retailer has to hold less cash. From a community perspective, money gets recycled in the community, instead of being spent where community members have previously had to go to get cash.

'We want the retailer to feel like a business partner, to promote the use of the machine to clients and ensure the machine is working so that clients are satisfied with the service,' explains Arnold. As such, in terms of the financial model, while the retailer pays a monthly rental for the Mini-ATM, FNB pays the retailer a rebate per withdrawal.

Because retailers often only have a certain amount of cash in their till at a time, it is important to manage customers' expectations to ensure that retailers can honour their withdrawals. FNB has therefore modified the Mini-ATM to include a tag indicating maximum daily withdrawal limits at specific times.

Challenges

FNB has had to address a number of challenges in the roll-out of Mini-ATMs. For example, microlenders sometimes take advantage of the proximity of Mini-ATMs to force payment from their clients or have also sometimes taken possession of customers' cards and PINs. Some retailers have demanded that customers buy something in their store before they hand over the cash. There was also potential for duplication of slips for fraudulent purposes.

FNB had to manage the use of fraudulent slips. It decided to modify the original device, which contained a single printer that produced a slip detailing the store name, the time and date of the transaction, and a number sequence, to include a second printer next to the till, which prints a slip that the merchant uses to match with the customer's slip. 'We also recognised the need to educate the retailer about checking the slip to prevent fraud,' says Arnold. Mini-ATMs are never installed at microlenders' premises, and suspected cases of card and PIN retention are reported to the regulatory authorities.

'The relationship between FNB and the retailer is critical to a successful Mini-ATM installation,' he says. 'Therefore the bank applies an extensive screening process to assess store location and to determine whether the retailer is trusted in the community. The retailer signs a contract outlining each party's duties and obligations. If the retailer proves untrustworthy, or unscrupulous, demanding customers shop in the store to receive their cash, for example, FNB removes the machine.' To date, FNB has removed fewer than five machines.

FNB has also sought to increase the number of transactions made from Mini-ATMs by each customer by decreasing transaction fees. 'When it was first launched, customers viewed the Mini-ATM as an extension of the ATM. The charges for using a Mini-ATM were priced at the same level as an ATM because, initially, the Mini-ATM was expensive to deploy,' says Arnold. 'However, in November 2004, we adjusted the Mini-ATM pricing strategy.'

The bank introduced a simpler pricing scheme: R1.50 for transactions between R10 and R500; and R5 for withdrawals between R500 and R1 000. 'Many cardholders in emerging markets disliked the previous percentage calculations,' explains Arnold. 'They want to know exactly how much the transaction will cost.'

The bank thought that if fees were less of an inhibitor, customers would use the device for more services. 'We assumed that people would change their behaviour and withdraw small amounts more often. But people drew large amounts less frequently,' says Arnold. 'In the rural communities people generally receive money through remittances or social grants. They then buy a monthly basket of goods, because travelling to stores in another town is time consuming and costly.' This trend of withdrawing larger amounts less frequently is not unique to the Mini-ATM, however. FNB is observing the same pattern at all of its ATMs, particularly when inflation increases the costs of basic goods.

In 2004, FNB conducted an industrial theatre campaign, presented in the relevant vernacular and incorporating characters from local television soap operas, to increase customers' understanding of Mini-ATMs. The bank also enhanced signage around the device. This campaign, coupled with the reduced transaction fee, led to double-digit growth in transaction volumes compared with single-digit growth the year before. This trend has continued.

Benefits to customers

The benefits of having easy access to cash via ATMs are well documented. These include access to banking for low-income households; reduced travelling time and transportation costs; revival of local economies because of cash recycling; improved turnover and decreased cost of cash for retailers; and commission for the retailer once break-even volumes are achieved.[10] In addition, customers start to understand ATM cards and PINs – a critical element in using financial services.

A small business owner in the Eastern Cape, Thabang Ntseno, has rented the FNB Mini-ATM for a modest monthly fee. He says the installation of the ATM has doubled his profits because he made money out of transactions, and customers also tended to buy more from his store. 'Customers can now draw money. They don't have to travel long distances to get cash and can immediately buy goods from my store, which is good for my business,' says Ntseno. 'I get about 10 people daily who make transactions from the Mini-ATM. From that I receive a rebate for every transaction made.'[11]

FNB pays commissions to retailers on a tiered system. Thus the retailers receive no commission for the first 350 transactions they process, and thereafter an increasing value at bands between 351–500, 501–1 000, and 1 001 and above.

FNB also entered into an agreement with the Eastern Cape provincial government in 2003 to open free bank accounts to facilitate the payment of social grants such as old-age pensions and child-support grants. FNB identified trading stores in remote rural areas in which to place 242 of its Mini-ATMs. Under the agreement, the provincial government subsidises the cost of these accounts. The account holders do not pay FNB ATM charges or monthly service fees. FNB plans to negotiate with other provincial governments to conclude similar social grant payment agreements.[12]

Bushunti Liwane, a pensioner from the Eastern Cape, says the ATM has saved him a lot in transport costs. 'Before [our pensions were paid directly into our bank accounts], the government truck used to bring our pension, but since the machine came here the process has been better. The store owner fetches us and brings us to the store to get our money,' he says. Liwane has a wife and seven dependants, and withdraws his entire grant to buy groceries for his family.

Nobukela Ndlothovu, who receives social grants for both her children, comments on the convenience of the Mini-ATM. 'It is now better and faster and we can sit down while waiting. Before we used to stand in a long line waiting in the sun for our money … sometimes the government truck did not arrive,' she says.

'The more devices in areas, and the more government enables the delivery of pensions and social grants electronically, the easier it becomes for recipients, provided merchants have cash in the store,' says Elizabeth Hazell, head of ATM strategy at FNB.

This means merchants have to have cash in their tills to fulfil the demands made by pensioners withdrawing their monthly pension, which could amount to large sums of money. Some retailers make special trips to the bank to acquire additional cash to pay out pensions. Although this adds a security risk, the return for store owners is increased turnover.

'There has only been one claim in three years for retailer cash loss,' says Arnold. Most retailers find that their float is sufficient because as pensions are paid, store turnover increases. 'Pensioners generally spend their pension on food on the day they receive a payout to avoid having to travel back to the store again during the month. On pension day, money velocity in the store is much higher, with the same cash often moving between the retailer and multiple pensioners in one day,' he says

According to Hazell, a high concentration of devices and payments improves everyone's lives. 'But once you are involved in a community providing a service, it is very difficult to exit. This is why we conduct detailed site assessments before deployment.'

Success for FNB

The Mini-ATM strategy falls within FNB's mass portfolio strategy, a market it refers to internally as the 'smart segment'. This services individuals earning less than R81 000 a year.[13] The bank's target markets for Mini-ATM deployment are those in rural and underserved areas, where customers are ATM cardholders, pension and social grant recipients, or Mzansi account holders,[14] as well as small retailers in these areas, catchments where ATMs are not viable, and low-income communities.

During the 2007 financial year, the segment's profits increased significantly, mainly as a result of strong growth in non-interest income, which increased 27 % and was driven primarily by a 22 % growth in income-generating transactions for ATM and debit cards, and a 60 % growth in prepaid airtime transactions.

Because of the link to Saswitch, customers from all banks can use an FNB Mini-ATM, and the split of non-FNB customers who use Mini-ATMs is higher than that on conventional ATMs. About 80 % of transactions on a full FNB ATM are from its own customers, while 20 % are Saswitch transactions. On the Mini-ATM, the split increases significantly, even though the Saswitch withdrawal charges are higher. Each bank that issues cards sets the withdrawal fee itself. Other banks generally set Mini-ATM withdrawal fees at the same level as Saswitch full ATM transactions. But this varies by bank, product and pricing packages and it is difficult to calculate a general figure.

Hazell notes that rural customers sometimes open FNB accounts, or switch bank accounts if an FNB Mini-ATM opens in their area. 'Where FNB deploys a device, a non-FNB account holder may open an FNB bank account in order to be able to use the device at a lower cost. Non-FNB customers may also swap from another bank to FNB to benefit from lower withdrawal charges,' she says. 'In rural areas people may open accounts because of the presence of a Mini-ATM – this is less of an influence in urban areas where there is greater density of ATMs.'

FNB's Mini-ATMs have enabled it to extend its reach in previously underserviced areas, and the bank has the highest reach into LSM1–5 in terms of the charter targets. Arnold notes that transaction growth on the Mini-ATM continues, demonstrating that there is a need for such a service.[15] The bank therefore regards the Mini-ATM as a key component in its strategy to provide services to previously unbanked people in remote rural areas.[16]

FNB has deployed more than 200 Mini-ATMs into Lesotho, Botswana, Namibia and Swaziland, with a further 100 being deployed to Namibia.

The private company – ATM Solutions

Established in 1999, ATM Solutions is the largest independent deployer of ATMs in South Africa. It is not a bank, but its network of ATMs, which are linked to Saswitch, can be used by customers of all of the banks in South Africa. It rents out its ATMs to retailers and corporates who see the benefit of having an ATM on their premises.

The company did not actively set out to extend access to financial services to underserviced areas. Instead, because of its merchant-orientated strategy, its expansion tracks that of the retail chains and other organisations that house its ATMs. Because of this, 32 % of the company's ATMs are now located in rural and previously underserviced areas.

Some of ATM Solutions' devices are therefore servicing a market previously ignored by the banks, says ATM Solutions co-founder, Steven Kark, pointing out that this is a problem which has been exacerbated by banks closing branches in these areas, thereby further reducing accessibility. 'In some areas, we have installed machines where facilities cannot be found within even 100 kilometres,' he says.

The history of ATM Solutions

The ATM Solutions story began with an article in *Forbes* magazine that highlighted the success of independent ATM deployers in the US. After a field trip to see for themselves, and an assessment of the local market, the founders of ATM Solutions, Kark and Rowan Swartz, were convinced that this model could work in South Africa. They saw an opportunity to meet the enormous demand expressed by retailers and customers for in-store cash withdrawal facilities, which no one else was addressing at the time.[17]

In their view – aside from the issues of the cost of the ATM machine, the need to install a leased line telephone connection, 24x7 maintenance contracts, and the costs of monitoring and replenishing the machines – one of the most important contributors to the high break-even point for ATMs was the banking approach itself. As a consequence, explains Kark, banks were reluctant to place machines in certain off-premise locations, away from bank branches in retail stores 'thereby essentially ignoring a massive potential customer – the retailer'. Kark and Swartz believed that, in addition to targeting an untapped retail market, off-premise ATMs would also bring convenient banking to a greater part of the population.

Kark and Swartz used an integrated access device as a base to develop their own model, which reduced the cost of deploying ATMs to roughly one half of the cost to the banks. In turn, this reduced the transaction break-even point, and meant that ATM Solutions could deploy ATMs where banks could not.

They were not deterred by the discouraging views of the dominant banks, and installed their first off-premise ATM in 2000. Within two years, the company had won contracts from clients such as Engen, Caltex and Total (all petrol companies) as well as 7-Eleven and Makro (retail chains), and Netcare (a chain of private hospitals). Within four years, the company had captured 30 % of the highly regulated, big-bank-dominated market. The company controls about 48 % of the off-premise ATM market in South Africa – that is, ATMs located away from bank branches. It is also the largest supplier of ATMs to petroleum retailers. The company was profitable in its second financial year. From the first machine installation in March 2000, the company now has a network of more than 4 000 machines dispensing R1.6 billion cash each month.[18]

ATM Solutions is the largest independent provider of in-store ATMs in southern Africa.

Access into Saswitch

One of the hurdles the company had to overcome was that, because it is not a bank, it had to have access to Saswitch via an acquiring bank so that it could process transactions. But the major South African banks were sceptical of ATM Solutions' proposal to operate a bank-branded, off-premise ATM network on a joint basis. This led to an agreement between ATM Solutions and Saambou Bank (the seventh-largest bank in South Africa at the time) in February 2000, in terms of which Saambou received a percentage of the transaction fees.

In February 2002, Saambou went into curatorship, but by then ATM Solutions' market presence had positioned the company as an attractive partner for the banks, and all four of the big banks expressed an interest in becoming the transaction-acquiring bank for ATM Solutions. ATM Solutions chose to sign an agreement with Absa in May 2002.

Since then seven banks – Absa, Standard, Nedbank, Teba, Bidvest, Mercantile and Ithala – have outsourced deployment of ATMs to ATM Solutions, and ATM Solutions has expanded to have a presence in other African countries.

ATM Solutions' business model

From its inception, the company focused on deploying the maximum number of machines in the shortest possible time so as to seize and consolidate market share, secure its position and create a barrier to entry. The strategy was to target merchants who required an ATM, and customers who required ATM services.

ATM Solutions offers three options: fully-cashed ATMs, merchant-cashed ATMs and Mini-ATMs. To increase foot traffic into outlets that house its Cash Express machines, ATM Solutions has incorporated value-added services into the ATMs. As such, its machines are able to sell airtime for Vodacom, MTN, Cell C and Telkom, and electricity. It has also included the EasyPay bill payment system on the machines, which allows customers to pay accounts ranging from telephone and electricity bills to TV licences and traffic fines.

The company manages the entire deployment, service and maintenance process. Merchants pay a rental fee for the ATM and then receive a rebate per transaction. The rebate increases as transaction volumes increase. Merchants can select to cash the machines themselves, which saves them having to pay bank charges when they deposit cash into the bank, or use ATM Solutions' cashing service. The company manages cash requirements for 60 % of the machines in the network.

ATM Solutions does all the monitoring, data mining, reporting and maintenance of the machines, and provides all the necessary support functions. This is to make its service offering as hassle free as possible for the organisations that rent its machines. To lower installation, ongoing maintenance and transaction costs, the machines use alternate wireless communication systems, providing response times that are almost equivalent to those on a leased line, at greatly reduced costs.

ATM Solutions owns and manages each aspect of the value chain. This includes ATM location assessment, which looks at predicted transaction volumes, ATM visibility and average monthly foot traffic through the location. Otherwise, the only function which ATM Solutions outsources is the physical transportation and replenishment of cash.

Providing services in rural areas

In addition to the merchant-led deployment of ATMs, which has seen ATM Solutions servicing rural areas, the company has installed about 200 strategic machines in rural areas at its own cost, or at a subsidised cost, out of a commitment to social upliftment and community development.[19]

Most merchants in remote areas rent the ATM. 'Only 200 transactions a month are needed to make installation cost effective, which means even small retailers can afford to host them,' explains Kark. 'Retailers also use their own cash to load the ATMs, so they are effectively banking their proceeds every time a customer makes a cash withdrawal.'

The owner of the farm stall in Lime Acres in the remote Kalahari region of South Africa's Northern Cape province says the installation of an ATM by ATM Solutions has attracted people to the shop, who withdraw money and then spend some of it in the store.

ATM Solutions can process transactions from any location.

The ATM machine installed at the Lucky 7 convenience store in Graafwater, about 300 km north of Cape Town, has also benefited the local community. 'The biggest town, Clanwilliam, is about 32 kilometres away,' explains the store owner. 'There is no public transport in the area and it can cost up to R150 per person for a one-way trip to Clanwilliam. Graafwater is the poorest community in the Western Cape and many people had to go to Clanwilliam to draw money to buy groceries. Now customers save money on transport and they can draw as little or as much money as they need. The community is ecstatic. My business has also increased due to more foot traffic in the store,' he says.

The owner of the OBC chicken store in Mabopane, a township outside Pretoria, says having an ATM reduces the risks associated with having cash, and he saves money on deposit fees. 'The machine also alleviates the long queues at the bank ATMs,' he says.

According to Kark, the company is also helping banks increase their rural footprint. About 60 % of the group's cash dispensers are outside the metropolitan areas. 'The ATMs are significantly cheaper to operate than the larger machines banks install, making cash-dispensing machines much more cost effective to roll out to a wider network.'

Qolora community benefits

The community of Qolora is about 70 km south of East London in the Eastern Cape, in one of the poorest regions of South Africa. FNB has deployed eight Mini-ATMs in this area, with the closest conventional ATM being in Butterworth, 40 km away.

The average cost of a return trip to Butterworth is R38. Should pensioners collect their pensions from Butterworth, they usually take a younger family member with them to help carry their food purchases on the return trip. Therefore the cost of a trip into Butterworth to draw pension money and buy monthly food supplies equates to R76, almost a tenth of the value of the monthly grant, which stood at R820 in 2006. The average cost of a return trip to East London, the nearest major city, is R66.

Having the Mini-ATMs in the village means that pensioners – indeed any community member wishing to withdraw money from a bank account – can save significantly on transport. This, says Arnold, is having a profound effect on the lives of people living in Qolora. He points out that with R66, the price of the return trip to East London, someone can buy 2.5 kg of sugar, 2.5 kg of maize meal, 2.5 kg of samp, five cans of beans, five packets of soup, two packets of tea, two litres of milk and two loaves of bread.

Russell Hulley, who owns Qolora Store, a general dealer and hardware shop, was initially hesitant about installing an ATM, but was amazed at how fast his customers adapted to the technology. He says the Mini-ATM has brought great benefit to his business, and to his customers as well, who no longer have to make the trip to Butterworth to do their banking. 'Also, doing their business in Butterworth exposed the people to criminals who stole their money at the ATMs and they were pick-pocketed on the taxis,' he says.

Conclusion

Deploying Mini-ATMs or ATMs in remote, previously underserviced areas improves people's lives. It makes access to cash, which for this market is 'king', easier and in some cases cheaper. For individuals, a main benefit is the saving on transport costs and the freedom this gives them to do other things with the money saved. For merchants, money is recycled in stores, trading volumes increase because of greater customer numbers and they also earn rebates on transaction fees. Communities benefit too in that trading increases in the area spurring the microeconomy of the community.

Whether the ATMs are financially profitable for the organisations deploying them is more difficult to answer, even with the lower break-even volumes required, as the organisations are reluctant to reveal figures. Certainly some of them are, but in areas where transaction volumes are very low, there may be a trade-off between the non-financial benefits and financial profitability.

For the banks, providing easier access to ATM services draws people into the banking system, educates them about using cards, PINs, savings and interest, and also generates brand equity in a segment where the future generation is the emerging market.

Hollard and Pep: *Prêt-a-porter*, cash-based insurance

> South African insurance company Hollard, in partnership with retail chain Pep, sells packaged insurance at an affordable price to low- and middle-income earners. Insurance companies are seeking alternative distribution channels because the economics of traditional broker-led distribution do not work for selling insurance to low-income consumers. Also, insurance often requires premiums to be deducted from a bank account, and this excludes the unbanked. Despite sensitive legal issues, such as who provides advice to the consumer in an environment where financial literacy is often weak, Pep and Hollard have worked out an arrangement for prepaying insurance that ensures that even unbanked consumers can get access to funeral or accident cover.

In March 2006, Pep, a division of Pepkor Limited, in partnership with Hollard Insurance, one of South Africa's largest privately owned insurance companies, launched a range of insurance policies activated and distributed like cellphone starter packs.[20] For several years consumer research conducted by Pep had shown a customer need for financial services of various kinds, and the company therefore actively looked for a partner that could match its customer-service-driven approach.[21]

The aim of the venture is to make buying insurance easier, more affordable and more accessible for people who do not have bank accounts, and thus no debit-order facilities, easily traceable addresses or payslips. Until now, such people were not able to buy formal insurance.

The insurance starter pack is a South African first in retailing and insurance. It originally offered a choice of family funeral, personal accident and cellphone insurance, or a combination thereof, at R19.99 a month per product. The response exceeded Hollard and Pep's expectations, not only in terms of customer response, but also because of the new business opportunities that it has opened up.

The Pep/ Hollard insurance products were the first cash-based policies available through a South African clothing retailer.

Within the first 11 months, more than 130 000 customers bought a starter pack from Pep. By the end of 2008 this number had increased to over 250 000. Funeral cover has been the most popular product, accounting for 89 % of product take-up. The simplicity of the product and ease of use to the customer are key.

In November 2008, as a result of the initial experience and further research, the product range was relaunched. The new policies cover funeral insurance, which is a well-understood concept and one that continually came up in research as a customer need, and accidental death. Premiums now range from R19.99 to R69.99 depending on whether cover is for seniors (65 to 75 years old) or families (policyholder, partner and up to five children). Personal accident insurance and cellphone insurance have been dropped from the range.

The starter pack is an innovative distribution device that includes a barcoded card containing a unique policy number. To activate the policy and to pay premiums in the future – in cash – customers present the insurance card at normal till points each month at any one of Pep's stores countrywide.

Policies are distributed through Pep stores and people do not need a bank account to buy one.

Trendsetters

Hollard is a privately owned company founded in 1980. It provides short-term, or general, insurance and life assurance products, and has grown into one of South Africa's largest insurers by focusing on niche distribution channels. The company attributes its success to strategic distribution partnerships and suitable brand matching: it develops its products and service delivery to match the brand image of its partners, and only enters partnerships when brand images are complementary or aligned.

Pep is a division of the retailing group Pepkor. It is a cash-based retailer that focuses on the lower end of the market, and has 1 159 stores nationwide, many of which are in South Africa's small towns where they are often the only such store. Hollard was already involved in a business venture with clothing chain Ackermans, which is also part of the

Pepkor Group, and thus the venture with Pep was a natural extension of this relationship as both parties identified opportunities in the cash-based market.

Under the terms of the venture – which is the first retail, cash-based insurance initiative in South Africa – Pep provides the retail, distribution and client-centric understanding, and Hollard the technical expertise.

Pep is Hollard's only cash-based retail partnership, and the insurance policies were the first cash-based policies available through a South African clothing retailer.

Prêt-a-porter insurance for the bottom of the pyramid

Pep and Hollard saw several opportunities in this market, which is what motivated the companies to develop a suitable product: the products provide real benefits for people who need them; they add value to the individual brands; and they create an opportunity to profile a cash market in terms of demographics and buying patterns.

There was a clear need for insurance in the lower-income group, confirmed by the initial take-up of the Pep Family Funeral cover in particular. The challenge was to establish a trustworthy distribution channel to serve the low-income market, and the Pep/Hollard partnership achieves this goal. Virtual cover is a difficult concept for customers to understand – they want to see 'bricks and mortar', and customers know that the Pep store is trustworthy. In addition, Pep's distribution and systems provide economies of scale that help make the insurance accessible and affordable.

The starter-pack concept is well suited to the target market. Most clients are prepaid cellphone users, and are comfortable and familiar with the prepaid type of concept. In addition, because funeral insurance is such a well understood concept, it does not need to be sold – in other words, staff do not generally need to spend a large amount of time and effort explaining the product and the mechanisms of payment.

The Pep/Hollard insurance products broadly target individuals in LSM1–6, with a national spread. Most of them are unbanked, and it is estimated that 17 million people fall into this category. The target market earns an average household monthly income between R2 000 and R5 000.

The products compete with other cash-based insurance products, such as those provided by burial societies and stokvels, and with other types of insurance sold through other retailers. Where burial societies charge between R80 and R140 a month for the same amount of cover offered by Hollard, Hollard and Pep's existing distribution and administration systems enable them to ensure that their product is much cheaper.

How it works

The insurance packs are generally placed on a rack at the till, and leaflets are available on a stand at the door of the shop giving more information about the products.[22]

While Hollard's business objective is to make underwriting profits, it is conscious of ethical and regulatory issues, and all products meet required standards, such as waiting periods and periods of grace. The products also fall within the Life Offices' Association of South Africa (LOA) standards in terms of pricing and benefits provided.

Instant activation takes place at the till point – but there is still the mandatory 30-day cooling-off period, during which the policy may be cancelled.[23] Pep staff may sell the product, but legally they cannot give advice. As their role is administrative, they do not have to be registered as agents in terms of the Financial Advisory and Intermediary Services Act (FICA). The model is structured so that advice is provided only on request via the dedicated call centre. The client has to contact the helpline to clarify any confusing aspects about the policy. Once the insurance has been activated, the Hollard call centre contacts the new client within 48 hours to provide more details about how the policy works.

To prevent policies from lapsing, a few days before the policy expires, the client receives an SMS reminder to pay the premium. If clients do not pay the premium within 30 days of the due date, they are required to pay the full outstanding premium to avoid the reinstatement of the waiting period that was applicable when the insurance was purchased.

Claims are not logged or paid at Pep outlets. To make a claim, clients or their family members contact a claims number. Customer research has shown that clients find that the process of purchasing the products, making a claim and receiving a payout is convenient.

Starter-pack insurance packs are displayed and sold in Pep stores. The policies are activated at the till.

Challenges

Hollard intends this product to be a volume-sustainable insurance offering that is affordable and accessible to the lower-income market. But it has faced several hurdles in operating in this market, primarily to do with ensuring that members pay their monthly premiums, and educating members about the products and insurance in general. The company also faces the challenges of preventing insurance fraud, and obtaining accurate client contact details where fixed or easily traceable addresses are not always available or permanent.

While policies must be legally accurate, they also need to be comprehensible for customers. Although the infrastructural reach and the fact that the premiums are collected in cash are factors that make this model work in the low-income market, there is still a challenge in terms of efficient communication with the clients. Policies are in English, but call-centre consultants can handle queries in any language, and the company plans to include the option of sending a client a copy of the policy in all of South Africa's 11 official languages.

Education is an ongoing concern, and Hollard plans to conduct community education through the media and in-store. Hollard has also changed the in-store marketing material to include posters reminding customers to pay their premiums and introduced in-store radio reminders. A new mechanism also enables clients to pay a few months' premiums upfront.

An efficient value-added model

For Hollard and Pep, the intention of these sales is also to create underwriting profits. A profit margin is built into the risk premium, which is calculated by applying actuarial models using insurance experience and trending to predict losses. The underwriting profits are shared within the joint venture.

One of the advantages of this venture for both Hollard and Pep is that it is not burdened with high distribution costs. Cost savings are achieved through the countrywide Pep store platform that provides an efficient distribution network to sell policies, collect premiums and acquire policyholder information. As all Pep infrastructure is established and sales staff are already in place, the only real cost to Pep is the addition of the two new products to the total Pep inventory of products, as well as the adaptation of their current systems.

For Hollard, the advantages in partnering with Pep lie in the wide distribution and Pep's staff training and buy-in. Pep notes that with respect to their staff–customer relationships, when it introduces a good product, staff members buy it first and word-of-mouth endorsement of the product then ensures sales.

Pep and Hollard regard the model as adding value to their brands. The joint venture has also created a growing database with information on just under 200 000 premium-paying, monthly policyholders. This data provides a valuable research tool for developing other relevant insurance and retail products, and generating new policy sales. The information gathered is valuable to Hollard and Pep as a customer-profiling and communications tool.

Such has been the success of this venture that Hollard is assessing product enhancements and new products to grow and improve on the existing offering within the constraints of simplicity, good service and consumer needs.

Endnotes

[1] FirstRand (2007).
[2] Porteous & Hazelhurst (2004).
[3] Fisher-French (2005).
[4] Mogaki (2005).
[5] Global System for Mobile Communications and General Packet Radio Service.
[6] ICT World (2005).
[7] Fleishmann (2005).
[8] Van Zyl (2005).
[9] Arnold (2006).
[10] Ibid.
[11] Mogaki (2005).
[12] Mail & Guardian (undated).
[13] FirstRand (2007).
[14] The entry-level bank account introduced by the banking industry as a Financial Sector Charter initiative.

15 Arnold (2006).
16 Van Zyl (2005).
17 ATM Solutions (2003).
18 Ibid.
19 Ibid.
20 Ford (2006).
21 Information from an interview with Robert Inglis, retail portfolio manager Hollard (March 2007) and update interview with Derek Cikes, general manager personal finance solutions Hollard; Louis Brand, commercial director Pep Stores; and John Edwards, financial services manager, Pep Stores (November 2008).
22 FinMark Trust (2006).
23 Ford (2006).

Chapter Five
Remittances and payments

The role of money transfers, or person-to-person payments, in the financial lives of poor people has become increasingly well documented in recent years. International remittances have drawn particular attention. For many developing countries, this source of finance far outstrips overseas development assistance and foreign direct investment combined. As such, there has been considerable emphasis on reducing the cost of remittances, with websites such as Send Money Home offering remitters an easy way to compare the different costs of sending small amounts of money to their families elsewhere, whether through a bank, a specialist remittance company or over the internet.

Migrancy, and therefore the direction of remittance flows, is not only a North–South phenomenon. Intra-regional migrancy, for example, stimulating remittance flows from South Africa to other countries in the region, and in-country migrancy[1] both underscore the need for remitters to be able to access a choice of affordable, formal remittance services to avoid having to use informal ways of transferring money that may be more unreliable.

The case study of Dahabshiil highlights the viability of privately run money transfer services even in an environment as complex and politically precarious as Somalia. The article by Fred Ahwireng-Obeng focuses on intra-regional remittances in sub-Saharan Africa, and the one by David Porteous considers the emerging field of government-to-person payments – how some governments in Africa are forming joint ventures with private suppliers (banks or technology providers) to deliver social payments to vulnerable citizens.

Dahabshiil: Sending money home in a conflict area

> To many, Somalia is synonymous with chaos and disintegration. To Dahabshiil, it is a market for a thriving money transfer business that provides a much-needed source of income to its customer base. Around 40 % of Africa's land mass and population are covered by countries that could be described as post-conflict, failing or fragile. Somalia has demonstrated in other sectors, notably telecommunications but also water, that it is possible for the private sector to do business in the near total absence of formal government. Dahabshiil tells a similar story from the perspective of the financial sector where traditional rules of society influence the way business is done.

The conflict in Somalia over the past decade has rendered the task of central government virtually impossible. In the lead-up to the conflict, persistent fiscal mismanagement, deteriorating physical infrastructure and public services, and high levels of corruption brought negative economic growth between 1988 and 1990. By 2004, Somalia had a per-capita income of a mere US$226. Nearly 47 % of the economically active population was unemployed. Despite the absence of central monetary and fiscal control during the conflict-ridden years, however, the private sector in Somalia has become increasingly dynamic.

A significant contribution to private sector growth has been the influx of remittance monies from diaspora communities to Somalia, estimated to be around US$500 million a year, contributing around 40 % of GDP. Estimates of remittance flows into Somalia must, however, be treated with caution. It is commonly said that the flow is about US$1 billion a year, but that represents the gross flows through the remittance companies. It includes money that goes to Somali communities in neighbouring countries, such as Kenya and Ethiopia, and counterpart transfers that are part of normal business transactions. The UNDP estimates that the net flows to households in the territory of Somalia, as a contribution to gross national income, are between US$300-US$500 million a year, and probably at the lower end of that range.

Remittances represent a vital lifeline for ordinary Somalis caught in the middle of warring clans and political factions. According to long-standing tradition, almost everyone in the diaspora is expected to send money home – and this is particularly so for those living in high-income countries. Based on surveys conducted by Dahabshiil in 2004, both women (47 %) and men (53 %) are equally likely to send money home. The average amount of most transactions is US$100, which is the typical amount that an average family needs to live on for a month in Somalia.

The recipients of these remittances live throughout the world, but most are in Somalia itself, and in Ethiopia, Kenya and Sudan. The overwhelming majority – 92 % – are urban. This is probably because most of the Somali diaspora are also from urban backgrounds, and send money to their relatives living in urban areas to pay for rent, food, school fees, medical bills and other supplies. The rural population is more likely to engage in subsistence agriculture to meet its basic needs. Women and men are equally likely to be recipients of remittances from abroad.

World Bank research showed that remittances accounted for nearly 40 % of urban household incomes in Somalia in 2004. In particular, remittances have supported the resurgence of the education sector in Somaliland. In Hargeisa, for example, 'remittances often play a central role in the livelihoods of those that receive them and help finance education, in some cases allowing the family to choose higher cost forms of education. Children in the households of people receiving remittances have relatively good school attendance rates. Moreover migrants often encourage families to whom they send money to educate their children'.[2]

Money transfer companies like Dahabshiil have successfully carved out a profitable and expanding niche market by tapping into the cultural expectations of the Somali diaspora community. By adapting the traditional *hawala* system of money transfer[3] to provide a reliable and efficient service in a post-conflict environment, Dahabshiil has ensured its profitability and sustainability.

Company background of Dahabshiil

Dahabshiil is a family business, originally founded by Mohamed Said Duale in 1970. He started trading as a remittance broker, selling imported goods from Gulf States on behalf of migrant workers and transferring the proceeds back to their families.

In 1970, Dahabshiil opened its first shop in Burao, the capital city of the Togdheer province in Northwest Somalia. Over the next 18 years, Mohamed and his son, Abdirashid, expanded the business to become the largest remittance business in the Horn of Africa. Subsequently, the business expanded into an international money transfer company with a large network of agents in the remittance source countries of North America, Europe and the Gulf. The first international network was established in the UK in 1989.

Twenty years on from the Somali civil war, Dahabshiil has more than 1 000 payout locations across the world, with 400 in the Horn of Africa, and provides a crucial money transfer service for those living in the African region. The company employs more than 2 000 people across 54 countries, with head offices in London and Dubai, and provides services to some of the world's leading humanitarian organisations, including the United Nations, Oxfam, the Department for International Development and Save the Children. Dahabshiil also supports the Somali community both in Africa and abroad, investing 5 % of its annual profit in community regeneration projects involving the development of schools, hospitals, agriculture and sanitation.

The business has zero debt, remains family-owned and is committed to its fair commission fee policy. It aims to meet the needs of the Horn of Arica migrant community by facilitating the sending of money home to their families and friends, and is diversifying its operations, with plans to establish private banks in the Horn of Africa. In January 2009, Dahabshiil received a license to offer banking services in Djibouti.

The remittance process is initiated by contacting one of Dahabshiil's worldwide agents. At the time of the transaction, information is taken from the sender, including personal details, identity, amount and destination, and the sender gives the money to the agent, being the sum to be transferred and the remittance fee of 1 %-5 %, depending on the amount. Using a proprietary web-based money transfer platform with automated compliance features, the agent transmits information about all the remittances commissioned from him daily to Dahabshiil's headquarters in London. The agent also deposits the collected money into a bank account, to be transferred to the central Dahabshiil account electronically. Dahabshiil's headquarters sorts and filters information at the central processing unit, and notifies both the paying agent and the beneficiary of the value of the transfer. In the case of Somalia, the communication may be through regional offices. The appropriate amounts are transferred to the bank accounts of the paying agents, or to a Dahabshiil account from which the agent is paid in cash. The paying agent contacts the beneficiary and verifies his or her identity. Once this is satisfactorily established, the beneficiary is paid the transferred sum in US dollars. Finally, the sender is informed that the payment has been successfully completed, and the relevant records are updated.

Key constraints

Dahabshiil's key difficulties in reaching out and providing financial services to potential clients include both technical and security issues in Somalia. Another key constraint is technological infrastructure. Although the proliferation of e-mail and mobile phones has greatly shrunk distances and made transactions easier, the costs of both accessing and maintaining this infrastructure can sometimes prove prohibitive. This is a particular problem in Somalia, where damage to the physical and communications infrastructure was extensive during the civil war. The transfer of remittances to Somalia does occasionally require physical cash to be transferred, and fluctuations in cash flows can sometimes create challenges particularly in South Central Somalia.

Dahabshiil also has to contend with significant legal hurdles, which intensified following the terrorist attacks on the US on 11 September 2001. Some remittance companies were closed down altogether after 9/11, and Dahabshiil and other financial services companies underwent extensive scrutiny. In response, Dahabshiil has established processes that have gone a long way to meet stringent international regulatory requirements.

Its other business includes banking, foreign exchange, telecommunications and real estate. Dahabshiil is a member of international money transfer associations including the International Association of Money Transfer Networks.

Dahabshiil takes meticulous care at the points of collection and payment, and proper documentation is provided at every level of the remittance process to ensure compliance. All the Dahabshiil offices have been duly licensed by the respective countries and robust anti-money laundering procedures are followed. Indeed, all Dahabshiil staff and agents undertake rigorous training to ensure they are able to implement robust strategy to prevent illegal use of the services.

The World Bank estimates that remittances are worth about US$1 billion (£610 million) a year reached Somalia from émigrés in Britain, the United States, Canada, Europe and the Gulf. Industry experts reckon that Dahabshiil may be responsible for handling two thirds of that amount.

Dahabshiil has succeeded as a commercially driven venture in one of the most inhospitable and hazardous environments in the world for business, and has provided a critical lifeline for Somalia's urban families.

ESSAY
Features and functioning of the *hawala* remittance system in sub-Saharan Africa

Frederick Ahwireng-Obeng and David T Mutombo – Frederick Ahwireng-Obeng PhD (Leeds, UK) is Professor of Economics, Wits Business School, Johannesburg, South Africa; David T Mutombo is an MBA graduate of the Wits Business School

Migrant remittance is a significant contributor to poverty alleviation in the developing world, especially Asia, Latin America and Africa. Between 7 % and 10 % of annual remittances, totaling about US$80 billion, is injected into African economies, 60 % of this transferred through informal rather than formal conduits. The reasons for this include low banking penetration of the continent and high costs of remittance through the formal system.[4] Indeed, informal funds transfer systems (IFTS) provide remittance services to remote regions of Africa not serviced by formal banking institutions. They are, however, vulnerable to abuse in carrying out illegal activities, and international efforts are in place to counter this trend. African countries appear to have the political will to contribute to this project, but they lack the capacity to supervise efficiently.

The problem confronting policymakers, supervisory and monitoring authorities is that there are various practices of informal remittance, each process varying from continent to continent in functionality and attributes. It is, therefore, difficult and ineffectual to enforce blanket legislative and regulatory measures against them.

This article evaluates the findings of a field survey to investigate the characteristic features and functioning of the *hawala* system of informal transfer of funds in sub-Saharan Africa. The scope of investigation is limited to *hawala* subsidiaries based in South Africa, and operating between South Africa and Nigeria, Angola, Ghana and the Democratic Republic of Congo. The study focuses only on funds transferred from South Africa to these countries, and it is assumed that the *hawala* businesses encountered in the survey share characteristics fairly similar to those operating elsewhere on the continent. It is further assumed that knowledge of the various features will be helpful in designing appropriate regulatory measures.

The informal *hawala* systems allows people to transfer money between sub-Saharan countries.

Characteristics of the *hawala* financial system

The *hawala* remittance system may be distinguished from other financial systems in many ways: by how it works; its attractive attributes; its apparent illegality and detrimental effects on the economies of the countries involved; and its strong links with business.

How the hawala system works

A practical way of explaining how *hawala* works is to demonstrate how money may be transferred without it actually moving between two parties in different locations. Kwabena (K) is a Ghanaian tailor living in Johannesburg. His younger cousin Yaw (Y) lives with the family at Assin Fosu in the central region of Ghana. K wants to send R10 000 to Y but because he lives in South Africa illegally and does not possess the necessary identification documents, going to the bank to transfer the money is not an option for him. Besides, he is aware that the banks not only charge high commissions and offer poor exchange rates, but are also painfully slow and bureaucratic. He therefore approaches a *hawala* agent, Kwasi Poku (KP), trading as KP Imports and Exports cc. KP offers the following terms:

- He will charge a 3–5 % negotiable commission for handling the transaction including delivery;
- Delivery is to be made within 24 hours;
- The amount transferred may be collected in any currency including cedi, the Ghanaian currency. It will indeed be delivered to Y since it exceeds US$500; and
- The rand/dollar exchange rate offered at the time was R6.20 per dollar (where R7.00 per dollar is offered by the banks).

Under these terms, K can send Y US$1 612.90 instead of US$1 428.57. K agrees to the terms and the *hawala* transaction proceeds as follows:

- K gives R10 000 to KP who, in turn, gives K an authentication code.
- KP then contacts Danso (D) in Cape Coast (capital of the central region of Ghana) with the details including the code, and instructs him to arrange to have either US$1 612.90 or the cedi equivalent delivered to Y (at Assin Foso) who needs to disclose the code to receive the funds.

Regarding settlement, KP has a liability to D, and he can redeem his position in a number of ways, such as financial, or goods and service transfers, or by transferring the liability to other intermediaries. For example, KP can settle his liability to D through reverse *hawala* or exporting goods. Assuming he imports foodstuffs from Ghana and exports a variety of manufactured products of South African origin, he can manipulate invoices to bring about the settlement. To enable him to pay back the R10 000, KP will ship manufactured goods worth R20 000 and under-invoice it as R10 000. The extra value of goods (R10 000) is the money that KP owes D. Similarly, in the reverse direction, D will over-invoice the value of foodstuffs he will send to KP from Ghana. In this case if D owes KP the equivalent of R10 000, he will over-invoice his imports as R20 000 to enable him to repay the R10 000 worth of manufactured goods received from KP.

The reverse *hawala* operation is often used for investment or for recovering education, travel or medical expenses by people from countries subjected to foreign exchange restrictions and capital controls. If a customer, Abena (A) in Ghana, wants to transfer funds to her son, Boakyie (B), studying at a South African university, she provides, in this example, Danso (D) with the equivalent amount in Ghanaian currency, the cedi, and requests that the rand equivalent be paid to her son, B, in South Africa. D may use KP directly if funds are available. If not, another agent in the network who has or is expecting funds may be used indirectly. Thus, neither reverse *hawala* transactions nor the settlement of liabilities necessarily involves the same *hawala* agents.[5]

Why is hawala so popular?

Increasing global migration has raised the need for adequate, affordable and convenient cross-border financial transfer facilities for purposes of family remittances and small business transactions. This is particularly true for Angola, the DRC, Ghana and Nigeria among several other African countries where formal banking systems are less developed than in South Africa. Thus, informal funds transfer systems, such as *hawala*, dominate these countries. *Hawala* has expanded rapidly in recent years and is much preferred to formal banking because it is more convenient, faster and cheaper to transact, and is less bureaucratic. Three factors largely account for *hawala*'s cost effectiveness.

As shown in the illustration of how the system works (see Figure 5.1), K saves US$184.33 on the exchange rate alone, and the service charge of 3 % to 5 % is not only much lower than the banks would demand, but also negotiable. Furthermore, by running the *hawala* business side by side with a formally registered business, the *hawala* component enjoys low overheads and avoids tax.

In the same example, the remittance from Johannesburg is delivered to the remote regional town of Assin Foso within 24 hours. Undoubtedly, this remarkable efficiency contrasts with the week or so it takes to complete a similar transaction through the formal banking system. A related merit of *hawala* is its reliability. Formal financial transactions usually involve two or more banks or branches, thus risking the real possibility of losing money 'in transit'. Again, *hawala* transactions entail little or no bureaucracy such as documenting and verifying customer identification details;

and the agents do not have to keep detailed records of individual transactions. In this example, K, the remitter, remains anonymous, and KP, the agent, is spared the nightmares of obligatory bureaucracy. Thus, *hawala* is convenient to both parties. Its attractiveness derives from these competitive advantages over formal financial transfer mechanisms. However, these micro level characteristic features are much less attractive from macroeconomic and legal perspectives.

Figure 5.1 Schematic representation of a *hawala* transaction

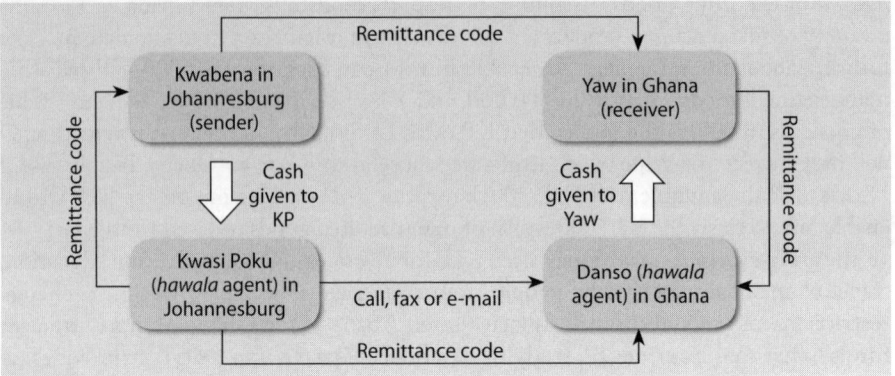

Source: Adapted from El Qorchi (2002)

What is wrong with the hawala mechanism?

From regulatory and legal perspectives, *hawala* is illegal. This is paradoxical because transactions such as K's are as well intended as they appear legitimate. Besides, they have saved many African countries, such as Zimbabwe, from total economic collapse, and have contributed to reducing poverty in several others. *Hawala*'s main problem is two-fold. First, the lack of customer identification renders it vulnerable for use in money laundering and the financing of terrorism. Second, its failure to insist on adequate recordkeeping has detrimental macroeconomic implications – both monetary and fiscal. Ironically, attempts to enforce stringent regulations to counteract these illegal activities tend to reinforce preference for the system.

Hawala undertakings are essentially balance of payment (BoP) transactions as they are linked to changes in international assets and liabilities, although these changes are not assimilated into actual BoP accounting data. For a typical African country, this creates a distorted picture of its true BoP position. The existence of foreign exchange control in most African countries, given the low banking penetration, increases the tendency to misuse *hawala* for money laundering. In countries such as the DRC and Angola where no controls exist, the incentive for extensive misuse of the *hawala* mechanism is even greater.

Money laundering consists of three phases: placement, layering and integration. *Hawala* may contribute to the process in all its phases. Since *hawala* is generally linked to genuine, formal businesses entitled to make cash bank deposits from time to time, it is difficult to determine whether such deposits originate from their own income-generating activities or from sources elsewhere. A key aspect of layering is the transfer of money from one account to another. Traditional banking creates two problems for layering.

First, unusually large deposits arouse suspicion. Moreover, the paper trail that formal transactions create provides ample evidence for investigators to trace the origins of the funds. The *hawala* mechanism, however, leaves a sparse or confusing paper trail. When invoice manipulation is used, the mixture of legal goods and illegal money leaves a trail in the international shipping network which is much more complicated than a simple wire transfer. In the integration stage, the launderer may invest in legal assets, enjoy the ill-gotten gains or invest in such illegal activities as narcotics trafficking and the financing of terrorism. Given the close links with legitimate business, *hawala* facilitates integration in all its forms. In the South Africa–Ghana transaction, K could transfer money from South Africa to Ghana, and transact a reverse *hawala* from Ghana to South Africa as part of 'normal' investment activities.

Since *hawala* transactions involve speculative practices in foreign exchange, they contribute to parallel exchange markets to siphon off the supply of much-needed foreign currency reserves from official sources. Finally, *hawala* activities contribute to loss of government revenue. To the extent that *hawala* operators do not pay taxes, both remitting and receiving countries lose tax revenues. Their activities lead also to loss of business for the formal banking sector and consequently reduce government income from these institutions.[6]

Contemporary policy initiatives

Regulatory and legislative measures designed to control the activities of IFTS, including *hawalas*, are aimed at enforcing exchange control, and fighting money laundering and the financing of terrorism. Countries, however, differ in their policies towards cross-border remittances with varying outcomes. In South Africa, the licence to operate as a foreign-exchange dealer or to transfer funds is limited to the banks. IFTS are prohibited altogether. Other countries – Ghana and Nigeria included – have passed legislation that requires money-transfer organisations to register with government, and adhere to certain regulations. The third category includes countries such as Angola and the DRC, which have no proper regulation of funds transfer so that formal and informal organisations compete freely. In this self-regulated environment, some *hawala* organisations have operated successfully. Several others have, however, been abused to advance such illegal activities as smuggling, circumventing customs duties and tax evasion.

Essentially, the regulatory framework in the first two categories requires compliance with the following three conditions: report suspicious transactions; keep proper records according to legislation; and conduct customer due diligence. In South Africa, the impact of these stringent requirements on the informal banking sector is drastic. Only about 5 % of remittances from South Africa to Southern African Development Community (SADC) countries pass through formal channels, and more than 60 % of all remittances flowing out of the country evade the regulated financial system.[7]

To sum up, the *hawala* system of remittance has a number of attractions alongside negative characteristics. The following are the main positive features:

- Relatively low remittance service fees in comparison with the banks.
- Speedy transfer of funds.
- Convenience for clients because of the minimum bureaucratic practices.
- Lack of recordkeeping, which reduces operational costs.

The undesirable characteristics include:

- Misuse for channelling funds to terrorist organisations.
- Misuse for money laundering.
- Misuse for foreign exchange diversion, tax evasion and smuggling.
- Distortion of the balance of payments accounts.

Field survey

Survey method

Given the generic attributes of the *hawala* system, the researchers explored each factor for its distinctive African features through personal interviews with 41 *hawala* agents in Johannesburg (see Table 5.1). The research employed a qualitative approach with the aid of semi-structured questionnaires and a combination of random and purposive sampling. Questionnaire responses were then coded and evaluated.

Table 5.1 Interviewed *hawala* agents operating in Johannesburg

Remittance destination from South Africa	Number of *hawala* agents interviewed
DRC (Democratic Republic of Congo)	13
Nigeria	12
Ghana	8
Angola	8
Total	41

Source: Authors

Survey findings

The field survey proved useful in elaborating on the positive and negative attributes of the *hawala* system contextualised in the African milieu. It also provided relevant practical examples from the practitioners' own experience.

Positive characteristics (sources of competitive advantage)

Cost effectiveness: The rationale for regarding cost effectiveness as a competitive advantage is two-fold. To begin with, the 3–5 % average service fee charged by *hawala* agents by far outperforms bank charges. For example, for a R250 transfer from South Africa to Angola, a *hawala* agent will charge up to R12.50, which is well below the average of R40 charged by formal financial institutions. Besides, *hawala* operators are flexible and are prepared to negotiate down the charges as the amount increases.

Speed of transaction: For *hawala* agents, it takes a simple cellphone or e-mail message to transmit information about a remittance transaction between countries. For those transacting from South Africa to Ghana and the DRC, the money is actually delivered to the recipient if it exceeds the equivalent of US$500. Another aspect of the speed of transaction is linked to their physical locations. *Hawalas* operate in central business districts as well as remote areas. In DRC, despite being a heavily populated country, banks operate in Kinshasa and Lubumbashi only. The rest of the country relies on *hawalas* to transfer money from elsewhere.

Convenience of transaction: All 41 respondents confirmed that they offer remittance services without conducting thorough customer due diligence. This is convenient for most Nigerians and Congolese living in South Africa without proper identification documents. Angolan *hawala* agents revealed that they place no limitation on their operating hours. They receive clients at odd hours, during weekends and on public holidays.

Minimum recordkeeping: All respondents considered recordkeeping as the most risky and dangerous aspect of their operations. As a result, they would rather not keep any record of their transactions except in a few cases where only names and cellphone numbers of the depositor and recipient as well as the transfer code are kept on record. No identification is required of the depositor or recipient. The normal practice is that the transfer code is not recorded on a computer or in a transaction book, and any proof of a transaction is destroyed once the funds are received. Where a record of transaction exists, it is removed from the premises shortly after it is completed. The agencies encountered in the survey operated under the guise of formally registered businesses. Most of the DRC and Angolan agencies operated as import–export companies, the Nigerian agencies as freight and courier companies, and the Ghanaian agencies as dealers in diversified ethnic African products. They all kept proper records for the formal component of their operations.

Hawala payments are popular because they are convenient, fast and do not need identification documents.

Negative characteristics (illegal outcomes of the system)

Misuse for channeling funds to terrorist organisations: All respondents, without exception, denied that African *hawalas* are used as conduits for financing terrorism. They argued that there is no terrorism in sub-Saharan Africa and that *hawalas* in Muslim countries, not those in Christian countries like the ones selected for the survey, are involved in terrorism. Besides, the average value of funds transferred in a simple transaction was only between US$87.00 and US$223.00 (see Table 5.2) and could not be considered sufficient to provide the financial support needed by terrorist organisations to function.

Table 5.2 Average value of funds transferred per transaction

Transacting countries	South Africa and Nigeria	South Africa and DRC	South Africa and Ghana	South Africa and Angola
Amount transacted (ZAR)	134	87	125	223

Source: Authors

Foreign exchange diversion: The survey confirms that sub-Saharan African *hawalas* are deeply involved in currency trading not as a core function but as an activity to give them the flexibility that adds to their competitive advantage. Their primary source of income is the service fee they charge for transferring money from one country to another. But, unlike their formal counterparts who accept payment in the currency of the country where they operate and make payment in the official currency of the recipient country, they (the informals) operate differently. They accept and make payments in any currency, including the major world currencies – the US dollar, the British pound and the European euro. This means that if the initial transaction is made in South African Rand, for example, the recipient in the DRC, Nigeria, Angola or Ghana is paid in either the recipient country's currency or in a major world currency.

Tax evasion: All respondents conceded that they do not pay tax on their *hawala* operations. An exception to this practice occurs when clients prefer not to present themselves physically at the *hawala* premises for personal reasons. In such a case, the client deposits the money into the formal business account of the *hawala* agent (since informal businesses do not keep bank accounts). Proof of payment and details of the recipient are faxed or e-mailed to the *hawala* agent. Eventually, the deposit, having been made into the account of the registered business, becomes tax deductible.

Exclusion from the balance of payments accounts: The fact that *hawala* operators are neither registered nor licensed suggests that such transactions are not reflected in the BoP accounts. The agents did not dispute this fact, but argued that the total value of their operations was so negligible that they would not make a notable difference in the BoP accounts. This view is rather short-sighted since the total population of *hawalas* and other informal businesses is unknown.

Misuse for money laundering: The *hawala* system is susceptible and can easily be misused for money laundering. This is another suggestion that the respondents never disputed. The system, as currently practised, allows anyone to send any amount of money to any destination serviced by a *hawala*. The amount involved is not questioned and the source is not queried. Worse still, *hawala* agents have no incentive to report any suspicious transaction or conduct customer due diligence as long as they remain unregistered or unlicensed.

Regulatory and miscellaneous factors

Respondents were fully aware of the regulatory framework that guides the transfer of funds between countries through financial institutions. They had, in principle, no objections to meeting the requirements once they were registered. They, however, considered the conditions rather expensive to implement and practically unrealistic to comply with, therefore there is a need to loosen up these regulations.

Miscellaneous factors that might influence the future prospects of the *hawala* business include the application of new information technology to the remittance industry. This would enable them to lower cross-border transfer fees, and offer better exchange rates and expansion of financial services to remote areas. The respondents were of the view that these efforts would not threaten their business because they did not consider themselves to be in competition with the banks on the basis of geographical spread. Furthermore, the probability of a rollout of banks to the remote villages of Africa is very low.

On the likely impact of new technology, they welcomed the prospects that it might enhance the competitiveness of the *hawala* industry by improving recordkeeping, as well as the speed and convenience of remittance.

Conclusion and policy implications

This article has adopted a qualitative approach to characterise the African version of the worldwide *hawala* remittance system regarding its functioning, attractions and negative impacts. By interviewing practising *hawala* agents rather than academic experts, conclusions and policy directions drawn from the study are practically relevant.

The *hawala* remittance system plays an important role in Africa by providing a cheap, fast and convenient way to transfer money between African countries, or between them and the rest of the world. The limited presence of financial institutions on the continent renders this role so crucial that without the *hawalas* the continent would be deprived of billions of dollars needed for subsistence, business and economic development.

Despite these attractions, *hawalas* are open to money laundering, the channelling of funds to terrorist organisations, illegal foreign-exchange trade and diversion, and tax evasion. There is also a concern that they are excluded from the BoP accounts. These weaknesses are the target of international efforts to regulate the *hawalas* by implementing a policy package which requires *hawala* operators to license or register their businesses, report suspicious transactions, conduct full customer due diligence and keep adequate transaction records. This is tailored to meet international Financial Action Task Force (FATF)[8] and Anti-Money Laundering (AML)[9] regulations and improve country ratings.

The expected impact of the policy framework is that being registered and keeping proper records will eliminate tax evasion, the negative effects on the BOP accounts and foreign-exchange diversion. Conducting full customer due diligence and reporting suspicious transactions will prevent misuse for money laundering and funding terrorism at the cost of convenience (see Tables 5.3 and 5.4). The problem, however, is that African countries lack the capacity to implement the level of supervision required. Experience has shown also that incentives, rather than punitive measures, work better.

Two current developments could make a difference to the remittance industry. The introduction of new technology could facilitate and reduce the cost of recordkeeping, improve the speed of transfer and reduce transaction charges for both formal and informal institutions. Furthermore, recent efforts by the banks to lower transfer charges and offer better exchange rates could intensify competition with *hawalas* for the advantages of low transfer charges. It is unlikely, however, that expansion of formal financial services to remote Africa will be rapid enough to eliminate the role of the *hawalas* from African economies.

Table 5.3 Relationship between positive and negative characteristics

Negative characteristics / Positive characteristics	Negative effect on BoP accounts	Misuse for financing terrorism	Misuse for money laundering	Foreign-exchange diversion	Tax evasion
Minimum recordkeeping	✓				✓
Speed					
Convenience		✓	✓		
Low transaction charges					
Flexibility (not registered)				✓	

✓ = positive correlation
Source: Authors

Table 5.4 Relationship between positive characteristics and miscellaneous factors

Miscellaneous factors / Positive characteristics	Low transfer charges and better exchange rates	Expanded services to remote areas	New technology
Minimum recordkeeping			✓
Speed			✓
Convenience			
Low transaction charges	✓		✓
Flexibility			

✓ = positive correlation
Source: Authors

A deeper understanding of the informal remittance industry in Africa will benefit from a more rigorous scenario analysis of interactions among the driving forces of the *hawala* system identified in this study research.

ESSAY

G2P schemes: A business opportunity for financial services at the very base of the pyramid

David Porteous – *Founder and director of Bankable Frontier Associates, a consultancy based in Boston, USA*

In most regions of the world, other than South Asia, microfinance barely touches the very poor. Indeed, people at the very base of the pyramid have often been considered beyond the reach of formal financial services, since they have so little cash to manage. In addition, they often live in rural areas with low market density, or in urban areas with poor infrastructure. Instead, they have eked out a subsistence existence, and occasionally received free goods, such as food aid, from government or donor programmes, sometimes in return for work.

Several powerful forces are changing this traditional picture and creating new opportunities for financial institutions, governments and poor people at the very base of the pyramid. Some of these forces, like urbanisation, which is drawing people into denser areas, and wireless communications, which are connecting them in cost-effective ways, are well known; their implications for financial services have been addressed elsewhere.[10] This article focuses on a third force, which, though less evident at present, is already proving to be very powerful in linking very poor people to financial services in a sustainable way: the rise of social transfer schemes in developing countries.

Social transfer schemes are one part of a wider range of social protection arrangements by which governments can provide benefits to their citizens (see *Understanding social transfer schemes*). In line with common parlance in electronic commerce such as 'person-to-person' (for mechanisms allowing person-to-person commerce or transfers), we will call social transfers G2P (that is, government-to-person) schemes. While developed countries are defined by their elaborate social welfare schemes, developing countries have usually lacked these forms of social safety net. In the past 10 years or so, in part as a response to rising social pressures, governments of several large middle-income developing countries – Brazil, Mexico and South Africa – have created or significantly expanded their own G2P programmes, with particular reliance on cash transfer schemes. As many as one in five people in these countries are already receiving a regular cash transfer in some form from the government.

A number of evaluations have found positive developmental benefits of cash transfers in different settings.[11] As a result, bilateral and multilateral donors have increasingly sought to extend these programmes in low-income countries as well. Today, donor-funded G2P schemes are being implemented, or at least piloted in places like the DRC, Zambia, Malawi and Kenya, and this trend is likely to continue. As a report by the UK's DFID states, '[t]he Commission for Africa identified social transfers as a key tool in tackling extreme poverty in sub-Saharan Africa … The greater use of social transfers in developing countries worldwide is endorsed by the World Bank's *World Development Report for 2006* which recognises their potential impact on poverty and inequality as well as their contribution to promoting and distributing growth'.

Understanding social transfer schemes

Social transfer schemes are one type of *social assistance,* which is in itself part of the broader category of social protection. A DFID Briefing Note defines these categories further: 'Social assistance is a set of instruments by which the state (or NGOs) transfers non-contributory benefits to those judged to be poor or vulnerable by society. Social transfers provide relatively small, but regular and predictable transfers in cash, vouchers or food directly to households or individuals. Examples include social pensions, child benefits, disability allowances and regular food or voucher distribution. Conditional cash transfers are one form of cash transfer in which the transfer is made conditional on the beneficiary fulfilling some requirement linked to the development impact, such as children attending school regularly or health clinic periodically.'

Source: DFID (2006)

Cash transfer schemes inject money into poor local economies that are often barely monetised. By placing purchasing power in the hands of the very poor, these schemes turn poor people into consumers who can choose what they will buy. This in itself is highly significant for BOP (base of the pyramid) markets, although some of the implications of this monetisation are still little understood. These demand further research and are not the focus of this article: instead, we highlight the specific opportunities created through new G2P schemes for financial institutions to provide appropriate financial services to very poor recipients who were previously viewed as being out of reach of formal markets. This article first describes the opportunity created by new payment mechanisms for social transfers, and then gives several examples of how countries and donors are encouraging innovation and how firms are taking advantage of the opportunity.

Payment mechanisms for social transfers: Pulling and pushing

In most social transfer schemes in developing countries today, beneficiaries are paid out in cash, often using a pay-point set-up, or else general public infrastructure, such a post office, at which a voucher, such as a cheque, can be redeemed. Regardless of the payout location, the beneficiary is required to come to a particular place, often at a particular time. Consequently, we have dubbed this a 'pull' approach.[12] Although pull methodologies are most common (see Table 5.5), they carry substantial disadvantages for the payer and payee: they can be expensive to administer and are subject to fraud by officials along the cash-handling chain. Beneficiaries receiving a relatively large cash lump sum at known payout times are at risk of theft, especially if they live in high-crime communities. Pull approaches also may require the recipients to spend time and money to travel to the payment location, and often to wait in line there.

The rise of electronic banking in developing countries has increasingly opened the door to an alternative: these 'push' approaches allow funds to be credited (or 'pushed', hence the name) to the electronic bank account of the beneficiary. From there, the beneficiary may make withdrawals or payments as needed, using standard banking infrastructure such as ATMs and even POS machines. A push approach requires that a financial institution issue the account. In most countries, only regulated entities such as banks are allowed to take deposits, although in some places, prepaid cards can be issued by employers, governments or third parties without a bank licence.

Before opening a bank account for a client, a bank must first be reasonably convinced that the account will generate sufficient revenue over time, whether from fees on the transactions, from the value of the float balance or from cross-selling other services. In the past, because of their low or no profitability, opening low-value accounts was left to state-owned banks. Indeed, banks like Caixa in Brazil and Bansefi in Mexico remain important for low-end deposit clients. However, merely having an account is not enough. The account is useless to beneficiaries if they cannot access the funds in the account in a convenient and affordable manner. If poor clients have to travel considerable distances to the nearest town to reach a bank branch or ATM, and/or pay a large fee for withdrawals, this would not make sense. For this reason, while state bank Bansefi in Mexico pays almost half of the beneficiaries under the Oportunidades G2P scheme, only a fifth choose to have a Bansefi bank account.

Table 5.5 Major schemes and their payment mechanisms

	Brazil	Colombia	Mexico	South Africa
Social transfer scheme	Bolsa Familia	Families in Action	Oportunidades	Old-age pension; child-support grants
Nature of beneficiaries	Qualifying households with children	Qualifying households with children	Qualifying households with children	The elderly and children under 14 on means-test basis
Number of beneficiaries/ recipients	8.7 million	50 000 eligible, 301 000 paid	Five million	9.2 million beneficiaries; 6.5 million recipients
Amount/nature of grant	Average US$30 per student per month conditional	US$6 or US$12 per child per month to mothers; conditional	US$104 per elementary student; US$177 for high school; conditional	Old age: US$140 per month; child support: US$30 per child per month; unconditional
Frequency	Monthly	Bi-monthly	Bi-monthly	Monthly
Payment method	Push: paid by state bank (Caixa) to electronic benefit card, from which it must be claimed in three months from one of 32 000 Caixa POS or ATMs	Pull: 100 % over the counter at seven banks (mainly state, but also private)	Pull: 75 % (Telco and Bansefi) Push: 25 % into bank accounts mainly at state-owned bank Bansefi	Pull: 79 %, via three private payment contractors Push: 21 % into bank accounts, at private banks (14 %) and state Postbank (7 %)
Total cost to deliver		Per payment via state bank: US$1.74 + 5-day float	Average cost to pay one grant: US$1.80 (2005 figures)	Average cost to pay cash US$4; Monthly subsidy of basic bank account: US$2 (non-cash)

Source: Bankable Frontier Associates (2006)

Two factors are changing this picture and creating new opportunities around G2P schemes for private and state-owned banks alike. First, new distribution channels are being created so that clients can access banking services through agents. This approach has been called 'transformational branchless banking'.[13] To serve as points at which clients can deposit or withdraw cash, local merchants acting as bank agents need nothing more than a POS terminal. Even a mobile phone may now serve as a low-cost point-of-sale device.[14] Because the fixed costs of establishing and maintaining this network are much lower than with dedicated bank infrastructure, the network can extend into much less dense areas. In Brazil, social benefits can be withdrawn using a social benefit card through the range of banking channels operated by Caixa, including ATMs and banking correspondents which are now present in all of Brazil's many municipalities. In South Africa, private payment provider Net1 has established a new merchant network in beneficiary areas, capable of accepting beneficiary smartcards and providing cash back (see *Net and BRAC in the box*). Agents share a portion of each transaction fee with the financial institution, and hence are more enthusiastic about participating.

Social cash transfers are an effective way of injecting small but regular amounts of money into poor communities.

Net1 and BRAC

Net 1 is a payments company which has turned its patents for a proprietary smart card payment technology, called the Universal Electronic Payments Scheme (UEPS), into a large profitable business which now supplies a range of payment and alternative banking solutions. A Net1 subsidiary, Cash Paymaster Services, is the largest payment service provider of social grants in South Africa, making almost four million payments per month in 2006, for which the South African Social Security Agency pays on average US$3.50. Beneficiaries receive a smart card which can be used for ID purposes at dedicated pay-points, as well as for purchases or cash withdrawals at a merchant network in rural areas created by Net1. Net1 now reports a merchant network of 2 500 merchants, through which one million grants are withdrawn per month. Net1 has also developed credit and insurance offerings to recipients which, based on usage projections, more than double its revenue per beneficiary card per month to US$11.

Net1's UEPS products are also being implemented in a range of other countries, including Namibia, Malawi, Ghana and Colombia. The Dowa Emergency cash transfer scheme in Malawi used a UEPS smart card to make the payments. Listed on NASDAQ since 2004, Net1 has seen its share price treble, and it has a market capitalisation of US$1.7 billion. Net1 has successfully demonstrated that there is a profitable market for G2P payments. While UEPS has received plaudits for its robustness, the proprietary nature of its solution has also been criticised as adding to the cost of deployment.

> The offering of some added financial services, such as credit or life insurance, to certain categories of transfer beneficiary, such as old-age pensioners, can be controversial. However, some microfinance organisations have found ways to link the provision of microsavings and even microloans to some transfer recipients in a way which helps them to get out of poverty and away from dependence on the transfers alone. The most successful case, highlighted in Hashemi and Rosenberg (2006), is the Income Generation for Vulnerable Group Development (IGVGD) scheme operated by BRAC, a large NGO in Bangladesh. The main beneficiaries of this scheme are destitute rural women to whom the government provides free grain (not cash – this is not a cash transfer scheme) for 18 months. During this period, BRAC collects microsavings from the women and provides training in how to start income-generation projects. Thereafter, they can access a microloan, much smaller than the usual BRAC loan, with which they can purchase stock or equipment to start income-generating projects. The full cost of these loans is subsidised with grants. Reviews to date show great impact: nearly two-thirds of 1.6 million participants in the programme have graduated to become normal microfinance clients of BRAC. In this case, no bank account is involved; but IGVGD does demonstrate the possibility of offering wider financial services even to very poor beneficiaries of transfer schemes.

Source: Net1

Second, governments are seeing the opportunity to reduce costs of paying out transfers, while at the same time achieving additional developmental impact. Paying to open a bank account for a beneficiary generally reduces the cost of each subsequent transfer compared with the cost of a cash payment, and may offer additional benefits through offering the beneficiary access to other formal financial services. In South Africa, several large commercial banks have offered a basic transaction account for social transfer recipients with a linked debit card and no minimum balance requirement. While the beneficiary can make a prescribed number of withdrawals (usually two) and certain other transactions for free every month, the government agency pays the bank a bundled fee of around US$2 per account per month. This compares well with the average of around US$4 a month for the alternative of cash payment. Account-holder recipients may access additional banking services via the account, although they must pay for these separately. For example, family members may now send remittances by depositing into the same account. All parties have the prospect of gaining from such arrangements:

- For the bank, the US$2 per account in reliable regular fee income from a low-risk source (government) has proven to be a sufficiently attractive source of income;
- For government, the costs per payment for the G2P scheme may be halved, and greater development impact may be possible; and
- The beneficiary now has a safe place to keep funds and receive other sources of money, in addition to the social transfer.

This push approach has been implemented on a large scale by Allpay, a subsidiary of Absa Bank, itself a subsidiary of the multinational Barclays Bank. Allpay has issued its VISA-branded Sekulula card account to two-thirds of the transfer recipients in one populous province – Gauteng. Other banks such as Standard Bank and FNB also offer basic bank accounts for G2P beneficiaries in certain other provinces.

Figure 5.2 The ladder of basic financial products

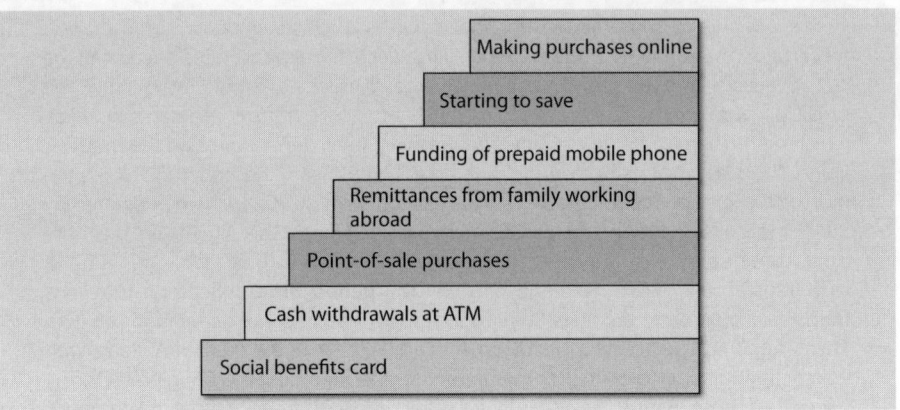

Source: Net1

Adding on other financial services: Climbing the ladder

Providing a social benefits card with basic bank-account properties is potentially the first step on the ladder of receiving access to other financial services (see Figure 5.2). FinScope surveys have found that there is a hierarchy of product use within defined categories of financial services, for example within the transaction category, starting with a simple basic service such as an ATM card and leading on to further use of new services. Additional services could include instruments to make other payments – such as topping up a prepaid mobile phone account – or to receive from other sources, such as family and friends in remote locations, even internationally. Account holders may also be offered specialised savings facilities, since, after initial cycles of cashing out the entire transfer at once, account-holding beneficiaries are likely to start leaving small balances in the account. Some providers like Net1 have gone further to offer credit and even insurance products, the instalments of which can be paid cost effectively from the account (see *Net1 and BRAC in the box*).

Conclusion

The growth of G2P schemes in developing countries creates major opportunities to promote financial inclusion at the very base of the pyramid. Building on the success of programmes like Sekulula, international card associations such as VISA have identified the opportunity for their members to issue debit or prepaid card accounts for these purposes.[15] It is not always easy, however, to move to new, more efficient electronic payment instruments and channels into environments in which basic infrastructure is lacking: wireless coverage may be rapidly increasing, even in rural areas, offering the opportunity of using mobile phones to transact, but the electrical grid does not cover many rural areas, hence there is a need for alternative power solutions. In addition, reliance on local merchants as cash-out points does not solve all operational risks for providers, compared with the alternative of paying beneficiaries in cash from armoured mobile vans: for example, how much cash does a merchant need to have on hand to be able to cover peak withdrawal cycles following the introduction of transfers? Often, this can only be found out by trial and error at the start of such schemes.

> **Supporting G2P innovation: Kenya's Social Protection Payments Challenge Fund**
>
> In Kenya, the orphans and vulnerable children programme is a cash transfer programme which has been piloted on a limited basis since 2006. Another transfer scheme, called the Hunger Safety Net (HSN), began a pilot in early 2009, focusing on very poor and often nomadic households in the drought-affected arid and semi-arid northern parts of the country. The pilot scheme will serve about 60 000 recipients over three years to test all aspects of the scheme prior to general rollout from 2011. With other donors, DFID has committed substantial funding for pilot and rollout.
>
> Despite rapid growth in recent years, the Kenyan banking system still has limited reach, serving less than one in five adults, and there is limited infrastructure in the areas in which beneficiaries live. To encourage the development of innovative approaches for the payment of the grants under these two pilots, FSD Kenya, a donor-funded trust promoting financial sector deepening, launched a challenge fund with international microfinance resource centre CGAP. This fund helped to raise levels of interest and awareness in approaches to paying transfers which promote financial inclusion as well. In the tender for payments services for HSN, numerous international and local providers competed to provide a basic account to each of the recipients, and to pay one million transfers during the life of the pilot. The tender was won by local retail bank, Equity Bank, which has developed an innovative smart-card-based solution for offline point-of-sale use in HSN areas.

The costs and risks can therefore deter private providers from innovating in some environments. For this reason, donors are starting to incentivise the development of new approaches to G2P.

An example of a new donor-funded G2P scheme in Kenya, the HSN programme, is highlighted in the box, *Supporting G2P innovation: Kenya's Social Protection Payments Challenge Fund*. HSN will provide small transfers in arid areas with little physical infrastructure and in some places, high security risks. The combination of factors would in the past have favoured a high-cost, cash-payout-only approach. However, the diffusion of technology in retail banking, together with some targeted innovation support from donors, led to active interest in the payment services contract from a range of local and international providers. The final payment arrangements include the creation of a new point-of-sale infrastructure through which local merchants will pay out many of the transfers from basic bank accounts offered by a large domestic retail bank. Small as this pilot is at first, it offers a picture of a possible, indeed likely, future in this sector: where financial institutions see G2P schemes as good business opportunities, and where donors see the chance to advance wider goals, such as financial inclusion and financial sector development, at the same time as protecting some of the most vulnerable.

Endnotes

[1] See http://www.financialdiaries.com for an analysis of the extent of the dependency of rural communities on remittances (whether social grants or other forms of remittance) from urban areas.

[2] Maimbo (2006).

3. *Hawala* brokers, or *hawaladars*, function with no promissory instruments. The system is based on trust. Tribal and clan-based identities are important as the system does not depend on the legal enforceability of claims, and can operate even in the absence of a legal and juridical environment. No record is produced of individual transactions – only a running tally of the amount owed by one broker to another is kept. Settlements of debts between *hawala* brokers can take a variety of forms, not necessarily in the form of direct cash transactions.
4. Sander (2003).
5. El Qorchi & Maimbo (2003), and Wilson (2002).
6. Ibid.
7. Goderama & Montsi (2003).
8. FATF is an intergovernmental body founded by the G7 in 1989. Its objective in developing countries is to combat money laundering and terrorist financing.
9. AML regulations refer to legal controls that require formal financial and other regulated entities to prevent and/or report money-laundering transactions. AML came into prominence after the 11 September attacks in the US in 2001.
10. See, for example, Littlefield, Helms and Porteous (2006) on the forces affecting financial access in future.
11. As a recent example, see De Koker, De Waal and Vorster (2006), which concludes from a large-scale survey of beneficiaries that 'cash benefits prove to be an important medium for the realization of socio-economic rights … social assistance improves poor families ability to provide for their basic needs'.
12. BFA (2006).
13. Lyman, Pickens & Porteous (2008).
14. Mobile phones are reportedly being used in the payment of demobilised soldiers under the Multi-country Demobilisation and Reintegration Programme, another form of G2P scheme, in Democratic Republic of Congo by m-payment provider Celpay.
15. See, for example, the presentation by Laura Cuda at the CGAP/IFC Conference, September 2007, available via http://siteresources.worldbank.org/FSLP/Resources/LauraCuda_FSandSocialProtections.pdf.

Chapter Six

Mobile phone banking

The explosion in the use of mobile phones across Africa has led many to speculate that mobile banking will become a major phenomenon across the continent. From only 16 million mobile users in 2000, there are now 300 million users[1]. Most of these have leapfrogged fixed-line telephony and so it is tempting to think these technologically conversant consumers will also leapfrog traditional banking and use their mobile phones not just to download and pay for airtime, as is commonplace today, but to make all sorts of other payments as well, to make balance enquiries and to even subscribe for a loan.

Many hope that m-banking, using mobile phones to effect banking transactions, will vastly improve access to financial services for the poor because it overcomes the problem of distance and could radically reduce the cost at which financial services are delivered. However, though the promise is great, the operational and regulatory challenges in m-banking are formidable and there is considerable uncertainty about the types of business model that will emerge as winners in this increasingly competitive field. Interestingly, it is an area in which the telecommunications companies could be the ones calling the shots, as Al Hammond suggests in his essay. Just as the banks see great opportunity in banking the unbanked through mobile phones, there is also the threat of powerful competition moving in to cut them out as intermediaries, target their customers directly and seize part of their revenue.

Mobile banking: Living up to its promise?

> M-banking is in its infancy although the numbers using phones to transfer money or airtime or check account balances are growing rapidly. Five different approaches are profiled in this case study, which addresses important questions such as whether the convenience and pricing of m-banking will appeal mainly to those who already have bank accounts or whether it will also appeal to the unbanked. Facilitating the adoption of m-banking by the unbanked is surely a priority for governments and other agencies with an interest in seeing a rapid improvement in access levels in Africa. But, as the case study makes clear, the operational challenges in rolling out this kind of banking system are very real.

As the rollout of mobile networks has gained momentum across the African continent, reaching into areas where it has been too costly to deploy fixed-line and physical infrastructure, so has excitement about the prospect of using mobile technology to make financial services more widely accessible on a cost-effective basis.

This enthusiasm is fuelled by evidence of the positive economic impact that mobile phones bring to areas that have not previously had telecommunications services. They have created business opportunities, and generated incomes and revenues, particularly in low-income countries. The *World Telecommunication/ICT Development Report 2006* suggests that mobile phones could do for underserved areas what fixed telephone lines did in many other regions years ago: widen markets, create better information flow, lower transaction costs, and connect people while saving time and money spent to travel to see someone.

The report goes on to say that the prospect of change as a result of m-banking goes further. Low-income countries may leapfrog the deployment of widespread earlier generation infrastructure, such as ATMs and dedicated electronic POS devices, and go straight to mobile technology. Across the spectrum, therefore, from development and not-for-profit organisations, to financial services organisations, mobile telecommunications companies and entrepreneurs with a social conscience, all have seen the opportunities and are looking for ways to exploit them on a sustainable basis.

The lessons from those that have entered the market early show that m-banking does indeed have substantial potential to make financial services more accessible to a wider range of people, and that it can be done sustainably. At the same time, the market is not without its challenges.

M-banking defined

The term 'm-banking' is used to refer to a wide range of financial services and transactions that use mobile phones as the primary customer interface:

- **M-commerce:** Payments for goods and services that are deducted from available airtime;
- **M-payments:** A wallet with transactional capability that allows payments from a phone; and
- **M-banking:** Access to a bank account from the phone through which most banking transactions can be done.

For clarity, 'm-banking' is used as a generic term in this case study to refer to all of these services, and 'm-commerce' or 'm-payments' when the specific meaning of these terms is intended.

M-banking can also be segmented, based on the intention of the organisation in offering the service. Jenny Hoffmann, ex-head of MTN Banking in South Africa, says that organisations may see m-banking as either a supplement to, or substitute for, existing banking services.[2] Mobile banking expert David Porteous classifies these approaches respectively as either additive or transformational. Banks following an additive approach see the mobile phone as simply another channel from which existing clients can access banking services. The purpose is not to open up new markets, but to serve an existing one. Organisations following a transformational model specifically intend to open up new markets by targeting the unbanked.[3]

The mobile promise

The growth in the mobile industry in the developing world has been such that in 2006, for the first time since mobile phones appeared on the market, there were more mobile phone users in developing countries than there were in developed ones. More than 800 million mobile phones were sold in developing countries between 2003 and 2006.[4] In 2004 about 15 million people signed up for new mobile phone subscriptions in Africa – more than the entire number of telephone subscribers on the continent in 1996, both fixed and mobile.⁵ Africa has seen dramatic growth in mobile telephony, with 300 million mobile subscribers (about 30 % penetration), and it is still growing, says Yolande van Wyk, Head of Strategic Projects at FNB Mobile and Transact Solutions, and in comparison with the internet, mobile technology has lower social- and income-related barriers. Outside of South Africa, very few Africans have access to the internet – and mobile handsets are more easily shared.

Mobile phone banking is expanding access to financial services.

In addition, as Porteous points out, mobile networks offer a sophisticated technology platform onto which other services such as m-banking can be built at a very low cost. Hoffmann notes that for the poor, and particularly the poor living in remote areas, one of the key barriers to accessing financial services is the price of being banked: including both the fees charged by the financial institutions, and the time and money required to access the infrastructure. FinMark Trust estimates that most low-income people can afford to spend only 2 % of personal annual income on banking services,⁶ but for banks, to roll out physical infrastructure to bring banking closer to the people is expensive. Using the existing mobile infrastructure therefore provides an opportunity to overcome this challenge.⁷

The key is the overlap between the number of people who have mobile phones and the number who do not have access to formal financial services. FinMark Trust has estimated that as many as 20 % of unbanked Africans have mobile phones. The Consultative Group to Assist the Poor (CGAP) notes that mobile phone network operators already know how to handle cash transactions, and low-income customers are already familiar with mobile phones. It says that this could facilitate the take-up of m-banking in developing countries.⁸

Five organisations illustrating a variety of approaches adapted to m-banking on the African continent are Celpay in the Democratic Republic of the Congo (DRC) and Zambia, Vodafone/Safaricom in Kenya, and First National Bank (FNB), MTN Banking and Wizzit in South Africa.

Celpay

Celtel, a pan-African mobile network operator, launched Celpay in Zambia and the DRC in 2002 and 2004 respectively. These are two countries with quite different economic and financial services environments, but where large portions of the population do not have bank accounts or access to financial services.

The DRC is among the poorest countries in the world. According to the *Index of Economic Freedom: 2007* report, infrastructure is extremely poor, the banking system is unstable, and bank operations have been hurt by war, political instability, frequent policy changes, unpredictable monetary policy, hyperinflation and unrecoverable loans.[9] The country is the size of Western Europe and has a population of between 60 and 70 million, but it has only 12 banks, with fewer than 60 000 accounts. Most commercial banks focus on international companies, top-tier local corporations, the public sector and a few wealthy individuals. The requirements for opening an account generally involve minimum deposits of between US$1 000 and US$5 000.[10] As such, most of the population is unbanked or underbanked, and most credit is informal, although there is a growing network of microfinance and credit institutions in the country.[11]

In contrast, Zambia is said to have one of the more liberal banking regimes in southern Africa, and the *Index* notes that banking supervision and regulations have improved in recent years. In 2006, there were 11 operational commercial banks, including several foreign-owned ones.[12] Nevertheless, according to FinScope Zambia 2005, penetration of financial products into the community remains low. In 2005, only 13 % of people had a savings account, two-thirds of Zambians were not receiving any formal financial services, and 11 % received financial services from informal providers only. In total, 14 % of adults had bank accounts.[13]

Using Porteous's segmentation of m-banking, Celpay is potentially transformational in nature, and definitely not additive, as its services are not being offered as an adjunct to existing banking services. When Celtel started Celpay, its intention was to facilitate the prepaid airtime sales process. The vast distances in the DRC made it logistically difficult to work with vouchers, and the company was looking for an alternative to the voucher system. In addition, it wanted to give customers more ways of buying airtime than just going to a Celtel outlet, says Lazarus Muchenje, Celpay CEO. The solution to both problems was to enable customers to open a bank account which they could access from their mobile phones. This would allow the transfer of funds from this account to Celtel's account regardless of where customers were. It would also solve the voucher problem by enabling Celtel to credit customers' mobile phone accounts with airtime when it received payment. Celtel therefore started Celpay, launching it first in Zambia and then in the DRC a year later.

In 2005, two years after Celpay was launched, Celtel divested itself of non-core assets and sold Celpay to FirstRand Bank, one of the biggest South African-based banking groups. At the time, EB Nieuwoudt, then CEO of FirstRand Africa and Emerging Markets, noted that because the building blocks for consumer banking were not yet in place in many African countries, this acquisition was an opportunity to take advantage of technology and lay the foundation for introducing more conventional banking products into these markets in the future.[14] Today, Celpay is an independent company with its group head office in The Hague in the Netherlands, having relinquished ties with FirstRand in 2008.

Celpay offers deposit taking and a range of payment services. Customers can deposit and withdraw cash at participating banks and Celpay outlets. It has a full mobile banking platform that could expand to include services such as debit orders should Celpay want it to. The system requires a 64k SIM card[15] with the mobile banking platform programmed into it. None of the networks in the DRC or Zambia supplies such SIM cards automatically. Thus, when customers open a Celpay account, they receive a new SIM card that adds the necessary software to their phone as well as an individual bank account number. Because Celpay does not have a banking licence, it has to partner with registered banks in the DRC and Zambia, where the funds for Celpay accounts are held in pool accounts.

Celpay requires no minimum balance and there is no fixed monthly fee. Revenue is generated from fees per transaction and commission from mobile network operators on airtime. The system operates on a multi-fee structure, and costs vary according to the type of transaction made. Muchenje says fees are based on the cost to the company as well as 'what the market will accept'.

One of the biggest markets for Celpay accounts is m-payments between large suppliers with big distribution networks, such as soft-drink distributors, breweries, petroleum suppliers and mobile network operators, and their smaller customers. The system Celpay has developed allows customers to order supplies remotely, and pay for them and provide proof of payment simultaneously, thus significantly streamlining the conventional ordering and payment process. While m-payments through Celpay are normally charged to the initiator of the payment, under this system, transaction fees are charged to the supplier. Muchenje says suppliers are happy to pay these fees because of the benefits. 'The breweries have seen massive value from this initiative, as it has substantially improved the financial leg of their supply chain management,' he explains.

Muchenje adds that business-to-business m-payments through Celpay have brought a wide range of people into the banking system in the DRC and Zambia who were not included before. He says that small, medium and micro enterprises (SMMEs) in these countries generally did not have bank accounts, because they did not want to pay the bank charges or because they were too small to be of any interest to the conventional banks. This system has encouraged them to open accounts.

Celpay's accounts are worth almost US$25 million a month in Zambia, and it is doing two million transactions a month in the DRC. Muchenje says that Celpay is almost at break-even, and the company was expected to reach this by the end of 2008.

Vodafone/Safaricom

Safaricom, the Kenyan subsidiary of the UK-based international mobile network operator Vodafone, launched the pilot of M-Pesa, a mobile money transfer service, in November 2005. The success of the pilot was such that Safaricom launched M-Pesa throughout Kenya in March 2007. The response was enthusiastic. In the first 18 weeks more than 200 000 customers registered to use the system (about 1 500 a day) and more than 150 000 customers who were not registered received money through M-Pesa. Newspaper articles at the time quoted one customer as saying that he was saving KSh3 000 each weekend by being able to use M-Pesa to send money to his daughters, rather than pay the transport costs for a relative to take the money to them. By June 2007, M-Pesa had started to make inroads into the business-to-person transfer arena. Safaricom had also started talks with the breweries to establish a system similar to that used by Celpay, in terms of which small-business customers could pay the breweries using M-Pesa.

After one year of operation the service had attracted two million customers, and this has now grown to more than 6.5 million. Vodafone and Safaricom are also expanding the system's functionality to enable bill and salary payments, and they are piloting international remittance services.

After one year of operation the M-Pesa money transfer service had attracted two million customers.

The idea for M-Pesa originated in 2002, when Nick Hughes, then head of Social Products and Enterprises at Vodfone, attended the World Summit on Sustainable Development. There the UK's Department for International Development (DFID) introduced him to the Financial Sector Deepening Challenge Fund, in terms of which DFID planned to give grants to private sector organisations involved in projects aimed at making financial services more accessible to poor people. Vodafone had already been doing some research into mobile person-to-person funds transfer. It presented the concept to DFID, and received funding to pilot the project with Safaricom in Kenya.

According to the *Index of Economic Freedom: 2007*, Kenya's financial system is one of the most developed in sub-Saharan Africa. Despite this, the FinAccess Survey, conducted in the second half of 2006, found that only 19 % of Kenya's population uses formal financial services such as regulated banks, buildings societies or Postbank, and that 38 % use no financial products at all. In the northeastern part of the country, there were only three bank branches, and none of the population there had a bank account. Physical access to formal financial services is one of the main hindrances to being able to use financial services. The number of banks and ATMs in Kenya is limited and many rural populations are too small for bank outlets to be viable. Moreover, the survey found that most bank accounts are relatively expensive to acquire and maintain.

Hughes says that Vodafone's research and early-stage pilot studies found that Kenyans are interested in being able to transfer money from person to person, and that this need was greater than the desire to have a bank account. According to the FinAccess survey, people tend to use informal ways of sending money within Kenya – through a family member or friend (58 %), or through a bus company (27 %). M-Pesa has therefore specifically been designed for those who do not use or have access to conventional banking, and it provides a mobile money transfer service rather than banking services. As such, its services fall within the realm of m-commerce – '… this is mobile payment,' says Hughes, 'it is not m-banking' – but they are potentially transformational in nature by virtue of the fact that M-Pesa is available to people who do not have bank accounts.

Only Safaricom customers may transfer money using M-Pesa (a term combining *pesa*, the Swahili word for 'money', with M for 'mobile'), although transfer recipients do not have to be Safaricom customers. They may transfer up to KSh35 000, and to initiate a transfer they put money into a specially created M-Pesa account by depositing cash with one of the local agents nationwide. Customers then send a text message with a four-digit PIN code to the transfer recipient's mobile phone so that the recipient can redeem the sum in cash at an M-Pesa agent. M-Pesa can also be used as a form of e-money,[16] as it allows Safaricom customers to put virtual money on their own phone and withdraw it at an agent when it is needed. They do not need a bank account to perform transactions, only a mobile phone. Getting an M-Pesa account is free and if customers need a new SIM card to perform the transactions, Safaricom does not charge them for the card. Charges are per transaction and are levied on the person sending the money.

In October 2008, there were more than 3 000 M-Pesa agents nationwide – well in excess of the number of Kenyan bank branches. Not all traditional Safaricom agencies have the capacity to become M-Pesa agents, says Hughes, because they are simply too small. Agents include petrol stations, larger retail outlets and several banking/financial service partners such as the post office.

Vodafone commented in June 2007 that it was still early days and clearly too soon for the product to be turning a profit. Nevertheless, the company was satisfied that M-Pesa would meet its business expectations for the current financial year. Hughes predicts that M-Pesa will reach breakeven within two years, and he is hoping that M-Pesa will generate between three and four chargeable transactions per customer per month. However, Vodafone and Safaricom see the benefits of M-Pesa as being more than just profitability. They believe that it provides an excellent value-added service for its customers, many of whom do not have access to formal banking. They believe that M-Pesa will increase customer loyalty, and encourage those who do not have a Safaricom account to consider becoming customers.

The concept of mobile money transfers has, however, been attractive enough that in Kenya the cellular company Zain has launched a money transfer service called Zap in competition with M-Pesa.

Early in 2008, Vodafone extended its service to Tanzania in partnership with Vodacom, the South African-based cellular service provider in which Vodafone has a controlling share. The service has also been made available in Afghanistan, where it is branded M-Paisa.

One of the key strategic developments that Vodafone would like to see from this project is the extension of the M-Pesa concept to international remittances, thus enabling people to send relatively small amounts of money across borders cost effectively. Because of the charges levied by conventional remittance organisations, it is simply not viable to send small amounts at present, says Hughes. Vodafone believes that because it uses an existing distribution network with low running costs, it will be in a position to offer international remittance services more cheaply, and it will be able to make things easier for people on the collection side of the transaction. To this end Vodafone and Safaricom have partnered with Western Union to pilot international remittances between the UK and Kenya.

Note: At the time of going to print, Nick Hughes no longer worked for Vodafone. Cenk Sedar had taken his place as Mobile Payments Director.

FNB Cellphone Banking

First National Bank (FNB), MTN Banking and Wizzit all operate in South Africa. FNB has rolled out mobile banking in Botswana and Namibia as well, and all of the other big four banks in South Africa (Absa, FNB, Nedbank and Standard Bank) have an m-banking offering. The *Index of Economic Freedom: 2007* describes the country's financial system as 'the most advanced in Africa', and notes that financial regulations are generally consistent with international standards.[17] According to FinScope 2008 research, 63 % of adults have bank accounts – a far greater proportion than in the DRC, Kenya or Zambia. The banking sector is dominated by the big four banks, which together account for about 80 % of assets in the sector. The advances that formal banks have made into the unbanked sector of the South African market have been strongly, although not at all exclusively, motivated by meeting the requirements of the Financial Sector Charter, which came into effect in 2003, and set certain targets for extending financial services to financially marginalised communities.[18]

The international Financial Action Task Force requirements to fight organised crime and terrorism by preventing money laundering are followed by most countries across the globe. In South Africa, the Financial Intelligence Centre Act (FICA), promulgated in 2001, sets out certain requirements which banks have to adhere to when opening accounts. These have had a particular influence on m-banking ventures. FICA requires banks, in most instances, to actually see the person opening the account and to obtain certain supporting documentation, such as an identity document and proof of residential address. An exemption, known as Exemption 17, waives the requirement for proof of residence for certain types of accounts for which, among other limitations, the maximum daily transaction limit is R5 000. Applicants who are happy to have a maximum balance of R25 000 and a daily withdrawal limit of R1 000 do not have to come into a branch, although they still have to provide their identity number, which must be verified by the bank against a third-party database. Customers who do not want these restrictions have to go to a branch for a face-to-face application and provide proof of residence.

FNB is the oldest bank in South Africa and is a division of FirstRand Bank, the holding company of which is FirstRand Limited. FirstRand Bank was formed when FNB and Rand Merchant Bank merged in the late 1990s. Its m-banking service is additive, in that it is offered as another banking channel for its existing customer base. Nevertheless, FNB sees m-banking as a way to make banking easier and banking services more accessible to a wider section of the South African population. As such, it falls within the Mobile and Transact Solutions business unit of the bank, which develops and manages mobile-related products for FNB and its customers such as FNB Cellphone Banking and inContact.

FNB's m-banking product was launched in March 2005, with the threefold aim of providing a low-cost service (mobile phone banking is free to customers at present), extending access to financial services in compliance with the requirements of the Financial Sector Charter, and taking advantage of the fact that mobile phone use is so widespread across South Africa. Clients can access the full range of banking services from their mobile phones, except for cash withdrawal, which they can do from any FNB branch, ATM or Mini-ATM in the country.[19]

From the beginning, the idea was to make mobile banking accessible to everyone. 'So we had to be creative with technology and how we implemented it,' says Van Wyk. As a consequence, FNB uses Unstructured Supplementary Service Data (USSD) and SMS[20] technology, which are core to the GSM technology and available on all phones, as well as WAP (Wireless Application Protocol)[21] for those with more sophisticated phones.

Customers can register for the service at an ATM, on the internet, via the call centre or at a branch. At present, branch registrations top all the other registration channels. At the time of the launch, ATMs were the largest registration channel, but branch registrations overtook ATMs once FNB made it easier for customers to register for mobile banking in its branches. FNB says that registrations done at the branch generally result in higher activity for those customers.

Over half of the mobile banking base belongs to the mainstream market, with the rest falling into consumer and other niche segments. Van Wyk ascribes the relatively low initial take-up of m-banking to a need for more education on the availability of the service and greater customer awareness. It is not because people in this market are nervous of the technology that they do not use m-banking, she says, but because they do not know that it exists. An encouraging sign for FNB is that the number of transactions per active customer is increasing, and has grown from four or five a month in 2005 to about seven in 2007. More than a million transactions are now conducted through this channel every month.[22] In fact, take-up of the services has exceeded expectations, and FNB cellphone banking broke even less than a year after its launch.[23]

Cellphone banking is free to all its customers, and the unit generates revenue from prepaid services. Examples of such services include not only prepaid cellphone airtime, but also Telkom (landline) airtime, Globel airtime and prepayment of electricity. By far the biggest number of FNB mobile transactions come from airtime purchases, and Van Wyk says that m-banking has replaced ATMs as the primary vehicle used to purchase airtime. Prepaid services are important for another reason, says Van Wyk: they are highly effective in encouraging customers to use the m-banking channel as a whole, and account for more than half of FNB Cellphone Banking's transaction volumes.

In 2005, FNB launched mobile banking in Namibia and Botswana. Take-up in these countries has been above expectation, Van Wyk says. In expanding, FNB has found that customer awareness and easy registration are key to the success of mobile banking.

MTN Banking

MTN Banking is a 50/50 joint venture between MTN, one of the biggest mobile network operators in South Africa and on the continent of Africa, and the Standard Bank Group, another of the big four South African banks. It was launched in August 2005, although MTN had decided as far back as the late 1990s that it wanted to get into m-banking. This was because of the rising popularity of premium SMSs which are often used for m-commerce transactions. Organisations use premium SMSs for a variety of services, such as competitions, donations to good causes, ring tones, dating and daily horoscopes, all of which are activated or purchased by sending an SMS to what is termed a short-code number – normally five digits. The cost of the service, which the network provider pays directly to the provider of the service, is added to the standard SMS rate, and the total cost is either taken from the monetary value of the available airtime of a prepaid customer, or charged to the account of a contract customer.

Because of the commercial opportunities in this market, says Dave Parratt, business development executive of MTN Banking, MTN wanted to enter this market more aggressively, and the company needed to have bank-like protocols and knowledge to be able to do this with any degree of security. As things stand, airtime is a form of e-money which is unregulated and not recognised as valid currency in the South African environment.

Parratt adds that reducing the turnover of prepaid customers was a further motivation for offering banking services. This market is notoriously fickle, switching from one network to the other in search of cheaper call rates. The principle, says Parratt, is that people who bank with MTN Banking should remain subscribers for longer, and that if MTN customer turnover is reduced by even a very small proportion, this would bring significant extra revenue to MTN. For Standard Bank the partnership presented an opportunity to gain access to MTN's customer base of more than 12 million people and also to find new avenues to meet the charter requirements by accessing MTN's unbanked customers. As such, MTN Banking provides an entirely new banking channel. It is not additive in nature, and has at least a partially transformational intent.

MTN Banking gives MTN customers access to a fully functional MobileMoney bank account, to which they can link a choice of two cards: a cash card for withdrawals and deposits at Standard Bank ATMs; and a MasterCard debit card which can be used at the ATMs of other banks and at certain other outlets countrywide, as well as for point-of-sale payments. All customers can make person-to-person transfers from their phone to other MobileMoney account holders or any other bank's account holder in South Africa.

As with Celpay, charges are transaction based, and there is no minimum balance requirement and no monthly service fee. The aim at this stage, says Terry Timson, CEO of MTN Banking, is not so much to hold deposits as to mobilise revenue through transaction fees. The model is one of facilitating transactions so that money comes in and out of the accounts frequently.

MTN Banking makes use of the E17 FICA exemption and the guidelines issued by the South African Reserve Bank for non-face-to-face account opening[24] to allow customers to open an account using their phone. Another option was to come into a Standard Bank or MTN outlet where customers would be served by a FICA-trained consultant. By late 2007, however, MTN Banking had enhanced its recruitment model and moved from self-registering to assisted registering. It did this by putting a sales force into the field, chiefly in areas where people were previously unbanked, using its bright yellow branding and stalls and gazebos to attract new users. In this way it was able to register between 1 200 and 1 400 new users a day and grow its customer base through face-to-face sales. This saw MTN Banking growing its own banking customer base, separate from that of Standard Bank.

A year later, despite the high level of interest and engagement at point of sale, says Timson, actual use was disappointing, with insufficient volumes of transactions. Research showed that customers were using their cellphones to buy airtime and to transfer money. They were not embracing the full banking services on offer. 'Nonetheless,' says Timson, 'we have retained our full-service offering, but at the same time shifted our focus to servicing our active base of users, this being out of the 300 000 registered users, the 20 % who are active.' Between 30 % and 50 % of the active group are previously unbanked, according to Parratt.

Standard Bank has embarked on its own recruitment drive, with MTN MobileMoney providing service solutions through development and maintenance of the appropriate technologies. Nevertheless, MTN's joint venture with Standard Bank is still in place and has also seen MobileMoney create and develop for Standard Bank what Parratt says is a Grameen-type banking arrangement, where each South African village will have a community banker. Timson notes that this will also increase levels of education in the previously unbanked communities where education has been one of the critical issues identified as necessary for uptake and use.

MTN Banking has grown its customer base by putting a sales force into the field, mainly in areas where people were previously unbanked.

MTN's cellphone-user market is mainly made up of upper-income customers, but, says Timson, there is huge demand in the lower-income segment, hence both MTN and Standard Bank's efforts in this segment. 'The prognosis is still positive,' he says. 'It seems logical and inevitable that this segment will grow, that take-up and use will grow in the future.'

MTN Banking in the form of its MobileMoney product was, at the end of 2008, about to launch in five African countries using in-country enhancements and focusing on the lower end market where there is demand for airtime payments and money transfer or remittances. 'In a way,' says Timson, 'we are retro-fitting this model in South Africa where we have learnt that what people in this bracket want is a safe way to receive payment and a safe way to make payments.'

Wizzit

Wizzit also offers customers the full range of transactional banking services from their mobile phone. It is, however, somewhat different in nature from the other organisations profiled. It is an entrepreneurial venture that does not have the financial backing of a large bank or mobile network operator, and its primary target market is unbanked and underbanked people, although 20 % of its customers already had bank accounts. Its stated intention is to be transformational in nature. It was the first of its kind to launch in South Africa, and is globally regarded as a pioneer in this space. Formally, it is a division of the South African Bank of Athens Limited, one of the minnows in the South African banking industry, which provides the licence that allows Wizzit to operate. Functionally, it operates as a completely separate entity, and is the brainchild of two entrepreneurs, Brian Richardson and Charles Rowlinson.

The founders came up with the idea for the venture after a discussion with Cyril Ramaphosa, a businessman and prominent member of the African National Congress, when it became clear to them that poor South Africans were finding it difficult to open bank accounts, and that there would be real benefit to them if they could.[25] According to Richardson, they are social entrepreneurs, and extend their policy of benefiting the poor, where possible, by employing only those who have been previously unemployed.

In the beginning, Richardson and Rowlinson investigated the possibility of launching a smartcard-based bank, but the cost of this option meant that it would not be viable. They therefore decided to launch Wizzit as a mobile bank with no formal branches. Wizzit has trained a sales force of more than 3 000, known as Wizzkids, and has deposit-taking arrangements with the South African Post Office and Absa Bank – the bank with the biggest retail footprint in South Africa. It also has an arrangement with EasyPay, the largest bank-independent payment switch in the country, where customers can pay various accounts and bills either at pay-points in supermarkets and other outlets across the country, or directly from their cellphone. A call centre is available for clients experiencing problems. To ensure that technology does not hinder the opening of an account, Wizzit operates using a USSD continuous session channel, which can be used by any mobile phone, across all networks and on all SIM cards.

The Wizzkids buy account starter packs, which contain a Maestro debit card and PIN, a Wizzit PIN and instructions on how to get started. They then sell these starter packs to new customers for double what they paid Wizzit and keep the profit as a commission. As with Celpay, M-Pesa and MobileMoney, Wizzit requires no minimum balance and carries no monthly service fee – fees are charged per transaction. Banking services include transfers, debit orders, ATM cash withdrawals (using the Maestro card at any of the banks' ATMs), balance enquiries and cash back at point of sale. Value-added services include mobile phone airtime and prepaid electricity purchases.

Three years down the track, Richardson jokes that the people who told him he had to be half mad to start a venture of this nature were absolutely right. Because the venture needed a banking licence to operate, Richardson and Rowlinson approached the big four to form an alliance, but this did not form part of these banks' strategic thinking at the time. The partners therefore saw no option but to go it alone, with the Bank of Athens providing a licence, but without provision of funding being part of the deal. As a consequence, Wizzit has had to learn how to operate as a micro player in a market dominated by four large banks with bigger marketing budgets, all of which have since launched or strengthened their m-banking offerings.

Wizzit does all of its marketing by word of mouth, using the Wizzkids, who live in the communities they serve. Richardson says that this has been effective in building up trust for the brand, because the Wizzkids market to people they know and who trust them.

In addition, says Richardson, when he and Rowlinson started out they were doing something that had not been attempted before in South Africa – starting a purely mobile bank that targeted the unbanked. This meant that there was no precedent, no blueprint to follow and no way of predicting how the market would react. He cites an example of something that caught the company completely by surprise. As a way of gaining bank accounts, Wizzit has worked with farmers and their workers so that farmers can pay wages directly into the accounts of those workers who open Wizzit bank accounts. However, when farmworkers, many of whom are seasonal, leave the farm and start work on another farm, they open another Wizzit account believing that the accounts are linked to their employment at a particular farm. Richardson was dumbfounded when he realised that this was happening. 'How are you supposed to anticipate that?' he asks.

> **Wizzkid: Lucky Mahlangu**
>
> Lucky Mahlangu is a 27-year-old Wizzkid who lives in Vlaklaagte in Mpumalanga, about 160 kilometres northwest of Pretoria. Lucky was introduced to Wizzit and the potential of becoming a Wizzkid by a friend who had just opened a Wizzit account. He went for the one-day training and passed the test, and now works full time as a Wizzkid, opening between 50 and 80 accounts a month. He has sold accounts to all of his friends, and finds other clients by approaching schools and businesses in his area, as well as simply by word of mouth. He says this is still the most important mechanism.
>
> His biggest competitor, he says, is Go Banking, a joint venture between retailer Pick n Pay and Nedbank, because its fees are relatively low. He says, however, that Go Banking does not have the advantage of having people like him on the ground where the people live. In effect, a Wizzkid is like a 24x7 portable branch. Community members know where to find him. They can come to him directly if they want to open an account and they can also approach him if they are having a problem with their account, in which case he can refer them to the right person at the call centre.
>
> Lucky describes Vlaklaagte as 'deep rural', and says that banking facilities in the area are sparse. People who cannot make use of cellphone banking have to travel a fair distance to get to the nearest branch or ATM. Then, when dealing with the branches, they are constrained on weekdays by banking hours, and on Saturdays by the fact that banks are so busy. Thus, the convenience and freedom to transact that a Wizzit account brings can change people's lives, he says.
>
> For him the advantages of being a Wizzkid come not only in the form of the profit that he makes from selling the starter packs, but also because of the 'the benefit that you can bring to the community … people put you on a pedestal'.

A third challenge that Wizzit has faced has been operating as a bank without the luxury of an established brand name which people know and trust, or physical points of presence to create an identity for itself. In Wizzit's experience, points of presence tend to give a bank credibility.

Independent research for CGAP (2006)[26] has shown that Wizzit customers use the bank because it is 'cheaper' (70 %), 'safe' (69 %), 'convenient' (68 %) and 'fast' (68 %). Although customers must still visit bank branches or the post office for cash deposits, with m-banking they can use their mobile phones to check their account balance, make payments or transfer money to friends and family. On average, Wizzit users appear to conduct more banking transactions per month using the mobile phone than non-users do using all other channels.[27] Balance enquiries are the most frequent type of transaction (60 %), followed by Wizzit transfers (25 %) and airtime purchases (15 %). Customers use their debit cards mostly for drawing cash from ATMs, and do not seem to be that comfortable with point-of-sale purchases.[28] Richardson comments, however, that since the research was done, prepaid airtime purchases are almost certainly closer to 30 % of transactions, and that customers are becoming more confident about point-of-sale purchasing.

> **Wizzit client: Nobelungu Mboda**
>
> Nobelungu Mboda is 67 and works as a cleaner at a factory near Kagiso, a township to the west of Johannesburg. Although she needs her daughter's help to use her phone to do her banking, having a Wizzit account has given her the peace of mind that her money is safe, and the convenience of being able to pay her bills from home.
>
> Before she opened her Wizzit account two years ago, she used to deposit her money into her daughter's bank account or keep it in a tin under her bed. 'I didn't have much,' she says. She paid cash for everything, and whenever anyone gave her money, it was in the form of cash. Her wages came in cash in an envelope.
>
> However, her money would regularly get stolen, particularly on payday. It just was not safe to be dealing in cash so much anymore. She had not thought of opening a bank account before because she believed that the bank charges would be too high. However, when the Wizzkid explained Wizzit's fees, they seemed to be reasonable, so she opened an account. Now her salary is paid into the account, and she uses a range of facilities that Wizzit offers. She pays for her groceries using the debit card, and uses her cellphone to pay for bills and electricity.
>
> For Nobelungu, the biggest benefit of having a Wizzit account is knowing that her money is safe, while she pays affordable fees. It has transformed her payday experience from one of fear that her hard-earned money would get stolen to confidence that she will have money to contribute to the needs of her household.

For his part, Richardson is pleased with the way in which Wizzit has progressed: from opening 2 000 accounts a month when the bank was launched, the bank is now opening up to four times this a month. Their success has been such that towards the end of 2007 the World Bank, through its financing arm the International Finance Corporation, bought a 10 % stake in the business. Wizzit will use the funds to extend its services in South Africa and eventually in other countries, keeping its focus on the poor and rural communities.

At the end of 2008, Wizzit had plans to launch in one other African country and in Romania. Richardson says there is a big demand in Romania where there is a 99 % cellphone penetration, and 60 % of the population is unbanked.

Learning from experience

The experience of these five organisations has shown that cost to the consumer alone will not determine the take-up of m-banking in this market. Wizzit's strategy, for instance, is not necessarily to be the cheapest product, but to remain affordable to their consumers. Richardson says that their experience shows that when people do not have money they do not transact. Success, he says, also depends on trust and confidence built over time. Parratt of MTN Banking notes that cellphone banking is not necessarily a cheaper model. It still has to comply with banking regulations and, for instance, opening a face-to-face account requires the presence of a FICA-trained salesperson, who therefore would have to have a matriculation (school leaving) certificate, and be a South African citizen at least. 'This adds to the cost of sale,' he says. 'The process is overburdened with legal compliances.' (See Table 6.1.)

Table 6.1 Mobile banking pricing – selected products, 2008

Bank	MTN	Standard Bank		WIZZIT
Product	MobileMoney	E Plan	Mzansi Blue Account	
Minimum balance	None	R50.00	R20.00	None
Monthly service fee	None	R6.65	None	None
Debit card purchase	R1.00	R2.00	R2.00	R1.99
Prepaid purchases	Free	Free	Free	R0.20
ATM cash deposit	1 % (min R3.00)	0.9 % (min R3.10)	R4.20	
Withdrawals				
Own-bank ATM withdrawal	R5.00	R5.05	R4.20	n/a
Other bank ATM withdrawal	R10.00	R11.75	R4.20	R4.00 plus 99c per R100
Balance enquiries				
Cellphone balance enquiry	R1.00			R 0.99
ATM balance enquiry	R1.00	R1.15	R2.00 (1 free)	R4.00
Statements				
Cellphone statement	R1.00			n/a
ATM statement			R2.00 (1 free)	n/a
Transfers and payments				
Cellphone transfers	R3.00		n/a	R2.99 - R4.99
ATM transfers		R5.05		n/a
Cellphone account payments	R3.00		n/a	R4.99
ATM account payments		R5.05		n/a

Source: Authors

Note: Fees capped at R75.00

There appear to be three other factors that organisations have to contend with if they are to be successful in this market: ensuring ease of use, dealing with regulatory issues, and generating sufficient transaction volumes.

Ease of use

One lesson that all of these organisations have learned is the importance of keeping the m-banking or m-commerce process and product simple. Hoffmann ascribes the slow initial take-up of MTN MobileMoney to the strong focus on self-service as well as the complexity of the process. Customers had to set up their accounts themselves using their cellphones, and this made it more difficult and intimidating to open an account. MTN has subsequently remedied this by offering customers various options for opening their account. The importance of ease of use is borne out by research conducted for CGAP which found that both users and non-users of m-banking have difficulty with technology, may prefer human interaction to interaction with a machine, and may have trouble using m-banking.[29] This means that the process that customers have to follow to conduct transactions has to be as user friendly as possible. Furthermore, notes Hughes, it is important to ensure that the product itself is simple. The pilot phase of M-Pesa showed that the product was too complicated, he says, and Vodafone had to simplify it to make it more usable and relevant to the market.

As well as ensuring that the process is not intimidating for users, it is important to make sure that customers and potential customers can access the service from any mobile phone. This is illustrated by MTN MobileMoney and FNB m-banking's initial experiences of launching their products in the market. Their products could only be used on phones with 32k SIM cards, of which there were relatively few in the market at the time. The inconvenience of having to swap SIM cards meant that take-up was low and only started to increase when the products were relaunched using technology that could be accessed from any phone. Celpay gives its clients the 64k SIM cards that its platform needs, but Muchenje believes that to get mass take-up of Celpay, mobile networks would need to start to use the 64k SIM as standard procedure.

Related to ease of use and accessibility is making it as simple as possible for potential customers to sign up for the service. 'The secret of m-banking is to make it accessible and easy – no application to download to the phone; quick and easy registration,' says Van Wyk. MTN's mass recruitment drive in the townships in late 2007, using a salesforce to assist in registration, proves the point. 'Ease of registration,' says Timson, 'is an overriding issue.'

Regulatory environment

The regulatory environment may be both a help and a hindrance to ease of access. Muchenje notes that registration in South Africa is far easier than in the DRC and Zambia. South Africa, he says, is one of the few countries in Africa with a working system of identity documents. This makes meeting the legal requirements of knowing customers and verifying customer information much easier. Thus it is possible to register customers remotely in South Africa, whereas in countries without an ID system, such as Zambia and the DRC, it is hard to do even the basic verification. Celpay has to physically see everyone who applies for an account, which makes opening accounts more difficult.

Hoffmann observes that technology has outpaced regulatory guidelines, and current regulations therefore do not cater for the new technology. In most countries, for example, there are no regulations relating to e-money, and it is not seen as a legitimate form of currency.[30] 'You have to work with the regulator,' says Hughes. Muchenje adds that the biggest area of learning for Celpay has been about the importance of the regulatory environment. 'Regulation creates certainty,' he says. 'When you invest in a new business, you are investing in future profits. But if regulation gets put into place that outlaws e-money, we don't have a business.'

Having said this, Muchenje acknowledges that at the moment the governments of Africa have to deal with more pressing issues than financial regulations, which are relatively high level. 'We accept that we will need to guide governments in making the right laws,' he says.

Porteous summarises by saying that in any new market there needs to be a blend of legal and regulatory openness to create the space for organisations to experiment, with sufficient legal and regulatory certainty to take away the fear that there will be arbitrary or negative changes to the regulatory framework.

Generating volumes

Once people have opened accounts, the challenge is to get them to conduct enough transactions to make the venture profitable or sustainable. As m-banking models are based around fees per transaction, transaction volumes are central to profitability. All the m-banking providers studied have found it difficult to achieve the necessary volumes. In this, they are dealing with a combination of a lack of trust in the concept of m-banking, a culture that has not traditionally seen the need for banking and electronic payment services, a consequent lack of financial literacy, and the nature of the market they are serving – in which employment is cyclical or sporadic.

Richardson points out that trust is crucially important when dealing with people's money, and this has been a limiting factor for M-Pesa. Potential customers are not sure that the money they send will be handed over by the agents on the other side. As a consequence, they have adopted a wait-and-see attitude to the service, and have been sending smaller amounts to test the system.

Porteous's research has found that a high proportion of people with bank accounts either do not understand m-banking or else have never even heard about it, and that along with the high levels of ignorance, there is also low trust in the concept. Van Wyk says that awareness of m-banking is important, because this builds trust and understanding. As such, she believes that increased competition is good for the market, because it helps to create the necessary awareness. This is something which Richardson remarks on too, noting that although the increased activity in m-banking poses a threat to Wizzit, the greater awareness and trust created has also benefited the organisation, and client numbers have grown as a result. In other words, providers are making a new market, and the more awareness created in the market the better it is for all the early players, since the issue is customer acceptance rather than market share.

Lack of trust is compounded by the fact that the concept of using a bank is foreign to many people in the unbanked segment of the market. Changing mindsets and behaviour patterns is necessary before people start using mobile technology regularly to conduct financial transactions. 'Basically, we are trying to bring about behaviour change,' says Richardson. 'For generations cash has been king in this segment of the market and it has been kept under a mattress. Now people are asking, "Why should I use a cellphone and who is Wizzit?" Part of the challenge has been to uncover needs that people never thought they had. If you've never had a bank account, why do you need one?'

'Individual-to-individual transfers don't really exist in the DRC and Zambia,' adds Muchenje. 'For us, the challenge has not been the high cost of getting individuals on board. It has been the cost of changing the mentality of people so that they trust and are willing to use our service.'

Finally, the cyclical nature of finances in this market has made it difficult to increase transaction volumes. Van Wyk says that while it has not been difficult to get people to open accounts, it has been so to keep these accounts active because people open bank accounts when they have a job, and let them go dormant when they lose their jobs.

Real potential?

Is m-banking living up to its promise? Does it have the potential to transform the financial services arena in Africa? And can it enable private sector organisations to extend financial services to the financially marginalised profitably and on a large-scale? Porteous points out that m-banking initiatives in Africa are still relatively new, making it difficult to accurately assess its transformational potential. Nevertheless, it is possible to draw some conclusions.

The extent to which mobile infrastructure itself is accessible to the unbanked and underbanked places a natural limit on the potential of m-banking in Africa. Despite the phenomenal growth rates of cellphone use, penetration remains relatively low in this market segment. In South Africa, for example, FinScope 2004 analysed mobile phone use by FSM[31] groups, and found that 'access and usage of cellphones in FSM 1–4 [primarily the unbanked] is at most 50 %, but as low as 20 % in FSM 1'.[32] Thus, mobile infrastructure does not yet reach the 80 % in FSM 1 who do not have mobile phones.

In Kenya, where mobile phones outnumber landlines by 20 to one,[33] 45 % of the population still do not have access to mobile phones. In the country's rural areas, where most people live, 52 % of Kenyans do not have access to a mobile phone.[34] In Zambia about three million people own a cellphone. Access to a cellphone exceeds 40 % of the population in only three provinces (Central, Copperbelt and Lusaka), and is 10 % or less in four provinces, including the Eastern province, which has the second highest number of people next to the Copperbelt.[35] Thus a large proportion of the population does not have access either to mobile phones or to financial services.

Despite this, large numbers of people do have mobile phones but not bank accounts. Porteous points out, for example, that 4.8 million South African adults (people over 16) have mobile phones but no bank accounts. This is around 15 % of the adult population and almost a third of those who do not currently have bank accounts.[36] Thus, although mobile phone penetration may still be relatively low, they are still used every day by millions of people who have no bank accounts, and the number of people using a mobile phone is growing significantly every day (at 50 % every year in Africa).

Against this backdrop, however, take-up of m-banking on the continent has not been quick, or happened on a large scale yet. Only between 400 000 and 700 000 South Africans make regular use of m-banking, which is between 1 % and 2 % of the adult population of the country. However, a survey conducted by technology research organisation, World Wide Worx, found that use among urban dwellers is growing rapidly. In total, 17 % of respondents said they had used their cellphones for banking services in 2007 compared with 8 % the previous year. An additional 24 % were expected to start using m-banking in the near future.[37]

Penetration of MTN Mobile Banking into its existing customer base – both low and high income – is less than 2 %. FNB has fared better, and the largest number of m-banking clients comes from its mass-market segment. M-Pesa is probably the most encouraging new entrant to date – although its customer base is still small as a proportion of Kenya's adult population, growth has been remarkably quick.

Aside from the issues of trust and ease of use, Parratt says that the limiting factor is not what the technology can do; it is more a question of what the market is looking for. FinScope research backs this up, as it indicates a potential disconnection between what unbanked people want from a bank and what m-banking currently gives them. The FinScope Mobile Banking Survey showed that for m-banking users, convenience is the strongest motivation for having a bank account – 85 % of respondents classified this as their primary motive. Saving is only a secondary motivation. In contrast, those who do not have bank accounts say that their strongest motivation for opening an account would be to save (65 %). Only 40 % say that they would open a bank account for the sake of convenience.[38] People who use m-banking are also much more driven by the ability to make payments. In total, 56 % of those who use mobile banking say that making payments is a motivation for wanting the account, while only 7 % of those who do not have bank accounts say that this would motivate them to open one.

It is in this arena – that of real-time, person-to-person transfers – that Porteous believes the real transformational potential of m-banking lies. Richardson agrees. He says that this is where the mobile phone comes into its own, and he believes it could completely change the payment environment. The experience of M-Pesa bears this out. Although a relatively small proportion of the Kenyan population has used the service, it signed up more customers in four months than MTN Banking and Wizzit have managed to do in three years.

Porteous foresees that once real-time, person-to-person transfers are widely accepted, the reliance on branches and ATMs – banking's cash-handling channels – will change. There will be less need for cash if people widely accept instant bank transfers, he says, and people may serve as human ATMs, giving cash in exchange for a credit transfer which is validated on the phone in real time. He says that such a shift could be decisive in breaking down geographic barriers to access, as cash would become as accessible as the next m-banking user. It would also substantially reduce the cost of banking services, as cash deposits and withdrawals together currently constitute at least half of the typical monthly cost of running a basic bank account.

Conclusion

Although m-banking is in its early stages, those who have made the first forays into this market in Africa believe it has potential to open up markets where cost and accessibility have put up significant barriers to entry and, at the same time, to extend the reach of financial services to those who have been marginalised because of the constraints of physical banking infrastructure.

Muchenje believes that when it comes to reaching the poor, the m-banking model has significant advantages over conventional banking. Not only is it cheaper, it is also more flexible: because it starts from a base of new technology, it does not rely on other dependencies and it is not hampered by the requirements of conventional banking systems.

What m-banking has shown is the flaw in the belief that by simply making banking services accessible and more affordable, the unbanked and underbanked would jump at the chance to use them. It requires a concerted effort to design the appropriate products and build awareness, trust and understanding, before people will be confident enough in the concept on a wide scale.

ESSAY

Technology trends that will drive base of the pyramid financial services: Why telecoms, not banks, are the key to the future

Allen L Hammond – *Senior Entrepreneur at Ashoka. He was formerly vice-president for innovation and the director of the Development through Enterprise project at the World Resources Institute*

Arguably the most important recent innovation in financial services for the poor came from outside the banking community. Over the past 30 years, the rise of microfinance has helped many base of the pyramid (BOP) households to improve their livelihoods and even, in some cases, to climb out of poverty. Initially grant driven and led by mostly not-for-profit organisations, microfinance is increasingly becoming a commercial activity with significant involvement by banks. And with an industry-wide client base of around 80 million borrowers, it is clear that Mohammed Yunus, as one of the pioneers of microfinance through the Grameen Bank he founded, deserved his Nobel Prize. Banks may well be the future of microfinance, but they were not the source of the innovation.

The next really important innovation in financial services for the poor will also come mainly from outside the banking community. That innovation is mobile phone banking – already fully commercial in the Philippines, South Africa and Kenya, and gathering momentum virtually everywhere in the developing world. While banks may play an important role in this activity, they are unlikely to be the real drivers and, without significant changes, may be sidelined by the owners of the technology that makes it possible, namely the mobile telecom companies that own the networks capable of reaching several billion unbanked people, and the servers capable of processing many billions of tiny transactions, or startup m-transaction companies that figure out innovative ways to use those networks.

Enabling technology trends

There are several technology and business trends worth tracking. One is the build-out of mobile telecom networks, arguably the most remarkable – and largest – technological phenomenon on the planet. There are already more than 1.5 billion mobile phones in use in developing countries, and that number is likely to reach 2.5 billion within the next five years. More than 80 % of new customers worldwide will come from developing countries and, since nearly everyone in developing countries who is not part of the BOP already has a mobile phone, that growth will come almost entirely from adding BOP customers. Growth is still explosive – in India, mobile companies are adding eight million new customers a month, and planned to build more than 30 000 additional cell towers in 2008. Mobile companies in Africa planned to invest US$50 billion to expand their networks from 2008 to 2012, double the rate of investment of the previous five years.[39]

A recent study showed that the share of BOP household expenditures on information and communications technology services (mainly mobile telephony) rises eight-fold between the lowest and the highest income segments of the BOP – a far more dramatic increase than any other sector, and a pattern of spending preference that underscores the huge latent demand that remains to be tapped.[40] This is especially so in Asia and Africa, where BOP populations and markets are dominantly rural and not yet well served by mobile networks. Nonetheless, by connecting BOP households to livelihoods and other sources of income, voice and text-messaging services alone are having a profound beneficial effect on the BOP.

A second trend is the increasing technological sophistication of mobile handsets, even as prices decline. Virtually all basic handsets now include voice and data capability and significant memory; many are multimode, capable of working over more than one frequency band; cameras are an increasingly common feature, even for low-end handsets. Some high-end handsets include Wi-Fi capability,[41], and there appears to be no technological reason why internet-enabled mobile handsets, such as multimode handsets with a Wi-Fi radio, cannot easily be made available to low-end customers as well. One estimate is that the cost, in quantity, of adding a Wi-Fi chip to a handset is about US$5. Moreover, costs of entry-level handsets continue to decline: US$30 GSM phones are common, and Vodafone introduced a US$20 handset in India in 2008. The processing power of handsets is also increasing rapidly, and is expected to equal that of today's PC within about five years. Mobile phones are becoming inexpensive, internet-enabled, multimedia-capable computing devices, with a replacement market approaching one billion phones a year, so it is not hard to think of them as portable banking terminals.

Technology is making it possible to provide services in remote rural areas.

Of course, mobile phone networks do not yet cover many rural areas in developing countries, and may never do so. The costs of installing a mobile network, usually more than US$100 000 per cell tower, including diesel generators, may simply be prohibitive, especially where sparse populations and low incomes mean that a positive return on investment will take a long time. Even where mobile networks exist, many BOP households cannot afford the service, which is why a third technology trend may prove important, especially for BOP financial services – the growing capability and very low costs of advanced fixed wireless networks, especially Wi-Fi or WiMax networks, but including advanced Very Small Aperture Terminal (VSAT) networks. These technologies are based on open standards and attract many manufacturers, and hence have declined in cost rapidly.

They also are optimised for data – they are broadband networks capable of carrying a much higher volume of internet or data traffic than the proprietary cellular networks commonly deployed by mobile telecoms. That makes them ideal for a wide range of services, including Voice over Internet Protocol (VoIP) – commonly called internet telephony – and it may turn out that these advanced networks are especially well suited as a way to extend mobile telephony into more remote rural areas.

The World Resources Institute, in partnership with US and Australian development agencies, a provincial government and a mobile telecom company – as well as Intel and other equipment vendors – have deployed just such a Wi-Fi/VoIP network in a poor rural part of Vietnam. The pilot uses advanced mesh Wi-Fi technology to link together a group of rural villages, and advanced Wi-Fi backhaul technology to link those villages to existing optical fibre. It provides voice service using VoIP on Wi-Fi-enabled phones, and can also provide internet access where there are PCs. The structure of the network makes it possible to provide local calling – within a group of villages – virtually for free (in effect, these villages are all within a large Wi-Fi hotspot), while charging normal prepaid tolls for calls to more distant locations. Since about half of the phone calls in most local networks stay local, this is a powerful incentive to own a phone. But the most interesting characteristic of the network is its low cost: we estimate that the capital investment required to build this network to cover every rural village in a mountainous province with a population of about a million is less than US$3 per person, or less than one fifth the cost of a conventional cellular network.

An additional characteristic of the Wi-Fi networks is their low power requirements. They can be powered with solar cells instead of diesel generators when no access to the electrical grid is available, making them more environmentally benign as well. We believe that mobile telecom companies will be able to profitably provide services even in remote rural areas. With Wi-Fi-enabled mobile handsets, the phones will work on either the village Wi-Fi network or the urban cellular network. In fact, most users will not know or care which network the phone is using – as long as it works.

It may seem strange to suggest building a modern broadband network with cutting-edge technology in the world's poorest areas. Yet the justification, I believe, is that the technology, or rather the services it enables, is simply more valuable in such places. BOP communities stand to benefit more than developed urban locations that already have a variety of options for connectivity. When you have no phone service and no internet access, that first connection makes a huge difference – and is only affordable with the very latest technology. The demand for affordable phone services and for internet access in BOP markets is large and largely unmet. As it turns out, more than half a dozen of the world's leading mobile phone companies active in developing countries have expressed interest in this approach and in visiting the Vietnam pilot to see for themselves both how it works and the extent of customer acceptance.

Mobile banking

What are the implications of these technology trends for mobile banking, and especially for extending banking services to low-income rural areas? Let me start with an example from my recent work in Vietnam. If you are out on the streets around midnight in Hanoi,

Vietnam's capital, you cannot miss the thousands of motorbikes streaming into the city, so loaded with produce that the driver is nearly invisible. These farmers are taking their produce to wholesale markets that operate at night, so that the products reach stores and restaurants in time for the next morning. The farmers, however, do not stay – they turn over their crop of flowers or vegetables to the owner of a market stall, and then start the often long journey back to their rural village. When do they get paid for their crop? Usually not until the next time they come back into the city, which might be a week or a month later, when they return with their next load. Suppose they could get paid the next morning, as soon as their crop is sold by the market stall, on their mobile phone?

That mobile phone banking will benefit rural BOP families seems clear. The continuing rapid growth of mobile telecom networks and customers provides an enormous potential market for banking services – the 2.5 billion people in developing countries expected to become mobile phone customers within five years. The growing processing power and sophistication of mobile handset technology will make a wider range of services possible, and decreasing costs will put mobile handsets within reach of a wider market. Possible services include advanced transactions security and voice recognition/voice synthesis that could benefit BOP customers (for example by coaching illiterate customers through a banking transaction). Extending mobile networks with Wi-Fi or other fixed wireless technologies and with internet telephony can provide cover in more remote or sparsely populated areas, as well as lower costs for local calling. Thus the conditions could hardly be more favourable for extending financial services to the vast number of people in developing countries who are presently unbanked.

Two basic mobile banking models have been deployed: bank-centric models that work under the banking licence of a single bank and will work on one, or frequently multiple, mobile telecom networks; and telecom-centric models that work on a single telecom network but are compatible with multiple banks or banking networks. Wizzit, a start-up company in South Africa, uses a bank-centric model that can work with multiple mobile networks; the Smart money network in the Philippines is also bank-centric, but works only on the Smart Telecom mobile network; and M-Pesa in Kenya is bank-centric, but works only on the Vodafone (Safaricom) mobile network. G-cash, deployed on the Globe Telecom mobile network, is a telecom-centric model that works with multiple banks. These models have been discussed elsewhere and I will not elaborate on them here. But it is perhaps useful to note that Vodafone expected about 200 000 customers at the end of the first year of operation of its M-Pesa system in Kenya, but found itself dealing with long lines of eager customers that resulted in 200 000 customers in four months. Growth has continued to be rapid. There is no shortage of demand for mobile banking services.

These models may well be rapidly replicated. Globe is franchising G-cash to other mobile companies; Wizzit plans to do the same; Vodafone is planning to replicate M-Pesa on other Vodafone networks in developing countries. Other models will appear. All Mexican banks, for example, have signed onto a common platform for m-transactions, and will shortly begin deploying mobile banking services. Several South African banks offer their own mobile banking services, although Wizzit has undercut them in price and appears to be growing more rapidly. There is movement toward mobile banking in Nigeria and Pakistan, and in a number of other countries. We are probably entering an era of rapid experimentation and competition from which the winning models will emerge. It is plausible that over the next five years we will see one billion unbanked people gain access to financial services via mobile phone banking.

Nonetheless, it is significant that the driving force in each of these pioneering models is either a mobile telecom company or an independent start-up, not a bank. Mobile banking for the BOP will work only when transaction costs are kept low, and it is mobile telecom companies, not banks, that are used to manage billions of voice- or text-message transactions and millions of very small customer accounts. The leading customers for Hewlett Packard's high-end servers in developing countries are not banks, but mobile telecom companies. And it is more typically telecom companies or start-ups that track technology trends carefully and are comfortable with deploying cutting-edge technologies. Mobile telecom companies in developing countries already understand that their growth is dependent on serving BOP customers, and they are eagerly looking for value-added services to offer to them. From that perspective, mobile banking looks like a killer application, one that will drive phone use and increased individual phone ownership – you might share your phone, but you are less likely to share your wallet.

Another way to look at the institutional nature of the players is to note that mobile banking is a new business with unknowns and risks. Mobile telecom companies are quite entrepreneurial; banks generally are not. Banks might need to create separate divisions to become successful players in mobile banking, just as many have had to become microfinance players. It is important that banks do become active players, not just accept a passive role, simply because mobile banking is likely to become such a large activity. But organisational and business process change is likely to be necessary for banks to capture a meaningful share of this space. One way to measure this is to examine the range of services likely to be offered via mobile banking platforms – and also likely to find wide market acceptance in the BOP – as well as some of the challenges to the successful scale-up of these activities.

Mobile transactions

Mobile banking provides a way to offer a wide range of financial services. In addition to cash management, loan and bill payments, direct deposits of salaries or of receipts from retail sales or other commercial transactions, mobile networks can also offer remittances and money transfers and, either directly or via a linked debit card, facilitate cashless consumer purchases. In Kenya, Vodafone found that some M-Pesa customers were using the system to provide a safe way to carry funds from one location to another. They would deposit cash into the system, and then draw it out again on reaching their destination. Typically, both bank branches and a wide range of retail shops provide cash-in and cash-out locations, where mobile banking customers can exchange cash for digital credits or vice versa. In the Philippines, Smart Money customers are notified of a remittance from a relative overseas via a text message, and can pick up their cash at any McDonald's or at a large number of *sari-sari* convenience kiosks, or have it credited directly to their debit card. Given the large and rapidly growing volume of both international remittances (estimated at US$300 billion a year) and domestic money transfers, and the hazards of carrying cash in many parts of the developing world, these services will find ready markets.

Mobile phones can also provide a marketing and sales platform for additional financial services, such as insurance (life insurance, health insurance, crop or weather insurance), since they can readily provide information on, or answer questions about, specific products in local languages. Such information is especially easy to provide with the VoIP systems already described as part of village Wi-Fi networks, since they can be programmed into the VoIP switches. Moreover, the transaction records, including payment or remittance records, of a customer's mobile phone account may work as a substitute credit rating that could qualify a mobile banking customer for a microloan – applied for, approved, and paid out over the mobile platform. Both of these examples illustrate how mobile transactions could dramatically lower transaction costs compared to conventional banking methods, thus making BOP banking services more affordable to customers and more profitable to banks. However, they both entail significant changes in business process for banking institutions.

Barriers to mobile banking

A key barrier to the rapid expansion of mobile banking is lack of familiarity with the technologies and business models on the part of both banks and telecom companies, and the necessity of establishing partnerships that involve both kinds of companies. As awareness spreads of the success of mobile banking efforts, and of the details of specific models, these hesitations are beginning to disappear. Competition and the fear of being left behind will increasingly spur innovation.

A more significant barrier is regulatory approval, especially by central banks and sometimes by telecom regulatory authorities. Central banks, and the US Treasury Department, are concerned that mobile banking must adequately protect customers and the banking system against fraud, money laundering and other criminal activities such as the transfer of funds by terrorist organisations. At present, security for mobile banking transactions rests on several parallel approaches: device-based security, such as the unique SIM card within each mobile handset that identifies the customer who owns the phone; know-your-customer requirements, especially for the retail cash-in/cash-out points where customers are usually required to have a traditional bank account and establish their identity to the bank to open the account; and pattern-recognition software that tracks transactions to ensure that limits on the size and frequency of transactions do not exceed regulatory limits that might suggest money-laundering activity.

Many central banks in developing countries have not established rules for mobile phone banking, nor set in place some version of the transaction security system described above. As mobile banking is still in its infancy, serious criminal attention to defeating these systems, for example by hacking SIM cards so as to 'establish' fake accounts or take over legitimate accounts, has probably not reached the levels likely to occur eventually. Building capacity in central banks and spreading awareness of safeguards and how they need to be implemented is important to accelerate the spread of mobile banking.

There may also be a role for technology. There has been a lot of work on biometric identity systems in recent years, and it may prove possible to adapt some of that technology to the mobile handset platform in ways that shift security from device based to transaction based. Let me give a hypothetical example. Earlier work at the Massachusetts Institute of Technology Media Lab established that a digital picture of a face combined with a digital sample of a voice, when processed with appropriate algorithms, yielded a better biometric ID – a unique pattern for each individual – than a fingerprint. Since mobile phones with a camera can both take a picture of the face and capture a voice sample, it is possible that this biometric approach could be adapted to run on a mobile handset, then transmit the resulting biometric ID for comparison with the ID stored in a bank server to authenticate a transaction. That would replace the device-based security safeguard with something much more robust. A number of other biometric approaches are also being tried, and it is too early to say whether any of them will prove to be feasible and affordable. But with the processing power of handsets rising rapidly, it may just be a matter of when, not if, biometric approaches could add to the security arsenal.

The handset manufacturers have a major role to play. As they begin to anticipate the demand for a wider range of services on handsets – mobile banking; mobile educational services, particularly for informal, out-of-the-classroom education; and mobile entertainment – they are in position to develop technology solutions that can facilitate new applications, especially those of interest for BOP markets, where virtually all the growth in handsets will take place.

Where could banks take the lead?

If, as I have argued, banks are not likely to be in the forefront of mobile phone banking, as paradoxical as that may sound, where could they lead? Banks are already moving rapidly into microfinance, where they have the capability to bring scale well beyond what microfinance institutions can do. Mobile phone banking will accelerate that trend, allowing very low transaction costs, especially for loan repayments. An even larger BOP opportunity, however, is the mobilisation of investment capital for small and medium sized businesses, especially those that serve BOP markets, and often create badly needed jobs for BOP communities. A particular gap is the range above microfinance, but below the investment size now readily serviced by a wide range of commercial entities – say US$100 000 to US$5 million. This mesofinance gap is critical to creating inclusive growth, since it is in this range that most real businesses are started – those that can create significant employment opportunities, scale of service or product delivery, and wealth. Investing in or mobilising private capital to invest in ventures of this size may seem a stretch for commercial banks, but a number of African banks have joined with the Shell Foundation to do just that, and the Asian Development Bank is investing, usually with private sector partners, in similar SME investment funds in parts of Asia. Both models employ dedicated local fund managers – separate from the banks or other investors – and both report successful returns, even with investment sizes as low as US$300 000.

The advantage for banks in venturing into this territory, which in some ways is far closer to their traditional business model than either microfinance or mobile phone banking, is that by helping grow local businesses, they also grow entities that will need their banking services and that grow the local economy – that is, the investment doubles as a form of market development, quite apart from its financial returns. Given the paucity of angel investors and organised venture capital funds in most developing countries, there are in fact few other entities that could lead the growth of SME investment – banks are perhaps the essential player. And given the BOP-heavy structure of the populations and economies of most developing countries, it is likely that most SMEs will focus on serving BOP markets, where they have the comparative advantage of being close to the market. Banks that are willing to lead and that learn how to play successfully in SME finance are likely to do extremely well, because the opportunity is immense.

Endnotes

[1] International Telecommunications Union (2007).
[2] Hoffman (2006).

3 Porteous (2006).
4 Ivatury & Pickens (2006a).
5 Porteous (2006).
6 Ivatury & Pickens (2006a).
7 Porteous & Wishart (2006).
8 Ivatury & Pickens (2006b).
9 The Heritage Foundation & The Wall Street (2007).
10 http://www.procredit-holding.com, Congo link.
11 The Heritage Foundation & The Wall Street (2007).
12 Ibid.
13 Eighty 20 Consulting (2007).
14 FirstRand (2005).
15 SIM (Subscriber Identity Module) is a mini smartcard used in GSM mobile phones that contains operator and subscriber specific data that enables users to be authenticated.
16 A monetary value that is stored electronically on a technical device (either card-based or network-based) and that can be readily exchanged.
17 The Heritage Foundation & The Wall Street (2007).
18 Porteous & Hazelhurst (2004).
19 Information from a 2007 presentation by Yolande van Wyk.
20 USSD (Unstructured Supplementary Service Data) is a technology used by the mobile network to send information between a mobile phone and an application on a network, for example a banking application at a bank. It is a menu-driven form of SMS (short message service) whereby customers receive a text menu on their phone as opposed to a string of words.
21 WAP (Wireless Application Protocol) is a set of communication standards to enable the accessing of online internet services from a mobile phone.
22 World Wide Worx (2007).
23 FNB (2006).
24 South African Reserve Bank (undated).
25 Mitchell & Heil (2006).
26 Ivatury & Pickens (2006b).
27 Ivatury & Pickens (2006a).
28 ECI*Africa* (2005).
29 Ivatury and Pickens (2006a).
30 Hoffman (2006).
31 The FSM divided consumers into different segments on criteria including financial penetration; physical access; financial discipline; knowledge of, and control of, finance; connectedness; and optimism and financial astuteness. On this basis, eight cohorts are identified, from FSM 1–8, with the highest number reserved for the most financially sophisticated clients. FSM 1–3 are the least financially sophisticated, and most of the unbanked fall into these.
32 Feasibility (2005).
33 Information provided by Vodafone, June 2007.
34 Financial Sector Deepening (2007).
35 Eighty 20 Consulting (2007).
36 Porteous (2007).
37 World Wide Worx (2007).
38 Porteous (2007).
39 Phillips (2007).
40 Hammond et al (2007).
41 Wi-Fi is the wireless standard already widely deployed employed in hotspots, and in homes and offices; WiMax is its more sophisticated (and expensive) cousin, designed to handle the multiple reflections of wireless signals encountered in urban environments and to provide slightly longer range. Compared to Wi-Fi, its complexity and cost are at present a disadvantage in rural areas of developing countries, although costs are expected to continue declining.

Chapter Seven
Technology suppliers

The case studies in this chapter focus on the contribution of two companies that do not provide financial services but provide the technology that facilitates the delivery of financial services. Both companies are actively collaborating with financial services organisations to expand financial outreach.

New technology in and of itself will not expand financial access. Technology can help expand financial access by enabling providers to capture a bigger market by expanding their outreach, or to drive greater efficiencies from a market that might otherwise be insufficiently profitable. In other words, technology can benefit both the front and the back end of a financial services business. Cointel extended the application of its technology from enabling airtime purchases to be made using credit cards to enabling airtime to be paid for using a pre-funded bank account. This will dramatically extend the reach of its technology into a market that would not typically have credit cards. Ferlo's model is not just to drive inefficiency out of a single organisation's processes but, by building and operating a platform that all MFIs in Senegal can use, to drive it out of an entire industry.

Cointel: Enabling m-commerce

> Cointel provides enabling technology for mobile commerce – in other words the technology that allows the transactions that take place using mobile phones to happen. Cointel is well placed to take advantage of the predicted boom in m-commerce in Africa. Its story captures many of the strands that bind the debate on the potential for m-commerce and m-banking: the importance of interoperability, the need for large organisations to want to do things differently, the need to map a technology solution on to end users' requirements (not the other way round), and the importance of customer education. It also demonstrates the role that this kind of technology can play in creating and sustaining small business activity in Africa.

When Gary Nunez, Mark Attieh, Leon Richards and Ahmed Ayob got together in Nunez's spare bedroom to form Cointel in 1996, it was not their mission to provide m-commerce services to the poor. This evolved over time, as the potential of Simplus, the m-commerce technology platform that they developed, became evident.

Simplus allows consumers to conduct secure payment transactions using their cellphones. Through partnerships with financial institutions, it therefore creates the opportunity to make banking services accessible to people in South Africa and its neighbouring countries who have cellphones but no access to conventional financial services.[1]

The Simplus technology platform

Cointel originally entered the market with the launch of a product called Autocharge. Autocharge replaced the need to purchase prepaid cellphone airtime recharge vouchers, and allowed end users to buy airtime directly from their cellphones, with payment being charged to their credit card. The technology platform that Nunez and company developed for Autocharge evolved to support other offerings, and was later branded Simplus.

Simplus makes it possible to effect payment using a cellphone instead of a credit or debit card. The platform offers all the functionality that an ATM provides, except for the dispensing of cash. Simplus therefore allows person-to-person, business-to-business and business-to-consumer financial transactions to take place using a cellphone.[2]

The platform accommodates any make, model and generation of mobile phone or SIM card. 'This is critical in emerging markets, where handsets are usually older-generation models,' says Nunez. 'In addition, certain networks in African countries have less functionality than South African networks. Cointel can implement the Simplus platform in any location where GSM is present. The original intention was that customers should never have to change the SIM or device. We recognised this as an important starting point in the prepaid market.'

Cointel's evolution into the bottom of the pyramid

When Cointel developed Autocharge in the late 1990s, few prepaid cellphone customers had credit cards. Despite this, Cointel's founders were thinking about how the concept of prepaying for services could couple with the cashless environment of cellphone-based payment to solve many telecom and financial services challenges – and ultimately provide banking services to people typically not considered creditworthy.

Appropriate technology is making it possible for small businesses like *spaza* shops to access financial services.

Cointel's research revealed that the owners of *shebeens*[3] and *spaza* shops,[4] food and beverage companies, and petroleum distributors liked the idea that a customer could order and pay, and receive confirmation of this using a cellphone.[5] However, the need for an individual to have a credit or debit card from which payment could be derived was limiting.

Cointel's business challenge was not about how to get the technology to work – Nunez and his colleagues knew their technology worked. It related to finding a way of working with financial institutions to enable people to use the technology. The company faced the challenge of how, in a developing country, low-income consumers could use an electronic payment system that provided instant access to services while simultaneously ensuring the payment was actually transferred into the seller's bank account.

To overcome this obstacle, Cointel, MasterCard and Absa developed a 'virtual card' product, which involved cellphone users being given a MasterCard Absa account with which they could prefund their account. In some cases, there was no card at all. Thus, payment could be initiated from the cellphone user's account to a beneficiary's account using a cellphone, as long as there were funds available.

With the MasterCard Absa solution in place, Cointel also created a framework for small businesses to act as middlemen selling airtime from Vodacom (South Africa's largest cellphone network) to other mobile users. By making a free cellphone call, the business could transfer airtime to a customer's cellphone. In turn, the customer could use his cellphone to pay the full retail price for the airtime, while Vodacom automatically debited the wholesale cost price from the entrepreneur's bank account, thus creating an instant profit for the entrepreneur.

At the time, Vodacom was managing a growing number of community service franchisees who operated 22 000 community payphones. Whereas the payphones of fixed-line operator Telkom and mobile phone network MTN were standalone units, to create employment and avoid problems such as vandalism, Vodacom payphones were supervised and its payphone shops run by entrepreneurs.

One of Vodacom's main problems was how to make it easier for its franchisees to buy airtime. As things stood, they physically had to go to a bank to transfer funds into Vodacom's account and fax proof of this deposit to Vodacom before their phones would be credited with the airtime.

A variation on Cointel's Autocharge concept provided the solution. In partnership with Absa and MasterCard, Cointel provided tailor-made bank accounts to the community phone-shop franchisees. This meant that, by dialling in to the Simplus platform from a cellphone or through the internet, franchisees could top up the airtime of all or some of their phones, while payment was automatically debited from their prefunded account. In 2007, about 40 000 franchisees had these bank accounts. Under the terms of its agreement with Vodacom, Cointel charges a management fee based on a percentage of volume recharged.

The system benefits not only Vodacom, but its franchisees as well. Edith Manyame, a Vodacom franchisee in Alexandra, a township in the north of Johannesburg, since 1999, comments on how much more convenient this system is. 'Previously I had to make a deposit into a Vodacom account, fax my deposit slip through and then wait for my airtime to be loaded. Now buying airtime is quicker and simpler,' she says.[6] This system has been expanded to other prepaid environments including Telkom's PrepaidFone and Eskom's prepaid electricity.

Expansion beyond South African borders

In South Africa, Simplus is also being used by the smaller banks to facilitate m-banking, although the big four banks, Absa, FNB, Standard Bank and Nedbank, have developed their own enabling software. Outside South Africa, Cointel is partnering with the network operator and large banks in Namibia, where it has sold Simplus to Mobile Telecommunications Limited (MTC), the only mobile network in that country, which has partnered with Bank Windhoek and FNB Namibia to provide m-banking services to its customers.

In 2007, MTC and Cointel were also developing a distributed airtime solution to enable the sale of airtime directly from a cellphone to an MTC customer. It would work like Autocharge, but allow the customer to resell airtime and make a profit. MTC therefore structured a financial model to cater for a sales margin for these resellers, giving them the ability to earn revenue out of the electronic sale of airtime.[7]

A springboard into banking the unbanked

The FinScope 2004 study showed that 31 % of South Africa's 15.8 million unbanked people have access to a cellphone. Cointel saw this as an opportunity to exploit the popularity of this device and extend m-commerce to the unbanked using Simplus.[8] 'The local prepaid top-up market is the first step in introducing mobile payments on a broader scale, given the size and growth potential of the cellphone market,' Nunez explains. 'With cellphone usage in South Africa experiencing unprecedented growth, mobile commerce initiatives are expected to develop significantly in future.'[9]

The venture with Vodacom franchisees has given a number of small businesses, which might not otherwise have qualified for a bank account, access to transactional capability.[10] Nunez adds that exposure to the MasterCard Absa accounts often encourages people to open conventional accounts. 'When payphone operators receive an account to transact airtime, it exposes them to banking,' he says. 'Sixty to seventy per cent of users subsequently open a normal bank account to do other banking.'

Although Nunez regards m-commerce as still in its infancy in South Africa, he is confident that it will develop into a massive market opportunity because anyone with a cellphone and a bank account can do their banking using a cellphone.

He admits, however, that successful uptake of the technology depends on customer and end-user education. 'Many users have never banked and do not understand issues such as the costs of opening an account, and network charges. Often users have never used their mobile phone to do banking. While education is the responsibility of the entity implementing the system, without end user demand for the product, the bank may not want to offer the services.'

'A critical factor for mobile commerce success is to provide value-adds for the end user,' he says. 'So banks that want to service the unbanked have to change their banking model.'

NOTE: In August 2007, Vodacom, which already had a 70 % share in Cointel's holding company, Smartphone SP (Pty) Ltd, acquired the remaining shares in Smartphone.

Ferlo: A smartcard solution in Senegal

> Ferlo is essentially a story about the benefits a shared payments infrastructure can bring to a widely dispersed microfinance industry such as the one in Senegal. Ferlo is a technology provider, providing a payments system that not only extends access, and improves the quality of access, but also allows microfinance institutions to operate more efficiently. The study describes how the implementation costs need to be shared equitably between the provider and the beneficiaries, and also creatively so as to ensure that the user base develops critical mass.

The Ferlo project is a joint venture between AfriCap, a specialised MFI investment fund, and Senegalese technology firm ByteTech, which specialises in electronic payment systems. The two companies decided to install and operate an electronic payment platform that could be used by all MFIs in Senegal. A pilot project was launched in 2004 to test the viability of a shared platform for the industry, with ByteTech providing the intellectual property and AfriCap the operating capital.[11] Following the success of the pilot, a private company incorporated in Senegal was established in September 2005.

The main product is a smartcard called MoneaCard, which provides electronic payments to the MFIs. It can be used as a credit card, a savings card, to transfer funds and for internal payments. It is backed by a network of POS terminals, ATMs and reloading points.

The MoneaCard smartcard provides microfinance institutions with access to services such as savings, credit, funds transfer and internal payments.

The immediate goal is to reduce costs, improve efficiency and increase access to microfinance for the financially underserved Senegalese population. The ultimate aim of the project is to allow any MFI in the eight countries in UEOMA, (West African Economic and Monetary Union), which have the same currency and common central bank rules, to issue cards to their clients. This target market is 1 500 MFIs, three million potential cardholders and 3 500 POS outlets.

Sector background

The microfinance sector in Senegal is one of the most dynamic in UEOMA. It has a solid core of profitable institutions that compete with banks to finance the top-rated SMEs. The way the microfinance sector is regulated makes it difficult for commercial banks to grant microcredit, as to do so they would need to create dedicated financial institutions similar in structure to MFIs.[12] Senegal's microfinance sector has grown strongly since 2000.

The Senegalese economy has also expanded, achieving an annual average growth of approximately 4 % and per-capita GDP growth of 1.5 % in real terms.[13] The penetration rate of MFIs rose from 16 % of all households in 2000 to 25 % in 2003, and outstanding MFI credit expanded 3.3 times faster than bank credit in the same period.

Despite the growth in credit through MFIs, SME access to credit in Senegal is still burdened by the relatively high costs of financial intermediation. A lack of crucial infrastructure hampers rural access to financial services, and this is compounded by many people remaining outside the formal economy and an over-reliance on cash as the accepted method of payment. Innovative microfinance products, in particular those that extend access to financial services to the rural population, which were 58 % of the total population in 2005, could transform the financial sector in Senegal.

Technology as a strategic tool

Ferlo aims to modernise business transactions through a multifunctional smartcard system that facilitates access to financial transactions. A bottleneck at cash distribution points will be relieved by providing an online and offline payment transaction system. For instance, large companies could use the system for billing customers, employers could use it for payroll services, and financial institutions could offer convenient national and international payment transfers. The system could thus facilitate an overall increase in the volume of financial and non-financial transactions through an electronic platform, while substantially reducing transaction costs. In the long run, Ferlo could also provide the basis for generating the market intelligence necessary to develop a financially viable credit bureau that will help the development of a real credit market in the country and the region.

Figure 7.1 Transactions architecture

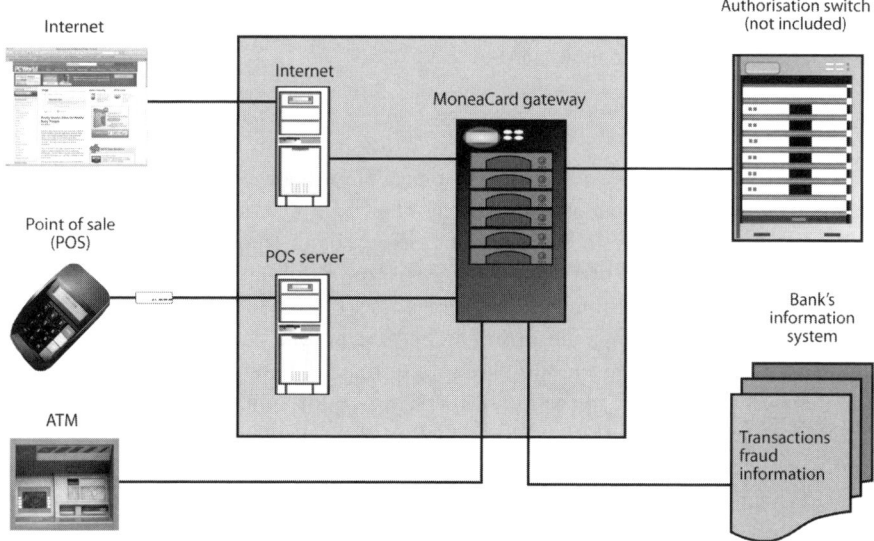

Source: Ferlo

In the business model used, Ferlo does not sell a platform; rather, it acquires transactions from different points, such as an internet café, a POS device or an ATM, and delivers those transactions to subscriber MFIs. The operation of the shared platform is outsourced to ByteTech. MoneaCard is a multifunctional smartcard that gives users access to five basic services: membership, savings, credit, funds transfer and internal payments. Because smartcard technology was chosen over magnetic strip-card technology, this functionality can be increased significantly over time.

How it works in practice

The pilot began in March 2004 for nine months. One thousand smartcards were distributed to potential clients, and 20 POS terminals, three ATMs, four reloading points and one card pre-personalisation centre were established. The personalisation centre is used by MFIs to upload their information, and Ferlo returns information relevant only to their clients. It is a closed-user system, so no MFI has access to another MFI's client information, neither can clients from one MFI make a transaction into another MFI. An international standard service platform is being used, which provides the opportunity for interconnectivity with other platforms, such as an authorisation switch for a Visa programme.

The smartcard complies with International Standards Organisation's ISO 7816 standards, as used by Europay-MasterCard-Visa. These technical specifications allow future introduction of other products based on similar technology in other parts of the world. The communication between the cards is established through a terminal (ATM or POS, or a PC equipped with a card reader). All the operations are encrypted with special keys, adding a much needed element of security and fraud protection. During the transaction, a complete snapshot is recorded as a numerical certificate in the card's microprocessor memory. This information contains basic data such as the date, the hour, the client code, the retailer code and the amount paid. Collecting this kind of data develops an essential baseline for future investments in this sector, particularly since this type of data has always been estimated in the past.

Business model

The business model is based on an MFI entry ticket. There is a subscription fee of US$2 270, and annual maintenance and management fees of US$1 360. Each client card costs US$9. Two important decisions were made about pricing before launching the pilot. First, to remove as many barriers to entry as possible, AfriCap subsidised the subscription fees and the annual management fees during the pilot phase. However, MFIs know the full cost and they know that AfriCap is subsidising it. Second, to avoid access to the product being entirely free, the cards for the end user are sold to the MFI. In normal business, the MFI would then sell the cards on to their customers, but Ferlo's contract with MFIs stipulates that the MFIs must pay for the cards on behalf of their clients, and not pass on that cost during the pilot phase. Ferlo did this because it wanted to capture transaction volume quickly: if clients had had to pay for the cards, take-up would have been slower. Also, since this was only a pilot and no one knew if it would succeed, selling the benefits of the card to end users would have been difficult. Ferlo and each MFI share the revenue because it is a partnership. A small flat fee is charged on each client transaction at a POS, ATM or cybercafé, 80 % of which goes to Ferlo and 20 % to the client's MFI (see Table 7.1). There is a lot of discussion about whether this is an appropriate split and whether larger MFIs should get a bigger slice.

Table 7.1 POS, ATM and internet charges

Service	POS	ATM	Internet	Cost in CFA
Payment by merchant	Yes	Yes	Yes	300
Recharging e-purse	Yes	Yes	Yes	200
Recharging client account	Yes	Yes	Yes	200
Cash withdrawal	No	Yes	No	200
Cash deposit	Yes	Yes	Yes	200
Health insurance	Yes	No	No	500
Sale of prepaid phone card	Yes	Yes	Yes	350

Source: Ferlo

Based on the pilot scheme, it is clear that both MFIs and customers can benefit.

- For the MFIs, operational costs were significantly reduced, while operational efficiency simultaneously improved.
- MFIs found that their revenues also increased over the term of the pilot, and they managed to generate new sources of revenue.
- For clients of microfinance services, access to financial capital for remote based clients immediately improved.
- There was an observed improvement in customer loyalty among existing clients.
- The introduction of technological solutions for microcredit services attracted a new category of urban clients.
- Clients also responded well to the added benefits of enhanced security features for their money, combined with access to their cash 24 hours a day, seven days a week.

The success of the pilot has since led to an increase in the number of clients with MoneaCards to 7 041, and a general increase in the technological infrastructure to 45 POS terminals installed, a further 65 committed, eight ATMs, 40 reloading points, and a second card pre-personalisation centre. As a result, revenue and profits have increased by 7 %.

By December 2008, the number of clients affiliated to Ferlo had increased significantly – the number of cards issued by MFIs was 5 819 while the number of cards directly issued by Ferlo was 6 105. In total, almost 12 000 clients were using Ferlo's services by the end of 2008 – an increase of 169 % on December 2007. Ferlo's technological infrastructure was also increased to cope with rising demand of services – from 45 POS terminals in 2007 to 96 in 2008; from 40 top-up points to 87 in the same period; and from eight ATMs to 12. These figures reflect the increase to six in the number of MFIs connected to the Ferlo platform.

The success of the pilot scheme is also reflected in the number of new applications of Ferlo cards. One of them is the Restaurant Card, launched in November 2008, which can be used in 21 restaurants in Senegal. In 2009, Ferlo plans to launch other similar products like a student card, a petrol card, a regional prepaid card and a fund transfer card.

The regional prepaid card comes out of Ferlo's expansion into other countries in Africa. Ferlo Senegal has created a branch in Burkina Faso, which is the first step towards further penetration in the UEOMA region. In this region Ferlo joined the Interbank Electronic banking group in December 2008, which guarantees the approval of the Ferlo card in all ATMs and outlets of the consortium of 87 banks that are members of the group.[14] Similarly, Ferlo Cameroon has been created in partnership with ADSNET to replicate the Ferlo experience in the Central African Economic and Monetary Community region.

Lessons

One of the key lessons is that this system is easily to replicate. The technological platform did not have to be modified to piggyback existing infrastructure, which enabled the most up-to-date configurations to be installed right away. This serves two purposes: it enables customers and users to take advantage of the most advanced technology to facilitate their transfers; and it creates favourable conditions to attract further investment and engagement from other formal financial institutions.

Another important lesson is that smartcard and innovative technology can benefit MFIs: the business model has been accepted by stakeholders, and these participants are among the leading MFIs in Senegal today.

Endnotes

1. *Financial Mail* (2004).
2. Simplus website.
3. South African term for drinking establishment.
4. South African term for small roadside trading outlets, typically selling fruit, sweets and other snacks but often airtime too.
5. Planting (2004).
6. Ibid.
7. Jello Marketing (2005).
8. Finmark (2005).
9. *Financial Mail* (2004).
10. Finmark (2005).
11. The pilot scheme in 2004 included four of the major Senegalese MFIs as participants. ACEP, CMD, PAMECAS and PAME-AGETIP boasted a combined loan portfolio of over US$70 million, and reached out to more than 67 000 clients in the country in 2006 alone.
12. The MFIs that are based on mutual or co-operative models have become regulated through the West African Monetary Union's 1994 PARMEC law. This has helped solidify the status of MFIs in Senegal, and enabled the microfinance industry to become an essential subsector of the formal financial sector in the region.
13. Data from the IMF Financial Sector Assessment, December 2004.
14. For the whole list of banks affiliated to this network, see http://www.gim-uemoa.org/fr/index.php.

Chapter Eight
Rural banking

Like SME banking, rural banking is often considered one of the more challenging financial markets. Not only do providers have to contend with the usual problems that any supplier of financial services may face when dealing with rural outreach (sparse populations, intermittent power supplies, poor road networks), the financial health of their predominantly agricultural customer base is also deeply affected by factors outside its control, such as climatic conditions, prices for agricultural produce and inputs that are often determined centrally, not locally. The case studies in this chapter show how financial services can help farmers and rural communities in many different ways, especially by providing short-term finance that helps them manage the peaks and troughs of the agricultural cycle.

These case studies are very different: the first looks at an apex organisation providing a payments infrastructure for an existing network of rural banks; the second looks at a community bank; and the third the subsidiary of a multinational providing mainstream banking services to salaried workers as well as warehouse finance to farmers. Despite their rural focus, these case studies confirm that, in some respects, rural banking is no different from other forms of banking: the development of successful products and services depends on an intimate understanding of the specific needs of the customer.

Rural banks provide essential services in remote areas.

ARB Apex Bank: Supporting rural banking services

> Ghana's numerous rural banks benefit greatly from being deeply rooted in their local communities, but their disparate nature is also their weakness: they are disconnected from the rest of the banking system and, remaining small, cannot take advantage of the economies of scale that larger financial institutions enjoy. The result is that the cost of service delivery remains high. The idea behind ARB Apex Bank, a kind of central bank for, and owned by, the rural banks, was that shared infrastructure and services would mitigate these structural weaknesses. The ARB Apex Bank provides the rural bank network with a payments system, treasury services, cash handling, training and computerisation.

Ghana's rural population accounts for about 60 % of the total population, and 60 % of Ghana's poor live in rural areas. Against the backdrop of rural households having limited access to financial services, Ghana's 123 rural and community banks (RCBs) are transforming the banking landscape for this market.

- The RCBs extend the reach of financial intermediation to many people with their extensive network of branches serving widely dispersed customers.
- They perform a key role in the rural economy by facilitating the purchases of cocoa and coffee crops, and the financing of agricultural production at the micro level.
- they teach banking habits, encourage savings and provide access to credit, and establish sound creditor–borrower relationships among the wider population.

Rural banks are essentially owned by their communities, which also form the bulk of their depositors. The secret of their success lies in their intimate relationship with the communities they serve, which enables them to practice effective Know Your Customer principles and prudent lending.

One of the weaknesses of RCBs is that they are small-scale enterprises, and therefore face the normal problems of small credit institutions. These range from the lack of a centralised facility to clear cheques or access credit for on-lending, to the limitations of their operations as standalone entities, which make it difficult for them to individually establish links with the rest of the banking sector. They were and are still doing business in the context of a predominantly cash-based payments system that involves high transactions costs, and precludes the economies of scale necessary for RCBs to reduce the costs of financial intermediation.

In the rural areas, the problem is exacerbated by the way the cocoa sector is operated. Between the 1980s and early 1990s, the number of rural banks expanded rapidly in response to the introduction of a payment system for buying cocoa from farmers using special cheques that had to be deposited into the farmers' bank accounts. Liberalisation of the marketing of cocoa brought in other buyers who started paying cash to farmers to beat their competition. Farmers preferred this cash payment. To purchase the cocoa crop, the Ghana Cocoa Board syndicates a loan – this amounted to US$700 million in 2004 or 25 % of the money supply. By 2008 the loan had increased to US$900 million. This loan is paid to the central bank in exchange for the cedis (the local currency) needed to purchase the crop from the farmers. The bulk of the cocoa purchases take place in the fourth quarter of the year, and this usually results in a large injection of cash into the economy, outside the banking system since the cocoa farmers have traditionally been paid in cash. This reinforces the cash nature of the Ghanaian economy, and complicates monetary management.

Initially, some RCBs looked to the commercial banks to provide them with cheque-clearing and cash-supply services, but this did not solve the problem. Not only was it costly for an individual RCB to use the services of a commercial bank, but the RCBs also came to realise that these very commercial banks were competing in the same markets in which some of the RCBs were operating.

Setting up a centralised bank

To remove these constraints on the RCBs, the Association of Rural Banks mooted the establishment of the ARB Apex Bank in 2000 to function as a mini-central bank for the rural banking sector, and began operations in July 2002. The bank was set up with the support of the donor community, primarily through the Rural Financial Services Project facility, and is wholly and equally owned by the different rural and community banks. The ARB Apex Bank is based on principles similar to those which informed the foundation of banks like Rabobank in the Netherlands and Raiffeisen in Austria, which is the central institution of a co-operative banking group. ARB is now the largest banking network in Ghana, covering 123 banks and more than 560 banking offices throughout the country.

The ARB Apex Bank operates a payments system for the RCBs, and has thus enabled these banks to integrate into the national clearing system. It also handles cash delivery to and from the RCBs, which has improved cash management within the rural banking sector.

To help increase the operational efficiency of the rural banks and facilitate their further integration into the national payment system, ARB Apex Bank has also promoted the computerisation of all rural banks in Ghana, allowing the different branches and offices to offer real time banking operations across the different agencies. This will allow bank customers to access their accounts at any of the branches and through point-of-sale terminals and ATMs, irrespective of where their accounts are domiciled.

This programme, funded under the US Millennium Challenge Account, is expected to create a rural banking sector that is connected in a wide area network, allowing RCB clients easy access to banking services across the country. A major advantage of such integration will be that it will allow cocoa farmers to have the payments for their crops credited to their bank accounts as soon as the purchases are made, thus avoiding the need to receive and carry large amounts of cash.

By the end of 2008, the number of licensed buying companies channelling funds through the bank to the RCBs for the purchase of cocoa had reached 11. The introduction of the Akuafo cheque service, where the bank plays an intermediary role, has greatly improved the delivery time and adequate supply of cash to the cocoa producers.

Given that these rural banks operate in areas where qualified banking personnel are hard to find, ARB Apex Bank provides regular training for staff and directors of the RCBs. The training is designed both to improve the quality of service provided by the RCBs and to develop their human resource capacities to cope with the modernisation of the system that it is helping to bring about.

ARB Apex Bank also offers treasury management services, which include brokerage services for the purchase of treasury bills and bonds issued by the government, maintenance of the Central Securities Depository, rediscounting of treasury bills, and the provision of products and services to address the short-term investment needs of those rural banks which have short-term excess liquidity. Along with these treasury management services, the ARB Apex Bank administers special funds from donor groups and government agencies, such as the microfinance schemes being implemented by the Department of Social Welfare. In this function, it acts as a conduit for funds provided for distribution to the rural areas, whether offered on commercial or concessional terms, thus allowing RCBs easier and more reliable access to funds for on-lending.

Making remittances easy

It is also part of the remit of ARB Apex Bank to develop innovative banking products designed to integrate the more remote rural areas of the country with the rest of the economy. The very existence of a centralised facility has enabled the RCBs to offer products and services that reflect exchanges made between the rural markets served by these banks and the rest of the economy. This is, for example, carried out through the Apex Link Domestic Funds Transfer, which makes use of the more than 560 offices and branches of RCBs to transfer funds to villages and towns in various parts of the country. The service addresses the needs of clients engaged in local trading activities as well as employed people who send remittances to their families in the villages. At the end of 2006, it was estimated that more than GH¢75 million (about US$82.5 million) had been channelled to communities in the rural areas through the Apex Link facility, according to Gloria Nikoi, former chairman of the bank's board of directors (now retired). About a quarter of this amount would have been lost to robberies on the highway had these transfers been made the old fashioned way. Today, Apex Link has become a household name to many Ghanaians.

The ARB Apex Bank also collaborates with a number of commercial banks and other registered money transfer companies to channel foreign remittances to their beneficiaries in the rural areas. Not only has this service enhanced the image of participating RCBs, but it has also cut transaction costs, especially for those living in far-flung villages – many people previously needed to travel long distances to reach the bigger town centres where they could receive the funds sent by family members working abroad.

To further bridge the divide between the rural and urban sectors in the country, ARB Apex Bank also recently introduced a new product called *Efie Ne Fie*, which means 'home is home'. This product enables individuals who are based in, or working in, cities like Accra to open savings accounts in the RCBs of the villages from which they hail. This is meant not only to encourage a culture of saving, but also to enable the transfer of money from urban to rural communities, and is envisaged as a means to promote local community development in the villages.

The ARB Apex Bank was established to fulfil a supervisory function for the RCBs.[1] As of March 2007, this function had not yet been effectively initiated by ARB Apex Bank, though in December 2006 parliament approved the instrument that bestows on the bank the power to inspect, regulate and supervise RCBs, subject to the supervisory authority of the Bank of Ghana. At present, the rural banks are required to submit their annual audited accounts to ARB Apex Bank for analysis, but on site inspection of the 123 rural banks is an activity which ARB Apex Bank is still unable to embark on. This, according to the bank's management, is attributable to the need for the institution to enhance capacity through the hiring of additional personnel with experience in banking supervision and inspection, and the lack of available funding to cover administrative costs related to the inspection of 123 RCBs spread throughout the country.

The institution's management thinks that it may take some time before this function can be fully assumed by the ARB Apex Bank, and this function still rests in the hands of the Bank of Ghana. Nevertheless, ARB Apex Bank remains active in its oversight function, and sees to it that prudent banking measures are set in place that will govern the activities of the different RCBs.

Slowly, the public is increasingly gaining confidence in the rural banking system, which the bank's management attributes not only to the work that it has carried out in the last few years but also to the readiness of RCBs to initiate reforms and participate in programmes to improve their services and overall banking operations. The 2006 performance figures show that total advances made by all RCBs have grown by almost 37 %, and total deposits likewise increased by almost 25 %. Despite this positive performance, the bank still continues to strongly communicate to the RCBs the need to strengthen their internal control mechanisms to minimise the incidence of fraud and risk, and ensure efficient operations.

Economies of scale

The experience of ARB Apex Bank in responding to the needs of the rural banks in Ghana provides an interesting example of the way individual small-scale rural banks may be enabled to take advantage of greater economies of scale to provide financial services.

The very existence of a central Apex facility promotes a higher level of efficiency in the delivery of services to rural bank customers. Significantly, this approach also enables these small-scale banks to link up effectively with other commercial financial institutions in the country, thereby promoting the integration of rural financial markets with the rest of the economy.

The establishment of ARB Apex Bank was meant to fill a void in the rural banking sector. In the first four years of operations the bank responded to the demands of RCBs, and even provided some of its services at a subsidised rate. This was necessary, especially in its initial years of operations when some of the rural banks serviced by ARB Apex Bank offices were outside the regional coverage, and the costs in delivering certain services were still high. During this period, operations were facilitated through support from donor agencies. The bank made an operational loss in its first year, which reflected the need for the institution to learn how to respond to the needs of RCBs, many of which were urgent in nature right at the beginning when the bank was still building its own internal capacity.

ARB Apex Bank is set on establishing itself as a sustainable and commercially viable institution: its management strongly recognises that this is the only way for it to have a lasting impact on the rural financial markets it seeks to serve. Furthermore, the bank is also aware that the donor-financing programmes supporting some of its activities will be available for only a limited period, after which it will be up to ARB Apex Bank to ensure that it continues to deliver the services needed by RCBs.

In 2006, the bank's total assets were registered at GH¢47.4 million (about US$52 million) and total deposits stood at GH¢34.2 million (about US$37.8 million), representing growth of more than 180 % in a span of two years.[2]

Non-funded income continued to grow in 2007 as a result of increased branch activities, rising volumes in local money transfers and commissions. By January 2008, the bank's total assets had grown by 9 % to GH¢51.5 million (about US$55 million). By January 2008, total equity was GH¢5 318.7 thousand compared to the December 2006 position of GH¢4 676.6 thousand (a 13 % increase).

Aware of the importance of accessible systems to remittances for poor households, ARB Apex Bank started collaborating in 2007 with commercial banks to channel foreign remittances through some RCBs. Some of the collaborating banks and other registered money transfer companies are the Metropolitan and Allied Bank and Merchant Bank

Ghana Ltd. The bank's commission income was expected to be bolstered in 2008 by its partnership with Western Union.

Apex has also introduced the Apex Certificate of Deposit (ACOD), which is a treasury product allowing RCBs to invest short term to earn interest. RCBs with excess liquidity can use the ACOD to earn extra income. The product has the flexibility of premature redemption if the rural/community bank requires liquidity to meet cash shortfalls. Weekly interest rates are sent to the RCBs through the bank's branches and clearing centres.

The expansion in its operations and the growth in services delivered to the RCBs are being supported by improvements in computerisation of its head office along with all the RCB branches. This is seen as an important milestone in the bank's drive to bring down costs and deliver its services more efficiently.

At this stage in its development, the bank's management is keen on gaining further access to funds to assist its efforts to build capacities within its organisation, particularly in relation to its supervisory function over rural banks. ARB Apex Bank claims that it has the information capital regarding rural markets and adequate knowledge about rural banking operations, which may be an advantage as the institution evolves its supervisory function. Nevertheless, this also needs to be weighed against a possible moral hazard – the ARB Apex Bank is after all an institution owned by the rural banks, which may therefore result in a conflict of interest should the execution of this supervisory function entail strict adherence to certain banking standards with which some poorly performing rural banks may not be able to comply.

That the ARB Apex Bank is an institution that reports to the Bank of Ghana, and that its governance structure is designed to represent the interest of most of the rural banks that are operating in compliance with banking rules and regulations, may act as a safeguard against this possible conflict of interest.

Mbinga Community Bank: Tailor-made financial services for rural clients

> Mbinga is a small microfinance bank in a remote part of Tanzania, but Mbinga District's geography is only one of the bank's operating challenges: another is the fact that many of its customers are heavily exposed to only one major source of income – coffee. Uncertain or fluctuating coffee prices are a perpetual worry for these customers, and so the bank has introduced a product that helps them maximise their profits from the coffee growing cycle. Mbinga attributes its success to being attentive to the particular needs of the community.

Mbinga district is in the coffee-producing region in southwest Tanzania, 1 100 kilometres from Dar es Salaam. It is bordered by Lake Malawi to the west and Mozambique to the south. According to the 2002 census, the population of Mbinga represented a little more than 1 % of the country's population, with a population density of only 18 people per square kilometre, the third lowest in the country, compared to the national average of 39 people per square kilometre. More than 92 % of the population lives in rural areas. Most of the roads are unpaved, making it difficult and expensive to travel around this remote area. Most economic activity is based around seasonal and single crops: in addition to coffee, the conditions in the region are suitable for tobacco and tea, and food crops such as mangoes, maize, sorghum, cassava and potatoes, as well as pyrethrum. There is an extensive artisanal fishing industry along the shore of Lake Malawi.

Sorting through the harvested coffee beans as they dry.

During the rainy season – the growing season – income tends to be low among farmers. They are often forced to pre-sell their coffee and other cash crops at low prices to earn enough income to meet their basic essential needs. This was exacerbated by a global overproduction of coffee, which saw prices stagnate globally and locally, from 2001 with farmers getting lower returns for their crops while contending with ever-increasing production costs.

The Mbinga Co-operative Union (MBICU) was formed in 1989 by the Ministry of Co-operatives to cater for the financial needs of coffee producers of the region. After the Tanzanian government liberalised the domestic coffee market in 1993, the MBICU could not compete with the private coffee buyers and went bankrupt.

Mbinga Community Bank (MCB) opened on 30 July 2003 to fill the void left by the collapse of the MBICU. The bank is licensed by the Central Bank of Tanzania as a Regional Unit bank with its headquarters in Mbinga Township. MCB shareholders comprise individuals, companies, co-operative societies, non-governmental organisations, savings and credit co-operatives, and the Mbinga District Council.

MCB is a fully fledged microfinance bank, offering loans and savings products. As of 30 October 2008, the bank had a total of 7 752 savers out of which 900 were 'group accounts', covering a membership of nearly 15 000 people. It also had more than 14 000 loan accounts, which cover microloans to individuals, small-business loans, productivity loans, loans provided to solidarity groups, and its overdraft facility (*kifuku*), which is also used by its farmer clients. The average loan is US$130, and the average savings balance US$160. Typically, MCB customers are rural smallholder farmers and fishermen, and the artisans and micro retail businesses that serve them, and their families. Being able to deliver a range of products relevant to this diverse client base is a key reason for MCB's success to date.

One of the most interesting and well received products developed by MCB is the overdraft account, or *kifuku*, which aims to address the liquidity problems of smallholder farmers in Mbinga during the rainy season. MCB realised that seasonal income fluctuations were negatively affecting its customers. During agriculturally unproductive months, farmers were in dire need of funds. By pre-selling their cash crops for lower prices, they were risking their future earnings and savings potential. The bank developed an overdraft service to protect its customers. By signing up for this account, a client can withdraw a fixed amount a month until the harvest season. This product has been well received by clients, and the demand for it is growing. Customers who have access to this product use the monthly funds to meet a variety of obligations, including paying for essentials such as hospital bills and school uniforms for their children.

The overdraft facility allows MCB to actively assist its customers, which in turn is helping its own business to grow. By waiting for better prices, for example, clients have been able to make larger deposits from coffee sales. In the 2006–2007 season, these reached TZS2.2 billion. This in turn has increased the bank's profit through interest and commissions charged. Mbinga, as a community bank, knows its customers, and has therefore been able to maintain a relatively low default rate for this poor rural area. The portfolio at risk over 30 days is 5 %, which while nowhere near the large microfinance lenders in the country such as PRIDE (0.44 %) or Selfina (0.04 %), bears comparison with similar institutions like Akiba Commercial Bank (4.9 %) or the Small Enterprise Development Agency (3 %), and is well ahead of some other microfinance providers like FINCA (19.86 %) or Faulu (14.34 %).[3]

MCB's decision to offer tailor-made financial services to its clients has shown dividends. Between 2005 and 2007, the number of borrowers grew from 5 328 to 8 712. It continues to reach more and more clients: its total number of borrowers for October 2008 represented an increase of more than 60 % in the previous 15 months. The bank reported having a total loan portfolio of US$1 million, as of October 2008, and total deposits of roughly US$1.3 million.

This development model is ensuring a steady increase in customers for MCB (see Table 8.1). The productivity loans and small-business loans continue to be the leaders in MCB's portfolio. However, all of the products are performing satisfactorily, according to the bank, and all were expected to improve by the end of 2008. The products are generating reasonable income for the bank in terms of interest and commissions charged.

Table 8.1 Mbinga Community Bank customer growth

Product	Number of customers 31 March 2007	Number of customers 31 December 2007	Number of customers 30 October 2008
Individual microloans	64	100	121
Small business loans	149	200	202
Productivity loans	8 190	10 000	11 310
Solidarity groups	120	500	1 650
Overdraft (*kifuku*) account	189	500	1 056
Total	8 712	11 300	14 279

Source: Mbinga Community Bank

Lessons

An important lesson that arises from MCB's experience is the need to do market research. This is essential to put the bank in touch with the problems its clients face, which can then be addressed during the design phase of any new product. MCB also emphasises the importance of IT infrastructure to roll out the products and maximise efficiency.

MCB has overcome a number of fundamental challenges to its growth. One of the most important has been the distances between communities. Mbinga District is vast and mountainous, covering 11 000 square kilometres. The farthest client MCB reaches is about 150 kilometres away from its bank branch. Most of the roads leading to the villages are in poor condition, which means that the journey can take longer than usual, especially during the rainy season. This has made both providing the services by MCB and accessing these services by clients difficult. This difficulty has been overcome largely by using mobile telecommunications. For example, farmer clients in more remote villages are contacted on mobile phones, and meetings with groups of clients can be pre-arranged. In these meetings, loan applications can be processed and savings balances accessed by individual clients. In some villages, however, there are no telephone services. Clients must travel to Mbinga Township, or the nearest village with a telephone service, to access savings balances and process loans. Clients often have to make such trips more than once, but are willing to do so despite the transaction costs because they value the perceived security of Mbinga accounts and the suitability of the bank's services to their financial needs.

The inability of MCB's clients to diversify economically is also a challenge for the bank's delivery of financial services. Most agricultural clients are dependent on single crops. For years, coffee has been the mainstay of Mbinga's economy. The global price fluctuations have had disastrous consequences on local incomes.

MCB's future is tied to the community it serves. By maintaining its close dialogue with its clients and responding to their needs, it believes it will be able to expand its businesses in Mbinga, and capture and maintain quality customers. MBC's staff maintains close contact with their customers, by telephone or by travelling to meet them. The 'community' flavour of the bank enables it to gain and maintain customers even in areas served by a branch of the National Microfinance Bank – the only national bank significantly represented in the region.

Stanbic in Africa: Broadening its reach to the unbanked

> Standard Bank is represented in more countries in Africa than any other South African bank. Its Ugandan subsidiary, Stanbic Bank Uganda, which listed in 2007 on the Uganda Stock Exchange, is easily the largest bank in Uganda, and is expanding its customer base by targeting the unbanked employees of large employers, including government institutions, and offering them on-site banking services, including personal microloans. It is also offering a warehouse receipts/guaranteed financing system for farmers in collaboration with USAID's Rural SPEED (Savings Promotion & Enhancement of Enterprise Development) programme. The current offering is for agro-credit guaranteed loans. These activities have brought the bank success, as its rapidly increasing low-income customer base demonstrates.

Since Stanbic Bank Uganda acquired the government-owned Uganda Commercial Bank (UCB) in 2002, the bank has grown substantially by targeting, among other segments, low-income salaried people. Stanbic Uganda offers three basic products: transactional accounts, microloans and credit life insurance (against death and permanent disability). In recent years, the bank has also partnered with USAID's Rural SPEED programme to extend financial services in non-traditional ways to rural communities in Uganda. Only 10 % of the country's rural residents currently have access to basic financial services, and Stanbic sees this partnership as a logical extension of its drive to enter the untapped rural market.

Company background

Stanbic Bank in Uganda forms part of the Standard Bank group, which is headquartered in Johannesburg, South Africa, and has a presence in 17 sub-Saharan countries and in 21 countries on other continents. An agreement with Standard Chartered Bank prevents Standard Bank from using the name 'Standard Bank' in the rest of Africa, hence the use of the name Stanbic Bank.

Stanbic established a presence in Uganda when the Standard Bank group bought the Grindlays network in Africa in October 1993. Uganda is a largely agricultural economy which has had strong economic growth in the past few years. However, the FinScope Uganda 2007 survey found that only 8 % of the population is formally employed – either in the public or private sector. It adds that 62 % of the economically active population receives no financial services at all, while only 18 % receive financial services from the formal sector.[4]

After opening in Uganda, Stanbic catered largely for the corporate market and upper-income earners. This changed in February 2002 when it acquired a 90 % share of UCB, which had 400 000 customers (mainly government employees who had to have accounts with the bank), and was by far the biggest bank in the country at that stage[5].

Competition exists in the form of Standard Chartered Bank, Barclays Bank (which has recently acquired Nile Commercial Bank) and Centenary Bank, formerly Centenary Rural Development Bank. However, Stanbic Bank Uganda is the dominant bank in Uganda with 70 branches spread all over the country and 138 ATMs (about 80 are in towns outside Kampala and Entebbe). On 25 January 2007, it was listed on the Uganda Stock Exchange with a market capitalisation of more than US$450 million.

Taking banking to the unbanked

When Stanbic bought UCB, it was in a state of disrepair and the staff lacked training. The purchase nevertheless presented Stanbic with the opportunity to cater for the ordinary, low-income, salaried Ugandan and to attract more people in this market into the bank.

Marius Wait, director of personal and business banking of Standard Bank Africa, and tasked with rolling out retail banking in the Standard Bank group in Africa, explains: 'With our experience in South Africa in autobanking and mass-marketing, we have learned that you can bank lower-income people who barely transact per month, but you need to deliver to them differently.'

To operate as cost effectively as possible, Stanbic steers away from brick-and-mortar branches. Branches are expensive to build and maintain and, notes Wait, it would be 'financial suicide' to use them to process only small accounts as they could not sustain the expense of a branch. In attracting new customers, the bank therefore targeted large employers, such as government institutions, the army, police force and prisons personnel, as well as private businesses. It offered them a means of disbursing wages and paying salaries safely, such as by opening bank accounts on site for all their employees. In this way, it acquired a large number of customers in a short space of time. Moreover, the bank extended its services to the whole spectrum of customers within an organisation, from cleaners and foremen to managers.

This simple strategy – selling on site in bulk to lower the unit costs – saved the bank the expense of opening more branches. The bank has opened only five more branches since it acquired UCB, while customers have benefited from not having to stand in a queue for four to five hours to cash salary cheques, as had been the case with UCB. Stanbic found that its customers' behaviour started to change when they opened transactional accounts. Once their salary was deposited by their employer, the average customers started withdrawing money only once a week from Stanbic's ATMs, and even managed to save a little. This is in sharp contrast to the cash-in-hand behaviour of the past, which had encouraged spending. Stanbic's savings account base amounts to about USh252 billion in deposits, and personal current accounts total about USh429 billion.

A crowd in Amuru district in northern Uganda gathers to find out more about Stanbic Bank.

The company soon also started to offer microloans – personal salaried loans – canvassing for customers through employers, as it had with transmission accounts. At the request of employers, instalments are deducted before the net salary is paid to the employee, an arrangement which presents the bank with a much lower risk.

Wait notes that the main challenge for financial institutions in Africa is the absence of credit bureaus to check credit records. For this reason, some employers are prepared to underwrite loans for their employees, keeping in mind, he says, that Ugandans tend to treasure their jobs and rarely resign. As for other microloan customers, once transactional accounts show a history of a regular income in the form of a salary cheque, Stanbic is also prepared to offer microloans to these customers without employer support.

By the end of 2006, the number of accounts had grown from 400 000 to about 900 000, and the number of customers from 210 000 to 550 000. About 70 % of the accounts are held by low-income people. Stanbic manages to open 1 000 accounts a day.

To make its accounts more accessible, the bank lowered its opening deposit requirement to only about US$7.22 (USh15 000).[6] However, according to a FinMark Trust survey, the average Ugandan income is only US$280 (USh483 300) a year.[7]

Stanbic Uganda also extends up to 500 microloans a day. The average size of a loan is US$1 100 (about USh2.2 million), but they range from US$275 (USh550 000) to much larger amounts. Loan terms may extend from 12 to 48 months, although rarely the latter. The loans are typically unsecured, and the annual interest rate is set at prime (16 %) plus between 2 % and 8 %. Customers are notified within 48 hours as to whether the loan has been approved, and it is paid out the day after. All the loans are underwritten by a life policy from a local insurance company. Stanbic also buys these policies and sells them on to customers.

'The transactional revenue, the loans revenue and the insurance policy revenue are small amounts, but it all adds up in the end to ensure a profitable business,' says Wait. 'We have proven that there is a case for banking for the lower-income group by selling them more than one product, originating cleverly, keeping the accounts active, ensuring we have a decent risk profile when we lend to them, and most importantly, having them transact outside of a branch, at the ATMs or at POS devices in shops, whether it is a debit card purchase or cash withdrawals.'

Commodity-backed finance

Stanbic's partnership with USAID/Rural SPEED is aimed at reaching farmers in Uganda. Agriculture is the country's main economic activity, but the financial sector has always perceived farmers as being too risky to deal with, especially if they are tenants who do not own land that can be used as collateral. The cyclical nature of farm income adds to farmers' problems because, since all the farmers deliver their crops simultaneously, prices are forced down, leaving the farmers no choice but to sell at any price they can get.

Stanbic was involved with Rural SPEED in piloting a warehouse receipts system that allowed farmers without collateral to store their crops in a secure warehouse until they could get a better price for them.

The bank has set aside US$200 000 to lend to farmers making use of this scheme. Uganda's agricultural sector contributes about 22 % to its GDP, but most of the agricultural activity is subsistence farming, and Stanbic believes therefore that farmers are mainly unbanked. However, this solution is for both the banked and unbanked farmers.

The scheme works in the following way. The farmer receives a certified receipt for the crop when he brings it to the warehouse. Stanbic uses the crop as collateral to extend a loan of up to 80 % of the value of the crop at the current price, which the farmer sells later when the price increases. The loan is paid back when the crop is sold, and the farmer is able to retain any surplus proceeds on the sale. The World Food Programme was also involved in the pilot and agreed to buy high-quality produce from the warehouse at a higher price than that offered by local traders.

The pilot project was successful, and similar programmes are now being developed in other parts of Uganda.

In March 2007, Stanbic signed an agreement with Rural SPEED to come up with innovative ways of improving access to banking services for rural people. Ideas have been discussed concerning using existing technology, such as POS machines or Mini-ATMs, that do not require any servicing or loading of cash, since these activities drive up costs. However, a pilot project in Botswana, where customers could swipe their cards at a POS machine in a shop, receive a slip from the machine and then obtain their cash from the cashier, revealed some potential problems. In some instances, for example, shop owners refused to pay out the money on presentation of the slip, or placed conditions on paying out the money, such as requiring the customer to purchase something from the store. Stanbic is therefore researching the options further to find solutions to be able to serve the rural market.

Conclusion

Stanbic Uganda's approach to the lower-income market has been two tiered: first, to penetrate small formal market and capture both salaried people and regular income earners, and, second, to penetrate the informal sector.

From its base of 400 000 UCB clients, Stanbic Uganda has more than doubled its low-income client base, and this sector is making a contribution to the bank's profitability, which increased from USh28.4 billion in 2003 to USh39.5 billion in 2006 and USh53.02 billion in 2007.

Endnotes

[1] In 1994, the Bank of Ghana withdrew its technical services to the RCBs, which prodded the establishment of an alternative facility that can help carry out the centralised functions as needed by the rural banking sector. The increasing number of RCBs and the peculiarities in the markets they serve posed challenges for the supervisory role of the Bank of Ghana.
[2] In terms of profitability, ARB Apex Bank had a return on equity (ROE) of 5.8 % and a return on assets (ROA) of 0.57 % in 2006.
[3] Figures from Mix Market, all for 2005.
[4] The Steadman Group (2007).
[5] Stanbic Uganda www.stanbicbank.co.ug/SBIC/Frontdoor_07_02/0,2493,9681341_9757102_0,00.html.
[6] Currency rate as at 9 July 2007.
[7] Bankable Frontier Associates (2007).

Chapter Nine

Insurance

Insurance penetration across Africa is so low that is hard not to conclude that insurance is one of the great new frontiers of finance in Africa. Use of insurance by individuals is practically non-existent in many countries, although pockets of cover do exist, such as funeral insurance in southern Africa, and vehicle insurance, which is often mandatory. Affordability is a major problem but so too is a basic lack of understanding about how insurance actually works. In many countries, structural factors conspire to inhibit the development of an insurance industry. These include absent or inappropriate regulation and underdeveloped capital markets, which means there are limited ways that insurance companies can invest the premiums, or long-term savings, of their clients.

However, millions of potential insurance clients contend daily with serious risks that could be mitigated through insurance – notably, risks associated with disease and the environment, such as floods and fire, and also personal security such as theft. Poor life expectancy should arguably encourage the development of the life insurance industry including its variant, credit life, which pays off a loan when the borrower dies.

The case studies in this chapter show how insurance can be made affordable, and how its benefits, with use, can become better understood.

Opportunity International's MicroEnsure: Providing a safety net for societies in need

> MicroEnsure, the profit-making insurance broking subsidiary of the non-profit microfinance giant Opportunity International has the classic bottom of the pyramid profile – very low margins compensated for by high volumes and products that poor people actually need and can understand. Undeterred by exceptionally low levels of insurance penetration in Africa, it now has big ambitions for its business on the continent.

Some may ask whether really poor households actually need insurance. Richard Leftley, president of Opportunity International's MicroEnsure, responds by saying that one only has to imagine the range of risks that people who are poorly nourished, live in informal housing and have limited access to healthcare have to face to know why the poor want to be insured.[1]

The figures back him up. MicroEnsure operates with microfinance institutions and increasingly with humanitarian organisations as distribution partners, and with local insurance companies and reinsurers across the globe. It has issued around one million policies to date covering about 3.5 million lives in Africa, the Philippines and India.

MicroEnsure background

Although profit driven, MicroEnsure has its roots in the microfinance NGO or non-government organisation Opportunity International (Opportunity), which was founded in 1971 to provide small business loans to people living in chronic poverty. Overwhelmed by the demand for microfinance, in 1998 Opportunity began sourcing partners around the world, looking for independent organisations with similar values, and the Opportunity Network was born. By mid-2008, Opportunity was operating as a global network of more than 40 MFIs, with lending operations in 27 countries.[2]

Opportunity started developing microinsurance products in 2002, in response to client need identified in Africa. Market research conducted by one of Opportunity's partners in Africa showed that, on average, 41 % of its clients could expect a death in the family within the course of a year, a phenomenon aggravated by the HIV/AIDS pandemic. Funerals are also expensive and can cost anything up to three months' disposable income. The combination of the cost and frequency of the funerals motivated Opportunity to provide highly scalable insurance products that poor people in Africa both need and can understand.[3] As a result it launched the Micro Insurance Agency in 2005, which subsequently became MicroEnsure.

MicroEnsure is a wholly owned subsidiary of Opportunity and acts as an independent microinsurance broker. It works in partnership with Opportunity's network partners (although these are free to take on any other insurance product that suits their needs), or with other organisations that serve the poor, such as MFIs from other networks, rural banks, savings and credit co-operatives, and humanitarian organisations.

MicroEnsure has subsidiaries in Ghana, Uganda, Tanzania, the Philippines and India, but serves the poor in 10 countries across the globe. The organisation plans to open at least three new subsidiaries a year with the help of a US$24.2 million grant from the Bill & Melinda Gates Foundation. MicroEnsure finds that its products are most successful where it has its own subsidiaries, and that it is extremely difficult to ensure that its products get off the ground when it tries to do so remotely, as a consultant.

MicroEnsure's strategic plan for the four years to the end of 2012 envisages establishing a presence in 11 new countries in Africa and Asia (14 additional countries), eventually covering more than 20 million lives. This will require substantial investment in infrastructure, and means that MicroEnsure will only be able to report a profit again in the third quarter of 2011.

No other brokers, agents or intermediaries are seeking to serve the low-income market in the countries where MicroEnsure is active at present, either on a global or a regional level, in the way in which MicroEnsure does. There are other competitors acting in other capacities, such as the American International Group and Allianz Zurich, which approach MFIs directly.

MicroEnsure is profit driven because Opportunity believes that this is the best way to pay for MicroEnsure's fixed and variable costs, and to provide for expansion. While unwilling to disclose overall profitability, MicroEnsure says that its pretax revenue of US$40 000 in the month of February 2007 from the three subsidiaries in Uganda, Ghana and Philippines, covered all fixed and variable costs associated with the three subsidiaries and the global team in that month.

How MicroEnsure operates

MicroEnsure uses a slightly adapted partner-agent model to structure its partnerships, which, says Leftley, is the simplest, cheapest and fastest way.[4] Its model comprises three partners: a distribution partner (usually a social aggregator such as an MFI, NGO or traditional *susu* collector who provides access to groups of clients); a licensed insurance company to carry the risk; and MicroEnsure. The organisation provides the product concept, or assists in developing the product in collaboration with the distribution partner and insurer. It also administers the technology-driven back-office system it has developed, and provides technical training and start-up assistance to its MFI partners.

The standard approach at the outset of a project is to carry out market research by working with an existing organisation to determine client needs. Regulatory requirements and the available supply of insurance locally are important elements that MicroEnsure considers.

Once the needs are determined, MicroEnsure will then, in partnership with the MFI, develop a suitable insurance product to offer the MFI's clients: one that will fit in with its existing processes and products. As many MFIs do not have the necessary expertise, most products are developed by MicroEnsure. Leftley notes that it is crucial to ensure that insurance experts are involved in all instances. He warns that, as a team, MicroEnsure has witnessed cases where products have been designed without the input of insurance experts, and the product has turned out to be illegal, unethical or financially unsustainable.

Once the product concept is ready, MicroEnsure approaches local and multinational insurers to find out whether they would be willing to underwrite the product or adapt one of their own products in return for a fee. Leftley notes: 'The challenge is to convince the insurance company to simplify their products to essential coverage. The more simple a product, the easier it is to explain, and the easier to understand, which leads to a higher client satisfaction rate. Fewer conditions mean that the claims process is easier and quicker to administer. This reduces the transaction cost and claims payment speed.'[5]

Typically, the products cost between US$1 and US$2 a month. For inpatient healthcare insurance, the amount will vary according to the number of family members covered, for example. Most of the premium covers the underwriting costs of the insurance partners. It also includes a mark-up added by the MFI partners to cover their own costs. Where MicroEnsure has subsidiaries, it prefers to receive its remuneration through commission from the local insurance company on the sale of the products that it has designed. In countries where it does not have a subsidiary, and its partners wish to use its services, it charges via a consultancy agreement.[6]

Premiums are collected mainly through an existing infrastructure, such as a loan repayment, by loading the cost into the interest rate charged on the loan, or the premiums are deducted from a savings account. Because the monthly premiums are so low, it is impossible to sell the products directly to individuals; they have to be grouped somehow to provide economies of scale. However, Leftley believes that advances in technology, such as cellphone technology, will in the near future permit affordable methods of distributing financial services to individuals.

As this is a very low-margin business, MicroEnsure has to keep costs to a minimum. A continuous challenge is to simplify the products, such as by offering minimum coverage instead of comprehensive coverage. This streamlines administration and reduces transaction costs.[7] MicroEnsure's definition of a successful product is one that is simple, flexible and scalable, but still meets most of its clients' needs.

Another ongoing challenge is finding new ways of managing the claims process so as to simplify this, since long waiting periods cause client dissatisfaction. Most claims are paid within 14 days of receiving the complete documentation, although Leftley admits that gathering the relevant documentation may sometimes take longer.

MicroEnsure's products

MicroEnsure's products broadly fit into the following categories: credit life (protecting MFIs against the inability of borrowers to repay loans because of death or disability); term life (also called funeral insurance); index-based crop insurance; livestock insurance; property insurance; packaged insurance (which combines various products); and, in the future, products sold directly to the public using cellphone technology.

Another innovative product is crop derivative insurance, which enables small farmers to insure their crops. Lending to farmers on smallholdings is often considered too risky, because a climatic event such as a drought may make it impossible for the farmer to repay a loan. MicroEnsure has designed crop insurance products that use a rain index to determine if and when a payout is due. This product protects the farmer and the lender, enabling rural credit programmes to expand with reduced risk. Although not available in the African market, the organisation has recently developed a typhoon weather index product for rice farmers in the Philippines using satellite tracking of the typhoon to trigger payouts. This is believed to be a world first.

MicroEnsure also offers inpatient healthcare insurance in India costing only US$7 per annum for a family of four. Cover for all the children in the family is mandatory, pre-existing conditions and maternity are covered, treatment is provided on a cashless basis, and premiums are made weekly. Leftley predicts that this will overtake life insurance over the next five years as the organisation's fastest-growing product. Life insurance makes up approximately 90 % of all insurance sold at present.

Lessons

A significant lesson that MicroEnsure has learned over the years is the need to invest heavily in training loan officers. This is because the loan officers, in turn, have to educate the clients. If loan officers cannot answer difficult questions, clients lose faith in the product. In 2008, MicroEnsure partnered with Microfinance Opportunities, a financial education consultancy, to develop a new microinsurance training programme to train the trainers. This is based on extensive research and testing, and will be adapted for all subsidiary offices globally. Client education materials have also been developed and will be translated into the local languages wherever products are introduced.

Market research is enormously important, both before the design of a new product and after implementation. An example is MicroEnsure's weather index crop insurance. Research into the effectiveness of an original three-phase model showed that, when there was very little rain at the beginning of a growing phase but a lot during the rest of the period, the model would mask the deficit and excess. The model was then refined to ensure a closer correlation between rainfall patterns and crop growing requirements. Further refinement has resulted in a more complex calculation that takes the weekly moving average and compares this with weekly water requirements.

Conclusion

MicroEnsure's activities are showing that the very poor not only need insurance but are prepared to buy it. The benefits are tangible: clients benefit from the payout when they suffer a setback. MicroEnsure has found that this in itself is a good marketing tool. Over time, uninsured community members see the advantage of payouts and also want to be insured.

One of MicroEnsure's partners, for example, reported that one of the main reasons clients gave for joining its credit programme was that it offered compulsory credit life insurance.

MicroEnsure's experience demonstrates that microinsurance is a volume business, and that if you have the expertise to get the products right, the volumes will ensure profitability. Serving the poor can be a profitable business, says Leftley, but it remains a business for the specialist.

MLife insurance company: Tackling microinsurance

> The NGO microfinance sector in Zambia has been under pressure for some years. Customer accounts are declining because of high delinquency, high staff turnover and death. HIV/AIDS has cut life expectancy. It follows that the incentive for an MFI to bundle an insurance product with a microloan would be strong. MLife offers two products: one pays off the loan if the borrower dies (credit life) and the other, funeral insurance, pays funeral costs and so shelters the estate of the deceased. While MLife has the right product, given the choice, borrowers would not buy the insurance and so it has been made a mandatory part of the sale of a microloan. This is not popular and does not help customers understand the benefits of insurance.

In 2001, Peri-Urban Lusaka Small Enterprise (PULSE) Holdings, one of Zambia's larger MFIs approached MLife Insurance Company Zambia (MLife) with a request to develop insurance products for its clients so as to protect its loan portfolio in the event of the death or illness of its clients. MLife, which had traditionally focused on larger clients, saw the opportunity to penetrate the low-income market as a major breakthrough and agreed.[8]

Six years later, MLife was working with five other MFIs, and its microinsurance client base had grown to more than 130 000 clients. Despite the numerous challenges that this sector presents, Agnes Chakonta, deputy general manager of MLife, sees significant potential in the venture.

Almost half of Zambia's working population works in the informal sector in small and microbusinesses.

Microinsurance in Zambia

Zambia is a small country in Central Africa covering 752 614 square kilometres. Its population is estimated at 11.9 million, and life expectancy is low – 42 years for both men and women.

The country is a major copper producer, and its economy is based on copper and agriculture. When the price of copper collapsed in 1975, so did the country's economy, and it moved from being potentially one of the continent's richest countries at independence in 1964 to one of the world's poorest. Other factors such as a colonial legacy, economic mismanagement, debt, refugees from the Democratic Republic of Congo and diseases such as HIV/AIDS and malaria have all contributed to its economic decline.

Millions of Zambians live below the World Bank poverty threshold of US$1 a day. According to the Central Statistical Office 2000 Census, overall poverty stands at 73 %, while extreme poverty is estimated at 58 %. Only 18.3 % of Zambia's working population is formally employed, 40 % is engaged in the informal sector (small and microbusiness ventures), and the rest is either unemployed (primarily in urban areas) or relies on subsistence agriculture.[9] Only 15 % of the adult population has a bank account. Key economic data are in Table 9.1.

Table 9.1 Key economic data – Zambia

Population (million), 2006	11.9
Urban population (%), 2000	35
Unemployment rate (%), 2000	50
Poverty (% population at US$1 a day), 2005	64
Poverty (% population below national poverty line), 2005	68
GDP (US$ billion), 2006	10.9
GDP growth rate (%), 2006	6
GNI per capita (US$), 2006	630
Inflation rate (%), November 2007	8.7
180-day deposit rate – deposits over K20 million1 (%), November 2007	6.2
Lending rate (%), November 2007	18.2

Sources: Central Statistical Office Zambia; World Bank World Development Indicators; CIA World Factbook

Microinsurance in Zambia is a relatively new industry consisting mainly of credit life and funeral cover for microborrowers and their family members. Credit life schemes pay off the loan amount in the event of the borrower's death and pay loan instalments when the client is ill. Insurance penetration is low in the country – between 1 % and 1.5 %.[10] Although microinsurance falls under the Zambian Department of Pensions and Insurance, no steps have yet been taken to regulate microinsurance in the country.

Most microinsurance is conducted using the partner–agent model. Insurers use MFIs to reach markets they could not reach on their own by capitalising on the client base of the MFI. In turn, the arrangement legally permits the MFI to sell microinsurance to protect its loan portfolios.

Only two of all the regulated private insurers in Zambia – MLife and NICO Insurance – serve the low-income market through partnerships with MFIs.[11]

Madison Insurance Company Zambia

Madison Insurance Company Zambia Ltd started out in 1992 as a subsidiary of Meridian International Bank. The Meridian Group collapsed in 1995, and Madison was acquired in a management buy-out. A new law proclaiming that no composite companies should operate in Zambia after December 2006 prompted Madison to split the existing company into two separate specialist companies earlier in 2006: MLife Insurance Company Zambia Limited and Madison General Insurance Company Zambia Limited.

MLife underwrites individual life insurance policies, group life insurance policies, credit life insurance policies, gratuity policies, funeral expenses insurance policies and personal as well as group pension plans. Before becoming involved in the microinsurance arena in 2001, the company focused on the corporate market and the higher end of the individual market.[12]

MLife and microinsurance

MLife offers the two standard microinsurance products, credit life and funeral insurance. It conducts most of its microfinance business through MFIs. Legally the MFIs are the policyholders. In practice, the MFIs act as insurance agents in return for either a fee or profit share.

Product development remains MLife's responsibility, with minimal input from the MFIs on premium rates and coverage. The MFIs are solely responsible for sales and servicing (the collection of premiums and claim settlements), client education and measuring client satisfaction. Clients live mainly in peri-urban areas and are mostly self-employed, operating small or micro enterprises.[13]

MLife has partnerships with six of the biggest microfinance institutions in Zambia: PRIDE Zambia, PULSE Holdings, Christian Enterprise Trust of Zambia (CETZAM), the Foundation for International Community Assistance (FINCA), Nkwena and Pan Africa Building Society.

MLife's first product for PULSE was an adaptation of a credit life policy that it had developed for commercial banks, the Credit Life Assurance Scheme. In 2002, PULSE, through its association with MLife, then introduced a funeral policy called *Thandizo*, meaning 'assistance', which covers the borrower and selected household members.

In 2004, CETZAM also decided to include credit life insurance as part of its product offerings, because NICO, the provider of its funeral policy, did not provide it. PRIDE Zambia and FINCA Zambia came on board soon afterwards. Each of these organisations has made taking out credit life and funeral cover for the principal borrower mandatory with every loan.

Profit distribution

MFIs' partners are compensated for their sales and service functions in one of two ways: an administration fee or profit-sharing. The profit-sharing scheme works as follows: MLife deducts 30 % of the premiums to cover its administrative costs; it then pays out claims and finally shares the balance evenly between itself and the MFI. The profit share is calculated at the end of each financial year and any losses are for MLife's account. Only two of the six MFIs have opted for the profit-sharing arrangement. The others receive a fixed fee of 10 % of the premiums collected. MLife prefers the fee approach because it is slightly easier to administer and at present more profitable to MLife, says Chakonta.

Challenges

This market is not without its challenges. Research conducted for CGAP, for example, has shown that MFI management, loan officers and their clients do not understand the products sufficiently. Credit officers are recruited to sell and manage the MFIs' core business – credit – and not for their knowledge of, or experience in, insurance. Therefore, the MFI loan officers do not give insurance products the focus they need. Few MFI clients really understand microinsurance, and many perceive it as a cost and not as a beneficial product. This is exacerbated by the fact that insurance is mandatory with a loan. Left as a voluntary purchase, most of the target market would not buy insurance. According to Chakonta this is understandable as every cent spent on insurance in reality can be a contribution to the next meal.

The MFIs do train the credit officers on the insurance products, and occasionally invite MLife to provide this training. However, the training is limited to information about the product features. Chakonta stresses that, as a consequence, MLife has become more involved with training, but the high turnover of loan officers means that keeping the MFI staff well trained remains a major problem.

The lack of information technology within the MFIs also makes the complicated paperwork of registering new clients and processing claims more onerous. Chakonta explains that MLife does not have up-to-date information on its microinsurance clients, as paperwork takes as long as five months to reach the company. This in turn affects the settlement of claims. In addition, settlements are delayed if the documentation provided by the MFIs is insufficient or incomplete.

In an attempt to shorten the claim period, some MFIs have opted to pay upfront and claim from MLife afterwards, as long as the documentation is correct. For its part, MLife has accommodated clients in rural areas by, for example, replacing the requirement of seeing a death certificate with written confirmation of the death from three public officials.

The MFIs have their own difficulties. For example, the client base of PULSE dropped from 3 063 in 2001 to only 1 945 towards the end of 2004. Research in 2002 by an independent company revealed high delinquency and default, low client retention, HIV/AIDS, fraud and high staff turnover. PULSE subsequently underwent a major restructuring that included product refinement, product diversification, policy changes, and institutional and staff changes.[14] However, this drop in the number of PULSE clients damaged the growth of MLife's microinsurance business at the time.

Looking to the future

Despite the challenges, this venture benefits all parties. The MFIs benefit because microinsurance lowers their credit risk and increases their profitability through the administration fee or profit share. In addition they are able to provide their customers with an extra service.

Clients and their families benefit by having their loans covered or a funeral policy in the event of death. As most MFIs issue loans through group lending using mutual guarantees, they expect the group to repay that member's debts in the event of death or illness. Microinsurance is crucial for keeping groups together and helping them continue after a member's death. Moreover, before insurance was introduced, the MFIs excluded potential borrowers suspected of being HIV positive. However, now that a group loan is covered by insurance, MFIs seemed less concerned about excluding members who might be HIV positive as long as they appear physically healthy.

For MLife, which recognised the opportunity in the low-income market in 2001, the venture has shown promise and contributes as much as 22 % to the company's overall income. Moreover, since 2002, the microfinance arm of the business had grown by more than 300 %. 'Although we have done reasonably well,' says Chakonta, 'we still need more volume,' adding that MLife is determined to tackle the issues in order to make the business grow.

One way in which MLife is considering expanding this business is by offering microinsurance through commercial microcredit providers, which are growing much faster than the NGO MFIs. Direct selling, using cellphone technology for example, is not an option at this point, because MLife does not have direct access to potential individual end users. Moreover, most of the target market still does not have access to a cellphone.[15] As a result, MLife is continuing to work with groups only. That said, because the MFIs have now started moving into the rural areas, MLife products are now covering a wider area as well.

Finally, as this model has been successfully implemented with most of the teething problems sorted out, MLife believes it could be replicated in other countries where MFI penetration is higher than in Zambia.

Microcare: Insurance for affordable access to quality healthcare in Uganda

> Most Ugandans see serious illness as the greatest risk to their household finances, perhaps not surprising in a country that has battled, with some success, against the HIV/AIDS pandemic. Health insurance therefore should be viable in Uganda, and Microcare is demonstrating that it can be. Microcare has two approaches: a community-based model in which groups pay premiums to a local hospital under a managed scheme, and a more profitable corporate model. Growth is coming from the corporate model but the company says the community-based model is financially self-standing. Microcare has made judicious use of donor funding, both for start-up and expansion and also as a guaranteed insurance fund for the community-based business.

In May 2000, Gerry Noble, an Irish physician and health-financing specialist, and Francis Somerwell, an IT specialist, were looking for a way to provide quality healthcare to the poor of Uganda at an affordable price. With donor support, they founded Microcare Limited, a non-profit company, and developed a managed group health scheme at a mission hospital in western Uganda and a multi-service-provider urban scheme for MFI clients and their families in Kampala. A key component of the project was technology designed to contain costs.

Funding was provided by the UK Department for International Development (DFID) Financial Deepening Challenge Fund (FDCF) in June 2004 to commercialise Microcare, with external insurance management input. With donor funding coming to an end in mid-2006, major management restructuring was required. Noble and Somerwell took back control of the company, and started running Microcare's two subsidiaries, Microcare Health Ltd and Microcare Insurance Ltd, as profit-orientated businesses focused on core expertise in health insurance. Microcare Insurance Ltd has rapidly become one of the largest insurance companies in Uganda, and the leader in health insurance in both the low-income and corporate markets.

Projected turnover in 2007 was more than double the USh3 billion[16] that was achieved in 2006, and the company moved into profitability. Although the corporate business is credited with the rapid growth and profits, it is risk management not subsidy that has made serving the low-income segment successful. 'If you make healthcare services available to poor people at a reasonable cost, they are willing to pay,' says Somerwell.

Political and socio-economic background

Uganda achieved independence from Britain in 1962. A period of political and economic turmoil followed until Lt Gen Yoweri Kaguta Museveni seized power in January 1986.[17]

With the support of the international community, Museveni introduced policies to rehabilitate and stabilise the economy. Over the past two decades the economy has performed well, and the real GDP growth rate for 2007 to 2009 is predicted to be 6.4 % on average. Poverty levels among the country's rapidly growing population of almost 30 million have declined, with 31.5 % living below the US$1 a day poverty line in 2006, compared with 56 % in 1992.[18] Despite this, the country is listed among the 50 least developed countries (LDCs) in the world. Per-capita income is about US$300 a year.

In total, 88 % of Ugandans live in rural areas.[19] Agriculture provides 80 % of employment, and most industries and services in the country depend on this sector.[20] While conducive to food production, Uganda's tropical climate, rivers and lakes also give rise to two of the country's main health concerns: malaria and water-borne diseases. Only 37 % of the population resides within five kilometres of a health facility that provides the national minimum heathcare package.[21]

According to Noble, Uganda has proved to be one of the most enlightened countries in the world regarding HIV/AIDS. As a result of proactive interventions, HIV/AIDS prevalence declined significantly from about 18 % in the early 1990s to 6.5 % in 2005.[22]

Table 9.2 Key economic data – Uganda

Population (million), 2005	26.8
Urban population (%), 2002	12
National unemployment rate (%), 2003	3.5
Urban unemployment rate (%), 2003	12.2
% of labour force classified as working poor*, 2003	36
Poverty (% population below the official poverty line), 2003	38
GDP (US$ billion), 2006	9.3

→

GDP growth rate (%), 2006	5.3
Forecast GDP growth rate (% per annum), 2007–2009	6.4
GNI per capita (US$), 2006	300
Inflation rate (%), November 2007	4.8
Deposit rate (%), April 2007	1.2
Lending rate (%), April 2007	18.8
Commercial bank time and savings deposits (USh billion), June 2006	857.31

Sources: Uganda Bureau of Statistics; Bank of Uganda; World Bank World Development Indicators

Note: *Defined as those earning an amount that was below the official poverty line of an average of $34 per capita per month (thus about US$1 per day)

Financial services for the poor

Only 38 % of the Ugandan population accesses financial services from the formal, semi-formal – MFIs, for instance – and informal sectors. Most people (58 %) use informal financial services such as savings and loan associations, and traditional groups that function within communities. The proportion of the rural population using financial services (35 %) is lower than in the urban areas, which are mainly concentrated in and around Kampala. The highest rural use is recorded in the more politically stable areas in the west of Uganda, which is also where Microcare works closely with communities.[23]

From the mid-1990s to the early 2000s, the Ugandan microfinance industry grew continuously. During this time, stakeholders collaborated to create a group of sustainable, commercially oriented MFIs, and to penetrate deeper into the rural areas. In 2003, the Ugandan parliament passed legislation that paved the way for the strongest MFIs to become regulated deposit-taking institutions, thereby shifting the focus to protecting the savings of the poor.[24]

In support of this move, Paul Rippey of the Financial Sector Deepening Project Uganda (FSDU) argues that microcredit is not a panacea for poverty. The myth, he says, is that people take loans to invest in a business when in fact the loans are often diverted to finance consumption. According to the FinScope Uganda 2007 study, the primary reasons that Ugandans save and borrow are to meet household expenses and to cover emergencies such as death and illness. Furthermore, Ugandans see serious illness as the greatest risk to their household finances.[25] Rippey believes that although savings and insurance are more difficult products to offer profitably than credit, this is where the focus should lie.

'For the poor, life is a risk'

Low-income households are vulnerable to risks and economic shocks, and take longer to recover from them.[26] 'For the poor, life is a risk,' says Vyasa Krishna, executive director for insurance at Microcare. FinScope Uganda found that in the event of acute adversity, poor Ugandans turn to informal savings and borrowing, or to selling their assets and livestock, thereby rapidly depleting their resources. Only 6 % of Ugandans have insurance, with affordability and lack of knowledge cited as the main reasons for not taking out insurance cover.[27]

According to Craig Churchill, chair of the Microinsurance Network (previously the CGAP working group on microinsurance) a major challenge in providing microinsurance – which is affordable insurance tailored to be relevant to the risks of low-income households[28] – is overcoming wariness among the poor of paying for intangible benefits that may never be claimed. He observes that while informal groups represent a form of insurance or risk pooling, the funds involved often only cover a small proportion of a loss.

When Noble founded Microcare in 2000, there were several community health financing schemes aimed at assisting the poor. Rather than entering the regulated insurance market at that time, Microcare's aim then was simply to augment the existing informal schemes for mitigating healthcare risks through improved management systems.

The Microcare story

In the late 1990s, Noble was involved as an Irish government volunteer in projects to finance hospitals and community health in Uganda. While co-ordinating a project for DFID, Noble and his colleague, Somerwell, realised that their prime objective – getting decent healthcare to low-income people at an affordable price – was at odds with the focus of their work, which was helping hospitals achieve institutional viability and sustainability. In an environment in which government healthcare infrastructure was inadequate at all levels, and patients tended to use private facilities, many of the sick, particularly in the rural areas, lacked the money to access medical care.[29]

In May 2000, Noble and Somerwell founded Microcare with donor funding.[30] They registered Microcare Limited as a non-profit organisation, and set it up as a microfinance initiative so that it fell under the Ugandan Ministry of Finance. In the first year, Noble and Somerwell concentrated on product and systems development, and initiated pilot studies for providing managed group health schemes to the poor.[31] In July 2001, they started introducing their products to two distinct groups. One was the *engozi* (burial societies) in the community around Kisiizi in western Uganda. There, Microcare took over the management of a mission hospital health scheme that already had 6 000 members. The other group consisted of MFI clients, and in particular those of FINCA, where Microcare acted as an intermediary between MFI client groups and the health service providers.

The burial societies of Kisiizi

In the mountainous region around Kisiizi in western Uganda, *engozi* is the vernacular word for 'a stretcher'. The burial societies are named *engozi* because the only way to transport the sick through the mountains to a medical facility is on a stretcher. As funerals are extremely important in Ugandan culture, communities have traditionally made provision for this expense. The burial societies collect funds, charge interest on loans and have mechanisms to guarantee repayment. 'They are very complex, but the critical thing is their existence. They are stable community organisations with a history of handling money and they trust each other,' says Noble.

Children from an orphan group whose health cover is paid for by a donor.

Somerwell explains their approach to the *engozi* in the early days. 'We asked them why they only collect money when people die and why they don't also collect money for when they are alive. They caught onto the concept of insurance quickly,' he says. The organisation then approached the local mission hospital with a proposition: what could the hospital do for a family who paid a guaranteed US$10 a year if there were thousands of such families? Financial sustainability had become a challenge for the mission hospital, and it welcomed the income source and contribution to monthly overheads.

In the meantime, Somerwell had been developing a health service management system (HSMS) to manage their initiatives and counteract the possibility of fraud. As a result, AON, an international insurance broker and risk management consultancy, approached Microcare to provide technical services for managing third-party administration (TPA) health funds for a few of its corporate clients. The Microcare system helped AON Uganda grow its TPA business, and created a revenue stream for Microcare.

In 2003, AON decided to divest itself of the less profitable TPA health funds business and, in keeping with a policy decision in AON internationally, focus on its core general insurance brokerage business. At the same time the FSDU encouraged Microcare to expand its activities, and indeed it provided a US$15 000 grant to develop a proposal for the FDCF. In May 2004 a grant of £730 000 was awarded by FDCF to Microcare through AON, which was appointed to supervise the expansion. The donor support was to pay for senior management costs for the first two years, administrative oversight and technical support from AON, and actuarial support. Microcare brought in commercial shareholders, setting up a for-profit company called Microcare Health Ltd, and in July 2004, AON handed its health management clients over to Microcare Health.

The new company's mission was to provide health plans, managed healthcare, preventive health measures, health education and mediation between health providers and beneficiaries.[32] Microcare Health then established Microcare Insurance Ltd, a for-profit insurance company. 'We set it up as a subsidiary of Microcare Health because it is much easier to have an insurance company that fulfils all the statutory regulatory requirements than having to fit a health management company into the Ugandan insurance regulations,' Noble explains.

Microcare Insurance secured a licence to operate as an insurance company in Uganda in December 2004. Over the next few months the new company negotiated and acquired commercial reinsurance, and in May 2005 it added health insurance to Microcare's offering.

In 2006, according to Noble, the AON managing director informed the Microcare board that the company was on the verge of insolvency. However, on closer inspection of the financial position, Noble discovered over US$500 000 in uncollected debt, which meant the business could be rescued. Noble and Somerwell gathered support from the commercial shareholders, and parted from AON by taking control of Microcare in July 2006 and replacing the chairman of the board and the managing director. As AON had been the conduit for the FDCF funding, this signaled the end of donor support.

Noble, now in control of the company, appointed an internal auditor to scrutinise the near insolvency. They found that the company was spending more on reinsurance cover than was necessary (much related to non-health business that was not performing) and that the uncollected debt was closer to US$800 000.

A 'capillary' model

Figure 9.1 Microinsurance economic segmentation

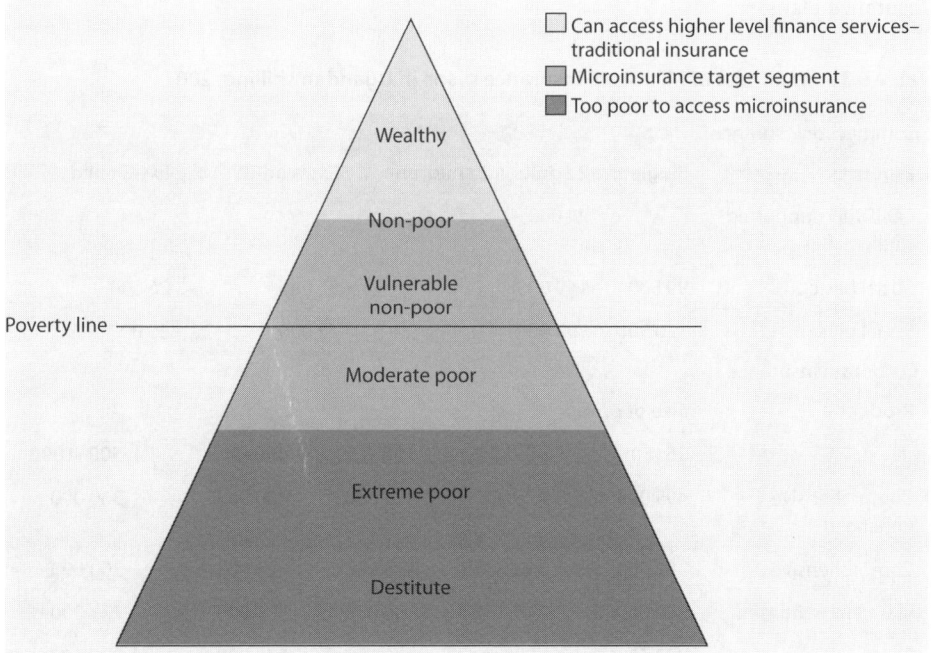

Source: Microcare

The new management set about remedying this and by December 2006 only US$15 000 of the uncollected debt was still outstanding. By June 2007, the uncollected debts from 2004, 2005 and 2006 had been reduced to US$2 000, the company had halved its reinsurance costs and reduced its operating costs, and Microcare had started becoming profitable. 'We had a good product, good people and good IT systems – probably the best in Africa for health management – it simply needed the cash flow to turn the company around,' says Noble.

Somerwell describes Microcare's approach as a capillary model (see Figure 9.1). He says that the top-down 'gravity model' is typically used for designing products for the poor, with products designed for the top end tailored to fit the bottom end. Microcare's model is to study the need and market of low-income people and design products for the poor, and then extend these products to higher-income segments. 'Gravity makes it easy to fall down, but capillary action pulls up,' he says.

The HSMS IT system that Somerwell developed to manage the mission-hospital health scheme in Kisiizi forms the foundation of the capillary model (see Figure 9.1), and has facilitated partnerships with service providers that serve both communities and corporates. Management of the company's operations falls under Microcare Health, but the multidisciplinary team of IT, health and insurance specialists combine to tailor products that suit customers' needs across a broad spectrum.

Products

Microcare's three main products are health insurance, TPA and the operation of company clinics.

Health insurance: This ranges from a basic product for the low-income market to a fully comprehensive plan for the top end. Table 9.3 shows the range and annual cost of insurance plans.

Table 9.3 Annual cost of Microcare insurance plans in Ugandan shilling, 2007

Community insurance				
Product	Single	2 adults + 2 children	Extra adult	Extra child
CORDAID-supported rural		24 000		
Social basic	99 500	149 000	52 000	26 000
Social plus	120 500	199 000	72 000	36 000
Corporate insurance				
Product	Size of group			
	25–50	50–100	100–250	250–500	500–1000
Comprehensive enhanced	495 000	475 000	425 000	400 000	360 000
Comprehensive	350 000	350 000	325 000	325 000	300 000
Standard enhanced	340 000	340 000	300 000	300 000	275 000
Standard	262 500	262 500	240 000	240 000	222 500
Basic	150 000	150 000	150 000	150 000	125 000

Source: Microcare

All products cover inpatient, outpatient, maternity, family planning, basic dental, optical and evacuation care. Cover for long-term HIV/AIDS treatment (antiretrovirals) and chronic medication applies only on enhanced products, but all products include inpatient treatment for the related medical conditions. Dependent children who are not the natural children of the principal client, for example orphans, can be included, as well as the parents of the client.

Viable health microinsurance necessitates rationing benefits to maintain premiums at affordable levels. For the client to express an interest in covering a perceived risk, the potential financial loss of the risk must be higher than the cost of the insurance.[33] Microcare tailors microinsurance accordingly, varying the priority given to different benefits depending on the group being insured. For example, chronic disease cover to benefit a few would put premiums beyond the reach of low-income groups. Consequently, clients agreed on this exclusion as the chronically ill are already paying for their medication.[34]

The same principle applies to insurance offered to corporates. 'When we visit a company, we analyse their needs and tailor our product to work within the company's budget,' explains Clare Mukuru, marketing manager of Microcare.

Products are also tailored to allow clients access to a specific level of healthcare service provider. In the urban areas there is a range of service providers and in Kampala different products entitle clients to use different facilities. In the rural areas there is rarely much choice when it comes to quality healthcare service providers. Microcare classifies providers according to their cost and quality. Top-of-the-range products cover access to all levels (A, B, C and D), while the low-income products cover access only to level D providers. 'You can choose to use any service provider, but we pay claims according to your level,' says Somerwell.

Third-party administration: Microcare Health manages health funds that company clients have created to cover the medical expenses of their staff. Although health funds are not insurance, the administrative burden and risks of ensuring that the right people receive the right treatment at the right price are similar to those of health insurance. For each health fund, Microcare keeps an escrow account, which is topped up periodically by the client. The company also manages the utilisation, costs and quality of service provision on behalf of the client.

Operation of company clinics: As Microcare Health has both administrative and medical expertise, it also manages in-house company clinics. However, this is not Microcare Health's core business, and Noble says the company accepts the work 'under duress' since Microcare is keen to avoid the conflicts of interest that commonly arise when the healthcare service provider is also the insurer.

Insurance risk management

According to Noble, adverse selection, moral hazard and fraud are common to all types of insurance, but are a particular problem in health insurance, as the service provider both determines the problem and benefits from the solution.[35]

Adverse selection happens when the health status of an insured group is worse than would be expected from the general population, and claims paid therefore exceed premiums received. As Microcare upholds a principle of equal access to medical care, it does not screen or exclude clients. This means that there are no exclusions for being HIV positive. It has therefore mitigated the risk of adverse selection by insuring only pre-existing groups formed for purposes other than health insurance – burial societies, MFI groups and employees of companies – and requiring a minimum of 50 insured lives per group. For MFIs, at least half the group and their families must join with a minimum of 20 families. 'And it has to be for the whole family, not just the elderly or the sick, who are a high risk,' says James Turner, Microcare operations manager.

Microcare charges annual premiums to reduce the risk of people taking out short-term membership for urgent medical care, and then dropping out of the system. But as Somerwell explains, 'People know how to live with problems like dental and eye problems. When you join a health programme, you want a clean up. In the first year the utilisation is very high.' Rather than charge a higher premium, however, Microcare absorbs the increased claims in the first year knowing that claims will slow down in the second year and that the client retention rate is high.

This mother of six had a c-section with her last child, which was covered by the scheme.

Moral hazard happens when members overuse health services because they are covered by insurance. Turner explains that to mitigate this risk, Microcare members in the rural burial society schemes pay a consultation fee ranging from USh500 to USh2 000 to encourage responsible use of their cover. 'Ugandans love health services and love to be treated whether by tablet or by injection, and this small fee is a way of screening. With emphasis on the word "small",' he adds.

Microcare uses experience-related pricing at annual premium reviews as another mechanism for controlling risk. In the first year, groups are charged standard rates, but once Microcare has a utilisation record, premiums are adjusted if necessary. This record, produced by the IT system, is central to Microcare's ability to prevent fraud, monitor the quality of care and control costs. By involving the clients and making them aware of their claims performance, overuse is discouraged.

The IT enabler

Unlike other forms of insurance where claims per customer are infrequent, health insurers expect multiple claims per family member every year. Managing the volume and integrity of claims can be daunting, but the IT system that Microcare developed helps the company address this.

All Microcare clients receive smartcards on enrolment. The smartcard is used for client identity verification and has photographs of the principal policyholder and all the dependants printed on it. It also shows the group or company to which the policyholder belongs. A microchip carries details on the insurance cover and up-to-date utilisation data.

Microcare has its own computerised check-in desk, run by a qualified Microcare nurse, at each of its major contracted hospitals and clinics. The check-in terminal is linked to the central Oracle database of client information at the Microcare head office. Client details are downloaded to the terminal, and utilisation data uploaded to the database at regular intervals. To alleviate problems associated with power outages, check-in desks are equipped with UPS power back-up or batteries with inverters, depending on the location. Some hospitals and clinics have generators. However, since the data transfer system is off-line it does not rely on continual connectivity.

Clients can move freely between service providers, even though the terminals are not permanently connected to the central database, as up-to-date information is available either from the downloads or on the smartcard. Uploads are triggered by the amount of new data on the terminal. Connectivity is established and the data is transmitted to the central database for processing. 'I collect all the transaction data in about 50 shillings of connectivity cost,' Somerwell explains.

On arrival at the service provider, the client presents the smartcard to the nurse. The nurse swipes it to verify the client's identity against the photograph on the card and on the terminal. The nurse also checks the client's cover under the scheme and use of cover to date.

After consulting a clinician, the client returns to the check-in desk, and claim details such as the clinician's name, the diagnosis, the tests administered and the drugs prescribed are entered into the system and processed. This ensures that only covered care is provided. The client is also informed if the treatment or drugs are not adequately covered by the remaining limits of the policy, and then has the choice of paying the difference, going to a cheaper service provider, or requesting less expensive treatment. 'The hospital and the patient work it out. The patient may get any treatment, but we pay only up to the limit,' explains Krishna.

The smartcard is updated and a medical treatment access card (MTAC) is printed in triplicate, with one copy given to the patient to keep, one copy kept by the hospital for their own records before drugs are issued or further treatment is administered, and one copy held by the service provider for billing purposes. At the end of each month, the service provider submits a bill to Microcare, supported by copy MTACs. The bill is then reconciled by Microcare Health and settled.

This process provides valuable actuarial data, and enables an audit of clinician performance and service provider costs.[36] 'It is our responsibility to control the costs and not allow people to abuse the system. Indirectly you save 30 % of the premium costs by avoiding abuses. Then we have done our job, because at the end of the day the poor people are paying the premium,' says Somerwell.

Service providers partners

An underlying principle at Microcare is giving clients a choice of service provider. It has therefore contracted a network of more than 170 service providers across Uganda. This principle differentiates Microcare's offering from other health management plans, such as Health Maintenance Organisations (HMOs) where clients receive all the care from a particular provider for a set annual fee.

Service providers are mostly private providers such as for-profit clinics and hospitals, and not-for-profit mission hospitals. Clients on the lower-income products predominately use the not-for-profit hospitals both in Kampala and in the rural areas. Microcare also partners with some government hospitals, such as the country's largest hospital, Mulago Hospital in Kampala. However, as the government has abolished user fees in government hospitals where all services, including drugs, are provided free of charge, only separately run private wards in these hospitals are permitted to receive payment for services from Microcare.

Another differentiating factor is the nature of Microcare's relationship with its service providers. 'I do not believe you can be the doctor and the insurer. That is one of the philosophical cornerstones that we have built our company on,' says Noble. He explains that there is a natural balance in the relationship between the insurer and the medical provider that contains costs and ensures quality service provision: an independent insurer will not accept unnecessary costs, but an insurer who also provides clinical services may compromise on quality by avoiding high-cost services.

Somerwell believes that the key to the success of the programme is having a network of service providers providing the level of service that Microcare promises. Noble believes that the biggest problem at Ugandan hospitals and clinics it that they often lack financial management capacity. Microcare facilitates positive cash flow for its service providers by providing a steady source of customers, and guaranteeing prompt payment. These allow providers to access loans and improve their facilities. The relationship is mutually beneficial as Microcare can, in turn, negotiate lower prices and stipulate minimum (or better) levels of service provision.

Selection of service providers is stringent, but constrained by supply, particularly in the rural areas. 'We pick the best of the bunch. The main requirements are that they are medically sound, have decent facilities and can account for what has been spent,' says Turner. Providers are then contracted to deliver services, and set prices according to Microcare's specifications.

'Inefficiency creates a stumbling block for providing services to the poor,' states Somerwell. Consequently Microcare Health takes a proactive role in driving standards up and costs down by training, advising and monitoring the service providers.

The model followed by most hospitals and clinics in Uganda – and which Microcare is actively advising its own providers to change – is to recover high inpatient costs from the outpatient department and the pharmacy, where mark-ups often exceed 100 %. Pharmaceuticals account for about 70 % of Microcare's payment to service providers, and are closely monitored for excessive mark-ups and exclusions, such as prescriptions for vitamins. 'There is a tendency in Uganda to over-prescribe things like vitamins, despite the fact that there is an abundance of fresh vegetables and fruit is falling off every tree,' says Turner.

Lindsay Davidson, healthcare manager at Microcare, says that service providers often submit invoices that do not comply with their Microcare contract. Although the IT system rejects non-compliant items, this requires additional administration. 'The only effective way to control it is to put a line through it and point them to the contract that they signed,' she says.

As well as monitoring service provider charges, Microcare Health can review the quality of clinical services from the information provided by the IT system. The staff from Microcare's medical department, who are all medical professionals, visit the service providers to monitor quality, advise on Microcare's expectations, and at times even offer medical expertise. 'We don't have a conflict of interest, so we can go in and do something about it when they are not complying,' says Davidson.

It is, however, not only service providers who inflate drug costs. The malaria parasite's resistance to chloroquine has compelled the ministry of health to recommend the more expensive artemether-based drugs for first-line treatment. The drugs are supplied by international drug manufacturers, are not subsidised, and have tripled the cost of treatment. As malaria is endemic in Uganda and the most commonly diagnosed disease among Microcare clients, the cost of the treatment presents a major threat to Microcare's efforts to provide affordable healthcare for the poor. It also makes the company's preventive healthcare initiatives an imperative.

Preventive healthcare

'If prevention is cheaper than cure, then as an insurer you should be in the prevention business, providing you have a stable client base,' says Noble. As preventable diseases, such as malaria, waterborne diseases and HIV/AIDS, cause a large percentage of Ugandan deaths, Microcare is trying to educate clients and intervene with measures to prevent disease, and thereby reduce claims in the long term.

Microcare subsidises and distributes mosquito nets to its clients, because the cost of one outpatient treatment for malaria exceeds the cost of an insecticide-treated net. 'If they use the mosquito nets, we can prevent at least one treatment per year for the average client,' Krishna explains. Distribution of nets and education about malaria go together, and Microcare is already seeing the benefit. Clients are seeking early treatment, which is cheaper than advanced treatment. Distribution of jerry cans and water purification tablets, aimed at reducing the incidence of waterborne diseases such as dysentery and cholera, are also being promoted for the low-income clients. Although Uganda has been proactive in HIV/AIDS prevention since 1986, there has recently been an upsurge in prevalence rates.[37] Microcare Health has introduced HIV awareness and voluntary counselling and testing (VCT) programmes, as stigma and the issue of confidentiality still hamper dealing with the disease, even in otherwise sophisticated corporates.

Donata Asaba, preventive health manager for Microcare, explains that the nets, jerry cans and health education sessions are tangible benefits which the company uses to market its product, but the long-term gain is what Microcare has in mind. 'We are looking at building good health practices, as we believe people can change their behaviour. And we hope that in the end they will remain with us and that they are healthy,' she says.

Engaging the communities

Microcare's early Kisiizi initiative was partly donor funded. It is now replicating the principles of the model with a profit motive in other communities. The combination of working with groups that had formed around a culture of saving, and partnering with a hospital committed to serving the community, has worked well. As a consequence, from the original 6 000 people covered by the Kisiizi hospital's health plan, more than 20 000 people are now covered by Microcare's health insurance in Kisiizi, and Microcare is expanding the programme to other service providers in the area. 'A lot of the lessons have been learned from working with those original people,' says Turner.

One of the lessons was that Microcare needed to partner with MFIs to help potential customers to gain access to savings and loan accounts. Somerwell explains that this became apparent on a visit to Kisiizi when a woman offered him some potatoes in exchange for insurance. 'We realised that we needed a microbank and we approached an MFI, Uganda Microfinance Limited (UML),' says Somerwell. Today, there is an UML branch next door to the Microcare offices at Kisiizi, and at Kisoro in western Uganda where Microcare subsequently started operations.

Another reason for partnering with MFIs is that they already work with informal-sector groups and thus potential customers for health insurance. As well as targeting microfinance groups in Kampala, where Microcare has almost 700 members, Microcare has targeted other kinds of groups. It has recruited customers from drama groups, a group formed to learn mathematics, and another formed to overcome harassment by the police in the marketplace.

> **Microcare client: The Tukolerewamu community group**
>
> A group of women are gathered under a tree in Rubaga, a Kampala suburb. It appears to be a social gathering, as the women converse and gesticulate enthusiastically. It is the weekly meeting of a group named *Tukolerewamu*, 'Let's work together'.
>
> Harriet Nantonga, the secretary of the group, relates how the women started out. 'The group was formed in 1998 with about 30 women. We did not come together in the interests of borrowing money. We first came together for unity, helping each other in case of problems. In this way each woman could put aside a little saving and organise a small business.'
>
> The group met for a year, each member saving USh1 000 a week. After a year FINCA stepped in and offered the group a USh100 000 loan to supplement their savings and set up small businesses. After they had paid back the first loan, FINCA increased the size of the next loan. This cycle of paying off and borrowing anew has continued for eight years.
>
> The women all have small businesses. Harriet has a retail shop, the treasurer sells used clothing, some sell agricultural produce, and others have poultry. FINCA introduced the group to Microcare. 'As we didn't have money to go to the hospital when we got sick, we got interested. FINCA gave us loans that we could pay off in instalments to join Microcare. The interest is 3 % a month. We are happy, because it is not that much,' Harriet explains.
>
> As the group sits and chats, the treasurer collects and records the loan repayments. After the meeting she will take the money to FINCA. The group appointed her their treasurer because she had studied accounting. 'She is trustworthy and she knows how to account for our money,' says Harriet.
>
> Although frustrated that the social basic package does not cover chronic disease medication, the chairperson and founder of the group acknowledges that the value of the services they receive is more than the premiums they pay. 'It gives you peace,' she says.

Godfrey Asiimwe, a Microcare field officer, is responsible for recruiting new groups, and providing customer care for existing ones in Kampala. In addition to educating potential and existing clients about health microinsurance, Asiimwe periodically attends group meetings to resolve problems and counsel clients when their insurance is due for renewal.

His work also benefits the MFIs. 'I help to connect the customers with the MFIs and make sure they pay back their health loan,' he says.

Frequency of income – and the effect this has on people's ability to pay the annual premium – is another motive for partnering with the MFIs. Informal group members typically earn income daily or weekly, and meet every week to save or repay loans. Not many of these clients have the full annual premium at their disposal when it is required, and therefore have to take a loan, and incur interest, to make the payment. Microcare works with the MFIs to provide separate loans for annual insurance cover so that clients can easily determine what their health insurance costs them.[38] Loans are paid back over four months to curtail interest costs.

MFIs also facilitate premium collection. Noble argues that transacting in cash is extremely expensive and encourages fraud. 'Rule number one at Microcare is that we never handle cash,' he says. Instead, the MFI writes a cheque for the annual premiums or transfers the money directly into Microcare's account.

Although the MFIs take on these financial risks, it works to their advantage to have customers who are insured against health risks. A pilot study conducted by Microcare and FINCA in 2000 shows that 40 % of defaulters cite sickness as the reason for not repaying their loans. Healthy customers are less likely to default on loan repayments, to undermine the solidarity of the group or to redirect business loans for health expenses.

Microcare client: AVSI Foundation

AVSI Foundation, an NGO that provides support to internally displaced people in war-ravaged northern Uganda, offers Microcare health insurance to its staff of 250 and their dependants. Although they have many staff members in Kampala, most are stationed in the north.

Charles Ombanya, human resource manager for AVSI, says that the company has tried all the health management options to ensure that it has healthy staff members. Before Microcare, AVSI gave its staff a cash medical allowance. The problem with this approach was that when people fell ill they would treat themselves rather than get the proper intervention to save on costs.

AVSI then tried TPA with Microcare. Although this was better than the cash allowance, says Ombanya, 'it is not always easy to get precise accountability in the hospitals'.

When Microcare started converting its TPA customers to insurance, AVSI was eager to make the move. As Microcare had not yet extended its operations to the north, AVSI introduced health insurance to the Kampala staff only. Microcare has formed partnerships with upcountry hospitals and health centres, and AVSI has gradually introduced health insurance to the rest of the staff.

There have been a few hiccups such as overuse, which happened because neither the staff nor the service providers fully understood the limits and the exclusions. The photographs on the smartcards have also not eliminated fraud entirely, and there have been instances of look-alikes using the cards.

Service provision at the level that Microcare demands is still limited in the north of the country. Ombanya has scouted the area for potential Microcare partners but found most places wanting. 'We may need to establish a clinic in one of the towns with *Médecins sans Frontières*,' he says.

AVSI has embarked on a programme to educate the staff about health insurance and is considering expanding their package to increase the dental, optical and chronic disease coverage. 'Overall,' says Ombanya, 'things are looking good'.

The corporates

The success of IT-supported, community health-financing management in Kisiizi and Kampala drew Microcare into the corporate market. Its ability to contain costs and manage risk while giving clients a choice of service providers remains the thrust of this expansion.

Mukuru explains that initially companies could not distinguish between Microcare's product and the HMO schemes to which they were accustomed. She says the HMOs were also underpriced, which meant that to compete, Microcare could not rely solely on the quality of its products, and had to get its pricing right.

Microcare's portfolio of blue-chip TPA clients helped give the company credibility, and also provided a starting point for selling health insurance in the corporate market. As TPA funds give employees unlimited access to healthcare, it is in these claims that the most fraud is detected. By introducing smartcards and a choice of monitored service providers, Microcare has managed to curtail abuse, but Turner explains that confidentiality often creates a dilemma for Microcare's medical department. 'A doctor signs off that the treatment has happened. If you refuse to pay it, then you penalise the employee. If you pay it, you might be paying fraudulent claims,' he says.

Claims that appear to be fraudulent are referred back to the TPA client (usually through their human resources department), Microcare pays the service providers if the funds are available, but delayed replenishment of the fund by the corporate client often causes stresses with the service providers. The need to frequently top up funds that have been depleted by use and the unpredictability of TPA requirements provide strong incentives for companies to convert to insurance, according to James Turner. While some have chosen to remain with TPA, according to Davidson, others have converted to insurance, the primary reason being the benefit of a fixed health budget.

Risk management, says Noble, is recognising that it is not only the cost of intervention that has an impact on health cost, but also the cost of non-intervention. 'Companies must determine the optimal intervention strategy to mitigate and manage that risk,' he adds. As employers in Uganda start seeing the advantages of insurance, Mukuru says that she and her team are cherry picking in the corporate market through direct sales and marketing.

Noble attributes growth in the corporate segment to Microcare's relationships with its clients. 'Our retention rate is extremely high, which is important in this business,' he says. At present, the number of Microcare corporate clients has grown to 170, and the number of lives being covered to around 60 000.

Edging into profitability

Most of Microcare's expansion has happened since the 2006 shakeup. Turnover for that year was USh3 billion, and Amin Manji, Microcare's financial consultant, projected a turnover of almost USh8 billion for the year ended 31 December 2007. 'In 2005, I thought that it was not a viable business, because it was running at a loss. In 2006 there was a huge improvement, and now it is profitable,' he says.

Reinsurance is a significant proportion of the cost of health insurance, and reserve requirements are high. While the Dutch Catholic development organisation Cordaid (Catholic Organisation for Relief and Development Aid) provides a guaranteed fund for community insurance, commercial insurance is reinsured separately with commercial reinsurers. Up to 10 % of premiums go to stop-loss reinsurance, and 40 % of the premium has to be maintained in reserve.

To date Microcare has not needed to claim on its stop-loss reinsurance and has only used its reserves. Manji explains that hunger to grow is the rationale for this policy. 'If you claim from the reinsurance you won't be looking in the market,' he says. Table 9.4 shows Microcare's reserve profile.

Table 9.4 Microcare Group's financial profile, June 2007

	Microcare Health	Microcare Insurance
Assets	USh29.7 million	USh80.7 million
Paid-up capital	USh1.44 billion	USh1 billion
Investment worth	nil	USh253 million

Source: Microcare

Note: Microcare Insurance is the registered insurance company, underwriter and manager of broker relationships. Microcare Health delivers health provider contracts and liaison, and all support services.

The claims ratio on Microcare's corporate insurance is between 50 % and 55 %. Krishna ascribes this to the effectiveness of the IT system and says that it is a remarkable achievement, since claims ratios for medical insurance often exceed 95 % and even 100 %. At the level of community insurance, premiums collected exceed claims by approximately 5 % only, despite the low premiums. According to Manji, Microcare's profit is around 7 %, and he believes the company can achieve a level of 12 % by reducing overheads and continuing on its growth path.

Although Microcare is recovering community insurance administrative costs from profits in the corporate segment, Somerwell and Krishna are both adamant that corporate insurance does not subsidise community insurance. Poor people are paying for their medical care, they say, and the company is using overhead costs optimally by bringing in high volumes in both sectors.

Looking ahead

Noble is looking at ways to improve delivery by healthcare service providers and to expand Microcare's service provider network. He envisions a triangular relationship between Microcare, service providers and health sector investors. 'What we would bring to the party is guaranteed payments to the financier. So, if you want to invest in a hospital, you would get first bite of the cherry every month,' he explains. The benefits for Microcare would be improved facilities and service to clients, as well as lower costs, since service providers would benefit from Microcare's leverage to negotiate lower interest rates on loans and thus reduce their own overheads.

Although the Ugandan government has proposed a national health insurance scheme (NHIS) under which employers will contribute 4 % of every employee's gross salary, and employees will contribute an additional 4 % to a National Hospital Insurance Fund, Noble does not believe that it will affect Microcare's expansion in the corporate market as the cover would be limited. 'Companies are still going to have to provide healthcare for their workers, and their expectations are higher than the NHIS programme can deliver.

They are not going to settle for standing in a queue in a government hospital, or a much more limited range of treatments from the private providers,' he says.

Expansion into other East African countries is on the cards, but only once Microcare finds sufficient funding for initial market surveys and start-up costs. Noble believes any initiatives that Microcare undertakes must be ultimately self-sustaining and says that, while he would look to donor grant funding for initial research and development, other socially orientated investment sources are needed to provide a cost effective form of venture capital. 'Healthcare is not something that traditional venture capital is interested in or used to, so the terms would be detrimental,' he explains.

Deeper penetration into low-income groups in Uganda lies at the heart of Microcare's expansion plans. 'The reason we have consolidated our position in the apex market is to stabilise our company so that we can push downmarket,' says Noble. Microcare intends expanding aggressively into informal sector groups. For example, the taxi drivers' association has 60 000 members and already has a collection mechanism in place through its own social benefit fund.

Other groups in Microcare's sight are market-stall owners, fishermen and agricultural co-operatives. Somerwell describes a potential method of collecting premiums in agricultural co-operatives. 'A farmer supplies milk, but each week the proceeds from the first few litres go towards his health insurance and he receives cash payment for the rest,' he says.

As the success of health insurance in the agricultural sector depends on the farmers' ability to continue paying premiums, Microcare is also investigating insurance to overcome disruption to agricultural production. Most Ugandans derive their income from their animals and the productive capacity of their land. Agricultural insurance would stabilise their income and make their productive assets secure so that they could be used as collateral for borrowing. In the event of a loss, farmers currently have to sell off their productive assets for survival. 'With insurance, the farmers can get money from the banks and plant for the next year,' says Krishna.

'Once we have addressed their vulnerability by covering their health, their burial and also their livelihood with an affordable insurance product, then these low-income people can also live a risk-free life,' Somerwell explains.

Conclusion

Microcare's capillary model creates a symbiotic relationship between serving the top and the bottom of the pyramid. The drive to make healthcare affordable at the bottom simultaneously addresses the needs at the top, while profits earned at the top provide the resources to intensify Microcare's impact and outreach at the bottom.

Noble isolates the reason for the organisation's success: 'It is because we are a health, insurance and IT company combined,' he says. There are several factors that have contributed to serving the whole pyramid profitably. The first is to have the controls in place to mitigate the risk. The second is efficient premium collection and prompt payment of service providers – essential to ensure that the service provider and the clients do not lose confidence in Microcare.

The third is volume. 'We are not a boutique,' says Noble. 'We are Microcare, but we are not micro. The "micro" in microinsurance refers to the income of the target client base, not the scale of operation of the insurer. In fact the bigger you are as an insurer, the more efficient you should become, the better the risk pooling is and the more affordable you can make your product for the low-income client. By the end of this year, in terms of turnover, we will be in the top five or six insurance companies in Uganda, and a leading regional player in terms of health insurance volume.'

And the most important lesson he and Somerwell have learned is not to surrender control of the company to others. 'With your own money, you can take the time to do it the way you want to do it,' he concludes.

Note

In 2009 the Microcare group faced two disputes which had implications for its ability to continue to do business in the future. Six large hospitals sued the organisation for non-payment of claims dating back for many months. Microcare insisted that the claims in question were not genuine and that it therefore had no obligation to pay them. In August 2009 the hospitals' case was withdrawn and the High Court awarded legal costs against them.

The second was not resolved as successfully. In February 2009, the Uganda Insurance Commission (UIC) refused to renew Microcare's licence to operate as an insurer. Microcare Insurance challenged the decision in the High Court, saying that the UIC had not followed either the correct statutory procedures or accepted international accounting standards. The court agreed to hold a judicial review of the UIC's actions, and in late March 2009 it reinstated Microcare's licence, preventing interference with the business until such a time as an application was heard for judicial review. On 22 October 2009, the High Court dismissed Microcare's case on the preliminary objection that it had not exhausted all other channels of intervention before seeking judicial review, however, the judge still give Microcare the option to seek a second judicial review if not satisfied with the outcome of an appeal to the Minister of Finance. The UIC subsequently ordered that until the licence is renewed, Microcare could neither write new insurance policies nor renew any existing ones, although it could continue honouring claims on the policies already in force.

In the interim, Microcare had been looking for an external funder and on 3 November 2009 it was announced that the International Medical Group (IMG) was to take over Microcare Insurance Ltd. IMG, which owes the International Hospital, Kampala and International Air Ambulance, said that it would invest the necessary capital (about USh1.8 billion) so that Microcare could meet the UIC's licensing requirements. Microcare Health will continue to operate as a separate entity, as a technical support organisation in microinsurance development both locally and internationally, especially focusing on systems needs.

Endnotes

[1] Leftley & Mapfumo (2006).
[2] Leftley (2006a).
[3] Leftley (2005).
[4] Leftley & Mapfumo (2006).
[5] Leftley (2005).
[6] Leftley & Mapfumo (2006).
[7] Leftley (2006b).
[8] Manje (2005).
[9] Manje (2005).
[10] Ibid.
[11] Four insurance companies offering a combination of products: Zambia State Insurance Corporation Limited, Madison Insurance Company Limited, Professional Insurance Corporation Limited and ZIGI Insurance Company Limited; one life insurance company:

African Life Assurance Limited; three general (non-life) insurance companies: NICO Insurance Company Limited, Goldman Insurance Company Limited and Cavmont-Capital Insurance Limited; and one reinsurance company: ZimRe (Z) Limited.

12 Madison Life Insurance Company Zambia (2006).
13 Manje (2005).
14 Ibid.
15 Adongo (2007).
16 October 2007 – US$1 = USh1 725.00.
17 CIA World Factbook.
18 World Bank Country Brief.
19 Uganda Census 2002, in The Steadman Group (Uganda) Limited (2007).
20 The Steadman Group (Uganda) Limited (2007).
21 Avsi Uganda (2006).
22 World Bank Country Brief.
23 The Steadman Group (Uganda) Limited (2007).
24 Goodwin-Groen, Bruett & Latortue (2004).
25 The Steadman Group (Uganda) Limited (2007).
26 Cohen & Sebstad (2006).
27 The Steadman Group (Uganda) Limited (2007).
28 Churchill (2006).
29 United Nations (2002).
30 Austrian Development Bureau, European Union/Government of Uganda Suffice Program and the Mc Knight Foundation (USA). Source: Noble (2001).
31 Noble (2001).
32 Microcare (2004).
33 Churchill (ed.) (2006).
34 Radermacher, Dror & Noble (2006).
35 Ibid.
36 Leftley & Mapfumo (2006).
37 World Bank Country Brief.
38 Radermacher, Dror & Noble (2006).

Chapter Ten

Sustaining markets

Long-term sources of finance and consumer protection, especially with the introduction of credit to people, often for the first time, are essential for building an inclusive financial system and sustaining financial markets. The two case studies in this chapter look at different aspects of capital and credit markets.

Without sources of long-term finance, such as pension funds and insurance companies, there is limited scope for developing a mortgage market or private equity. Without the range of investment options associated with capital markets, pension funds and insurance companies are constrained in their ability to generate adequate long-term returns to cover people's financial needs in their retirement.

Where there are well-functioning capital markets, professional investors have come to appreciate the attractions of microfinance as an asset class in its own right and so, across the world, asset managers have been chasing equity investments in microfinance banks or, as in the case of Faulu Kenya, investing in the long-term debt of MFIs. This is a positive development especially if, as in Faulu's case, it results in domestic demand for long-term capital being matched by domestic supply.

There has been a dramatic increase in commercial microlending – typically, short-term unsecured loans. Mostly, but not always, these loans are used to buy consumer goods. Often they are simply used to cover a temporary shortfall in household income. The boom in this type of lending raises two issues. First, the proliferation of different sources of credit in the market with the risk of 'roundtripping', where loans are paid off by other loans, underscores the importance of credible borrower information. Second, overindebtedness becomes a real threat, and the need for debt counselling services grows. It could be said that debt counselling is a case of shutting the stable door after the horse has bolted. But even with robust consumer protection measures in place (and non-bank commercial microlenders in many African countries are operating in an entirely unregulated market), the implications of taking on credit mean there will still be a demand for efficiently supplied debt counselling services to help consumers out of their debt trap. The Summit Financial Partners case study proposes one way to do this – and to do so sustainably.

Faulu Kenya: Finding finance after grant funding

> The upsurge of interest in microfinance over the past decade has meant that microfinance institutions can access more types of capital instruments from a wider range of investors than ever before. Faulu Kenya has grown in just 15 years from a donor-funded microlending pilot programme to becoming the issuer of a five-year local currency bond on Kenya's capital markets. The success of Faulu illustrates how donor funding can be used successfully to 'crowd in' local funding – through their investment in the Faulu bond, Kenya's pension funds and commercial banks are being connected with the country's unbanked population.

When Monicah Wanjiku's retail clothing business was stagnating, she thought she had reached a dead end. For a long time business had been slow because she had no capital to expand. In 2000 Monicah heard about Faulu, one of Kenya's leading microfinance institutions, with whom she now has a flourishing relationship. As a member of the Bidii Self-Help Group, she took a loan of KSh20 000, then the equivalent of US$250, to restock her retail clothes shop. Monicah then took a series of loans from Faulu and was lending KSh300 000 (US$4 000) by her sixth loan cycle. Her business has grown steadily and she has managed to pay off each of her loans before the scheduled time. The business allows her to feed the whole family and to educate her children. Monicah now employs five people and has bought a commercial van for transport. She has financed her business growth solely with Faulu's support, and is now in a position to access formal banking credit on an individual lending basis if she wishes to, something unthinkable a few years ago. Like many of Faulu's customers, Monicah continues borrowing from Faulu out of strong loyalty and because of the convenient repayment terms Faulu offers.

Faulu uses the group lending model backed by consultants who provide advice and support.

This is not the end of the story for Monicah: 'My greatest ambition is to import goods for my business, buy a plot and build a house and educate my family the best way possible … What I like about Faulu is that, if you are determined to work hard, then they will facilitate you, no matter how small your business is. I have managed to stand firm financially. I like the way they provide loans to business holders, and their money is quickly processed without the normal lengthy banking procedures. I like the way loans are repaid on a weekly basis.'

Faulu's lending model

The word *faulu* means 'success' or 'to succeed' in Kiswahili, and Faulu has succeeded in becoming one of the largest microfinance institutions in Kenya. Its core activity is granting credit to solidarity groups – only a small proportion of its portfolio is lending to individuals.

As part of the lending activity, Faulu loan officers also act as business consultants. They meet weekly with the borrower groups, and analyse their performance, providing advice and support when needed. This approach has ensured low portfolio-at-risk ratios and a high level of operational sustainability.[1] Faulu is also involved in vocational training, such as a training course for SMEs in Nairobi jointly sponsored by Jomo Kenyatta University of Agriculture and Technology and Faulu Kenya, and agricultural skills training for the rural areas.

Funding microfinance institutions in Kenya

Over the last 20 years, MFIs in Kenya have largely developed through grant funding. Faulu Kenya started off in 1992 as a pilot microlending programme of Food for the Hungry International (FHI), a Christian relief and development organisation based in Thailand with operations throughout the world. The pilot programme upscaled in 1995 with significant funding from USAID and the UK's DFID, and by 1998 had registered significant growth. In the late 1990s, key donors started to press client MFIs to work towards financial sustainability. The path to sustainability was not easy for institutions previously focused on free-spending outreach drives. Those that had succeeded in significantly expanding their operations were faced with the need to find alternative sources of capital as donor funds became insufficient to sustain the growth momentum. During this period, many MFIs took the opportunity to become limited liability companies with a share capital. K-Rep, for example, became Kenya's first microfinance bank, securing a banking licence in 1999 and broadening its shareholder base with a number of international and Kenya-based investors. The board of Faulu realised that unless it could ensure reliable capital for on-lending at a competitive cost, the MFI would lose considerable ground to organisations such as K-Rep, Family Finance and Equity Bank.

In 1999, Faulu Kenya Limited was incorporated as a private company with 100 % of its share capital owned by FHI. This allowed Faulu Kenya to start sourcing commercial funding, which it did initially in 2000 with a subsidised loan of US$145 000 from the EU. This was followed by another EU loan of US$500 000 in 2001, and in 2002 two commercial banks provided credit lines worth US$4 million secured against existing assets – that is, the existing debtor book – with some backing from a donor guarantee. In 2003, this was supplemented by a Blue Orchard's Dexia Microfinance Fund 18-month hard currency term loan of $450 000 structured as a promissory note, also granted on the strength of Faulu Kenya's balance sheet. In total, Faulu Kenya raised US$5.1 million in external funding between 2000 and 2003, during which period its loan book grew from US$2.5 million to US$7.2 million.

These early borrowing experiences gave Faulu the confidence to take the bold step of accessing the capital markets for longer-term debt finance at lower cost.

Faulu raises a bond issue

One of the more remarkable features of the global microfinance movement is that an intrinsically pro-poor mechanism should have evolved to capture the imagination of investors in mainstream capital markets. The landscape of microfinance funding options is varied (see Figure 10.1), ranging from investors with a social mission to alleviate poverty, such as international donor agencies and foundations, to those with more commercial motivations, such as commercial investors and domestic capital markets, and the options in-between.

Figure 10.1 The landscape of funding options for microfinance

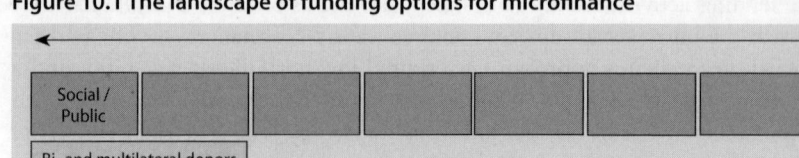

Source: CGAP (2006)

Note: IFI = international financial institutions (investment arms of public bilateral or multilateral institutions)

A few leading MFIs have used debt instruments on local capital markets. For instance, Compartamos in Mexico, Mibanco in Peru, and Women's World Banking, Cali in Colombia have placed bonds on their local markets, based partially on ratings from mainstream rating agencies like Standard & Poor's, Fitch, and Moody's. On the equity side, in 1997 BancoSol became a pioneer as a microfinance institution transforming into a bank – getting listed on the Bolivian stock exchange and issuing the equivalent of US$3 million in bonds. The ProCredit Bank family in Eastern Europe have also raised capital in the capital markets. In June 2004, ProCredit Bank (Ukraine) issued US$6.8 million in three-year bonds. It is important to note that these deals have also benefited from at least initial partial guarantees from donors and international financial institutions (IFIs).[2]

After researching the capital markets, Faulu Kenya decided to raise a five-year bond, supported by Agence Française de Dévéloppement, which offered to guarantee 75 % of the bond.[3] This guarantee was fundamental to the success of the bond. Investors would not have had the confidence to invest in Faulu bonds had the guarantee not been in place. After all, long-term finance is riskier than short-term finance, and the coupon that Faulu Kenya would have had to promise investors to attract them would have made this form of finance prohibitively expensive. A technical team from Stanbic Bank Kenya Limited and its parent, Standard Bank of South Africa, arranged the Kshs500 million (US$7 million) bond. Philip Odera, Stanbic Bank Kenya's managing director, commented at the time: 'This transaction is one of the most important ever undertaken by any bank in Africa. It addresses one of the major challenges facing Africa: how to direct credit at affordable pricing to enterprising people who up until now have been starved of credit. It is in line with both the United Nations Millennium Development Goal to halve global poverty by 2015, and with the Kenya Government's Poverty Reduction Strategy.'

The team started work in September 2004, and the issue was launched in March 2005. By the end of March the issue was oversubscribed by 111 %. The entire KSh500 million was placed by 4 April 2005, and trading in the bond on the Nairobi Stock Exchange started on 11 April 2005. A number of pension funds, two MFI wholesale institutions and two commercial banks were the main primary investors.

Faulu's exponential growth from 2005 to 2008 is the best proof of the success of its bond issue in 2005. In December 2005, Faulu had only 39 000 credit clients but this increased rapidly to 68 000 and 90 000 in 2006 and 2007 respectively, with average loans of US$550 split 70/30 between urban and rural areas.

By October 2008, Faulu had already surpassed its 2008 year-end target of 150 000 credit customers, notching up more than 151 185 clients. Similarly the staff numbers also grew from 130 in 2004 to 632 in October 2008. Faulu's presence around the country has grown and as at November 2008, there were 72 branch and marketing offices in seven of the eight Kenyan provinces. Faulu believes it is on track to achieve its target of serving up to 800 000 clients by the end of 2011.

Key to achieving this goal is the transformation of Faulu into a full financial intermediary. The strategy involves different aspects of transformation:

- **Institutional preparedness:** Refining governance structures, and changing its legal structure to one proposed by the regulatory authorities.
- **Market research and product development:** Reviewing and refining the existing credit products, developing appropriate savings and money transfer products, and new credit products based on the market research.
- **Re-branding:** Positioning itself as a full financial intermediary.
- **Process mapping and risk management:** Reviewing its financial and operational processes and systems, and refining these to ensure efficiency and to meet regulatory requirements.
- **Treasury management:** Overseeing the establishment of a treasury function with a mandate to maximise revenues, manage liquidity risk and comply with regulatory requirements.
- **Review of human resources:** Identifying competence gaps and developing a plan to meet these, either through training or recruitment.

These tasks were carried out with the support of the Financial Sector Deepening initiative. Faulu confirmed that, as at November 2008, 90 % of the above initiatives had been carried out successfully. The institution applied for a deposit-taking licence from the Central Bank of Kenya on 9 July 2008. This was granted in May 2009, making Faulu the first MFI in Kenya to be licensed by the central bank. There is a view among some observers that regulators are perhaps too stringent in their supervision of the MFIs, vetting them according to the standards applicable to a full commercial bank, thus causing delays in the issuing of licences.

Lessons

There are a number of important lessons from Faulu's bond issue experience. Some of these are particular to Faulu; others reinforce the lessons from MFIs' experiences with capital markets elsewhere:

- This was the first such bond issue in Africa and it provides a valid African model for other MFIs to replicate. This landmark issue allowed Faulu Kenya to secure the long-term resources it needs at a lower cost than conventional bank finance.
- Faulu has demonstrated that it is possible for an MFI to transform its capital structure over time such that it can meet the rigorous requirements of a capital market listing.
- Donor agencies looking for a way to help MFIs after the initial set-up and early growth stages can assist them to forge a long-term relationship with domestic investors

to leverage local resources, and in Faulu Kenya they have an African precedent to follow.
- Local investors can diversify their investment portfolios with a long-term security in an economic sub-sector not previously covered. As the Faulu Kenya case shows, pension funds and other institutional investors with long-term liabilities to match are keen to invest in bonds such as these.
- The Faulu Kenya guarantee was effective in crowding in local resources that would not have been committed in the absence of the guarantee. By 2006, there were between US$300 and US$500 million of funds committed in loan guarantees for microfinance, but so far only a few MFIs have used guarantees to float bonds on their domestic capital markets. Guarantees for loans or bonds can be cumbersome and costly to set up, hence when deciding on this mechanism both the guarantor and the investee MFI must be sophisticated enough to implement the guarantee.
- One of the barriers to floating MFI bonds is the very high transactions costs associated with raising small amounts of capital. By issuing a sizable bond, Faulu Kenya can concentrate on fulfilling its business objectives without the distraction of constant fundraising; and the bond origination costs are more easily accommodated than for a small issue.
- Another barrier that stops more MFIs from issuing bonds is the maturity of the domestic capital markets and the legal and regulatory framework in which the MFIs and the market participants operate.
- The public scrutiny of Faulu Kenya's performance over the next five years will require the organisation to keep improving as it commits to meeting investor expectations. Spillover effects could benefit microfinance in Kenya and other countries as markets take note of this emerging investment opportunity.
- A local currency bond is less expensive and complex than hard currency debt finance that more often than not has to be hedged against exchange losses.
- Bond issues such as this allow capital markets to play their part in the fight against poverty by indirectly deploying capital into the microenterprise sector, an important sector for economic development and poverty reduction, especially in Africa.

The key to the success of this experience appears to be banks and investors truly willing to enter into new markets, and the design of the guarantee itself. If too much of the liability is guaranteed, the investor might feel it is acceptable to discontinue the relationship in the absence of the guarantee. Investors have to take on some of the risk – with Faulu, the oversubscription on issuance indicated the favourable risk appetite of the Kenyan market.

Summit Financial Partners: A rescue remedy

Booming consumer credit markets in Africa have unquestionably led to widespread overindebtedness in many countries, notably in southern Africa, where payroll lending is prevalent. Lack of regulation and strong consumer demand for short-term loans have fuelled this boom in an environment where consumers' understanding of the consequences of overborrowing is often limited. Summit Financial Partners operates in this controversial part of the financial landscape. Its story demonstrates that not only NGOs can offer this type of service; profit-making businesses can too – and do it sustainably through combining a social mission with a strong desire to grow a healthy business.

A 1992 amendment to the Usury Act formalised microlending in South Africa, making finance available to a community that was unfamiliar with formal borrowing, and ignorant about the implications of defaulting on repayment. One result was an increasing problem of overindebtedness, often leading to a debt spiral. This is when borrowers are forced to borrow to help pay back loans, thus driving them deeper into debt, often aggravated by unscrupulous microlenders and debt collectors.

Clark Gardner, founder of Summit Financial Partners, saw the impact of uncontrolled microlending on people's lives, and shifted his focus from microlending to advising and educating borrowers, and assisting the victims of exploitative microlending practices.

While new legislation has been necessary to outlaw the worst abuses that have been taking place in microlending, Summit is an example of a sustainable market-led response that addresses, if not the root cause, then the symptoms of the problem. And in doing so it shows how the private sector, complementing new legislation, can offer a solution that helps to ensure the market system functions more effectively.

Summit's turnover has more than doubled annually since 2004, with a 75 % increase for the year ending February 2008. By early 2008, the company was showing an annual profit of almost R1.9 million, and was forecasting a profit of R3.5 million for the coming year. Gardner anticipates that in the market of nearly four million overindebted employees in South Africa, Summit will double in size within the next year and continue growing. 'If you want it to be sustainable, then it must be commercial,' says Gardner.

Industry background

Until the early 1990s, most South Africans were deprived not only of political power, but also of economic power and a means to accumulate assets.[4] As a whole, the highly sophisticated formal banking sector ignored this market, and instead the informal microlending sector, ranging from community programmes to loan sharks, met its demand for credit.

People fall into a debt trap when they start to borrow money to pay off other loans.

The 1992 exemption to the Usury Act removed the interest rate ceiling on small loans, making microlending viable and stimulating the development of a vibrant microlending industry in both the formal and informal sectors. Loans were easily available and actively marketed to people who previously had little or no access to credit.[5] Borrowers were less concerned about the interest charged than the benefit derived from access to loans, and two types of loan providers evolved: cash loan operators, who made short-term loans of 30 days or less, and term lenders, who made longer-term loans and based repayment on payroll deductions.[6]

While high interest rates mitigated risks, salaried employees with bank accounts were of particular interest to microlenders: term lenders collected repayments through payroll deductions and debit orders; and borrowers relinquished ATM cards and PIN numbers to cash lenders who withdrew repayments as soon as the borrower's salary was deposited into the account.[7]

In response to concern over the exploitation of borrowers, a further exemption to the Usury Act in 1999 provided for a regulatory body, the Micro Finance Regulatory Council (MFRC), to oversee microlending. The exemption put in place regulations regarding the awarding of microloans and the method of collection, and set a ceiling on the interest rates. Furthermore, microlenders had to register with the MFRC and could no longer take possession of ATM cards and PIN numbers. However, Gardner argues, changes in the laws and regulations are only as effective as the extent to which they are enforced.

Of the estimated 3 500 firms in the formal microlending industry, only 1 334 registered with the MFRC. Many microlenders closed down as they were no longer viable, while others continued operating illegally.[8] In 2000, the Department of Trade and Industry identified two concerns relating to borrowers: overindebtedness, causing debt spiral; and exploitation by aggressive lenders who were overselling credit and charging high interest rates[9] and collection fees. Of particular concern was the long-term indebtedness of term borrowers who, after payroll deductions, were left with minimal net take-home salaries and were forced to take short-term debt at higher interest rates for survival.[10]

Garnishment – the use of a court order to deduct debt repayments against an employee's income prior to the employee receiving earnings – is not unique to South Africa. As in other countries where this is used to recover debt, legislation states that garnishee order deductions cannot result in employees taking home less than is required to maintain themselves and their dependants. According to Gardner, in South Africa this restriction is ignored by the magistrates and clerks of the court who process the orders. Furthermore, consumers have neither the knowledge of their rights and recourse nor the resources to dispute the practice.

Company background

In 1998, while Gardner was completing his articles to qualify as a chartered accountant (CA), he witnessed the effect of uncontrolled microlending on the employees in his father's factory. As there was no central register of loans in the country, term lender representatives whose incentives were based on commission sold loans to employees indiscriminately, without determining the employee's existing repayment commitments.

Gardner noticed that some employees were taking home virtually no income after garnishee orders had been deducted against their salaries. On closer investigation, he discovered that many of these overindebted employees were in a debt spiral. He intervened by consolidating the debt and making loans available to the employees at the same interest rate at which he acquired the finance. This relief made such an impact that the union approached Gardner and suggested that he expand and commercialise his involvement.

Gardner grew up in a community where most of the families experienced financial distress, and he wanted to make a difference. After qualifying in the top 10 in the board exam, rather than accepting offers to join a company, he aimed to have his own business. When the union approached him, he saw the opportunity to realise his ambition. He established Limpio Financial Services (bought by Summit Financial Partners in 2000), a microlending company, which reached employees through a relationship with their employers. 'As you have the security of the deduction, you have reduced your risk, so you can charge mutually beneficial rates. It supports both parties,' he explains.

However, Gardner soon realised that this did not prevent employees from borrowing from the loan sharks and falling back into the same indebtedness trap. Believing he was doing more harm than good, he identified the need for preventative measures, and shifted his focus to debt counselling and financial training in the companies whose employees he had been serving through microloans. 'They loved what we stood for and they were excited by these new solutions,' he said.

In 2004, Gardner officially severed his ties with microlending, and established a new company under the same name to pursue his passion: financial wellbeing.

Financial wellbeing

Gardner sees financial wellbeing as comprising three elements: preventative financial literacy; reactive financial counselling (including debt relief); and administering and auditing garnishee orders. Summit differentiates its offering in the market by offering a holistic approach. 'We do an impact study and tackle their debt problem, staff loans and garnishee orders,' Gardner explains.

Financial literacy training entails teaching employees about the benefits of saving rather than borrowing for consumption. Gardner notes that it is essential to use appropriate techniques to convey this message to the relevant target market. 'For instance, with the lower-income market, we make use of visuals, practical examples, scenarios and interactive discussions,' he says. Furthermore, Summit's trainers educate retrenched employees on how to start their own businesses, and provide support through a call centre for six months thereafter. Summit develops all its own materials, and is an accredited provider of training for debt counsellors.

Financial literacy training is of little value if it does not change behaviour, says Gardner. It is for this reason that the financial counselling arm was established. This arm gives consumers access to financial advice that assists them to manage and measure their cash flows for three months after the financial literacy workshop. Gardner's aim is that during these three months, consumers will change their behaviour and start to manage their finances more effectively.

Debt counselling involves face-to-face counselling of people in distress caused by debt – and assistance in restructuring of debt. This can be initiated by a management referral, through the garnishee orders audit or by the employee. Counselling includes helping employees to identify ways to supplement their income by using the skills or assets they have and providing debt rearrangements with creditors, support to challenge irregularities within such debt, wealth creation advice and support via the call centre.

Administering and auditing garnishee orders is outsourced by companies to Summit in its entirety, and Summit's garnishee auditors scrutinise these for irregularities. Gardner elaborates, 'One in three garnishee orders overstate collections by R1 500. On average, it is R500 per garnishee and there are two million garnishee orders out there. That means R1 billion is going illegally into the pockets of creditors instead of really distressed borrowers.'

Customers

Gardner set out to improve the lives of indebted employees. Acknowledging that sustainability and profit go hand in hand, his solution targets employers who are willing to pay to effect this improvement for a number of reasons. The first is the productivity of employees who are living with negative cash flows. 'Not being able to put food on the table for the last week of the month causes significant stress and absenteeism,' Gardner says. The second reason is high staff turnover caused by employees resigning to realise retirement funds to pay off their debt, or losing their jobs as a consequence of desperation theft.

A third reason is concern over the wellbeing of employees who have either lost or resigned from their jobs. Often these people are forced into further borrowing to survive, committing crimes or, in some instances, suicide. The fourth reason is that employers often feel they have a social responsibility to provide financial advice and support to their employees. 'The employer is feeling it and really wants to de-risk the employees and see that they take home a salary,' Gardner adds. Finally, Gardner has a personal motivation for targeting the company. 'The company pays me a retainer. We will *never* sell a product to an employee,' he says.

The agreement between Summit and the employer depends on the service. The employer pays a retainer, based on the number of employees, for debt counselling and for administering and auditing garnishee orders. Summit charges separately for any training it conducts.

Successful partnerships

ICAS, the largest provider of corporate wellbeing services in southern Africa and Europe, has a similar vision, and offers psychosocial support, preventative healthcare, legal wellbeing and trauma support services as employee wellbeing interventions. Through an exclusive outsourcing agreement with Summit, ICAS has added financial wellbeing to its offering, and Summit has gained access to a distribution channel of more than 400 companies representing 500 000 employees.

Whereas Summit previously used ICAS's infrastructure, with its staff of 35 back-office employees and 20 trainers on contract, the organisation now has its own infrastructure, with trainers throughout the country and a 30-seat call centre. However, it still uses ICAS psychologists to deal with the emotional or psycho-social issues that may be at the root of clients' overspending. 'As 22 % of negative cash flow problems are a result of a psychosocial or emotional problem, we can address the source,' Gardner explains.

Summit has also formed another important alliance with the Life Offices' Association (LOA), now merged with other South African industry bodies into the Association for Savings and Investment, which represents all the life insurance companies in the country, and derives most of its revenues from deductions against the payroll of government employees. 'All government employees can now access financial literacy training, paid for by the LOA,' says Gardner. 'In fact, well over 25 000 government employees have now been trained through this programme, with most government departments involved. We have reached employees throughout the country, with 50 % of participants living in rural areas.'

Unethical practices

Gardner's challenge is to fight exploitation of borrowers by unregistered lenders charging interest rates in breach of the Usury Act, unethical collection practices and the predatory marketing practices of an industry pushing credit. He cites an example of a person who took out a loan of R20 000, payable over three years at R1 000 a month. When the borrower defaulted after the fourth payment, the lender's attorneys presented a repayment plan instructing the employer to deduct R1 200 a month over almost 14 years: a total of R162 000, of which R115 000 was interest. 'The clerk of the court is stamping these orders regardless of whether they are valid or invalid,' he says.

Gardner is adamant that the Department of Justice is not doing enough to change this situation. 'We have presented to parliament, the justice department, treasury and the regulator in an attempt to change the manner in which these orders are granted, with little to no success,' he says. 'We are therefore now purely focused on challenging the lenders and collectors via the court or media in order to get them to stop abusing the consumer.'

He adds, 'The government may not be doing anything to stop the abuse of those in serious debt, but National Treasury has provided its approval of, and support for, our solution to be implemented on government's payroll to eliminate the effects of this abuse on its employees.'

Another mechanism for exploiting uninformed borrowers is forcing them to sign blank 'consent to judgment' and garnishee orders at the time of originating the loan. Consequently, lenders do not have to wait for the borrower to default before collecting exorbitant amounts – and legal fees – against the unsuspecting borrower's salary. 'And it's not only individual lenders. It is also listed companies,' Gardner says. This problem, he believes, had not been adequately addressed, as the regulator and the justice system are not communicating effectively about this issue.

It is not only lower-paid employees who find themselves at the mercy of undiscerning lenders. The tendency to exhibit success through the acquisition of portable assets has brought many from the rising black middle class to Summit's door with judgments against their names. Rather than seeing these as economically active potential customers for home and car loans, the banks are issuing credit cards indiscriminately for short-term gains. 'You can make money in this market without damaging people. If [lenders] lower their margins and tighten their credit borrowing so that their bad debts are lower, it would still be a successful business,' says Gardner.

While restructuring debt has been difficult, the new National Credit Act, which came into effect in its entirety in June 2007, provides for restructuring by debt counsellors either through consent of creditors or approval by the Magistrate's Court. This, according to Gardner, will give Summit more 'bite' in its fight.

'However, while the act does have greater clarity on the process to be followed to obtain a judgment when a borrower defaults, and while it explains what an invalid loan is and the restrictions on the amount of interest to be charged, these stipulations are still not enforced in the courts. I can show you R800 000's worth of loans that are invalid, charging in excess of the interest rate ceilings, but being awarded garnishee deductions … and this is only for one lender deducting at one employer,' he says.

Growth

Summit measures its impact through course evaluations by trainees, reversal of negative cash flows, and the amount it saves employees through the garnishee audit process. Course evaluations are not only positive, but also often request that training is extended to spouses and the community. As a result, Summit now extends the courses to families by providing trainees with simple, visual money management books that they can take to their homes and communities, and use to teach others.

In 85 % of debt counselling cases, cash flows turn positive and stay positive. Gardner describes the success of a particular garnishee audit handled a few years ago. 'The company paid us R90 000 for the service and a quarter of the way into the project, we had saved R340 000 for the employees,' he says.

'We have refunded or saved employees over R2.5 million in the past 12 months alone. We have provided more than 25 000 clients with financial wellbeing solutions through our telecare service, and reduced employers' staff turnover and stock losses or fraud numbers significantly by addressing over indebtedness.'

Gardner believes that the present worldwide financial crisis will dramatically affect South Africans, and will result in further problems for consumers. 'The international market meltdown will affect corporate South Africans' access to capital, which includes the banks. The banks will be more cautious and will tighten their credit-granting criteria. However, I do believe this would have happened in any event, as credit granting in South Africa has been very aggressive over the past three years and has taken its toll on the consumer. The result is that we have many more South Africans who are financially distressed, and the financial institutions are experiencing higher levels of default and bad debt,' he says.

'However, this will only increase the need for Summit's solutions and currently, the demand is greater than we can cope with. Our solution is now expanding to banks that want their clients to access our solution, as this will result in a more economically active client in the long-term and less bad debt for them in the short term.'

Success is also measured in terms of growth and profitability. 'I am not a charitable angel. I am a capitalist and I love business,' says Gardner. The future looks promising: in addition to the pipeline of over 400 companies, the vast population of overindebted South African employees means that the company does not have to look beyond the country's borders for the next three years. 'However, as a result of ICAS International requesting our solutions, we are now exploring opportunities in India and the UK.'

'India is a similar environment to South Africa with a small portion of very wealthy individuals and a mass market of lower-income individuals. That might be next, using the same model of working through the employer and employee wellbeing programmes. Later we will go through Africa.'

Endnotes

[1] PAR > 30 days ratio 2.5 % in 2002 and under 10 % in 2006. This increase in PAR > 30 days is congruent with the big increase in size of portfolio. In Kenya the banking sector averages a NPL ratio of around 15 %, and the microfinance sector has an average PAR > 90 day of 22 %. Operational sufficiency over 100 % since 2000.
[2] CGAP (2006).
[3] The guarantee covers capital and interest up to 75 % of the issues only.
[4] Terreblanche (2002: 6).
[5] Porteous & Hazelhurst (2004: 89).
[6] Ebony Consulting International (2000) and Usury Report at www.acts.co.za/usury/index/htm.

7 Porteous & Hazelhurst (2004).
8 Ibid.
9 Interest rates varied from effective rates of 60 % for long-term loans (up to three years) to rates exceeding 1 000 % for short-term loans of less than a week.
10 Ebony Consulting International (2000).

Glossary of terms

Access frontier: The access frontier approach segments the market for a particular product into five groups: those who now use it, those who could have it but do not want it, those who do not have access today but could do so in the absence of certain constraints, and, finally, those outside of the reach of the market because they are simply too poor.

Bottom of the pyramid: This refers to the poorer socio-economic groups in a society that were traditionally ignored because business thought they were too poor; however, they are increasingly being deliberately targeted as a potential market (also referred to as the 'base of the pyramid' or 'BOP').

E-money: This is a monetary value that is stored electronically on a technical device (either card- or network based) and that can be readily exchanged.

E-purse: This is a function on a chip card which allows monetary value to be stored. It is an alternative to cash that can be used to pay for goods and services. The card can be disposable or reloadable, and the stored value is reduced as payments are made (also known as an e-wallet).

E-commerce: This refers to transactions that are conducted over an electronic network where the buyer and merchant are not at the same physical location.

Financial inclusion: As financial exclusion is increasingly seen as both a symptom and a cause of poverty, most developing countries have financial inclusion as a goal. This means giving people access to appropriate financial products and services, such as savings, transaction banking, credit and insurance.

LSM (Living Standards Measure): LSM is used in South Africa by the advertising and marketing industries to segment the market according to such factors as ownership of consumer goods and access to services. There are 10 LSMs, and LSM1–5 is the low-income market in South Africa, today comprising half the adult population.

M-banking: This refers to the provision of banking services through a mobile phone. These services can be **transformational** in that they target unbanked people or **additive** in that they are an additional channel a bank offers to its existing customer base.

Merry-go-round: A rotating saving club in Kenya. Each member pays in an agreed amount every month. The total amount collected is given, in turn, to one of the club members.

Missing middle: This refers to people in the middle of the income spectrum, ignored by the commercial banks, whose needs may be more complex than can be satisfied by traditional microfinance. Such people may include self-employed traders, artisans and low-end government employees.

Payroll loans: These are loans provided in partnership with employers to people such as lower-paid government employees without collateral, and entail repayment through deductions from their salaries.

Second-tier banks: Such banks are restricted in their activities by regulation but can take deposits and do some lending. Their set-up and operating costs may be low, because they may operate on the back of other businesses. **Third-tier banks** are member-based banks, such as co-operative banks, which take deposits from, and lend to, their members only.

Stokvel: This is an informal savings society in which members contribute regularly and receive payouts in rotation (South Africa).

Tontines: This is a term used in several Francophone countries to describe the type of rotating savings and credit association known elsewhere as merry-go-rounds or *stokvel*. They are also sometimes referred to as *njangis*.

Vault cash: This is the sum of all cash held by financial institutions in central vaults, branches, ATMs, and cash in transit in an armoured carrier.

Technical terms related to mobile phone telephony

GSM (Global System for Mobile Communications): GSM is a cellular network, which means that mobile phones connect to it by searching for cells in the immediate vicinity. It is the most popular standard for mobile phones in the world. Its promoter, the GSM Association, estimates that 80 % of the global mobile market uses the standard.

GPRS (general packet radio service): This is a type of telecommunications technology that allows fast connectivity at a relatively low cost and can be used in areas where there is a cellular network but no landlines.

Integrated access device: Also known as IAD, this is a device that sends information from the customer's premises on to a single telephone line for transmission to a carrier or service provider.

International ISO 7816 standards: To promote interoperability among smartcards and readers, the International Organization for Standardization (ISO) developed the ISO 7816 standard for integrated circuit cards with contacts. These specifications focused on interoperability at the physical, electrical, and data-link protocol levels.

IP protocol: The internet protocol (IP) is the method or protocol by which data is sent from one computer to another on the internet.

SIM (subscriber identity module) card: A mini smartcard used in GSM mobile phones. It contains operator and subscriber specific data that enables users to be authenticated and voice or data sessions to be encrypted over the air.

SMS: This stands for 'short message service' and is a communications protocol allowing the interchange of short text messages between mobile telephone devices.

SNA protocol: System Network Architecture by IBM is a suite of protocols mainly used with IBM mainframe and AS/400 computers.

USSD: This stands for 'unstructured supplementary service data' and is a technology used by the mobile network to send information between a mobile phone and an application on a network, for example a banking application at a bank. It is a menu-driven form of SMS whereby a customer receives a text menu on their phone as opposed to a string of words.

WAP (wireless application protocol): This is a set of communication standards to enable the accessing of online internet services from a mobile phone.

Wi-Fi: This is the wireless standard already widely deployed in hotspots and in homes and offices; WiMax is its more sophisticated (and expensive) cousin, designed to handle the multiple reflections of wireless signals encountered in urban environments and to provide a slightly longer range. Its complexity and cost are at present a disadvantage in rural areas of developing countries, compared to Wi-Fi, although costs are expected to continue declining.

VoIP (Voice over Internet Protocol): This is a general term for a family of transmission technologies for delivery of voice communications over IP networks such as the internet or other packet-switched networks.

VSAT (very small aperture terminals): This refers to a two-way satellite-to-ground system which uses a small disc antenna. It is usually used to transmit narrow-band data such as those from point-of-sale transactions or to provide internet access to remote locations.

References

Absa Group (2007). 'Annual report 2007'. Available from www.absa.co.za.
Adongo, J (2007). 'The potential for mobile phone banking in Zambia'. Research for FinMark Trust Zambia. Available from www.finscopeafrica.com.
Africa Project Development Facility (2005). Available from www.gmfield.info.
Al Amana (2006). 'Annual report 2006'. Available from www.alamana.org.
Apea, C & Sezibera J (2002). 'Some causes of bank failure, a case study of Ghana Co-operative Bank'. International Accounting and Finance Master's thesis no. 2002: 54.
Arnold, M (2006). 'Presenting FNB Mini-ATM'. Company presentation.
Aryeetey, E (2005). 'Sub-Saharan Africa in informal finance for private sector development in sub-Saharan Africa'. *Journal of Microfinance* vol. 7, no. 1. Brigham Young University, Utah.
ATM Solutions (2003). 'Non-listed company award submission document'. Company document.
Avsi Uganda (2006). 'Annual report 2006 – The human challenge'. Available from www.avsi.org.
Ayadi, A (2006). 'Challenges and opportunities to enhancing access to finance for SMEs through factoring'. African Development Bank. Available from www.adb.org.
Bank Administration Institute (2001). White Paper: 'Competition, innovation and strategy in the financial services industry'. Available from www.bai.org.
Bank of Ghana, www.bog.gov.gh.
Bank of Namibia, www.bon.com.na.
Bank of Uganda, www.bou.or.ug.
Bank Windhoek (2007). 'Annual report 2007'. Available from www.bankwindhoek.com.na.
Bank Windhoek (Online, a). 'EasySave – Banking the unbanked in a uniquely Namibian way'. *Money Matters*, issue 7. Available from www.bankwindhoek.com.na.
Bank Windhoek (Online, b). 'EasyCredit – Taking the lead with accessible and affordable banking'. *Money Matters*, Issue 20. Available from www.bankwindhoek.com.na.
Bank Windhoek (2006). 'Annual report 2006'. Available from www.bankwindhoek.com.na.
Bank Windhoek (2007). 'Reflecting on 25 years of banking'. *Money Matters*, issue 48. Available from www.bankwindhoek.com.na.
Bankable Frontier Associates (2006). 'Scoping report on the payment of social transfers through the financial system'. Paper commissioned for DFID (Available from www.bankablefrontier.com.
Bankable Frontier Associates (2007). 'Financial service access and usage in southern and East Africa – What do FinScope Surveys tell us?' Research for FinMark Trust. Available from www.finscopeafrica.com.
Barajas, A, Steiner, R & Salazar, N (2000). 'Foreign investment in Colombia's financial sector' in Claessens, S & Jansen, M (Eds) *The internationalization of financial services: Issues and lessons for developing countries*. Kluwer Academic Press. Boston, MA.

Barnard Jacobs Mellet (2006). 'African Bank Investments: Many snouts in the trough'. Research document circulated to clients.

Barth, J, Caprio, G & Levine, R (2001). 'The regulation and supervision of banks around the world: A new database' in Litan R E & Herring R (Eds), *Integrating emerging market countries into the global financial system*. Brookings Institution Press, Washington, DC.

BBC Country profiles, www.news.bbc.co.uk.

Beck, T, Demirguc-Kunt, A, Peria, M & Soledad, M (2006). 'Banking services for everyone? Barriers to bank access and use around the world'. World Bank Policy Research Paper 4079.

Beck, T, Demirguc-Kunt, A & Peria, M (2005). 'Reaching out – Access to and use of banking services across countries'. Available from www.microfinancegateway.org.

Bhattacharya, A, Lovell, C & Sahay, P (1997). 'The impact of liberalisation on the productive efficiency of Indian commercial banks'. *European Journal of Operational Research*, vol. 98, no. 2. pp. 332–345.

Bonin, J P & Abel, I (2000). 'Retail banking in Hungary: A foreign affair?' Prepared as a background paper for World Bank, World Development Report 2002: Institutions for Markets. Wesleyan University, Connecticut.

Brownbridge, M & Gayi, S (1999). 'Progress, constraints and limitations of financial sector reforms in the least developed countries'. Institute for Development Policy and Management. Available from www.microfinancegateway.org.

Brownbridge, M (1998). 'Financial distress in local banks in Kenya, Nigeria, Uganda and Zambia: Causes and implications for regulatory policy'. *Development Policy Review*, vol. 16, no. 2.

Calderisi, R (2007). *The trouble with Africa – Why foreign aid isn't working*. St Martins Press, New York.

Cali, M, Ellis, K & Te Velde, D W (2008). 'The contribution of services to development and the role of trade liberalisation and regulation'. ODI Working Paper 298, Overseas Development Institute, London.

Central Bank of Egypt, www.cbe.org.eg.

Central Statistics Office Zambia, www.zamstats.gov.zm.

CGAP (2006). *Access for all – A bold vision for microfinance*. World Bank. Washington DC.

CGAP (2006). 'Setting out scenarios for the future of microfinance'. CGAP Note 39 (Financial Inclusion 2015). Available from www.cgap.org.

Christen, R P & Pearce, D (2004). 'Lessons learned from Nkwe Enterprise Finance'. *Development Southern Africa*, vol. 21, no. 5. pp. 815–830.

Christensen, C M (1997). 'The innovator's dilemma – when new technologies cause great firms to fail'. Harvard Business School Press, Boston.

Churchill C (Ed) (2006). *Protecting the poor – A microinsurance compendium*. Munich Re Foundation and ILO. Available from www.munichre-foundation.org.

Churchill C (2006). 'What is insurance for the poor?' in *Protecting the Poor – A Microinsurance Compendium*, Churchill C, (Ed). Munich Re Foundation and ILO. Available from www.munichre-foundation.org.

CIA World Fact Book, www.cia.gov.

Claessens S, Demirguc-Kunt, A & Huizinga, H (2000). 'The role of foreign banks in domestic banking systems' in Claessens, S & Jansen, M (Eds) *The Internationalization of Financial Services: Issues and Lessons for Developing Countries*. Kluwer Academic Press, Boston, MA.

Claessens, S (2005). 'Universal access to financial services: A review of the issues and public policy objectives' in *Liberalisation and Universal Access to Basic Services*. World Bank. Available from www.microfinancegateway.org.

Clarke, G, Cull, R, D'Amato, L & Molinari, A (2000). 'On the kindness of strangers? The Iipact of foreign entry on domestic banks in Argentina' in Claessens, S & Jansen, M (Eds) *The Internationalization of Financial Services: Issues and Lessons for Developing Countries*. Kluwer Academic Press, Boston MA.

Clarke, G, Cull, R. & Peria, M (2001). 'Does foreign bank penetration reduce access to credit in developing countries?' World Bank Policy Research Working Paper 2716, Washington DC. Available from www.microfinancegateway.org.

Cohen, M & Sebstad, J (2006). 'The demand for microinsurance'. *Protecting the Poor – A Microinsurance Compendium*, Churchill, C (Ed). Munich Re Foundation and ILO. Available from www.munichre-foundation.org.

Collier, P (2007). *The Bottom Billion – Why the Poorest Countries are Failing and what can be done about It*. Oxford University Press US, New York.

Coppoolse, M (2007). 'Microfinance: An emerging asset class for equity and debt investors'. A White Paper published by Microcapital. Available from www.microcapital.org.

Cracknell, D (2004). 'Electronic banking for the poor – panacea, potential and pitfalls' in *Small Enterprise Development*, vol. 5, no. 4.

De Koker, C, De Waal, L & Vorster, J (2006). 'A profile of social security beneficiaries in South Africa, vol. 3'. Department of Social Development, Republic of South Africa. Available from www.welfare.gov.za.

De la Torre, A Gozzi J & Schmukler S L (2006). *Innovative Experiences in Access to Finance: Market Friendly Roles for the Visible Hand?* World Bank, Washington DC.

Demirguc-Kunt, A & Huizinga, H (2000). 'Determinants of commercial bank interest margins and profitability: Some international evidence'. World Bank Economic Review, vol. 13, no. 2. pp. 379–408.

Demirguc-Kunt, A (2007). 'Finance for all? Policies and pitfalls in expanding access'. World Bank Policy Research Report. Available from www.worldbank.org.

Demirguc-Kunt, A Levine, R & Min, GH (1999). 'Opening to foreign banks: Issues of stability, efficiency and growth' in *Proceedings of the Bank of Korea Conference on the Implications of Globalization of World Financial Markets*. Seoul, December 1998.

DFID Country Profiles, www.dfid.gov.uk/countries/africa.

DFID (2006). 'Social protection in poor countries'. *Social Protection Briefing Note Series*, Number 1. Available from www.dfid.gov.uk.

Easterly, W (2006). *The White Man's Burden: Why the West's Efforts to Aid the Rest Have Done So Much Ill and So Little Good*. Penguin Press, New York.

Ebony Consulting International (2000). 'Report on costs and interest rates in the small loans sector'. Study commissioned by the South African Department of Trade and Industry, as gazetted in *Government Gazette* no. 2138.

ECI Africa (2005). 'Report on customer acceptance behaviour of clients of Wizzit Bank'. Available from www.eciafrica.com.

Eighty 20 Consulting (2007). 'Access to financial products in Zambia: An analysis based on FinScope data, February 2007'. Available from www.finscope.co.za.

El Qorchi, M & Maimbo, S M (2003). *Informal Funds Transfer Systems – Analysis of the Informal 'Hawala' System*. International Monetary Fund, Washington DC.

El Qorchi, M (2002). 'How does this informal funds transfer system work and should it be regulated?' *Finance and Developments* 5, Vol. 39, no. 4. Available from www.imf.org.

Equity Bank (2006). Annual statements. Available from www.equitybank.co.ke.
Euromoney Yearbooks (2005). *World Leasing Yearbook 2005*. Available from www.investmentinfo.co.uk.
Feasibility (2005). 'The impact of the Dedicated Banks Bill on access to financial services'. Available from www.finmarktrust.org.za.
FinAccess, www.finscopeafrica.com.
FinAccess Survey (2006). Available from www.finscopeafrica.com.
Financial Mail (2004). 'Mastercard and Simplus develop M-Commerce solution with R1.6-billion turnover'. *Financial Mail*, 19 March.
Financial Sector Deepening (2007). 'FinAccess survey Kenya'. Available from www.fsdkenya.org.
Finmark Trust (2005). 'Cointel Simplus: Payphones'. FinMark Trust Innovation Series no. 2. Available from www.finmark.org.za.
FinMark Trust (2006). 'Pep and Hollard: Making insurance available to low-income earners'. Available from www.finmarktrust.org.za.
FinScope Namibia (2007). Available from www.finscopeafrica.co.za.
FinScope South Africa. Available from www.finscope.co.za.
FinScope Tanzania (2006). Available from www.finscopeafrica.com.
FinScope Uganda (2007). Available from www.finscopeafrica.com.
FinScope (2007). 'FinScope mobile banking pilot survey highlights'. Available from www.finscopeafrica.com.
FirstRand (2005). 'FirstRand expands further in Africa'. Available from www.firstrand.co.za.
FirstRand (2007). 'Annual report 2007'. Available from www.firstrand.co.za.
Fisher-French, M (2005). 'Getting mama her money'. *Mail & Guardian*, October 7 issue.
Fleishman, H (2005). 'FNB's Mini-ATM technology helps rural communities thrive'. Johannesburg, 21 January 2005. Available from www.itweb.co.za.
Fletcher, M, Freeman, R, Sultanov, M & Umarov, U (2005). 'Leasing in development – Guidelines for emerging economies'. IFC, World Bank Group Washington DC. Available from www.ifc.org.
FNB (2006). 'FNB cellphone banking profitable a year ahead of target'. Company statement. Available from www.fnb.co.za.
Ford, S (2006). 'Pep and Hollard partner to deliver SA's first "starter pack" insurance'. Press release.
Ghana Statistical Service (1999). 'Ghana living standards survey, round 4 (GLSS 4) 1988/89'. Available from www.worldbank.org.
Goderama, C & Montsi, F (2003). 'Towards effective control of money laundering in southern Africa'. *African Security Review*, vol. 11, no. 1. pp. 20–32. Available from www.iss.co.za.
Goodwin-Groen, R, Bruett, T & Latortue A (2004). 'Uganda microfinance sector effectiveness review'. CGAP. Available from www.fdsu.org.ug.
Government of Tanzania (2003). 'Comparison of national household budget surveys for 1990/91 and 2000/01'. Available from www.tanzania.go.tz.
Hammond, A, Kramer, W J, Tran, J, Katz, R & Walker, C (2007). 'The next 4 billion: Market size and business strategy at the base of the pyramid'. IFC and World Resources Institute, Washington DC. Available from www.wri.org.
Hashemi, S & Rosenberg, R (2006). 'Graduating the poorest into microfinance: Linking safety nets and financial services'. *CGAP Focus Note* no. 34. Available from www.cgap.org.

Heritage Foundation & *Wall Street Journal* (2007). '2007 Index of Economic Freedom'. Available from www.heritage.org.

Hoffman, J (2006). 'Mobile banking: Implementation choices. Working draft – Risk frontier consultants'. Available from www.finmarktrust.org.za.

Honohan, P (2007). 'Cross-country variation in household access to financial services'. World Bank conference on access to finance. Washington DC, 15–16 March 2007. Available from www.worldbank.org.

Honohan, P & Beck, T (2007). 'Making finance work for Africa'. World Bank Publications, Washington DC.

ICT World (2005). 'Mini ATMs for rural areas bridge digital divide'. Available from www.ictworld.co.za.

IFC MSME database. Available from www.ifc.org.

IFC (2007). 'Gender entrepreneurship markets country brief – Egypt 2007'. Available from www.ifc.org.

IMF (2008). 'International Monetary Fund report on South Africa'. Available from www.treasury.gov.za.

IMF and World Bank (2001). 'Poverty reduction strategy paper for Kenya'. Available from www.worldbank.org.yu.

IMF Financial Sector Assessment (2004). Available from www.imf.org.

IMF International Financial Statistics. Available from www.imfstatistics.org/imf.

IMF (2008). 'Regional economic outlook: Sub-Saharan Africa – October 2008'. IMF, Washington DC. Available from www.imf.org.

Industrial Development Corporation of South Africa. Available from www.idc.co.za.

International Telecommunications Union (2007). 'ITU World Telecommunications/ICT Indicators Database 2007'. Available from www.itu.int/.

Ivatury, G & Pickens, M (2006a). 'Mobile phone banking and low-income customers: Evidence from South Africa'. CGAP publication. Available from www.cgap.org.

Ivatury, G & Pickens, M (2006b). 'Mobile phones for microfinance'. CGAP brief. Available from www.cgap.org.

Jansen, M & Vennes, Y (2006). 'Liberalizing financial services trade in Africa: Going regional and multilateral'. Staff Working Paper ERSD-2006-03. World Trade Organization, Economic Research and Statistics Division, Geneva.

Jello Marketing (2005). 'Cointel provides m-commerce solutions to MTC in Namibia'. Available from www.itweb.co.za.

Jenkins, H (2000). 'Commercial banks' behaviour in micro and small enterprise finance'. Development Discussion Paper 741. Harvard Institute for International Development, Harvard University. Boston, MA.

Kabbucho, K, Sander, C & Mukwana, P (2003). 'Passing the buck, money transfer systems: The practice and potential for products in Kenya'. Paper for MicroSave. Available from www.microfinancegateway.org.

Kiraly, J, Majer, B, Matyas, L, Ocsi, B, Sugar, A & Varhegyi, E (2000). 'Experience with internationalization of financial service providers – Case study: Hungary' in Claessens, S & Jansen, M (Eds) *The Internationalization of Financial Services: Issues and Lessons for Developing Countries*. Kluwer Academic Press, Boston, MA.

Leftley, R (2005). 'Technical assistance for the promotion of microinsurance: The experience of OI' in CGAP *Working Group on Microinsurance: Good and Bad Practices*. Case study no. 11. CGAP, Washington, DC. Available from www.microfinancegateway.org.

Leftley, R (2006a). 'Overview of the MIA's operations'. Opportunity International Network. Company document.

Leftley, R (2006b). 'The wealth and opportunity of providing Insurance to the poor'. Opportunity International: Support Planning and Operations. Available from www.finmark.org.za.

Levine, R (1999). *Foreign Bank Entry and Capital Control Liberalization: Effects on Growth and Stability*. Mimeo.

Leftley, R & Mapfumo, S (2006). 'Effective microinsurance programs to reduce vulnerability'. Opportunity International Network. Available from www.microfinancegateway.org.

Littlefield, E, Helms, B & Porteous, D (2006). 'Financial Inclusion 2015 – four scenarios for the future of microfinance'. *CGAP Focus Note* no. 39. Available from www.cgap.org.

Lyman, T R, Pickens, & Porteous, D (2008). 'Regulating transformational branchless banking – Mobile phones and other technology to increase access to finance'. *CGAP Focus Note* no. 43. Available from www.cgap.org.

Madison Life Insurance Company Zambia (2006). 'Company profile'. Company document.

Mail & Guardian. (undated). 'FNB doubles size of cash machine network'.

Maimbo, S M (2006). 'Remittances and economic development in Somalia – An overview'. *World Bank, Conflict Prevention and Reduction*, Social Development Paper no. 38. Available from www.siteresources.worldbank.org.

Manje, L (2005). 'Madison Insurance Zambia'. CGAP Working Group of Microinsurance, Good and Bad Practices. Case study no. 10. CGAP, Washington. Available from www.microfinancegateway.org.

Manuel, T (2002). Address by the Minister of Finance Trevor Manuel to the Investment Management Imbizo – 2002. Available from www.finance.gov.za.

Marshall, M G (2005). 'Conflict trends in Africa 1946–2004: A macro-comparative perspective'. Paper for the UK government's Africa Conflict Prevention Pool.

Mattoo, A, Rathindran, R & Subramaniam, A (2001). 'Measuring services trade liberalization and its impact on economic growth'. Policy Research Working Paper no. 2655'. World Bank, Washington, DC.

MicroCapital (2007). *MicroCapital Monitor*, vol. 2, no. 10. Available from www.microcapital.org.

Microcare (2004). 'Presentation to Uganda Micro-Finance Forum'. Available from www.fdsu.org.ug.

Microfinance Information Exchange (2007). 'Mix Global 100: Rankings of microfinance institutions'. Available from www.microfinancegateway.org.

Mitchell, C & Heil, D (2006). 'Taking banking to the unbanked: Wizzit (B)'. Wits Business School case study, WBS 2006–16.

Mix Market, www.mixmarket.org.

Mogaki, I (2005). 'Banking boom in rural areas'. Available from www.itweb.co.za.

Namibia National Planning Commission. Available from www.npc.gov.na.

Namibia Trade Directory. (Online). 'Fast facts'. Available from www.tradedirectory.com.na.

Napier, M (2005). 'Engaging the private sector – The case for financial access charters in sub-Saharan Africa'. Paper for FinMark Trust. Available from www.finmarktrust.org.

Net1 Aplitec. 'Net1 strategy presentation'. Available from www.aplitec.co.za.

Noble, G (2001). 'Healthy, wealthy and wise: An introduction to microfinance based group health schemes'. Available from www.microfinancegateway.org.

OECD (2005). 'African economic outlook 2004/2005 – Burkina Faso'. OECD Publishing/African Development Bank. Available from www.oecdbookshop.org.

Oxford Policy Management (2007). 'Supply-side study of the inclusiveness of Zambia's financial system'. Report for FinMark Trust Zambia. Available from www.finmarktrust.org.

Peachey, S & Roe, A (2006). 'Access to finance – What does it mean and how do savings banks foster access?' For the *World Savings Bank Institute Perspectives Series* (no. 49). World Savings Bank Institute, Brussels.

Peachey, S (2006). 'Savings banks and the double bottom line – A profitable and accessible model of finance'. Paper for *World Savings Bank Institute Perspectives Series* (no. 52). World Savings Bank Institute, Brussels.

Phillips, T (2007). 'GSM Association' cited in *Balancing Act*, issue no. 378. London. Available from www.balancingact-africa.com.

PlaNet Finance (2007). 'Morocco – Microfinance in the rural areas'. Available from www.oecd.org.

Planting, S (2004). 'Signed, sealed and delivered over the cellphone'. *Financial Mail*, 7 May.

Porteous, D (2006). 'The enabling environment for mobile banking in Africa'. Report for Department for International Development (DFID). Available from www.dfid.gov.uk.

Porteous, D (2007). 'Just how transformational is m-banking?' Research report for FinMark Trust. Available from www.finscope.co.za.

Porteous, D & Wishart, N (2006). 'M-banking – A knowledge map and possible donor support strategies'. Washington DC, World Bank, 2006. Available from www.infodev.org.

Porteous, D with Hazelhurst, E (2004). 'Banking on change – Democratising finance in South Africa 1994–2004 and beyond'. Cape Town: Double Storey Books, Cape Town.

Radermacher, R, Dror, I & Noble, G (2006). 'Challenges and strategies to extend health insurance to the poor'. In *Protecting the Poor: A Microinsurance Compendium*, Churchill C, (Ed). Munich Re Foundation and ILO. Available from www.munichre-foundation.org.

Rutherford S (1999). 'The poor and their money – an essay about financial services for poor people'. Institute for Development Policy and Management, University of Manchester.

Rutherford, S (2001). 'The poor and their money'. Oxford India Paperbacks, New Delhi India. Available from www.uncdf.org.

Sachs, J D (2005). *The End of Poverty – Economic Possibilities for Our Time*. Penguin Press, New York.

Sander, C (2003). 'Capturing a market share? Migrant remittance transfers and commercialization of microfinance in Africa'. Available from www.microfinancegateway.org.

Sardanis, A (2007). *A Venture in Africa: The Challenges of African Business*. IB Tauris, London.

Sen, A (1999). *Development as Freedom*. Random House, New York.

Simplus, www.simplus.biz.

South African Advertising Research Foundation (2007). 'AMPS 2007 individual database'. Available from www.saarf.co.za.

South African Department of Trade and Industry. (Online). 'Namibia economic overview'. Available from www.dti.gov.za.

South African Reserve Bank (undated). 'Circular 6'. Available from www.reservebank.co.za.
South African Reserve Bank, www.reservebank.co.za.
Stanbic Uganda website, www.stanbicbank.co.ug.
Stats SA (2007). 'General Household Survey 2007'. (Online). Available from www.statssa.gov.za.
Stiglitz, J (2003). *The Roaring Nineties*. WW Norton & Company, New York.
Tanji, Y S (2006). '*Scenario de Transformation institutionelle de l'Association Al Amana en institution bancaire*'. Unpublished thesis.
Tanzania Postal Bank (2005). 'Annual report 2005'. Available from www.postalbank.co.tz.
Tanzania Postal Bank (2006). 'Annual report 2006'. Available from www.postalbank.co.tz.
Terreblanche, S (2002). 'A history of inequality in South Africa 1652–2002'. University of Natal Press, Scottsville.
The Steadman Group (Uganda) Limited (2007). 'FinScope Uganda: Demand, use and access to financial services in Uganda'. For DFID Financial Sector Deepening Project. Available from www.finscopeafrica.com.
The Steadman Group Uganda Limited (2007). 'FinScope Uganda' launch presentation. Available from www.finscopeafrica.com.
Townsend, S & Mosala, T (2006). 'Capitec Bank: Low-cost banking for Joe Average'. Available from www.caseplace.org.
Uganda Bureau of Statistics, www.ubos.org.
UNDP (2006). 'Human development report 2006'. Available from www.hdr.undp.org.
UNDP (2005a). 'Human development report'. Available from www.hdr.undp.org.
UNDP (2005b). 'Egypt human development report 2005'. Available from www.hdr.undp.org.
UNDP (2007). 'Human development report 2007/2008'. Available from www.hdr.undp.org.
United Nations (2002). 'Johannesburg Summit 2002 – Uganda country profile'. United Nations, New York. Available from www.un.org.
Van Zyl, R (2005). 'Banks spending billions on bringing services to South Africa's rural areas'. *The Herald*, 6 October.
Wilson, J F (2002). '"Hawala" and other informal payment systems: An economic perspective. Seminar on monetary and financial law'. International Monetary Fund. Available from www.imf.org.
World Bank (2006a). 'Doing business 2007 – How to reform'. World Bank, Washington DC.
World Bank Country Briefs, www.worldbank.org.
World Bank World Development Indicators. Available from www.worldbank.org.
World Bank (2005). 'A better investment climate for everyone' in *World Development Report* (2005). World Bank. Available from www.siteresources.worldbank.org.
World Bank (2006b). 'Financial Sector Development Policy Loan Project Document'. Available from www.web.worldbank.org.
World Bank (2007). 'Africa Development Indicators 2007'. World Bank, Washington DC.
World Resources Institute, www.wri.org.
World Wide Worx (2007). 'Mobility 2007'. Available from www.theworx.biz.

Index

Entries are listed in letter-by-letter alphabetical order. Page references in *italic* indicate where you can find a figure or table relating to the index entry term.

A

ABIL *see* African Bank Investments Limited (ABIL)
Absa Flexi Banking Services xv, 12, 13, 14, 16, *21*, 44-45, 58-59, *58*
   business outcomes 57-58
   delivery of services 55-57, *55*
   education 57
   history 51
   microloans 53-54
   portable branches 56, *56*
   products 53-54
   risk management 57
   segmenting of mass market 52
Absa Group
   financial features *47-49*
   history 47-49
   in mass market 50, *51*
   Mzansi initiative 49-50, *50*, 53
ACCION International xx, 15, 127-129
Ackermans 159-160
ADAF *see* Appropriate Development for Africa Foundation (ADAF)
Afghanistan, mobile phone banking in 191
Africa
   economic background 3-5
   financial services in 5-6
   population growth in 4-5
   reasons for success in 7-14
   urbanisation in 5
African Bank Investments Limited (ABIL) 50
AfriCap xxi, 216, 218
Afriland First Bank xv, 141-144
agricultural sector
   of Burkina Faso 100
   of Tanzania 226-227
   of Uganda 232, 243
airtime for cellphones 193, 214-215

Al Amana xvi, 13, 131-135, 140-141
   bankers' view of 139-140
   branch network *134*
   business model 137-139
   child labour 134-135
   clients (examples) 135, 137
   financial information *137*
   highlights from annual report *132*
   loan portfolio profile *131*
   mobile phone banking 136
   organisational structure *133*
   outreach strategy 135-137
   staff statistics *134*
   women customers 129, 133, 134
Allpay 54, 181
Appropriate Development for Africa Foundation (ADAF) xv, 125, 141-144
ARB Apex Bank xvi, 13, 15, 222-224
   economies of scale 225-226
   remittances 224-225
Association Al Amana pour la Promotion des Microentreprises *see* Al Amana
ATM Solutions xvii, 153-154
   access into Saswitch 154-155
   business model 155
   clients (examples) 156-157
   services in rural areas 155-157
Autocharge 213

B

bank failures 7-9
banking hours
   Barclays Bank Ghana 118-119, 125
   hawala remittance system 173
   Wizzit 197
Bank of Namibia (BoN) 77, 79
Bank Windhoek xvii, 11, 16, 76, 78-79, 85-86
   business outcomes 84
   challenges 84-85

expansion into rural areas 79
financial overview *78*
future plans 85
investigating unbanked market 79-80
local community engagement 80-81
products 82-84
recruitment strategy 81
temporary versus permanent branches 81-82
Banque Internationale de Burkina (BIB) 101, 107
Banque Marocaine du Commerce Extérieur (BMCE) 133, 138-140
Banque Misr *xvii*, 9, 11, 16, *20*, 88-89, 90, 98-99
business model 94-95
expansion of microlending programme 98
highlights from annual report *91*
launch of microlending programme 93
Luxor branch 95-98, *96-97*
management of microlending programme 94, *94*
proposition of microlending programme 91-93
reasons for success 95, 98-99
recruitment strategy 92-93, 95
women customers 95
Banque Populaire du Micro-Crédit 131
Barclays Bank Ghana *xviii*, 110-111, 114-116, *115*, 120-121, *123*
banking hours 118-119, 125
future plans 120
loan size 119
on-lending scheme 116-118, *116*
pilot projects 112-113
products 111
susu collectors 110-111, 113-114
training 116, 119, 125
BIB *see* Banque Internationale de Burkina (BIB)
biometric identity systems 209-210
BMCE *see* Banque Marocaine du Commerce Extérieur (BMCE)
BoN *see* Bank of Namibia (BoN)
bonds 263-266
Botswana 4, 232-233
Bottom Billion, The 4
BRAC 181
Brazil *179*, 180-181
burial societies 160, 245-246
Burkina Bail *xviii*, 3, *20*, 88, 99-100, 108-109
business model 103-104

challenges 107-108
clients (examples) 104-105
clients' impressions 107
company background 101-102
factoring 103, 106
future plans 108
key data *102*
leasing 103, 105-106
products 102-103
Burkina Faso 100-101, *101*
currency conversion *ix*
ByteTech *xxi*, 216, 218

C

Call Account 73
Cameroon 141
currency conversion *ix*
capacity building *see* training
capillary model *247*, 248
case studies
context for 3-5
selection of 2-3
CashBank 9
cellphones *see* mobile phone banking; mobile phones
Celpay *xix*, 188-189
Celtel *see* Celpay
child labour 134-135
Christian Enterprise Trust of Zambia (CETZAM) 240
coercion by government *see* government intervention
coffee industry 226-229 *see also* agricultural sector
Cointel *xix*, 10-11, 212-215
expansion beyond South Africa 214-215
Simplus technology platform 213
Community Bank *see* Mbinga Community Bank
community-based mutual funds *see* MC2
community engagement 80-81, 253-255
Community Reinvestment Act 43-44
Co-operative Banks Act 57
corporate citizenship 16
cross-disciplinary approach 10
currency conversions *ix*
customer needs 12

D

Dahabshiil *xix*, 164-167
Democratic Republic of Congo (DRC) 172, 173, 188-189, 202

Department for International Development (DFID) viii, 17, 79, 190, 243
development of new markets 12-13
DFID see Department for International Development (DFID)
direct mailing 61-62
dirigisme 19 see also government intervention
Domicile Savings Account 73
donors 16-18 see also funding
DRC see Democratic Republic of Congo (DRC)

E

Ecobank xx, 125-129
economic data
  Africa 4
  Burkina Faso *101*
  Egypt *89*
  Ghana *111*
  Kenya *24-25*
  Republic of Namibia 76-77, *77*
  South Africa *45*
  Tanzania *66*
  Uganda *243-244*
education see training
Efie Ne Fie 224
Egypt
  currency conversion *ix*
  economic data *89*
  poverty in 89, *90*
Electronic Banking for the Poor 147
End of Poverty, The 4
Environmental Quality International (EQI) 93
Equinox banking system 73-74
Equity Bank xx, 10, *20*, 23-24, 27-29, *28-29*, 39
  business model 31
  clients (examples) 32, 35
  competition 38
  customer service 33-34
  future plans 37-39
  growth in *30*
  marketing strategy 34-36
  mobile phone banking 35
  products 31-33
  recruitment strategy 30
  risk management 36-37
  turnaround strategy 29-31
  women customers 34

F

factoring 103, 106
Faulu Kenya *xxi*, 17, 261-266
  bonds 263-265
  clients (examples) 262
  funding 263-265, *264*
  lessons 265-266
  reasons for success 265
FBS see Absa Flexi Banking Services
FDCF see Financial Deepening Challenge Fund (FDCF)
female clients see women customers
Ferlo *xxi*, 215-220
  business model 218-220
  lessons 220
  pricing *219*
  sector background 216-217
  transactions architecture 217-218, *217*
FICA see Financial Intelligence Centre Act (FICA)
Financial Deepening Challenge Fund (FDCF) 17, 79, 190, 243
financial exclusion 41-44, *41*, *42*
financial inclusion, potential of 18-19
Financial Intelligence Centre Act (FICA) 192, 198
financial literacy see training
Financial Sector Charter, South Africa 16, 44, 46, 148
Financial Services Measure (FSM) 52, 202
FINCA see Foundation for International Community Assistance (FINCA)
FinScope 12, 44, 182
  Namibia (2004) 80, 82
  South Africa 46, 49, 147, 192, 202, 203, 215
  Tanzania (2007) 67
  Uganda (2007) 230, 244
  Zambia (2005) 188
First National Bank 147-148
  GrowthAssist product 9, 14
  Mini-ATMs *xxii*, 11, *21*, 146-147, 148-150, 157 see also ATM Solutions
    benefits to customers 151-152
    business model 150
    challenges 148-149, 150-151
    clients (examples) 151, 152
    social grant payments 152
    success of 152-153
  mobile phone banking *xxi*, 192-193
fixed wireless networks 206
FNB see First National Bank

Fondation Zakoura 131, 135, 139
FONDEP *see* Foundation for Local Development and Partnership (FONDEP)
foreign banks 39-44
  financial exclusion 41-42, *41, 42*
  government intervention 43-44
  impact on SMEs 41
Foundation for International Community Assistance (FINCA) 228, 240, 245, 254
Foundation for Local Development and Partnership (FONDEP) 131
FSM *see* Financial Services Measure (FSM)
funding 8-9, 263-265, *264 see also* donors
funeral cover *see* burial societies; Hollard Insurance and Pep Stores Partnership

G

G2P schemes 176-178, 182-183
  BRAC 181
  in Brazil 179-180, *179*
  Hunger Safety Net (HSN) 183
  in Kenya 183
  ladder of basic financial products 182, *182*
  in Mexico 178, *179*
  Net1 180
  payment mechanisms 178-181, *179*
  in South Africa *179*, 180, 181
garnishment 268, 270
G-cash 207
GCSCA *see* Ghana Co-operative Susu Collectors' Association (GCSCA)
General Household Survey, South Africa *46*
Ghana
  access to financial services 111-112, 222-223
  bank failures in 7
  currency conversion *ix*
  economic data *111*
Ghana Co-operative Susu Collectors' Association (GCSCA) 114-118, 121
government intervention 9, 19, 39, 43-44
government-to-person schemes *see* G2P schemes
group-based microcredit 72-73
GrowthAssist 9, 14

H

hawala remittance system 167-172, *170*
  field survey 172-175, *172, 174*
  negative characteristics 170-171, 173-174, *176*
  policy implications 175-176, *176*
  positive characteristics 172-173, *176*
  reasons for popularity of 169-170
HIV/AIDS 242, 243, 253
Hollard Insurance and Pep Stores Partnership *xxii*, 158-160
  advantages of 162
  challenges 161-162
  Hollard Insurance 159
  Pep Stores 159-160
  products 160-161
hours of banking *see* banking hours
Hunger Safety Net (HSN) 183

I

ICAS 270, 272
identity systems, biometric 209-210
IFC *see* International Finance Corporation (IFC)
IFTS *see* remittances and payments
Income Generation for Vulnerable Group Development (IGVGD) 181
India 204, 205, 237, 272
informal funds transfer systems (IFTS) *see* remittances and payments
innovation 11-12
Innovations for Poverty Action (IPA) 59-60, 63, 64
insurance 234 *see also* Hollard Insurance and Pep Stores Partnership; Microcare; MicroEnsure; MLife Insurance Company
  linkage banking and 122-125, *123*
International Finance Corporation (IFC) 91, 93, 128, 198
Internet access in Africa 5 *see also* technology
Internet Protocol (IP) 149
IPA *see* Innovations for Poverty Action (IPA)

K

Kenya
  bank failures in 7
  currency conversion *ix*
  economic data *24-25*
  financial sector in 25-26
  G2P schemes 183
  mobile phone banking 189-191, 202, 203, 208
  poverty in 24-25
  urbanisation in 25
Kenya Post Office Savings Bank 71
Kisiizi, Uganda 245-246, 253-254
K-Rep 263

L

leasing 103, 105-106
liberalisation 18
Life Offices' Association (LOA) 160, 270
linkage banking 110 *see also* Afriland First Bank; Al Amana; Barclays Bank Ghana; Ecobank
  insurance schemes and 122-125, *123*
literacy, financial *see* training
LOA *see* Life Offices' Association (LOA)
local community engagement 80-81
location 9

M

Madison Insurance Company Zambia 240
markets, development of new 12-13
mass banking 23 *see also* Absa Flexi Banking Services; Bank Windhoek; Equity Bank; foreign banks; randomised controlled trials (RCTs); Tanzania Postal Bank
m-banking *see* mobile phone banking
Mbinga Community Bank *xxiii*, 8, 9, 14, *20*, 226-229
  customer growth *228*
  lessons 229
MC2 141-144, *142*
Meridien BIAO banking group 8
Mexico 178, *179*
MFRC *see* Micro Finance Regulatory Council (MFRC)
Microcare *xxiii*, 3, 12, 15, 19, *20*, 242-248, 258-259
  capillary model *247*, 248
  clients (examples) 254, 255
  community engagement 253-255
  corporates 256
  disputes against 259
  financial profile 256-257, *257*
  future plans 257-258
  IT system 251
  preventive healthcare 253
  pricing *248*
  products 248-249, *248*
  risk management 249-250
  service providers partners 252-258
MicroEnsure *xxiii*, 10, *21*, 124, 234-238
  lessons 237
  products 237
Microfinance Opportunities 237
Micro Finance Regulatory Council (MFRC) 268

Micro Trust Fund Trust 144
migrant remittance *see* remittances and payments
Mini-ATMs *xxii*, 11, *21*, 146-147, 148-150, 157 *see also* ATM Solutions
  benefits to customers 151-152
  business model 150
  challenges 148-149, 150-151
  clients (examples) 151, 152
  social grant payments 152
  success of 152-153
MLife Insurance Company *xxiv*, *21*, 238
  challenges 241
  future plans 241-242
  Madison Insurance Company 240
  products 240
  profit distribution 240-241
mobile branches *see* portable branches
mobile phone banking 15, *21*, 185-187, 203-204 *see also* mobile phones; Wizzit
  in Afghanistan 191
  Al Amana 136
  Celpay *xix*, 188-189
  definition of 186
  in Democratic Republic of Congo (DRC) 188-189, 202
  ease of use 200
  Equity Bank 35
  First National Bank *xxi*, 192-193
  in Kenya 189-191, 202, 203, 208
  M-Pesa 1, 35, 189-191, 207
  MTN Banking *xxii*, 193-195
  potential of 202-203
  pricing 198-200, *199*
  regulatory environment 200-201
  Safaricom 189-191
  in South Africa 202-203
  in Tanzania 191
  technology trends 204-210
    barriers to mobile banking 209-210
    biometric identity systems 209-210
    cost of technology 205
    fixed wireless networks 206
    opportunities for banks 210
    transactions, types of 208-209
    Wi-Fi networks 206
  transaction volumes 201-202
  in Vietnam 206-207
  Vodafone *xxv*, 189-191
  Zain 191
  in Zambia 188-189, 202
  Zap 191
mobile phones

airtime purchases 193, 214-215
   use in Africa 5, 229
MoneaCard *see* Ferlo
money laundering
   Dahabshiil 167
   hawala remittance system 170-171, 174, 175
   mobile phone banking 209
money transfers *see* remittances and payments
Morocco 129, *130*, 131-133
   currency conversion *ix*
motivation of microfinance organisations 14-16
M-Pesa 1, 35, 189-191, 207
MTN Banking *xxii*, 193-195
M-Transact 35
Mutuelle Financière des Femmes Africaines (MUFFA) 144
mutuelles communautaires de croissance see MC2
Mzansi initiative 18-19, 49-50, *50*, 53

N

Namibia *see* Republic of Namibia
National Credit Act (NCA) 50, 53, 271
needs of customers 12
Net1 180
NICO Insurance 240
Nkwe Enterprise Finance 8, 9
Nkwena 240

O

operating effectiveness 8
operating hours *see* banking hours
Opportunity International *see* MicroEnsure

P

Pan Africa Building Society 240
Pep Stores *see* Hollard Insurance and Pep Stores Partnership
Peri-Urban Lusaka Small Enterprise (PULSE) Holdings 238, 240, 241
permanent versus mobile branches 81-82
   see also portable branches
person-to-person payments *see* remittances and payments
Philippines 64, 208, 237
political economy motivations 15-16
Poor and their Money, The 113
population growth in Africa 4-5
portable branches
   Absa Flexi Banking Services 56, *56*

Bank Windhoek 81-82
poverty *41*
   in Egypt 89-90, *90*
   in Kenya 24-25
   in Tanzania 66-67, *66*
   in Uganda 244-245
Poverty Action Lab 136
preventive healthcare 253
pricing 61-62
PRIDE 228, 240
product development 64
profit motive 14-15
Promotion of Rural Initiatives and Development Enterprises *see* PRIDE
PULSE *see* Peri-Urban Lusaka Small Enterprise (PULSE) Holdings

Q

Quick Account 73

R

randomised controlled trials (RCTs) 59-65
   direct mailing 61-62
   pricing 61-62
   product development 64
   risk assessment 62-64
recruitment strategy
   Bank Windhoek 81
   Banque Misr 92-93, 95
   Equity Bank 30
remittances and payments 164 *see also* Dahabshiil; G2P schemes; *hawala* remittance system
remote distribution 146 *see also* ATM Solutions; First National Bank; Hollard Insurance and Pep Stores Partnership
replicable models of innovation *20-21*
Republic of Namibia 76-78
   banking sector *77-78*
   currency conversion *ix*
   economic data 77
risk assessment 62-64
risk management
   Absa Flexi Banking Services 57
   Equity Bank 36-37
   Microcare 249-250
role clarity 8
rural banking 221 *see also* ARB Apex Bank; Mbinga Community Bank; Stanbic Bank Uganda

S

Saambou 9, 155

Safaricom 189-191
salary loans 72-73
SASSA *see* South African Social Security Agency (SASSA)
Saswitch 153, 154-155
Score 148, 150
SEED 64
Send Money Home 164
Senegal 215-220
   currency conversion *ix*
senior management support 13-14
SGMB *see* Société Générale Marocaine de Banques (SGMB)
Simplus *see* Cointel
small business banking *see* SME banking
Smart Money 207, 208
SME banking 41, 88 *see also* Banque Misr; Burkina Bail
social transfer schemes *see* G2P schemes
Société Générale Marocaine de Banques (SGMB) 138, 139
Somalia 164-165
South Africa 2, 8-14
   bank failures 8-9
   banking services 147
   currency conversion *ix*
   economic data 45
   G2P schemes *179*, 180, 181
   microlending industry 267-268
   mobile phone banking 202-203
      First National Bank *xxi*, 192-193
      MTN Banking *xxii*, 193-195
      Wizzit *see* Wizzit
   political background 45-46
   socio-economic background 45-46, *45*, *46*
South African Financial Sector Charter 16, 44, 46, 148
South African Social Security Agency (SASSA) 54, 180
South West Africa *see* Republic of Namibia
Stanbic Bank Uganda *xxiv*, *20*, 229-233
   commodity-backed finance 232-233
   products 230
Standard Bank *xxii*, 47, 77, 193-195, 230
Summit Financial Partners *xxiv*, 16, *20*, 266-272
   future plans 271-272
   partnerships 270
sustaining markets 261 *see also* Faulu Kenya; Summit Financial Partners
susu collectors 12, 110-111, 113-114

T

Tanzania
   currency conversion *ix*
   economic data 66
   mobile phone banking 191
   poverty in 65-67, *66*
   rural banking 226-227
Tanzania Postal Bank *xxv*, 65, 67-76
   asset/income mix *70*
   Call Account 73
   composition of lending to clients *71*
   deposit trends *68*
   Domicile Savings Account 73
   Equinox banking system 73-74
   financial indicators *69*
   group-based microcredit 72-73
   potential outreach 74
   Quick Account 73
   salary loans 72-73
   T-bill and loan yields *71*
   Uhuru card 73-74
technology 10-11 *see also* Internet access in Africa; mobile phone banking
technology suppliers 212 *see also* Cointel; Ferlo
telecommunications industry *see* mobile phone banking
temporary buildings *see* portable branches
'thick cultures' 11-12
training 13
   Absa Flexi Banking Services 55, 57
   Appropriate Development for Africa Foundation (ADAF) 143
   ARB Apex Bank 223
   Bank Windhoek 81
   Banque Misr 94-95
   Barclays Bank Ghana 116, 119, 125
   Dahabshiil 167
   Faulu Kenya 263
   financial literacy training 269, 272
   MicroEnsure 237
   MLife Insurance Company 241
Trouble with Africa, The 4

U

UEPS *see* Universal Electronic Payments Scheme (UEPS)
Uganda
   burial societies 245-246
   currency conversion *ix*
   economic data *243-244*
   financial services for poor 244-245

political and socio-economic background
    243–244
  rural banking 229–253
Uhuru card 73–74
UNDP see United Nations Development
    Programme (UNDP)
UniFer 4, 53, 57
United Nations Development Programme
    (UNDP) 34, 129
Universal Electronic Payments Scheme
    (UEPS) 180
urbanization 5, 29
US Millennium Challenge Account 273

White Man's Burden, The 30
Wi-Fi networks 206
Wizzit xxv, 11, 35, 195–198, 207
  banking hours 197
  clients (examples) 197, 198
women customers
  Ashland First Bank 141
  Al Amana 13, 129, 131, 133, 134
  Banque Misr 95, 96
  BRAC 181
  Equity Bank 44
  SEED 61